DISORDER AND HARMONY: 20TH CENTURY PERSPECTIVES ON ACCOUNTING HISTORY

Selected Papers from the 7th World Congress of Accounting Historians

CGA CANADA
Research Foundation
La Fondation de recherche

Edited by
Alan J. Richardson

Research Monograph Number 23

Canadian Cataloguing in Publication Data

World Congress of Accounting Historians (7th : 1996 :
Kingston, Ont.)
Disorder and harmony

(Research monograph ; no. 23)
Includes some text in French.
Includes bibliographical references.
ISBN 1-896436-98-6

1. Accounting—History—Congresses. 2. Taxation—History—Congresses. **I.** Richardson, Alan John, 1955- **II.** CGA-Canada Research Foundation. **III.** Title. **IV.** Series: Research monograph (CGA-Canada Research Foundation) ; no. 23.
HF5603.W68 1996 657'.09 C96-910359-X

Ordering information is available from:
CGA-Canada Research Foundation
700-1188 West Georgia Street
Vancouver, BC Canada V6E 4A2
Telephone: (604) 669-3555
Facsimile: (604) 689-5845
e-mail: lgoulet@cga-canada.org
sspector@cga-canada.org

ISBN 1-896436-98-6

The CGA-Canada Research Foundation was incorporated and registered as a charitable foundation on May 30, 1979. The creation of the foundation grew from the desire of members of the Certified General Accountants' Association of Canada to make a meaningful contribution to accounting research in Canada by sponsoring research which would advance the accounting community as a whole. It is our desire to encourage pure and applied research in the areas of auditing, accounting and finance.

This monograph is the twenty-third in a series to be published by the CGA-Canada Research Foundation as part of the Association's continuing research effort. Each monograph expresses the viewpoint of its authors, and has been neither approved nor disapproved by CGA-Canada. These monographs are intended to stimulate thought, discussion and debate on matters relating to accounting, auditing and finance. The Foundation welcomes comments from readers.

Ruby Howard, FCGA
President
CGA-Canada Research Foundation
July 1996

MONOGRAPHS PUBLISHED BY THE CGA-CANADA RESEARCH FOUNDATION

No. 1: Historical Cost Accounting and its Rationality, by Yuji Ijiri

No. 2: Accounting for Local Government in Canada: The State of the Art, by Arthur Beedle (Out of Print)

No. 3: Local Government Financial Management and Accounting: A Research Framework, by Katherine Graham (Out of Print)

No. 4: Accountants' Roles in Industrial Organizations and Access to Information, by Michael Newman, Carolyne Smart, Ilan Vertinsky and Vinay Kanetkar

No. 5: The Financial Reporting of Contingencies and Uncertainties: Theory and Practice, by Daniel Thornton

No. 6: Research in Audit Decision Making: Rationale, Evidence and Implications, by Robert Ashton (Out of Print)

No. 7: Modern Accounting Research: History, Survey, and Guide, second edition, by Richard Mattessich

No. 8: International Conflict of Accounting Standards, by Kenneth Most

No. 9: La comptabilité en périodes de changements de prix, deuxième édition, par Daniel Zéghal

No. 10: Risk Assessment in Accounting and Auditing, by Theodore Mock and Ilan Vertinsky

No. 11: The Serviceability of Financial Information: A Survey, by Raymond Chambers and Haim Falk

No. 12: Materiality: An Empirical Study of Actual Auditor Decisions, by Chris Robinson and Len Fertuck

No. 13: Product Differentiation in Auditing: Auditor Choice in the Market for Unseasoned New Issues, by Dan Simunic and Michael Stein

No. 14: Analytical Review Procedures and Processes in Auditing, by Stanley Biggs, Theodore Mock and Paul Watkins

No. 15: Le marché de la vérification au Canada, par Daniel Zéghal

No. 16: The Value of Communication in Agency Contracts: Theory and Experimental Evidence, by Joyce Berg, Lane Daley, Frank Gigler and Chandra Kanodia

No. 17: Accounting Research in the 1980s and its Future Relevance, by Richard Mattessich (aussi offert en français – N°. 17F)

No. 18: Accounting for Options: No Longer an Option, by Wanda Wallace and Duane Smith

No. 19: Experimental Tests of Auditing as a Credibility Generating Mechanism, by Nicholas Dopuch and Ron King

No. 20: The Management of Financial Disclosure: Theory and Perspectives, by Michael Gibbins, Alan J. Richardson and John Waterhouse

No. 21: Ethical Reasoning in Accounting and Auditing, by Lawrence A. Ponemon and David R. L. Gabhart

No. 22: The Ethical Foundations of Public Accounting, by James C. Gaa

No. 23: Disorder and Harmony: 20th Century Perspectives on Accounting History, edited by Alan J. Richardson

No. 24: Forthcoming

No. 25: Research Methods in Accounting: Issues and Debates, edited by Alan J. Richardson

Abstract

This monograph consists of selected papers from the 7th World Congress of Accounting Historians held August 11–13, 1996 at Queen's University, Kingston, Ontario, Canada. The World Congress is held every four years at varied locations under the authority of the Academy of Accounting Historians. Past congresses have been held in Japan (1992), Australia (1988), and Italy (1984). This is the first time the Congress has been held in Canada and only the second time in North America. The 8th World Congress will be held in Barcelona, Spain in the year 2000.

Over sixty papers were presented at the Congress in all areas of accounting history including financial accounting, management accounting, auditing, taxation, accounting regulation and the economic, behavioural and social consequences of accounting. The Congress featured plenary sessions by Daniel Wren, Maureen Berry, Barbara Merino and Gary Previts. The Congress also included special sessions on "Decimalized Plans of Accounts", "Accounting History on the Internet", and "The Emancipatory Potential of Accounting History". Abstracts of all papers presented at the Congress are included in an Appendix to the monograph.

The monograph includes fifteen refereed papers from the 7th World Congress and Daniel Wren's plenary address entitled "Connection: the shared heritage of accounting and management history". The papers published in this monograph are divided into six themes: cost and management accounting; accounting education; financial accounting and auditing; professional organizations; taxation; and accounting texts.

Résumé

Cette monographie réunit certaines des communications faites lors du septième World Congress of Accounting Historians, qui s'est tenu du 11 au 13 août 1996 à l'Université Queen, de Kingston (Ontario, Canada). Ce congrès, qui a lieu tous les quatre ans dans un lieu différent, est parrainé par l'Academy of Accounting Historians. Les congrès antérieurs se sont déroulés entre autres au Japon (1992), en Australie (1988) et en Italie (1984). C'était la première fois qu'il avait lieu au Canada, et seulement la deuxième fois en Amérique du Nord. Le huitième World Congress se tiendra à Barcelone (Espagne) en l'an 2000.

Le congrès a été le cadre de plus de soixante communications sur des sujets touchant à tous les domaines de l'histoire comptable, notamment la comptabilité financière, la comptabilité de gestion, la vérification, la fiscalité, la réglementation comptable et les incidences de la comptabilité sur l'économie, le comportement et la société. Le congrès comportait des séances plénières avec Daniel Wren, Maureen Berry, Barbara Merino et Gary Previts. Il comprenait également des sessions extraordinaires portant sur les plans comptables, le rôle émancipateur de l'histoire comptable et la manière d'obtenir, à l'aide d'Internet, des renseignements sur l'histoire comptable. La monographie offre, en annexe, la liste complète des communications faites lors de ce congrès.

La monographie présente quinze de ces communications, revues par un comité de lecture, ainsi que l'allocution prononcée par Daniel Wren à l'occasion d'une séance plénière et intitulée « Connections: The shared heritage of accounting and management history ». Ces communications sont classées selon six thèmes: comptabilité analytique et comptabilité de gestion, formation comptable, comptabilité générale et vérification, organismes professionnels, fiscalité et, enfin, ouvrages de comptabilité.

Preface and Acknowledgements

It is a great honour and privilege to host the 7th World Congress of Accounting Historians at Queen's University, Kingston, Canada. This is the first time that the Congress has been held in Canada and only the second time in North America.

The Congress is organized by the International Committee for Congresses of Accounting Historians and the Academy of Accounting Historians and held every four years. The history of the Congress is shown below.

- 2000 Barcelona, Spain
- **1996 Kingston, Canada**
- 1992 Kyoto, Japan
- 1988 Sydney, Australia
- 1984 Pisa, Italy
- 1980 London, England
- 1976 Atlanta, USA
- 1970 Brussels, Belgium

The 7th World Congress attracted papers in all areas of accounting history including financial accounting, management accounting, auditing, taxation, accounting regulation and the economic, behavioural and social consequences of accounting. The Congress also included plenary sessions featuring Professor Daniel Wren (University of Oklahoma), Maureen Berry (University of Illinois), Barbara Merino (University of North Texas), and Gary Previts (Case Western Reserve). This volume provides a selection of the papers presented at the Congress; a complete listing of papers is included as an appendix.

This conference has been eight years in the making. The first step was taken by John Williams (now at Nanyang University, Singapore) in 1988. He attended the 5th World Congress of Accounting Historians in Sydney, Australia to present a paper that I co-authored with him. The Congress made such an impression on him that John volunteered to hold the 7th World Congress at Queen's University with which he was then affiliated. The plan was that he and I would act as co-convenors. As time went by John followed his academic interests to Singapore but the die had been cast and the Congress would be in Kingston.

As the Congress planning unfolded I have been assisted by many individuals and organizations. I would like to formally recognize the Congress Program Advisory Board who were instrumental in developing and promoting the Congress. They are:

Ashton Bishop, School of Accounting, James Madison University, *Harrisonburg, Virginia*

Bruce Buchan, School of Business, Queen's University, *Kingston, Ontario*

Wai Fong Chua, School of Accounting, University of N.S.W., *Sydney, Australia*

David Cooper, School of Business, University of Alberta, *Edmonton, Alberta*

Anne Fortin, Dept. Des Sciences Comptable, University du Québec à *Montréal*

Michael Gaffikin, Department of Accountancy, University of Wollongong, *Wollongong, Australia*

Esteban H. Esteve, Banco de Espano, *Madrid, Spain*

Pang Yang Hoong, School of Accountancy, Nanyang University, *Singapore*

Alicja Jaruga, Department of Accounting, Łódź University, *Łódź, Poland*

Brian Jones, Faculty of Business, University of PEI, *Charlottetown, PEI*

Jeffrey Kantor, School of Business, University of Windsor, *Windsor Ontario*

Alan Mayper, College of Business Administration, University of North Texas, *Denton, Texas*

Christopher Napier, Dept. of Accounting and Finance, London School of Economics, *UK*

Hiroshi Okana, Osaka City University, *Japan*

Gary J. Previts, Weatherhead School of Management, Case Western Reserve University, *Cleveleand, Ohio*

Al Roberts, College of Business Administration, Georgia State University, *Atlanta, Georgia*

I have been assisted by individuals who provided reviews of specific papers. They are:

Ashton Bishop
David Cooper
Wai Fong Chua
Esteban Esteve
Mahmoud Ezzamel
Walker Fesmire
Tonya Flesher
Dale Flesher
Anne Fortin
Giuseppe Galassi
Robert Gibson
Roger Jachau
Alicja Jaruga
Jeffrey Kantor
Juan Lanero
Frank Lewis
Norm Macintosh
Laura MacDonald
Cheryl McWatters
Chris Napier
R.H. Parker
Gary Previts
Jeanette Sanfilippo
Michael Scorgie
Adrianne Slaymaker
David Smith
Dan Thornton
Stephen Walker

I would also like to acknowledge the administrative support provided by Christy den Haan-Veltman, Laura MacDonald who acted as registrar and kept my finances in order, and

Mary Brown who managed the mailing lists and the flow of correspondence. I am also grateful to Linda Freeman and Mike Kirkpatrick who handled the assembly of the monograph. Special thanks to Caroline Trevithick who worked with authors, particularly those with English as a second language, to ensure that their meaning was clear.

Finally, I wish to gratefully acknowledge the financial sponsors of this Congress. It was very gratifying to see the value of this Congress recognized by sponsors in times of funding cutbacks. I am particularly grateful to:

Social Sciences and Humanities Research Council of Canada
CGA-Canada Research Foundation
Certified General Accountants Association of Ontario
Society of Management Accountants of Ontario
Academy of Accounting Historians
Principal, Queen's University
School of Business, Queen's University.
Garland Publishing

In times of social change we look to the past for a better understanding of the road we have taken and the possibilities foregone. This century has been a time of great turmoil. We have witnessed great social experiments with equally great successes and failures. It has been a century of rationalization and accounting has been a central part of that process. This Congress has provided us with the opportunity to gather together and share our understanding of these developments.

The 8th World Congress of Accounting Historians will be held in Barcelona, Spain in August 2000. I wish Esteban H. Esteve success in organizing that event. I hope that you will join us on that occasion!

Contents

Introduction

The twentieth century has seen the coming of age of the accountancy profession. It has been a century of technical achievement and organizational development. We have devoted enormous fiscal and intellectual resources to creating standards for financial reporting and tools for management decision-making. We have also created professional associations and academic bodies which have established accreditation processes and lobbied for the improved status of accountants and accountancy. It has also been a century of crisis for the profession and has seen the social roles of accountancy subject to great scrutiny. Accounting has been implicated in the excesses of private enterprise and chastised for its inability to inform a broader range of social issues. As the century comes to a close it is appropriate to re-examine the history of accounting to better understand the forces that have shaped its development and will continue to affect its trajectory into the twenty-first century.

It has been said that every generation must rewrite its history. There are two readings of this quote. One is a cynical reading that history is arbitrarily rewritten to reflect the biases of a particular age. Recent feminist and minority critiques of traditional history have pointed out the ways in which their voices have been silenced or the ways in which history is written to justify the material and ideological positions of dominant groups. Undoubtedly this occurs, and one of the plenary sessions of the Congress by Barbara Merino and a follow-up session organized by David Cooper examine the critical (emancipatory) potential of accounting history.

A second reading of this quote is more charitable and recognizes two aspects of historical research. First, our knowledge of history is rarely complete. Research will uncover new documents or build a better understanding of the context of historical events which allows a refined understanding of both the facts of history and their meaning. Second, reality is more complex than any textual discipline can record. This means that historical research represents a choice of subject matter from among the myriad details left in time's wake. Each generation will look back from the context of its own problems and desires. We drive into the future staring intently into the rear-view mirror; the history which each generation chooses to write is that which they believes provides most insights into where they are going.

The papers published here and presented at the Congress provide a fascinating snapshot of the current state of the global economy and the range of issues which are in the collective conscious. For example, there are papers which examine historical barter accounting reflecting, perhaps, concern with the growing size of the underground economy. There are also papers which examine various aspects of taxation policy including the economic logic of tax systems and the distributive properties of those systems over the last two hundred years. These papers provide some perspective on the personal consequences of recent attempts by many governments to reduce their fiscal deficits. Several papers examine the history of public sector accounting and the connection between government policy and the information systems through which those policies are enforced. For example, there are papers which examine the way in which pollution control legislation is reflected in financial disclosures and analyses of the impact of concern for "sustainable development" on accounting theory. There are also papers which document the re-emergence of free markets (the global market) after an epoch of protectionism and regulation, and use the early years of accounting to identify the likely role of accounting in this new economy.

The Congress is an opportunity to reflect on the state of the profession, accounting education and scholarship. In many countries, the professional status of accounting is not institutionalized. For example, the title of "accountant" may be unrestricted or the standards of accounting may be set with little professional input. Understanding the process by which the profession has gained and maintained its status in one country may help others currently engaged in the professionalization process (or de-professionalization process!) to better understand the forces at play. The use of examination processes to test professional competence has been an important part of the professionalization process in most countries. In the United States, the CPA examination is one hundred years old this year. Two papers provide some background on the origins of this examination.

The Congress is also an opportunity to engage in traditional scholarship and to probe emerging paradigms. Several papers address issues raised by others, or re-examine old texts. These papers seek to correct the historical record or to develop a more subtle and insightful understanding of a well-known issue. Other papers challenge us to consider the implications of post-modern epistemology for historical work. The process of historical research, as opposed to the subject of historical research, can be enriched by borrowing from other disciplines. These papers point to sources of inspiration for historical researchers.

This monograph presents a cross-section of the papers presented at the Congress. At the end of the monograph you will find abstracts of all the papers presented. The papers are divided into six parts:

Part I: Cost and Management Accounting
Part II: Education

Part III: Financial Accounting and Auditing
Part IV: Professional Organizations
Part V: Taxation
Part VI: Texts.

The monograph begins with the plenary address given by Daniel Wren. We are grateful to Professor Wren for his permission to publish his address as part of this collection.

Plenary Address

Connections: The Shared Heritage of Accounting and Management History

Daniel A. Wren
University of Oklahoma

1.0 ABSTRACT

This is the plenary address to the 7th World Congress of Accounting Historians presented at Queen's University, Kingston on August 11, 1996.

2.0 INTRODUCTION

Silas Dunning, editor of the *Railroad Gazette*, said "The world advances in knowledge by recording, studying, and comparing experience" [quoted in Jenks, 1960, p. 425]. While this observation was made in 1872, I feel it is true today and that these meetings are a manifestation of our interest in comparing our experiences to promote a better understanding of our disciplines.

Basil Yamey has provided an interesting perspective with his selection of various art works that portray accounting and accountants [Yamey, 1989]. We see accountants present at important historical events and at rather mundane tasks. We see them worrying about how poorly their clients keep their records and we see how they may be viewed at tax preparation time. It would seem that little has changed.

The common feature that a management historian sees in these paintings is *information* — the accountant as a recorder of transactions, as a provider of organizational memory, and as a source of data for the use of others. Edwards and Newell provide a useful definition of managerial accounting as "the provision, for management, of statistical information for the purposes of planning, decision making, and controlling" [1994, p. 412]. My focus will be on the role that information and information technology have played in bringing management and accounting history together. This does not deny the importance of other aspects of accounting history but should enable me to sketch some of our shared heritage.

The true origins of our respective disciplines are unknown. This does not cast doubt on our legitimacy but illustrates that managers were managing and accountants were counting long before anyone was thoughtful enough to prepare a record of those activities. Some 4,000 years ago Hammurabi, King of Babylon, enacted a law about the proper handling of receipts and established for all time a fundamental rule of accounting, especially if you expect your travel expenses to be reimbursed by your university. Judging from Sumerian records, the early technology for recording transactions was a pointed stick (a stylus) and clay that would be baked for information storage purposes. Many of these ancient clay tablets exist today, and it is doubtful that our modern electromagnetic storage systems will match that record of durability.

Accounting historians disagree on when managerial accounting practices began: perhaps as early as sixteenth century Florence by the Medicis; or occurring with the Industrial Revolution and Great Britain in Josiah Wedgwood's pottery works, Boulton and Watt's Soho Foundry, and John Wilkinson's iron works; or in the mid-nineteenth century in the United States of America with the growth of railroads and of large scale enterprise [Pollard, 1965; Solomons, 1968; Chatfield, 1974; Johnson, 1987].

Books were kept to account for wages, material, and sales, but few managers used these accounts as an aid to decision making. Josiah Wedgwood, manufacturer of various pottery products, was one of those few and he refined his accounts until he was able to use them in setting prices, fixing worker piece rates, determining the percentage of selling expenses to sales, and tracing the embezzlement of certain funds by his head clerk [McKendrick, 1970].

In these early days management and accounting were deemed localized matters, not subject to generalization, and success was thought to depend on the personal qualities of the managers, not on their grasp of broader principles. Running a business was a personal art, not a discipline; pragmatic, not theoretical; and parochial, not universal. It is not surprising that it would be some time later before management and accounting would be examined more systematically.

The practice of merchants or manufacturers gathering information to use in making decisions is indeed as old, if not older, than the Medicis. If we are seeking the origins of more systematic study and the identification and publication of practices that appear to work better than others, however, I find the evidence supports more recent developments. The practice of managerial accounting is ancient, but it was more often than not specific to a firm and rarely received recognition elsewhere. In the development of railroads in the United States there is evidence to suggest the beginnings of systematic managerial accounting and a trail of developments that carry us from the mid-nineteenth to the early twentieth century.

3.0 THE RAILROADS

Historians are in agreement that the railroads were the world's first large-scale profit-seeking enterprise. There had been larger organizations previously — in government, the military, and the church, but none of these faced the same managerial problems as the railroads. These developments occurred almost concurrently in the United States and Great Britain with the steam powered locomotive, the iron rails, and flanged wheels of the engine and its train of passenger and freight cars.

Compared with previous profit-seeking enterprise, the railroads required the construction of a lengthy right of way across alien land, more investment in motive power and rolling stock, and a geographical dispersion of agents, telegraphers, and managers who would oversee this network. The larger initial investment, the increased fixed costs of operations, and the continuing need to repair and maintain the track and equipment presented managers with problems on a scale that previous organizations had not faced. The "make-up" of a train, i.e., the mix of passenger and freight cars, had to be decided; schedules had to be developed and coordinated to match capacity with market needs, and the safety of operations became paramount. Transactions in the sale of passenger tickets and freight bills were small and numerous — different from the sale of numerous bolts of cloth, or barrels of whale oil, or tons of coal. These transactions were not only increased relative to previous businesses, but were handled by freight and passenger agents who were operating without central control. Here, and for these reasons, we see the railroads begin to organize by forming departments to facilitate measurement and control.

The Baltimore and Ohio Railroad, under the leadership of Louis McLane and Benjamin Latrobe, was the first to departmentalize its operations in 1847. The "working of the road" (operations) became a separate department from that of the treasurer who was responsible for the collection and disbursement of revenue. The B&O, however, was not the largest railroad and did not reach Wheeling (West) Virginia until 1853.

Concurrent with the development of railroads we find a new information technology developing — the telegraph, an invention of Samuel F.B. Morse. Railroad roadbeds and their right of way provided a convenient pathway for the telegraph as well since its lines needed space free of interfering tree branches and other natural impediments. The telegraph would be used for personal and commercial messages and we will see how this information technology also became part of managerial accounting on the railroads.

3.1 Daniel C. McCallum

The innovator of systematic management and of accounting information on the railroads was a Scottish immigrant, Daniel C. McCallum. Self-educated, McCallum became a carpenter and architect, designing and building bridges for the New York and Erie Railroad. At that time, it was not unusual for skilled employees to be promoted to management and McCallum had worked his way up from a division superintendent position to general superintendent of the New York and Erie by 1854.

The Erie outstripped all other lines in length (nearly 500 miles) and had some 4,000 employees by 1851. Travel on the Erie was not easy — from the Duane Street Pier in New York City you needed to go twenty-four miles up the Hudson River by steamboat to Piermont, New York before a train was available to take you across the state to Dunkirk, on Lake Erie, another 466 miles according to the first timetable. If you chose, connections could be made at Dunkirk to travel by steamboat to Detroit in 35 hours, or Chicago in 50 hours, or Milwaukee in 60 hours.

The Erie, like many other railroads, was struggling with problems of organization, management, financial accountability, safety, and a familiar problem to travelers of all times, the loss of baggage. McCallum observed that operating a railroad over many miles was more difficult than for shorter lines, such as the B&O, but that any difference in costs or performance was not due to length but to the adoption of a "system."

McCallum recognized the importance of gathering information about railroad operations. In his Superintendent's Report of 1855 he stated:

> In my opinion, [for] a system of operations to be efficient and successful, the principal and responsible head of the running department [should have] a complete daily history of details in all their minutiae. Without such supervision, the procurement of a satisfactory annual statement must be regarded as extremely problematical. The fact that dividends are earned without such control does not disprove the position, as in many cases the extraordinarily remunerative nature of an enterprise may ensure satisfactory returns under the most loose and inefficient management ....
>
> It is very important that the principal officers should be in possession of all the information necessary to enable them to judge correctly as to the industry and efficiency of subordinates of every grade .... [*American Railroad Journal*, April 12, 1856, pp. 225-226]

McCallum's ideas seem to reach beyond the internal information needed by management to his concern that the "annual statement" could be misleading if it was not based on generating the proper information within the organization.

McCallum offered some general principles of organization and management:

> 1. A proper division of responsibilities.
> 2. Sufficient power conferred to enable the same to be fully carried out, that such responsibilities may be real in their character.
> 3. The means of knowing whether such responsibilities are faithfully executed.
> 4. Great promptness in the report of all derelictions of duty, that evils may at once be corrected.
> 5. Such information to be obtained through a system of daily reports and checks that will not embarrass principal officers, nor lessen their influence with their subordinates.
> 6. The adoption of a system, as a whole, which will not only enable the General Superintendent to detect errors immediately, but will also point out the delinquent. [*American Railroad Journal*, April 12, 1856, p. 226]

McCallum was the first to specify the methods and kinds of information needed to carry out these principles. Responsibilities would be placed in various positions; "power" (authority) needed to be established; and a "means of knowing" (a reporting system) that would be prompt and identify where (or who) corrective action needed to be taken.

The 1855 Superintendent's Report also mentioned how McCallum used the telegraph — apparently the first use of this technology for information management. In 1851, a telegraph line was completed along the New York and Erie right of way, primarily for commercial traffic before McCallum saw other possibilities. The use of the telegraph advanced by stages as McCallum discovered more practical applications. Initially, the system was designed to trace the progress of the trains as they moved through the various blocks of tracks under the direction of the telegraphers at those stations. Delays of more than ten minutes were to be reported; some trains were designated to "lay by" while others advanced along the single track; and departures from the posted time table were forbidden. Safety was paramount and the telegraph enabled train movements to occur more safely and in a timely manner.

As these basic problems were solved by the telegraphic communication, McCallum began gathering information by the various departments under his supervision. The connection between organization and information appears to begin on the railroads — that is, establishing various departments for the essential functions of railroad operations and placing responsibility for collecting certain types of information into that office [Chandler, 1965]. For example, McCallum's general ticket agent was responsible for setting passenger ticket prices, for supervising all ticket sales, and for reporting ticket sales revenue to the general superintendent. The general freight agent had similar duties for freight. Each division superintendent reported the miles ran and labour costs on their division; the master of repairs reported all repair expenses; and the general wood agent reported the number of cords of wood used per engine and the cost of the wood.

In the general superintendent's office, all of these reports were collected and aggregated by tons of freight, by the number of passengers, by cost per engine, by cost per miles run, and so on. One can only imagine how much paper these hourly, daily, and monthly reports could consume. The efforts of eight clerks were required, according to McCallum, to handle all of these reports from a railroad that was less than 500 miles long.

The results of these efforts were collected into what McCallum called "Statistical Accounts" which were to be used for planning, rate-making, and control. Comparative data allowed McCallum to gauge trends: for example, comparing 1854 with 1855, he could see that the number of passengers and of passenger train miles were decreasing while freight traffic had increased substantially.

McCallum resigned from the Erie in 1857 after a six-month-long strike by the locomotive engineers who objected to McCallum's enforcement of rules about safety. His career was not finished but his ideas about systematic management on the railroads would probably have fallen into the dustbin of history if his ideas had not received some noteworthy praise. We will see a series of connections following McCallum.

3.2 Henry Varnum Poor

An unsung hero in the history of our disciplines was not an accountant nor a manager but a journalist, Henry Varnum Poor, and he deserves mention in the history of financial as well as managerial accounting. When he became co-owner and editor of the *American Railroad Journal* in 1849, Poor observed the poor management, the high rate of accidents, and the financial abuse by speculators on US railroads. The New York and Erie was one of his favorite targets until McCallum became superintendent and began his reforms. From McCallum's work, Poor gleaned three fundamental principles: organization, communication, and information [Chandler, 1956]. Organization was basic: there had to be a careful division of labour from the president down to the common labourer, each with specific duties and responsibilities. Employees should be directly accountable to their immediate superiors; Poor repeatedly used the terms *responsibility* and *accountability* in his editorials. Communication meant devising a method of reporting throughout the organization to give top management a continuous and accurate accounting of operations. Again, the influence of McCallum and his use of the telegraph are clearly seen. Finally, information was "recorded communication"; the need for a set of operating reports to be compiled for costs, revenues, and rate making. This was McCallum's "statistics" and bears a resemblance to what we might call a data base.

Poor's *Journal* was the leading business periodical of its day and widely read outside as well as inside the transportation industry. Through Poor's editorials, the ideas of McCallum would have a far-reaching impact.

Before tracing other connections from Daniel McCallum, let us examine briefly the role of Henry Poor in the history of financial accounting. His editorials were intended for the railroad investor as well as managers and discussed developments, problems, and needed reforms. The *Journal* also presented detailed financial and operating data, such as the comparative statistics that McCallum compiled, so investors could make more informed decisions.

Poor complained that railroads did not separate construction from operating costs, thus screening the cost of operations from the investor. It was not an uncommon practice to put operating expenses in the construction account, thus showing higher profits from operations. This practice enabled the declaration of higher dividends that otherwise would have been unwarranted. (Does history provide explanations for why we have rules for accounting practice?)

A sidelight to illustrate: when the Central Pacific met the Union Pacific in Utah in 1869, some $2,200 was spent on champagne for the celebration. Did this go into the construction or the operating expense account? We cannot answer that, but the Union Pacific was capitalized at $110,000,000 and an estimated one-half of that was not the cost of construction. Perhaps we should say the stock was not "watered" but "champagned."

Henry Poor had faith that fully informed investors would make better decisions. For example, the performance data from the Erie were reported in Henry Poor's *Journal* to illustrate what data to collect and how they should be reported to inform other railroad managers as well as the public:

> Now, the public have it in their power to reform the management of railroad companies to a degree that will make productive most of our roads by *insisting* that in all cases full and lucid reports shall be frequently made. The reports of well managed companies would serve as standards to which all other companies would be obliged to conform. If one company gave to the public an exact picture of their internal management and by what process the cost of any branch of service was reduced to the minimum figure, all other companies, were the public properly alive to their interests, would have to make a similar exhibition. [*American Railroad Journal*, April 26, 1856, p. 265]

Poor gave a voice to McCallum's ideas and these would influence other developments. Henry Poor's legacy endures in other means — such as his *Manual of Railroads*, or *Standard and Poor's*, and others — but McCallum established the initial connection that information was accounting and management's shared heritage.

3.3 Further Developments in Railroad Accounting

McCallum's ideas and Poor's advocacy of them became identifiable as the field of "railroad accounting" and would be extended to other industries as we will see. Even though McCallum left the Erie in 1857, his ideas were adopted by J. Edgar Thomson, president of the Pennsylvania Railroad. McCallum's ideas of geographical departmentation, formal lines of authority and responsibility, communications, measuring performance, and cost accounting were all applied on the Pennsylvania. To these ideas Thomson added a separation of line and staff duties, clarifying McCallum's earlier ideas.

It was the Pennsylvania Railroad, not the Erie, that kept McCallum's ideas moving. A young telegrapher on the Pennsylvania would work his way up to a division superintendency and then take these ideas to an emerging industry — we will return to Andrew Carnegie shortly.

Albert Fink, an engineer and bridge-builder like McCallum, began his career on the Baltimore and Ohio and later became president of the Louisville and Nashville Railroad. He made advances in relating operating costs to freight and/or passenger traffic and coupled this with McCallum's information flows to advance the idea of control through statistics [Fink, 1875].

Internal auditing as a separate function also began on the railroads as early as 1847 on the Baltimore and Ohio. External independent auditing also appeared on the railroads as early as 1854 [Boockholdt, 1983], perhaps because of Poor's editorials advising shareholders to keep their eye on management.

3.4 From Railroads to Steel

It was suggested earlier that there was a connection between McCallum's ideas for the Erie, their adoption by the Pennsylvania Railroad, and a young man, Andrew Carnegie. Carnegie began as a telegrapher but by age 24 (in 1859) was superintendent of the Pennsylvania's Western Division, the largest division at that time. Applying his management skills he quadrupled division traffic, doubled the miles of track, and his division had the lowest ton per mile costs of any US railroad. Offered the position of general superintendent in 1865, he declined, saying he wished to pursue other interests — steel.

Carnegie used McCallum's ideas as he built his steel business: clear assignments of duties for accountability; promotion by merit; gathering costs for labour and material; statistics for measuring performance; cost-based pricing; and using the telegraph for negotiating sales, checking credit, taking orders, and providing shipping information. He belonged to the Bessemer Steel Association and refused to join a pool to share the market and fix prices. He rebelled, stating that he owned shares in each of their companies and had access to their financial reports. He knew their expenses (which Carnegie's competitors did not know) and promised to keep cutting his prices as he cut his costs. As one biographer summed up Carnegie's success:

> On the [Pennsylvania] railroad he assimilated the managerial skills ... that enabled him to become successively manager, capitalist, and entrepreneur. His most spectacular achievement — building Carnegie Steel into the world's largest steel producer — rested primarily on his successful transfer of the railroad's managerial methods to the manufacturing sector of the economy. [Livesay, 1975, p. 29]

McCallum, through the Carnegie connection, helped build the system of management and accounting that propelled the United States into the world's leading industrial power in steel before 1900.

4.0 THE ENGINEERS AND SHOP MANAGEMENT

The American Society of Mechanical Engineers (ASME) was formed in 1880 to address those issues of factory operation and management neglected by other engineering groups. A landmark meeting of the ASME was held in Chicago in 1886 and Henry R. Towne presented a paper entitled "The Engineer as an Economist." Towne proposed that the

ASME create an economic section to act as a clearinghouse and forum for shop management and shop accounting:

> Under the head of Shop Management fall the questions of organization, responsibility, reports, systems of contract and piece work, and all that relates to the executive management of works, mills and factories. Under the head of Shop Accounting fall the questions of time and wages systems, determination of costs, whether by piece or day-work, the distribution of the various expense-accounts, the ascertainment of profits, methods of book-keeping, and all that enters into the system of accounts which relates to the manufacturing departments of a business, and to the determination and record of its results.
>
> There already exists an enormous fund of information relating to such matters, based upon actual and most extensive experience. What is now needed is a medium for the interchange of this experience among those whom it interests and concerns. [Towne, 1886, p. 428]

Towne observed that there was an extensive record of experience about these subjects over the years but there had been no centre for collecting, exchanging, and discussing these ideas in a systematic fashion — which would be the role that Towne expected of the economic section of the ASME.

This idea of a "system" is central to subsequent developments; as one writer stated: "the utmost system [is] ... necessary in every detail [for] the economy and uniformity of production" [Smith, 1885, p. 1]. Thus *system* referred to the development of rules, standards, and procedures to handle the increased volume of activity in the production shop. Included in systematic management would be topics such as setting standards for tools, quality and quantity of work, coordination of work flow through routing and scheduling, wage incentives, accounting for costs, assigning responsibility, and handling labour problems such as soldiering [Litterer, 1961]. Towne's advice for engineers to think more about the economy of production fell on a fertile mind — Frederick W. Taylor.

4.1 The Basley-Taylor System

It is almost impossible to find a history of the late nineteenth and early twentieth century that does not mention Frederick Taylor, so I will try to follow a narrow theme about his contribution in connecting systematic management to systematic accounting.

Taylor's biographer, Frank B. Copley, calls Taylor "a pioneer in the development of modern industrial accounting" [1923, I, p. 363]. We will see that this is true but amend this statement to trace the basis of his ideas. As a manager at Midvale Steel, Taylor became interested in analyzing costs and classifying expenses but his ideas remained undeveloped for some time. In 1890, he became the general manager of the Manufacturing Investment Company's (MIC) paper and pulp mills in Appleton, Wisconsin and Madison, Maine. At MIC, R. D. Hayes, an engineer and experienced railroad manager (on the Missouri Pacific), revamped the company's bookkeeping system and hired William D. Basley to keep the system operating.

William Daniel Basley is one of those relatively unsung heros of this story. Basley was born in London but arrived in the United States in time to serve in the Union Army in the US Civil War [Wrege, 1983]. After the war he became a freight agent on the Newark and Hudson Railroad, owned by the Erie Railroad Company. The Erie, then under the control of Jay Gould, was still using the accounting forms and systems from the McCallum era. Basley apparently absorbed what he needed to know about accounting in order to become a public accountant in New York City and still later the internal auditor for the New York, Providence, and Boston Railroad.

In 1892, he became secretary and treasurer of the Manufacturing Investment Company, working in the New York office. At this point the chronology is tricky — so bear with me. It appears that Taylor did not pay much attention to what he called the "details of accounting" as general manager at MIC's mills, since the system that Hayes and Basley had started was operating satisfactorily.

In the summer of 1893, Taylor left the MIC to become a consultant and immediately became aware of the need to know more about accounting practices. He employed Basley, who still worked for the MIC, to tutor him in those accounting details that he had neglected previously. In addition to learning from Basley, Taylor "visited the offices of various railroads to look into their systems" [Copley, 1923, I, p. 392]. What Taylor learned was referred to as "bookkeeping under the Taylor System" and he described it as "in general the modern railroad system of accounting adapted and modified to suit the manufacturing business" [Copley, 1923, I, p. 364]. Again, we see the connection between Daniel McCallum and his heirs in the work of Hayes and Basley to Taylor.

Taylor started with Basley's ideas and observations of other railroads and extended these practices into manufacturing. In his report to Bethlehem Steel, his ideas were more related to providing information to top management as opposed to keeping the books. All records were to be generated and maintained to provide information to management; the costs should be accurate; the system should be "planned to render the temptation to steal as small as possible" and to prevent "complicity" in stealing; the reports should be prompt; and they should include information that indicated responsibilities [Copley, 1923, II, pp. 142–144]. Taylor saw that accounting was critical, not only for cost keeping, but in providing information to management about the condition of the business and its use of the firm's resources. He sought to analyze and classify expenses — for example, he collected these from various departments and classified them as shop (manufacturing) expenses, selling expenses, or administrative expenses.

His reporting system also included information about unusual costs or wastes and his idea of managing by exception:

> the manager should receive only condensed, summarized, and invariably comparative reports covering ... all of the exceptions to past averages or to the standards ... both the especially good and especially bad exceptions [Taylor, 1903, p. 126].

Accounting became an integral part of Taylor's consulting work. At the Steel Motor Company (a division of the Johnson Company), his costing system was installed and would become part of Pierre du Pont's system at the DuPont Powder Company [Johnson, 1975]. Russell Dunham, Pierre du Pont's senior accounting executive, also bought Taylor's ideas to the DuPont Powder Company from Bethlehem Steel where he had worked with Taylor [Chandler, 1977]. Followers of Taylor, such as H. K. Hathaway, continued to emphasize the accounting-management relationship well into the 1930s [Seay and Schoenfeldt, 1989]. And there were also—the neglected many.

4.2 The Neglected Many

The idea of connecting accounting information to management's need to plan, control, and make decisions was not unique to Taylor but pandemic to this era. I have attempted to avoid making this a history of cost accounting, yet to many of those discussed here information about costs were critical components of the information required by management to evaluate performance, make sales bids, economize efforts, safeguard assets, and so on. Too numerous to examine fully, there were other individuals of this period who saw management's need for accounting information.

Among this neglected many would be Henry Metcalfe, Joseph Slater Lewis, Alexander Hamilton Church, Charles Babbage, G. Charter Harrison, Frank Gilbreth, Harrington Emerson, Horace L. Arnold (who also wrote under the name, Henry Roland), and ... who of your favourites has been neglected?

5.0 CONCLUSIONS

The study of history reminds us that there is no last word. I have presented only a portion of how management and accounting history are connected through information. Managing, cost keeping, and bookkeeping are ancient in practice but only relatively recently did we begin to examine our disciplines in a more systematic fashion. I have suggested that it was on the railroads and as a result of their unique operational characteristics that accounting and management were connected by provisions for the information that was needed to manage this more complex organization.

These ideas would spread to other organizations that faced similar problems — other railroads, the emerging steel industry, and the workshop management movement. In journals and professional societies it was possible for individuals to exchange ideas, to debate which practices made more sense, and to disseminate these findings for use by others.

The development of our respective disciplines were in the actions and voices of railroad managers, journalists, and engineers. Formalization of these studies would come later in academia as practice preceded theory. Our purpose today is to do as Silas Dunning said over a century ago: to advance our knowledge by recording, studying, and comparing our experiences. I hope this congress will fulfill that goal.

REFERENCES

American Railroad Journal, Vol. 29 (April 12, 1856), pp. 225–226.

———. Vol. 29 (April 26, 1856), pp. 265.

Boockholdt, James L. "A Historical Perspective on the Auditor's Role: The Early Experience of the American Railroads," *The Accounting Historians Journal*, Vol. 10 (Spring, 1983), pp. 69–86.

Chandler, Alfred D. Jr. *Henry Varnum Poor: Business Editor, Analyst, and Reformer* (Cambridge, MA: Harvard University Press, 1956).

———. (ed.) *The Railroads: The Nation's First Big Business* (New York: Harcourt, Brace, and World, 1965), pp. 101–106.

———. *The Visible Hand: The Managerial Revolution in American Business* (Cambridge, MA: Harvard University Press, 1977).

Chatfield, Michael. *A History of Accounting Thought* (Hinsdale, IL: The Dryden Press, 1974).

Copley, Frank B. *Frederick W. Taylor: Father of Scientific Management* (Two Volumes) (New York: Harper and Brothers, 1923).

Dunning, J. Silas, quoted in Leland H. Jenks, "Early Phases of the Management Movement," *Administrative Science Quarterly*, Vol. 5 (December, 1960), pp. 421–447.

Edwards, J. R. and E. Newell. "The Development of Industrial Cost and Management Accounting before 1850," in *Accounting History*, R.H. Parker and B.S. Yamey, Eds. (Oxford: Clarendon Press, 1994).

Fink, Albert. *Cost of Railroad Transportation, Railroad Accounts, and Governmental Regulation of Railroad Tariffs* (Louisville, KY: John P. Morton and Company, 1875).

Johnson, H. Thomas. "Management Accounting in an Early Integrated Industrial: E.I. DuPont de Nemours Powder Company, 1903–1912," *Business History Review*, Vol. 49 (Summer, 1975), pp. 184–204.

———. *Relevance Lost: The Rise and Fall of Management Accounting* (Boston, MA: Harvard Business School Press, 1987).

Litterer, Joseph A. "Systematic Management: The Search for Order and Integration," *Business History Review*, Vol. 35 (Winter, 1961), pp. 461–476.

Livesay, Harold C. *Andrew Carnegie and the Rise of Big Business* (Boston: Little, Brown and Company, 1975).

McKendrick, Neil. "Josiah Wedgwood and Cost Accounting in the Industrial Revolution," *The Economic History Review*, 2nd series, Vol. 23 (April, 1970), pp. 45–67.

Pollard, Sidney. *The Genesis of Modern Management* (Cambridge, MA: Harvard University Press, 1965).

Seay, Robert A. and Roger C. Schoenfeldt. "H. K. Hathaway on Product Costing: Relevant Issues of Contemporary Concern," *The Accounting Historians Journal*, Vol. 16 (June, 1989), pp. 111–124.

Smith, Oberlin. "System in Machine Shops," *American Machinist*, Vol. 8 (October 31, 1885), pp. 1–3.

Solomons, David. "The Historical Development of Costing," in *Studies in Cost Analysis*, Second Edition, David Solomons, Ed. (Homewood, IL: Richard D. Irwin, 1968).

Taylor, Frederick W. *Shop Management* (New York: Harper and Row, 1903).

Towne, Henry R. "The Engineer as an Economist," *Transactions*, ASME, Vol. 7 (1886), pp. 428–429.

Wrege, Charles D. "Nineteenth Century Origins of 'Bookkeeping Under the Taylor System'," in *Proceedings of the Academy of Management*, K. H. Chung, Ed. (Dallas, TX: Academy of Management, 1983) pp. 106–110.

Yamey, Basil S. *Art and Accounting* (New Haven, CT: Yale University Press, 1989).

Part I:

Cost and Management Accounting

The Interaction between Accountants and Non-Accountants in the Creation of Managerial Reports:

Cases from the Belgian Colliery Industry

Ignace De Beelde
University of Ghent
Belgium

1.0 ABSTRACT

Cost and management accounting grew significantly in the nineteenth and twentieth centuries. Part of this development can be attributed to accountants, but engineers also seem to have played an important role. This paper focuses on the interaction between accountants and non-accountants in the creation of managerial reports in a number of Belgian colliery companies. The period studied is the first half of the twentieth century. The paper describes the results of an archival investigation of the managerial reports in these firms, lists the contents of these reports and looks for indications with respect to their origin. Overall, practice in these firms seems to have been variable, but in many firms the involvement of production departments appears to have been significant.

2.0 INTRODUCTION

The development of management accounting has been influenced by both accountants and non-accountants such as engineers [Loft, 1991; Solomons, 1968]. In a late-nineteenth early-twentieth century UK and US context, the influence of engineers seems to a large extent to be related to the scientific management movement [Nelson, 1974; Chandler, 1977; Kaplan, 1984]. In those two countries, accountants apparently became the dominant group during the first half of the twentieth century [Burchell *et al.*, 1980]. However, engineers kept a dominant position in some industries such as the British railway engineering industry, [Lawrenson, 1992]. These differences call for an investigation of the involvement of both engineers and accountants in managerial accounting and reporting practices in other countries and industries as well. Given different traditions in the management structure of companies [Granick, 1965] and in the professionalization of accountants, one can expect to find the relationship between both professional groups to be variable. The aim of this paper is to obtain evidence with respect to this relationship for the Belgian colliery industry in the first half of the twentieth century. One striking aspect of this industry was that all major management functions were in the hands of mining engineers: works' directors, managing directors and many members of administrators' boards all had a technical background. The dominant position of engineers seems to have been a distinguishing characteristic of the Belgian industry as a whole, a situation that continued well into the second half of this century [Granick, 1965]. However, the nature of colliery management apparently resulted in a similar dominance of engineers in other countries as well; also in the UK colliery concerns, management was mostly in the hands of technical people with mining engineering qualifications [Boyns and Wale, 1995]. Given this dominance, it seems possible that engineers also provided the information management needed to make decisions and to monitor the activities, information that is supposedly provided by management accounting systems.

This paper focuses on the creation of cost accounting data and related information. The development of more sophisticated cost accounting techniques was related to the scientific management movement [Chandler, 1977; Kaplan, 1984; Miller and O'Leary, 1994] and although it is unclear whether the ideas of F. W. Taylor, Harrington Emerson and others knew a wide application in Belgium before the Second World War, cost accounting textbooks of that period referred to techniques such as standard costing and efficiency measurement [De Beelde, 1995b]. Archival research shows that standard costing was not used in the colliery industry [De Beelde, 1995a]. Efficiency measures, however, were found in many colliery companies studied.

The remainder of this paper gives an overview of the internal reporting practices in some individual companies and looks for evidence of an interaction between accountants and engineers in the production of these reports. All these firms were rather small. Some were owned by local families, whereas others were part of larger industrial groups or holdings. The paper will conclude with an overview of some relevant data.

3.0 CASE 1: S.A. DES CARBONNAGES DE LA HAYE

The colliery company of La Haye was a small mine that originated in 1808 and that was mainly owned by local shareholders. The routine costing data available to its management were found in the monthly summaries of the operations [AEL(d), bundle 206, 1928–1930]. These included a preprinted form *Résumé des opérations du mois* and several other documents. The preprinted form included a sheet called "Unit cost" that gave gross and net extracted quantity, waste percentage, number of working days, net extraction and number of workers per day, net efficiency (*effet utile*) in kilograms, average wages and a breakdown of unit cost into thirteen cost types. Other sheets included in these monthly reports were details of the general coal account (sales, consumption, inventory and profits), invoices, client lists, a balance sheet and data on cash, financial assets and bank accounts. The documents also included a detailed survey of electricity consumption referring to the figures in the accounting books, a survey of the financial situation of the company and changes therein, a detailed balance and cost sheet, the results for the month with details on costs and inventory evolution and a list of transfers of coal and slack from one pit to another (amount and value).

The documents mentioned *Remis à Comptabilité* (handed over to accounting) and this suggests that they may have originated in another department. The unit cost breakdown for La Haye had the same structure as the extraction chapter in the accounting ledger but was completed with some data on efficiency and labour. Other data such as the evolution of the coal account and the monthly balance sheets also related to the "financial accounting system." Apparently there was an interaction in this company between the accounting department and those in the firm responsible for costing.

4.0 CASE 2: S.A. DES CHARBONNAGES DE GOSSON, LA HAYE & HORLOZ RÉUNIS

This company originated in 1930 as a result of the merger of four existing firms. The monthly *cédules de comptabilité* of Gosson, La Haye & Horloz Réunis included information on the pits of the company [AEL(d), bundle 299, 1931–1935, 1937]. The schedules listed the following items:

- balance of general accounts Coal and Briquettes, including among other items production quantity, sales, consumption, stock movement, unit cost and profit
- general information, such as number of days worked, daily production, average number of workers and cost of labour for different types of work
- coal: decomposition of unit cost (per pit) and total unit cost (per pit and total)
- balance sheet at the end of the month.

Except for the financial statements, all information was given for each pit separately. The actual title on the documents was *Résumé des opérations de ..., remis à Mr. Comptabilité* (summary of the operations of ... transferred to Mr. Accounting), suggesting that they were probably created outside the accounting department or that another department at least was involved in the creation of these documents.

For 1933, we also have a set of documents, called "summary unit cost" [AEL(d), bundle 300]. This document contained the same data on unit cost composition and on the evolution of the general coal account as the previous series. Figures were given for each pit (Gosson, Horloz, La Haye) and for the company as a whole. The table gave both total figures and figures per tonne. The sheet also included a General Coal Account Balance that gave the cash sales, credit sales, consumption, stock at the end of the month, total withdrawals (*sorties*), stock at beginning of the month, bought or transferred coal, total entries, production, unit cost and profit or loss for each seat. For each item quantity, average per tonne and total cost were reported.

The monthly reports on exploitation were mainly technical documents [AEL(d), bundles 641–675, 1932–1934]. They contained net production per day, evolution of the personnel, extraction and efficiency (*effet utile*), unit cost for the current and the previous month (and the difference between the two), preparatory works executed during the month and a survey of the work at the different exploitation seams. For unit cost, a distinction was made between underground wages, surface wages, coal consumption, electricity consumption and factory supplies. The structure of the available documents did not change over time.

Other series of documents were more voluminous. The annual reports on the company included more than 20 pages [AEL(d), bundles 756–773, 1937–1954]. They were typed instead of handwritten and contained much detailed financial information. From the documents themselves it was obvious that they were prepared for the meetings of the board of administrators. There were separate reports on total production, unit cost (with additional figures concerning wages), consumption of consumables, consumption of electricity, all kinds of gratifications to employees and evolution of the workforce. Much attention was paid to detailed production figures for the different seams and pits, to progress made in each layer of coal, to the evolution of stock for each variety of coal. There was a thorough analysis of the evolution of unit cost and the advancement of preparatory works. The documents tended to become even more detailed over the years. From 1941 onwards they contained a series of reports from the *Directeur des Travaux* and annual summaries of another series, the monthly reports on the company [AEL(d), bundles 774–787, 1941–1954]. For each year, the annual reports consisted of a collection of reports, about five centimetres thick. Their structure remained essentially unchanged, containing very detailed tables on different aspects of the exploitation. To illustrate their contents, the list of schedules for January 1941 included a report of the works director and a monthly report. The first sheet included the following items for each pit:

- net production, number of working days, daily production, details on numbers of different categories of workers, ratio of workers at the working places to total workers underground, and comments
- efficiency and average wages: including comparative data on previous month, for four categories of workers; with comments
- average weight of a *berlaine*, with comments
- breakdown of production (three coal categories)
- unit cost, with comparative data on previous month; broken down into wages underground, surface pit one and surface pit two; consumption of coal, electricity, wood and factory supplies; the sum of these gives a total unit cost; with comments
- monthly production and output per *abatteur*
- production per seam
- progress and output for each tunnel
- preparatory works (progress)
- first establishment (progress)
- surface: electricity consumption (comparison with previous month)
- power plant: production, coal consumption, cost of coal consumed, unit cost for one kWh
- drainage (with data on previous month)
- electricity consumption per pit
- notes on the working places: four pages with details on the working places
- maintenance of pits.

The monthly report included similar data but was more concise. It gave information on extracted quantities and days worked, analyses of coal, unit cost wages (not comparable with the unit cost calculation in the works director's report), efficiency of personnel and consumption of supplies, all with comments and comparative figures.

Sometimes reports relating to several months at a time were included. These reports said that they were made up for the meetings of the board of directors (*Comité de Direction*). They included the same schedules as the monthly documents, but also a summary scheme on unit cost with figures equal to those reported in the report of the works director, detailed lists of consumption of coal and supplies, a detailed schedule on the electricity production, a detail of social charges and other data on the workforce, coal production per seam and efficiency data with a three-page general discussion of the exploitation and situation of the company, including about five lines on expectations for the following months.

Most of the data found in the managerial reports were technically oriented; many data were collected to measure the efficiency of labour. Colliery management probably focussed on producing coal at a cost which was as low as possible. Given the dominance of wages in unit cost, this explained why in most reporting systems wages were detailed to a far greater extent than other expenses: labour expenses had to be controlled as much as possible to obtain maximum efficiency.

Some accounting data were comparable to the information found in traditional accounting books, such as the monthly balance sheets and details on the coal and by-products accounts. Many other data were much more detailed, especially in the extensive monthly and annual reports, and must therefore have been found in the "financial accounting system" itself rather than in underlying documents. Part of the documents was explicitly produced outside the accounting department, such as the reports of the works director. Information on the breakdown of unit cost might have been found in the industrial journal, although some differences were observed: the extraction expenses in the industrial journal, for example, do not seem to include free coal, which was in the cost sheets included in the labour expenses.

5.0 CASE 3: S.A. DES CHARBONNAGES D'ABHOOZ ET BONNE FOI HARENG

This firm was a small mining company, originating from several nineteenth century mergers and probably was owned by local shareholders. In the Charbonnages d'Abhooz et Bonne Foi Hareng, the members of the *Conseil Général* received a series of schedules on the situation of the company for the first semester of each year [AEL(a), bundle 844, 1895–1930]. The schedules contained comparative data with respect to production, average unit cost, average selling price, average profit per tonne, total profit, stock situation, direct extraction costs, preparatory works, drainage expenses, transport expenses, general expenses and capitalized *premier établissement* (formation) expenses. Besides these figures, the series included a balance sheet, a calculation of financial position and working capital and lists of debtors and creditors with reference to the general ledger.

The preceding documents were addressed to the *Conseil Général*, a body consisting of the administrators and the auditors of the company. Other documents were addressed only to the Board of Administrators, the *Conseil d'Administration*. Monthly reports are available for the period 1909–1916, annual reports for 1895–1930 [AEL(a), bundles 47–48 and bundles 49–83, respectively]. The monthly reports discussed the activities of the company during the past month. They were also copied in the minutes of the meetings of the *Conseil Général*. They were quite extensive, describing for each pit the state of the different seams that were exploited and the progress in works carried out. They included figures on the amount of coal extracted, efficiency and wages for cutters, *bosseyeurs*, underground, surface and total, unit cost (consisting of underground, surface and wood) and drainage at different levels underground. Besides these production data, the reports also provided information on the commercial situation [stock evolution (quantity and value), total profits, profits per tonne, unit cost, selling price, cash position and amounts to be paid]. Most of these figures were compared with the figures of the previous year and they were briefly discussed like all other financial data. The reports also included details of all sales transactions of the month. Sometimes, detailed reports on specific items were included, such as a report on the necessity and the consequences of considerable new investments in fixed assets [AEL(a), bundle 47, November 1909, pp. 160–170] and a report on the effects of the use of pick hammers on unit cost and coal quality [AEL(a), bundle 48, 1913, pp. 71–76]. The reports were signed by the *directeur gérant*, the managing director, except for the last report mentioned which was signed by the works director (the *directeur des travaux*).

The annual reports that were preserved were much more extensive (up to 90 pages) and cover a longer period. They included a discussion of the results of the year ending (production and profits), the allocation of profits, the works executed in each pit (drainage, extraction, fixed assets) and figures on profits, unit cost and stock. All of this took about six pages. The next section included a detailed discussion of the different "accounts that form in our books the assets and liabilities of the company at year end" [AEL(a), bundle 54, p. 6]. For each account, the opening and closing balance and a commentated overview of all transactions were included. This covered more than 40 pages and looks like a summary of the general ledger.

These reports ended with a statement on the financial position of the company that was merely a summary of the balance sheet, and a calculation of the net working capital. The report was signed by the managing director (*directeur-gérant*), the works director (*directeur des travaux*) and the bookkeeper (*chef comptable*). From 1908 onwards, the report also contained tables and diagrams for extraction, profit, value of extraction, exploitation cost, wages, gratifications, first establishment expenses and dividends, all computed per share, for each year since 1895 [AEL(a), bundle 62, p. 8 and following]. We also found a table for the same years giving extraction, value of extracted quantity, exploitation expenses, total wages and wages per tonne, first establishment expenses, social charges (total value and per tonne), unit cost, selling price, profit per tonne, total profit and drainage expenses. The structure of the reports remained fairly stable until 1930. After the first World War, they included more comparative data on prices, wages or costs. The report on 1919, for example, included a list of the evolution of wages and of prices for 31 categories of supplies, giving data on 1914, 1918 and 1919 [AEL(a), bundle 73]. These reports were not at the disposal of the Board of Administrators at the beginning of a new year. The report on 1900, for example, already mentioned total production and profit, whereas the minutes of the meeting of the Board on January 9, 1901, merely gave an estimate of total profit (profit until November + estimated profit for December) [AEL(a), bundle 4]. The report on 1900 was signed on February 20, 1901 and it was discussed by the Board of Directors on February 22.

For the period around the Second World War, the calculations of unit cost are preserved [AEL(a), bundles 84–94, 1939–1950]. The documents were probably made up at the end of the year and clarify the structure of unit cost calculation, giving historical figures for each month.

Another series has to be read in close relation to the previous one. It is a series of documents containing information on sales, consumption, unit cost, selling price, production, wages and efficiency [AEL(a), bundles 95–100, 1939–1950]. The tables were probably made up at year end, giving figures for each month. For sales and consumption, they detailed the total value of the consumption at the furnaces and fireplaces, free coal for labour and sales at different points of sale. Both total and unit profit figures were given for each pit and for each month. Unit cost was also computed for each month and for each pit, without any indication, however, whether this is a cost price per tonne. The reported cost price was very variable: a difference of 250% between the most expensive and the cheapest month was recorded in 1940. A possible explanation is the outbreak of the Second World War in May 1940. In the documents relating to 1947 however, similar variances could be found. For one pit, cost price even then varied between 509 and 1,011 Belgian francs (BEF). The composition of the unit cost figures also seems quite variable from one month to another. The percentages for the company as a whole in 1940 are included in Exhibit 1 by way of example. They are computed from the historical figures given in the documents; for total cost, the actual figure is given; for the breakdown of unit cost, the percentage of all components in total cost is given. Total unit cost was quite variable (an average of 201 BEF per tonne, standard deviation of 36 BEF). The share of direct costs varies between 61% and 76%. Total labour expenses amount to approximately 60% of unit cost.

Exhibit 1

Percentage Composition of Unit Cost Abhooz, 1940*

Month	Jan	Feb	March	April	May	June
wages underground	42	39	40	43	34	33
wages surface	6	5	5	6	6	8
factory supplies	10	10	11	15	11	8
coal consumption	4	2	3	2	4	5
electricity cons.	3	3	3	2	3	3
diverse costs	5	3	12	4	3	5
Precentage total direct cost	69	62	73	72	62	61
preparatory work	0	0	1	1	1	0
drainage	8	7	7	6	11	12
diverse expenses	6	6	5	5	5	4
general expenses	5	15	4	4	8	7
social charges	12	10	11	11	14	16
Hist. total cost per tonne	162	173	180	169	274	280

Month	July	August	Sept	Oct	Nov	Dec
wages underground	42	43	44	41	39	40
wages surface	6	6	6	6	5	7
factory supplies	12	12	12	12	13	13
coal consumption	4	4	4	3	3	4
electricity cons.	3	2	2	2	2	3
diverse costs	3	6	5	12	13	9
Percentage total direct cost	69	74	74	76	75	72
preparatory work	1	1	1	1	1	1
drainage	9	8	6	6	7	8
diverse expenses	5	4	4	4	4	5
general expenses	4	3	4	4	3	3
social charges	12	10	11	10	10	11
Hist. total cost per tonne	191	189	187	205	207	197

* [AEL(a), bundle 95]

To summarize, the quarterly schedules for the *Conseil Général* of Abhooz included only accounting figures (including balance sheets), and profit and cost price seem to have been the main measures for the success of the company. These documents did not include efficiency figures. Such figures were, however, central in the monthly reports for the *Conseil d'Administration* which were signed by the managing director. These reports nevertheless also included accounting data, at least until the First World War. The annual reports and several other series of documents confirm the importance of accounting information in addition to the more technical data. They also gave information on the changing valuation rules that were applied, especially concerning the capitalization of assets.

6.0 CASE 4: CHARBONNAGES RÉUNIS DE LA MINERIE

Again, this firm originated after several mergers in the nineteenth century; its exploitation, however, has much older antecedents. In the twentieth century production was quite low and the firm seems to have been owned by local capitalists.

Some reports that were preserved for the Charbonnages Réunis de la Minerie relate to only parts of this colliery. A first series of documents relates to the shafts Minerie, Dellicour and Neuwaide [AEL(e), bundle 322, 1861–1901]. Their layout remained unchanged over the whole period. For each fortnight we found extraction (hectolitre), rubble (hectolitre), a breakdown of expenses and a detail of cost price per tonne. It is unclear how unit cost was computed exactly: when total expenses are divided by total extraction, a unit cost figure is obtained which is higher than the figure reported in the register.

A second series relates to the Battice pit [AEL(e), bundle 323]. It contained a series of two-page handwritten documents that remained unchanged over the whole period. For each fortnight reported data included extraction, labour costs, number of workforce, number of days worked and surface exploited, per seam. Strangely enough, these documents included different information, although dealing with the same company and the same period. For Battice, only labour expenses were reported, whereas for the other pits, supplies consumption, preparatory works etc. were also registered.

The most important reports that were used by the management of the S.A. des Charbonnages Réunis de la Minerie and that were preserved, deal with the pre World War One period [AEL(e), bundles 314–321, 1861–1906]. These fortnightly reports on sales and unit cost contained the following tables: movement of coal stock, sales, general expenditures, debtor and creditor accounts, movement of factory supplies, unit cost per hectolitre and cash movement. These documents had to be signed by the managing director. No reference was made to the accounting department.

On the one hand, the information found in the Minerie reports was more detailed than that found in the "financial accounting" books. On the other hand, most of these data are accounting data, except the total extraction figure. Before 1908, the documents mainly included figures on expenses, sales, unit cost and cash position, while a profit figure is not included. After this year, figures on assets and profit were also reported. There were apparently no efficiency data reported but we have to bear in mind that our sources are quite limited for this mine.

7.0 CASE 5: CHARBONNAGE DU BOIS D'AVROY

The colliery company of Bois d'Avroy originated in 1885 as the result of a demerger of an existing iron working and colliery firm. It was owned by the Société Générale de Belgique, the largest Belgian holding company with very significant interests in Belgian coal and steel production.

Several documents addressed to the management of the company were preserved. The first series consisted of three-monthly reports, available from 1889 till 1923 and for three months of 1936 [AEL(c), bundles 14–16]. The schedules contained in these reports had a preprinted outline, which remained unchanged. The index for each report mentioned the following tables:

- balance sheet for the period (three months)
- operations during the period
- details of general costs
- debtor and creditor lists
- unit cost per pit
- coal sold and coal in stock
- coal consumption
- report of the engineer on the progress of the works.

The last four items are, however, missing. The contents of the documents that were preserved remained unchanged throughout the series, apart from some minor changes, such as the inclusion of an account "Electricity" from 1913 onward. These documents were identical to those prescribed by the Société Générale and provided management with detailed accounting information. These data probably originated in the accounting department itself: details of the different accounts had to be signed by the bookkeeper and by the director in charge, but this was not done in the documents consulted.

The company also produced other documents. For the beginning of the century, a series of monthly reports from the works director (*directeur des travaux*) existed [AEL(c), bundle 17, 1898–1910]. Apart from discussions of first establishment and preparatory works progress, these reports included data on production and efficiency for each pit and total unit cost with a discussion of the main influencing factors. Until 1904 they also included data sent to the *Inspection Générale*, probably a controlling body of the Société Générale de Belgique, the main shareholder of Bois d'Avroy. These data concerned the number of working days, daily production, production per worker, average daily wages and causes for variation in unit cost.

For the first decade of this century, there was also a handwritten series of documents on the exploitation and the financial situation of the company [AEL(c), bundle 18, 1903–1910]. This series included among other documents a *budget des dépenses* for 1904 [pp. 73–97]. The same was found for 1905 and 1906, although in a shorter version (a similar document was found in a series called *Rapports et correspondence* [AEL(c), bundle 19, pp. 458–460]). The *budget des dépenses* listed the cost of works executed in the year ending and the proposed expenditures for the budget year for the first establishment works and the preparatory works. The exploitation budget and the cokes production budget included production, unit cost and expenditures for the current year and for the next year (estimations). The budget had to be signed by the managing director and by the president of the Conseil d'Administration. All costs were very detailed, emphasizing the classification of accounts and their breakdown in articles as used in the three-monthly reports discussed before. Preparatory works were detailed for each coal seam and summarized for each pit. Apart from figures, there was also a short qualitative description of the works concerned. The exploitation budget unraveled total and unit cost in ten categories of direct costs (wages, oil and grease, iron, wood, diverse objects, workplace supplies, coal consumption, handling of coal, amortization of tools, diverse costs) and four categories of indirect costs (preparatory works, drainage costs, transports, general costs). Cost price was subtracted from sales price, giving total and unit profit. The sales price was estimated for each coal category and an average was given based on the estimated production for each category.

Calculations of unit cost were preserved from 1883 until 1959. The structure of unit cost calculation remained almost unchanged during the whole period under study [AEL(c), bundles 80–87 and 145–149]. Each month, unit cost was calculated for each pit. In a two-page document, production and number of days worked were mentioned.

Exploitation reports and financial reports were available from the last decade of the 19th century until about 1950, with a gap for the first decade of the 20th century [AEL(c), bundles 110–115]. For each pit the oldest reports mentioned production, number of days worked, average daily production, number of workers (underground), workers *à veine*, average coal grade, efficiency (tonnes/m^2, m^2/worker, tonnes/worker, tonnes/working day underground), total unit cost, direct costs (breakdown: wages underground, wages surface, supplies (oil, wood, metal, ropes, diverse), coal consumption, workplaces, handling of coal, equipment), indirect cost (preparatory works, drainage, transport, general costs) and results (profit or loss). All of these data were recorded on a monthly basis.

This information became slightly more detailed, especially where efficiency was concerned (efficiency/working day surface, working day underground, general efficiency). From 1928 onwards the documents included some separate, nonrecurrent tables such as a comparative unit cost table, giving monthly unit cost and production figures for 12 other coal mines, a table of the evolution in wages, and a comparison for this month and the same month two years ago of unit cost and coal and electricity consumption. From 1935 onwards, tables were included on workforce, production, workplaces, consumption, expenditures, further detailing the basic tables' data. A new table was entitled *Renseignements à fournir mensuellement à la comptabilité*. This table included the number of days worked, average daily production, details on the number of workers employed and the average daily wages (underground and surface). The inclusion of this table suggests that these schedules were not made up in the bookkeeping department.

During and after World War II, we find further additions to the basic table itself, although its general structure remained unchanged. New cost categories were added, such as amortization and administrative and industrial overheads. Selling prices and profit or loss/tonne were included, as well as a further table detailing sales, consumption, stock, extraction and efficiency.

All these tables had in common that they probably were made up at year end, summarizing other monthly or three-monthly tables. Some of the latter documents can be found in the registers entitled *Renseignements généraux* [AEL(c), bundles 116–119]. The registers essentially gave more information on and regrouped all data included in the exploitation reports.

In 1904, new ways of reporting were investigated. The management of the company asked to calculate unit cost for one pit for one month based on a different classification of accounts. The aim was to compare this new classification with the existing calculation [AEL(c), bundle 18, pp. 171–177]. The letter mentioned that the suggested system differed from the system used by the Société Générale.

We could summarize the preceding in the following way. Managerial information in Bois d'Avroy was very comprehensive. Most of the reports had a very stable structure and they contained both technical and accounting data. Accounting data included detailed surveys of financial accounts; they adopted the schemes imposed by the Société Générale. Technical information included detailed efficiency and unit cost data, and was probably made up by the production departments. Unit cost data were much more detailed than the information included in the accounting books.

8.0 CASE 6: CHARBONNAGE DES SIX-BONNIERS

The colliery firm of Six-Bonniers had no legal status like the other colliery companies discussed in this paper. Its ownership structure remained stable until its liquidation in 1948: a minority shareholder — a local family — and a majority shareholder, the iron and steel company of Ougrée-Marihaye, one of the major Belgian steel firms.

The main reporting medium to the management of the Six-Bonniers coal mine was monthly exploitation reports [AEL(f), bundle 610, 1911–1950]. These reports were short and typed, giving some figures and comments but few tables. Data included were net production (total and average per working day), sales and stock situation, evolution of workforce number and percentage of absenteeism, progress of preparatory works, new investments, sales figures, consumption of coal, waste percentage (coal handling) and from February 1921 onwards, results for the month. In some reports, comparative figures for the previous month were included. Until 1914, the report sometimes further included a list of sales, mentioning the name of the client and amount. These reports remained short and concise (two pages) and they referred to the monthly accounting statement, which will be discussed below. Each year, at year end, a more comprehensive report was made, giving information on production, sales, wages, personnel, coal price, first establishment works, exploitation, social security and profits, making a distinction between total profit and exploitation profit.

The monthly schedules were available from 1899 until 1948 [AEL(f), bundles 18–26]. Until April 1909, they detailed number of days worked, gross extraction, quantity of coal shipped and unit cost. The breakdown of unit cost distinguished between wages and supplies and between total cost and cost per tonne. Starting from May 1909, the structure of the schedule changed. From that moment onwards it consisted of eight tables and its general structure did not change for the rest of the period. It included a decomposition of wages, distinguishing 42 categories, a decomposition of supplies and general expenses, a detail of production with efficiency data, details on fixed assets and a balance sheet for the month.

At the end of the year, a balance sheet and profit and loss account were made up, which were intended for the management of the company [AEL(f), bundles 28–30]. The documents also included details on sales, operations and a table giving the results for the year mentioning "net extraction at selling price less consumption," cost price (+ allowances + coal handling expenses) and the difference between both, or the benefit of the year. The figures of the four schedules (balance sheet, sales, operations and results) could not be reconciled to each other. The figure registered in the operations table as "balance of p/l account" (19,958 BEF) differs strongly from the profit figure in the sales schedule (62,757 BEF) or in the results scheme (699,413 BEF).

In 1935, the group De Launoit acquired control over Ougrée-Marihaye, the main owner of Six-Bonniers. De Launoit reorganized Ougréze-Marihaye, creating among other things Cofinindus as a holding company for the whole group [Joye, 1964, pp. 30–33]. In the archives, we found some documents related to the control of Six-Bonniers by Cofinindus, with the schedules made up by Six-Bonniers itself. A first document dealt with 1935 and was signed by Herme, the inspector of Cofinindus. For 1937, 1938 and 1939 we had a typewritten document, stamped *Cofinindus-contrôle*. The documents contained lots of figures on the financial statements, in 1937, generally with comparative data on previous periods. Often they were further detailed and classified in a different manner than in the statements. The document criticized the accounting practices of the company:

> *Le poste 'amortissement sur matériel' était autrefois, comme l'indique son nom, un poste créditeur; devenu débiteur, il a passé à l'actif sans changer d'appellation, il est difficile de s'expliquer pourquoi, le fait étant ancien. Cette anomalie va disparaître : dès le nouvel exercice, ce poste recevra une désignation plus adéquate à la réalité, soit 'matériel en service.'*
>
> *'Prévisions fiscales'*
>
> *Cette désignation est également impropre. C'était bien, autrefois, au passif, une provision destinée à faire face à la taxe communale de démergement; cette taxe a été acquittée en son temps, mais la Société des SixBonniers a estimé qu'elle lui avait été appliquée à tort. Là aussi, une dénomination nouvelle eût été préférable. Ce poste va d'ailleurs être amorti et disparaître entièrement avec le nouvel exercice. [AEL(f), bundle 28, 'Bilans,' 1936/37, p. 7]*

The Cofinindus report of 1939 clearly showed that its authors acted as auditors of the Six-Bonniers company:

> *A cours de l'examen des différents postes du bilan, nous nous sommes fait produire diverses pièces justificatives et avons demandé certaines explications qui nous ont toujours été données très rapidement. Nous avons procédé à des sondages parmi les comptes des clients et des fournisseurs et nous avons examiné dans les livres d'inventaire la valeur attribuée à quelques articles par comparaison avec les prix actuels. Nous avons enfin procédé au reclassement de certains comptes afin de nous permettre de dresser le bilan suivant notre formule habituelle. [AEL(f), bundle 28, 'Bilans (Cofinindus),' April 30, 1939, p. 1]*

The monthly accounting schemes reported two unit cost breakdowns, the first one distinguishing wages, supplies and amortization, the other one exploitation, preparatory works, drainage, surface, general expenses, transport and handling, and amortization. It is quite remarkable that amortization was included and detailed (12 categories are reported). These schemes were probably made up by the accounting department since they were signed by the bookkeeper. Information for the amortization breakdown probably was found in underlying documents that were not preserved, since the accounting books did not report them in such detail.

Historical costing was used, except for general expenses for which a fixed rate was used during most months. Starting in 1909, these schemes became much more detailed, including, for example, 32 categories of wages. Most data, however, remained accounting data. Such detailed information certainly was not found in the accounting books, but must have been taken from underlying documents. Internal balance sheets illustrated the changes in accounting policy, mainly concerning capitalization of assets.

At the end of the 1930s, the company was controlled by Cofinindus. Available evidence shows that this control was quite detailed and also included the application of valuation rules and reporting practices.

9.0 CASE 7: S.A. DES CHARBONNAGES DE BONNE-ESPÉRANCE, BATTERIE ET VIOLETTE

The S.A. des Charbonnages de Bonne-Espérance, Batterie et Violette was one of the larger Belgian colliery companies. Although it was not under the direct control of one of the large holdings, its shareholders were mainly large industrial or financial groups or powerful families.

The Conseil d'Administration de Bonne-Espérance, Batterie et Violette received several reports on the situation of the company. Apart from some documents from the 19th century the first series that has been preserved contained only monthly reports from the early 1930s [AEL(b), bundle 85, 1930–1932]. These always included a survey of the exploitation works (including efficiency and unit cost comparisons with previous month, stock evolution, and results) and quite often also gave an outline of the first establishment works, in which actual costs were compared to the budget. From October 1932 onwards, diagrams were added to highlight production and sales figures.

For the whole first half of this century, extensive monthly reports in tabular form were preserved [AEL(b), bundles 449–1020]. They included balance sheets and additional information, unit cost, sales, inventory movement, unit cost (wages) and underground transport, an engineer's report and a report of the managing director. The latter included:

Engineer's report

- **Discussion of unit cost wages** (separate for each pit): Gave for each layer data for the current month and for previous months; mentioned number of days worked, average number of workers, production, cost of wages for each category of exploitation works and factory supplies (per tonne and per working day); the exploitation works and supplies were broken down as in a previous table "Unit cost wages."
- **Discussion of detail unit cost calculations** (separate for each pit): Same information as in "Detail of unit cost for work categories," but given for each layer, with comparative data for the previous periods.
- **Drainage**: Gave for the current and for previous months the number of pistonne blows, number of hours worked, number of stops, number of piston blows per minute, total quantity and quantity per 24 hours drained, drainage per tonne of coal produced.

Report of the *directeur-gérant*

- **Comparison of production and sales: current month, previous month and same month last year:** Included production and sales figures (quantity, average, percentage) for 11 coal qualities.

- **Comparison of stocks:** Gave stock at the end of the month at each pit and comparative figures for the 11 coal qualities already mentioned.
- **Coal consumed** (separately for each pit): Gave quantity, value and average value for coal consumption at preparatory works, drainage, extraction, sorting and general costs, with corresponding figures for previous month and previous year.
- **Profit comparison:** For each pit profit figure, production and value of coal per tonne were compared to figures on last month and last year.

These quite extensive schedules were supplemented with several separate tables, which provided details on general costs (14 items) and manufacturing (washing of coaldust, with washing expenses, estimate of the production value, estimate of coal supplies to washing unit).

At year end, an inventory of fixed and current assets and of liabilities was made and registered on inventory lists. To these lists were added a list of total debits and credits and their balances, and a profit and loss account [AEL(b), bundles 113–152, 1900–1939]. At the beginning of the century, the inventory lists were very detailed, listing all items for each fixed asset account, and including all clients and suppliers. This balance sheet was signed by the bookkeeper, the managing administrator and the other members of the Board of Administrators.

To summarize, monthly information for the management of this company included both reports on efficiency and unit cost and reports with financial accounting data. For first establishment expenses, budgets were made. Unit cost reports used different breakdowns. Also sales information distinguished coal types and selling points, and wages were highly detailed in more than one report. Finally, profit also was reported and at the end of the year, the managers received lists of total debits and credits with comments. This situation continued until the beginning of the 1930s. From then onwards, the scope of the information was greatly reduced. The reason why this happened is unclear: there were, for example, no major shifts in the management of the company.

10.0 CASE 8: S.A. DES CHARBONNAGES A. DUMONT

The firms discussed to this point were all part of the Lièges coalfield. The S.A. des Charbonnages A. Dumont is the only company discussed in this paper that is located in the Limburg coalfield. As exploitation of the Limburg coalfield only started in the twentieth century, A. Dumont was a more recent firm; it originated in 1907. It was also a much larger firm than the others discussed here and its owners were the large Belgian financial groups, mainly the Société Générale de Belgique. For André Dumont, no extensive series of management reports including or referring to accounting information could be consulted. However, some reports could be investigated.

A portfolio with notes of the managing director of the company contained an example of the monthly reports addressed to the works director [RAB, bundle 56, September 1931]. This report gave the following information:

- ratio net production/extraction
- ratio net production/gross production
- consumption of metallic frames
- consumption of mining wood per net tonne

- consumption of explosives per net tonne
- consumption of electricity and steam per net tonne
- consumption of electricity for ventilation.

The document also included comparative data for the last five months.

Some indirect information could be found on other reports, though. In a note dated September 3, 1931, addressed by the managing director to the works director, we found that the monthly report had to be completed with information on the "renewal equipment that should be repaired, that was repaired and that was consumed" *(matériel de renouvellement à réparer, réparé, utilisé*). The number of pieces received for repair, the number repaired and the number registered as waste had to be included, as well as all goods returned to warehouses, those goods which still had to be repaired and those gone out during the month. Data on goods returned to stock and goods delivered had to be obtained from the accounting department.

A series of documents containing summary annual reports was preserved in the Beveren archives [RAB, bundles 2997–2999, 1933–1971]. These reports were quite extensive. As an example, the data on 1933 included details on exploitation unit cost per month; wages underground and wages surface (making a distinction between 30 types of activities and for each activity number of days worked, wages, average wages, cost per tonne, percentages, average daily number of workers and number of workers per 100 tonnes); graphs on the average production, efficiency of cutters, efficiency of underground exploitation, efficiency of underground total and efficiency underground total and surface exploitation; average daily workforce for 78 types of activities; production figures; consumption for underground supporting works; data on coal handling; energy consumption and production data; technical data on the use of machines; graphs of the number of accidents; details on wages underground and distribution of total wages over 78 cost sections.

These tables were further extended during the remainder of the first half of the twentieth century. They included more graphs (e.g., for several production data per pit), and some new tables (e.g., comparing results and expenses and underground and surface works to those of the previous year). From 1939 onwards, there was also a document specifying the cost price, with a subtitle "monthly report of accounting department," apparently indicating that the accounting department was also involved in cost price calculation.

The evidence described above suggests that reports to the management were made up both by the accounting and the production departments. In this mine also, budgeting seems to have been limited to fixed assets. Wages were extremely detailed but many data also were available for other categories of expenses. For general expenses the Société Générale structure was used.

11.0 OVERVIEW AND GENERAL REMARKS

Exhibit 2 gives an overview of the type of documents that were discussed in detail in the preceding paragraphs. It also shows whether or not we had information about the origin of these documents. The data for A. Dumont are not easily comparable due to the different nature of the source material, so this company will be left out of the discussion that follows.

Exhibit 2
Summary of Reporting Practices

	La Haye	GLHHR	ABFH	Minerie	Bois d'A	Six B	BEBV	A Dumont
Extensive financial acc. data	BS	BS	X 4	X		X	BS	
Operational data in monistic chart	X	X	X	X	X	X	X	
Unit cost structure	Det	Det	Gen	Gen	Det	Det	Det	
Commercial data	X	X	X	X		X	X	
Technical data not in monistic chart	X	X	X	X	X	X	X	X
Reference to accounting department						X		
Reference to transfer to accounting department	X	X			X			
Reference to general manager			X	X			X	
Reference to production department		X			X		X	X

Notes:

This table includes only reports that were made up at least once a month.

Information for A. Dumont did not include actual reports; therefore the results are not comparable to the other firms.

The table generalizes the results of the research: the actual contents of the documents often changed over time.

Legend:

BS: balance Sheet included

Det: detailed breakdown included

Gen: general breakdown included

X: information present in preserved documents

The internal reports that were found in the archives of the colliery companies studied in this paper generally include financial accounting data. On the one hand, at least three of these firms created monthly balance sheets and in only one of them, financial accounting data were not presented to board members or directors on at least a monthly basis. On the other hand, all companies included technical or operational data that normally could have been included in a monistic chart of accounts and technical data which would not be included in a monistic chart. Richard [1995] shows that thinking in accounting in Belgium throughout the first half of the twentieth century was dominated by "formal monism," "an accounting system in which the accounting result (profit or loss) cannot be determined if *all* of the component accounts have not been established". A typical example of such a monistic approach to accounting was the chart of accounts that was published in 1926 by a leading Belgian practicing accountant, company manager and academic, H. Blairon. The chart, which was applied in many industries, was extremely detailed with respect to expenses. It made it possible to integrate unit cost calculation and the creation of balance sheets in one accounting system. Consequently, some managers probably did not feel a real need for a separate cost accounting system. However, the Blairon chart does not seem to have been very influential in the colliery industry, at least not in the period studied. Most of the colliery concerns used an accounting system that was to a large extent based on the schemes developed by the Société Générale de Belgique [Ansotte and Defrise, 1910]. In addition, however, this scheme was an example of "formal monism." The reports in all companies discussed previously included operational data that would have been found in these integrated accounting systems, suggesting the involvement of accountants in the production of these data. In most firms however, these integrated systems could produce only fairly general information, on the pit level or even on the firm level. In many cost sheets, information was much more detailed; some mines even produced data on the coal seam level. There was also much information in the cost sheets that was not included in the accounting books, especially technical data on efficiency, number of working days, workforce, quantity of water drained, etc. Such data are listed in the table as "technical data that are not found in a monistic chart." This then suggests the involvement of the production departments.

Detailed information on the structure of the cost of the coal was available to the management in most companies, although two of them provided only a general breakdown of unit cost. The cost categories found in the unit cost schedules often turned out to be comparable to the structure of the accounts in the ledgers, although they sometimes had a different degree of detail and although the figures which were reported in the different reports were not always comparable.

Evidence with respect to the involvement of accountants and/or engineers suggests several possible practices. In at least one firm, the accounting department seems to have played a major role in the creation of managerial reports. In most companies, however, we found indications of a significant involvement of the production department. The reports were signed by the works director, or called the "engineer's report," or transferred to the accounting department. The figures found in these reports often differ from those found in the accounting books, suggesting the use of different data sets. There is also a more material indication of the involvement of other employees: in all cases, the handwriting found in the reports differs from the one found in the accounting books from the same period. In the minutes of the meetings of the *Conseil d'Administration*, the reports are often referred to as the "engineer's report." As all of this suggests the involvement of engineers within the production departments, it becomes somewhat strange that these documents quite often also included pure financial accounting data, such as interim balance sheets or lists of total debits and credits. Evidence from the A. Dumont colliery suggests that data were transferred from one department to another and that both production and accounting departments were involved in the creation of cost information. The accounting department was responsible for the final report.

Kaplan [1984] says that in the US context, sophisticated cost accounting practices had been developed by 1925 and that cost accounting and financial accounting systems were kept separately, with the cost accounting system typically operated by the manufacturing departments. Our evidence suggests that Belgian colliery companies had accounting systems that were at least partially integrated and in which both accountants and engineers were involved. Such a conclusion seems somehow unexpected, keeping in mind the dominant position of engineers in Belgian firms referred to in the beginning of this paper, and the weak position of the Belgian accounting profession in this period [Mas, 1959]. Further archival research might shed more light on the precise nature of the role of both professional groups and their interaction. Now it looks as if practices differed between companies, but that creating managerial accounting reports was only rarely a task for just one of the two professional groups.

REFERENCES

AEL(a). Liège State Archives, Entreprises, Abhooz (various years).

AEL(b). Liège State Archives, Entreprises, Batterie (various years).

AEL(c). Liège State Archives, Entreprises, Bois d'Avroy (various years).

AEL(d). Liège State Archives, Entreprises, Gosson (various years).

AEL(e). Liège State Archives, Entreprises, Minerie (various years).

AEL(f). Liège State Archives, Entreprises, Six Bonniers (various years).

Ansotte, C. and A. Defrise. *Traité pratique de comptabilité industrielle* (Dour: A. Vaubert, 1910).

Blairon, H. *Cours complet de comptabilité des industries manufacturières (théorie — pratique — organisation)* (Brussels: La Revue Belge des Sciences Commerciales, 1926).

Boyns, T. and J. Wale. "The Development of Management Information Systems in the British Coal Industry c. 1900–1947," unpublished working paper, 1995.

Burchell, S., C. Clubb, A. Hopwood and J. Hughes. "The Roles of Accounting in Organizations and Society," *Accounting, Organizations and Society,* Vol. 5, No. 1 (1980), pp. 5–27.

Chandler, A. D. *The Visible Hand: The Managerial Revolution in American Business* (Boston, MA: Harvard University Press, 1977).

De Beelde, I. "Industrial Accounting Theory and Practice: Cost Accounting in the Belgian Coal Industry During the First Half of the Twentieth Century," *Accounting, Business and Financial History,* Vol. 5, No. 1 (1995a), pp. 71–108.

———. "The Evolution of Industrial Accounting Thought in Belgium in the First Half of the 20th Century: A Textbook Approach." Working Paper, 1995b, Faculty of Economic and Applied Economic Sciences, University of Ghent, 95/13.

Granick, D. *De onderneming in Europa: een Amerikaanse visie* (Utrecht: Marka, 1965).

Joye, P. *Les trusts en Belgique* (Bruxelles: Soc. Pop. d'Edition, 1964).

Kaplan, R. S. "The Evolution of Management Accounting," *The Accounting Review,* Vol. LIX, No. 3 (1984), pp. 390–418.

Lawrenson, D. M. "Britain's Railways: The Predominance of Engineering Over Accountancy During the Inter-War Period," *Critical Perspectives on Accounting*, Vol. 3 (1992), pp. 45–60.

Loft, A. "The History of Management Accounting: Relevance Found," in *Issues in Management Accounting*, D. Ashton, T. Hopper and R. W. Scapens, Eds. (London: Prentice Hall, 1991), pp. 17–38.

Mas, A. *Introduction à la revision des entreprises* (Gembloux: J. Duculot, 1959).

Miller, P. and T. O'Leary. "Governing the Calculable Person," in *Accounting as Social and Institutional Practice*, A. G. Hopwood and P. Miller, Eds. (Cambridge: University Press, 1994), pp. 98–115.

Nelson, D. "Scientific Management, Systematic Management and Labor, 1880-1915," *Business History Review*, Vol. XLVIII, No. 4 (1974), pp. 479–500.

RAB — Beveren State Archives, Archief Kempense Steenkoolmijnen, Waterschei (A. Dumont) (various years).

Richard, J. "The Evolution of Accounting Chart Models in Europe from 1900 to 1945," *The European Accounting Review*, Vol. IV, No. 1 (1995), pp. 87–124.

Solomons, D. "The Historical Development of Costing," in *Studies in Cost Analysis*, Second Edition, D. Solomons, Ed. (London: Sweet & Maxwell, 1968), pp. 3–49.

The Fall of Management Accounting: The NIRA and the Homogenization of Cost Practices in the United States

C. J. McNair
Babson College
Massachusetts

Richard Vangermeersch
University of Rhode Island

1.0 ABSTRACT

This paper explores the impact of societal trends on cost practices, and the management techniques used to support business structures, within the United States. Specifically, the influence of the National Industrial Recovery Act (NIRA) on the development of the competitive market, and the costing and pricing policies within it, is explored from the perspective of social rule system theory. It is argued that the NIRA, as enforced through the symbol of the "Blue Eagle" displaced the free market economy in the United States, leaving in its wake a pseudo-competitive market structure where full cost recovery and the earning of a fair and reasonable profit became the basis for market pricing and business management. The displacement of the competitive market by the NIRA is argued to account for the apparent loss of relevant costing theory and practice during this period, as well as the economic shocks currently hitting the United States in the wake of the developing global marketplace. The paper concludes by suggesting that relevant management accounting theory has to be reconstructed from a true competitive market framework.

2.0 INTRODUCTION

> The President said in his inaugural that he believed in putting first things first and the first thing in this great program is to get **Blue Eagles in every window**. The time for dealing with the chiseling fringe will come as soon as that is done .... [Hugh Johnson, *The Blue Eagle*, 1935, p. 265]

Over the past decade there has been an intense dialogue surrounding the relevance of current management accounting and control systems as well as a plethora of suggestions about how best to "fix" these ailing devices [Johnson and Kaplan, 1987; Cooper, 1989; Johnson, 1992; Shank and Govindarajan, 1993]. Throughout this dialogue, the focus has been on how to adapt accounting-based calculative practices to better provide the type of information needed by a company competing in the global marketplace. The economic impact of globalization provides the backdrop for the urgency and thrust of the messages delivered by the "new accountants." Unless changes are made to our "accountings," the future is projected to be bleak indeed.

The rapid decline of major industries (e.g., steel, home electronics, and automobiles), the displacement of major segments of the working population, and the rapid loss of competitive power caused by the onslaught of foreign competition are some of the powerful forces reshaping business practices in general in the United States. The radical upheaval in the American market that has followed on the heels of developing global markets harkens back to an earlier time of crisis in US economic history: the Great Depression of 1929. Both of these events represent significant shifts in the economic stature and health of the United States. These two periods are linked in many ways, as will be argued in the pages that follow. Specifically, it is suggested here that the market rules (formal and informal) set down in response to the economic crisis of the Depression set the stage for the current crisis in the United States.

To develop this argument, the following paper explores the development of the National Industrial Recovery Act (NIRA) and the de facto continuance of the Act through an informal social mechanism (the Blue Eagle). Having laid the groundwork for the discussion, the paper then explores the overall impact these combined forces had on the laissez faire capitalistic structure that lay at the heart of the market mechanism formed in the United States during its early history. Using the logic of social rule system theory [Burns and Flam, 1987a, 1987b, Burns, 1986], and the phrases and thoughts from original source documents from the period of the "New Deal" and the NIRA, this paper will explore the displacement of the competitive market, and the consequent abandonment of economic theories of cost in favor of full cost recovery, that this macroeconomic movement entailed.

By providing a historically- and economically-based analysis and explanation for the proliferation of full cost recovery practices, and the subsequent abandonment of economic, or market-driven, theories of cost, this paper stands to make a major contribution to our understanding of the historical development of management accounting and control practices. This enhanced understanding may support a constructive dialogue about the underlying assumptions, and implications, of the full cost recovery model and its potential for hampering the competitiveness of American companies in the global economy.

In the pages that follow, the major issues surrounding the Depression, the government's reaction to it (e.g., the "New Deal") and the formation of the NIRA is presented. The second part of the paper then moves into the specifics of the NIRA, and its long-term enforcement through the "Blue Eagle" symbol, exploring the apparent development of a pseudo-competitive market based on informal agreements to price above market using the full cost recovery costing model to define a "fair price." Finally, the argument turns toward the development of the global market and its apparent destruction of the social rule system denoted as the "Gentleman's Club," thus creating the demand for redevelopment of the economic theory of costs. In the end, the objective of this paper, then, is simply to present one plausible argument for the decline of cost management practices that provides a logical framework for its rebirth.

3.0 THE DEPRESSION AND NEW DEAL: A SYSTEM RULE THEORY PERSPECTIVE

> From a sociological perspective, market regulation, "collusion", and "interference with market forces and outcomes" are universal processes. They are part and parcel of the human production and strategic structuring of their conditions. The structuration of markets is largely, but not solely, a function of power, exchange, and conflict processes .... [Burns and Flam, 1987a, p. 124]

Social rule theory focuses on the development of markets as defined by the context, or cultures, in which they emerge (see Exhibit 1). This growing body of literature explores the socio-political processes relating to maintenance and change of market and related rule regimes [Burns and Flam, 1987a]. Market rule formation under this model can occur through legal and administrative rules created and implemented through political and government processes, the collusion of groups of sellers and/or buyers who establish rules of market entry and rules for procedures and transactions, the influence of norms, including informal rules, that are supported by a status group, and through the granting of credit and access to contracts within the economic system. As noted by Burns and Flam, such market rules affect transaction costs as well as imply the potential for increased prices through their impact on the supply and demand relationships within a market.

Exhibit 1
General Model of Market Structuration

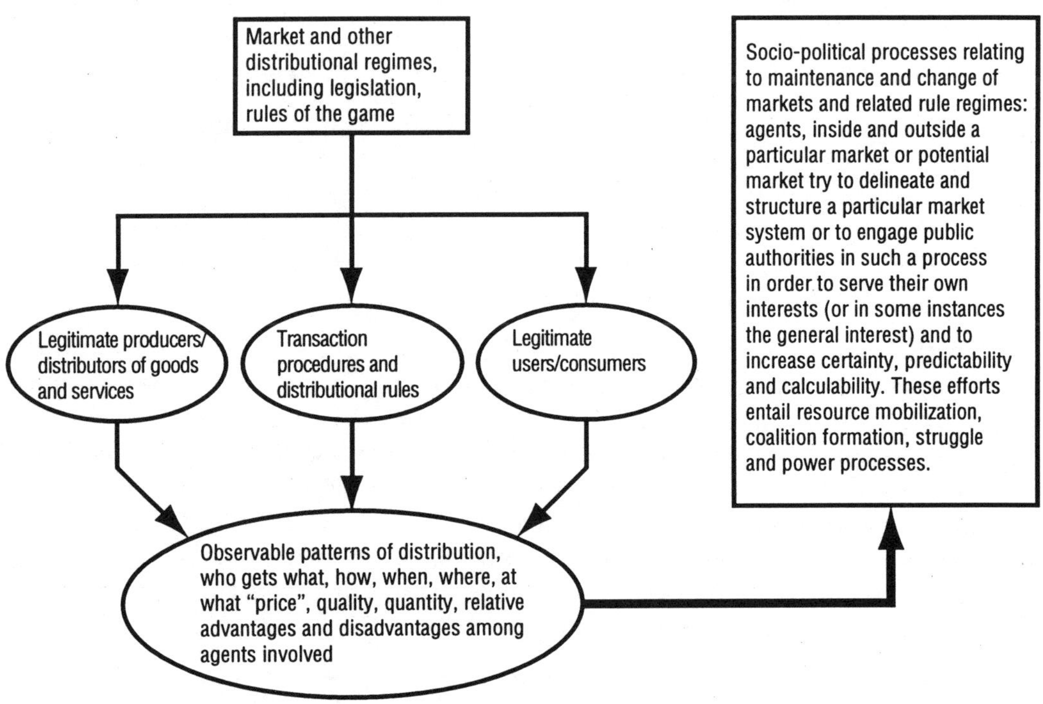

Source: Burns and Flam, "The Structuring of Markets and Other Distributive Systems," *The Shaping of Social Organizations,* (London: Sage Publications Ltd., 1987a), p. 126.

At the heart of this argument is the belief that "markets are social organizations, structured and regulated by more or less well-defined social rule systems" [Burns and Flam, 1987a, p. 125]. They go on to suggest that there are two basic ways that this market organization is brought about [Burns and Flam, 1987a, p. 127]:

1. Strategic structuring, informal or formal, whereby social agents, including the state, establish a rule regime regulating market access and transactions.

2. Emergent structuring, whereby participants discover or adopt certain similar strategies within bounded rationality and situations with certain opportunity structures and incentive structures. Social network and ecological properties result in relatively well-defined aggregate performance characteristics.

Social rule theory, then, provides a useful framework for analyzing the development of markets, as well as providing insights into the forces that can bring about changes in the social structuring, or rule systems, that govern their functioning.

3.1 Social Rule System Theory and the Creation of Markets in the United States

A laissez faire free market structure is one of the defining features of the capitalistic model developed and used to frame transactions within the United States during its early years [Brand, 1988]. Prothro, writing about this period, emphasizes that it was characterized by traditional business concerns with economic liberty and the preservation of private property, without a hint of any orientation toward, or desire for, increased business-government relations [Prothro, 1954]. Consistent with the "rugged individualism" that defined the developing social structure of the United States, markets, and the businesses which comprised them, were left to function with minimal interference from outside forces.

This "neoclassical" market model [Baker, 1984] builds upon a minimal set of market rules (seen more as forms of "interference" and "irrationality" than as mandates), open micro-networks and undifferentiated macro-networks of buyers and sellers as the basis of its structuration. Facing minimal transaction costs and situational constraints, a neoclassical market is depicted as one of "hyper-rationality" based on the tacit agreement of rule-abiding participants for its functioning [Baker, 1984].

Within the neoclassical model, transaction "costs" per se have little or no direct relationship to market prices. Market prices are set simply by the laws of basic supply and demand, unfettered by rules and regulations that would otherwise restrict the free flow of goods and services. Logically, then, "costs" of production would have information value only within the structure of the individual enterprise, leading to the potential for proliferation of costing practices. In other words, within the neoclassical structure, there is no reason to expect standardization in costing or accounting practices, unless such standardization supports the efforts of the micro-networks of buyers and sellers in reducing their market transaction costs [Burns and Flam, 1987a, 1987b; Burns, 1984].

It is interesting to note, given these comments, that a heterogeneity of costing practices designed around the unique needs of different companies, industries, and markets appears to be an economic fact prior to 1933 [Lyon, *et al.*, 1935]. It is this legacy of the free market system of the pre-Depression era, namely the existence of a diverse, rich costing theory tailored to specific business structures, that suggests that costing did not serve a constituent role in the early free market structure found in the United States. Instead, it appears to have been one of many calculative practices available to the burgeoning entrepreneurial venture focused on reaping profits from a free market economy. Cost accounting, and the management practices that it supported, were driven by the need for information to make decisions within the organization, not by government or professionally defined accounting rules.

3.2 Stability and Change in Social Market Systems

Social market systems are stable structures. Burns and Flam [1987a, p. 133] note that, "the stability of a market rule system — and its implementation structure — will obtain whenever: (1) no major interest finds the current regime disadvantageous; (2) those actors, either participating in the market or outside it, who oppose the present market rule system and might have an interest in change are unable to mobilize and exercise power to bring about change in market rules." In other words, a market structure, such as the laissez faire free market structure which developed in the United States after 1776, serves as a stabilizing force in an economy, a force which cannot be displaced without a major, or "meta" power shift. A favorable shift in the power base can provide those who disagree with the current system of rules and procedures with the power resources necessary to reframe, or overturn, the existing order [Burns and Flam, 1987a].

Within the United States, such a "meta-power shift" appears to have come about on the heels of the Great Depression of 1929 and the subsequent election of Franklin Roosevelt to the Presidency in 1932 [Brand, 1988; Himmelberg, 1976; Lyon and Abramson, 1936; Lyon, *et al.*, 1935]. The histories of this period suggest that Roosevelt was elected based on his promise to return the nation to prosperity in the aftermath of one of the most dramatic market failures of modern times.

The essence of Roosevelt's position was that free market capitalism had failed, as so strongly stated in a primary source document of the time [Johnson, 1935, p. 159]:

> Although tariffs and selective taxes and Adamson Acts and many other devices affect the natural laws of supply and demand, yet during the depression and up to March 4, 1933, few legislative steps were tried and the argument was "Let things alone and they will get all right because they always did, and because you cannot interfere with natural laws." That is the same philosophy that killed the savages .... It is fair to say that if we had let things alone for a few weeks longer we would have had to call somebody in — the undertaker and the riot squad.

By 1933, the United States was in the fourth year of the most serious economic depression it had ever faced. As suggested by Lyon, *et al.* [1935], it is this crisis that led to the election, and installation, of a new Administration that was skeptical of the rugged individualism of the past and convinced that a greater degree of collective action was the solution the ailing economy needed. The term "New Deal" became the hallmark phrase denoting the policies, rules, regulations, and sanctions that were to reshape the market structure of the United States.

3.3 Market Structuration and the NIRA

One of the central pieces of legislation of the "New Deal" was the National Industrial Recovery Act, or NIRA. The NIRA targeted the perceived "predatory competition" of the pre-Depression era that was argued by Roosevelt and his followers to be the major cause of this market failure [Johnson, 1935, p. 160]:

> If you want to know where the consuming power of America went, you need only

> look around you and see it congealed in icebergs of unnecessary building and unneeded plants — and in the dead leaves of the worthless securities which financed them.... How could we reverse our situation? Obviously, by a plan to obliterate its causes — an amendment to the rule of laissez faire....

Coupled with an increasing concern for the advancing "rationalization" of American industry between 1922 and 1929 (e.g., the displacement of men by machinery [Lyon, *et al.*, 1935, p. 6]), a defensible basis for redefining the rules of the marketplace was defined. The result was an attack on free market competition, the perceived causal factor in the economic collapse.

The NIRA was the backbone of this anti-free market movement, representing a visible and direct development of rules to reshape the market economy [Brand, 1988; Lyon, *et al.*, 1935; Johnson, 1935]. Lyon, *et al.*, [1935, p. 551] once again provide interesting insights into the logic of the times:

> Among the avowed purposes of the National Industrial Recovery Act none stands out more clearly than the declaration of intention to revise the nature of competition in American business ... its purpose was to "civilize industry," to "write a new merchant law" for American business .... As a consequence of this purpose of the law, NIRA codes have contained, either under the title of trade practices or otherwise, provisions designed to regulate trade activities. Indeed the codes are called codes of fair competition.

Roosevelt's own words suggest the intent and nature of the NIRA, as detailed by the following excerpt from the comments he made on June 16, 1933 while affixing his signature to this law:

> History probably will record the National Industrial Recovery Act as the most important and far-reaching lesiglation ever enacted by the American Congress. It represents a supreme effort to stabilize for all time the many factors which make for the prosperity of the nation and the preservation of American standards. Its goal is the assurance of reasonable profit to industry and living wages for labor, with the elimination of the piratical methods and practices which have not only harassed honest business but also contributed to the ills of labor.

One of the main enforcing mechanisms of the NIRA, as defined and structured by Hugh Johnson, its director, and the array of prominent individuals involved in its framing (Bernard Baruch, William Lybrand, Montgomery, Joseph Kennedy, John Lewis, Louis Kirstein, Arthur D. Whiteside, Malcolm Muir, and Major General C. C. Williams to name a few) was the development of a broad number of cost protection codes. In all, 352 separate code items dealing with the concept of "cost" were developed during the two short years the NIRA functioned [Lyon, *et al.*, 1935]. Once again, the source documents of the time provide evidence of the nature and intent of the NIRA's restructuring of the competitive market in the United States and the central role played in this restructuring by cost practices [Lyon, *et al.*, p. 585]:

> A less extreme, but far more frequent, transfer of power over prices is that achieved by prohibiting sales below individual cost, commonly known as cost protection .... To understand how no-sales-below-individual-cost provisions transfer power to determine prices, it is necessary to see that the decision as to what is an individual's cost has been transferred to a group. This is typically done by requiring that each individual include in his costs such elements as are specified in a uniform system of cost finding.

Developing uniform costing practices, then, served as the backbone of the NIRA's attack on the perceived inadequacies of the free market structure. In addition, as further reading underscores, it was not simply any form of costing which was to serve this purpose — it was *full cost recovery* that became the "accepted" means of measuring, and hence setting prices on the basis of, incurred costs. The implications of this change in the role, and method, of costing was clearly noted and understood by those shaping the economy as detailed once again by Lyon, *et al.* [1935, p. 588]:

> It is highly probable that in every instance in which the NIRA guaranteed cost protection to industries it was expected that such protection would bring about a price higher than the competitive price. It is needless to say, therefore, that it is in effect price fixing. Unless the cost systems, the use of which was required by individuals, included elements of cost that *were not being earned* [emphasis added], there would be no demand on the part of industries for such provisions. The precise extent to which no-sales-below-individual-cost provisions bring prices above competitive prices depends in part upon the elements included in costs .... An analysis of the first 16 accounting systems approved indicates that in each cost system elements of "cost" specified not only all direct labor and material costs, but a large proportion of indirect manufacturing expenses....

It would appear that within the formation and functioning of the NIRA, full cost recovery practices were to play a pivotal role in redefining the competitive market place. As such, then, the NIRA appears to provide a potential explanation for the apparently radical, and troubling, shift away from a rich, economics-based theory of costing, as detailed and promoted by Church [1930], Gantt [1915], and Clark [1923], toward the modern accounting-centred system. It was a change designed, not to improve business performance, but rather to radically change the structure of the laissez faire free market system that was the foundation of the American economy.

4.0 REFORMING THE MARKET: THE BLUE EAGLE TAKES OFF

> The clothes would have looked different, the women's skirts a little shorter, the men's coats sporting small black-velvet collars, perhaps. The automobiles would have been square and black. The shop windows would have carried the blue eagle of the National Recovery Act. There would have been small differences, but a city does not really change much over the years, because a city is only a collection of people and people are timeless. And the way the automobile came around the corner, it could have been 1937. [Ed McBain, *Killer's Payoff*, 1974, p. 5]

At this point in the argument, it is important to acknowledge the transitory nature of the NIRA. Signed into "law" as a temporary action in June of 1933, the NIRA was terminated in 1935 on the heels of a series of legal and legislative battles that brought its constitutionality directly into question, as suggested by the following: "The NIRA was declared unconstitutional as an excessive delegation of law-making power to private groups and government agencies" [Lowi, 1971, p. 75]. Cut short by the Supreme Court's decision in the *United States* v. *Schechter Poultry Corporation*, the NIRA faced growing resistance from big business during 1934 and 1935, and was ultimately abandoned [Brand, 1988].

To the casual observer of the period, then, the NIRA is a transitory blip in the operation of the free market that had some interesting cost implications. The framers of the NIRA, though, were not so naive in their attempts to reshape the economy. While the formal legislative structure of the NIRA was dismantled, it was not the only way the Act, and its intentions, were enforced. Specifically, the development of the National Recovery Administration (the administrative arm of the NIRA) by Hugh Johnson was framed around the use of a symbol: The Blue Eagle. It is the Blue Eagle, and its ongoing use throughout the period leading up to and immediately following World War II that provides the second, and perhaps most interesting part of the unfolding drama.

Returning to social system rule theory [Burns and Flam, 1987a,b], the role that social rules, both formal and informal, play in the structuration of markets opens the door to recognizing the potentially powerful, but informal, enforcement mechanism the Blue Eagle represented. To understand how a symbol could hold such sway over a population, it is only necessary to remember the nature of the 1930s and the dominance symbols exerted over the major political and economic movements of the time. First to come to mind, of course, is the *swastika*, which was so effectively used by Hitler to mobilize the German nation. The Nazi party gained its prominence, not by promising to conquer the world, but by restoring some semblance of order and prosperity to a German economy decimated by World War I and the retributions and restrictions placed on it by its conquerors. Hitler rose to power on the wave of promised economic reforms that gave the population hope ... and bread. The swastika was the symbolic representation of Hitler's promises to the German population.

Similarly, the *hammer* and *sickle* was embraced by the Russians in the aftermath of their social and economic upheaval following World War I, while the *fascis*, or Roman club, was embraced by Mussolini. The 1930s, then, was an era of symbols that were used to move nations. As such, the significance of the Blue Eagle, and its ongoing presence within the American arena in the wake of the overturning of the NIRA raises at least the potential for the informal continuance of the market procedures and transactions, such as full cost recovery, that lay at the heart of this act.

Burns and Flam [1987a] make a point of stating that unwritten rules and informal norms are one way that rule regimes can pursue the active shaping of supply and demand curves through the active determination of, or interference with, market prices. In other words, it appears possible that the influence of the NIRA on both the market, and the costing practices which defined it, may have remained in force through the operation of an informal set of rules that were conveyed through the Blue Eagle symbol. The opening quotation to this section, found in a mystery novel, suggests that the Blue Eagle was an important force in 1937, perceived as one and the same as the NIRA which spawned it. If the NIRA disappeared in 1935, then why did this well-known author tie it to a scene in 1937? To make the presumption of the Blue Eagle and its ongoing use to tacitly enforce the New Deal economics, and to suggest that this symbol was the source of the decay of management accounting practices, though, are two very different things. Making this second connection returns us to the source documents that effectively capture the intent and mood of the times.

4.1 The Birth of the Blue Eagle

> In war, as in the gloom of night attack, soldiers wear a bright badge to be sure that comrades do not fire on comrades. On that principle those who cooperate in this program must know each other at a glance. [Franklin Roosevelt, Fireside Chat, July 24, 1933]

To understand the role played by the Blue Eagle in enforcing the intent, if not the letter of the law written in the NIRA codes, it is best to turn to the autobiography of Hugh Johnson, the man who was charged by Roosevelt with the formation, operation, and success of the NIRA.

His book, aptly named *The Blue Eagle from Egg to Earth*, provides unusual, and at times troubling, insights into the logic and motivations of the individuals shaping the New Deal era.

As Chapter 21 unfolds, Johnson is focusing on the reasons for the Blue Eagle, and the precedence for its use. Quoting from a speech delivered by B.M. Baruch on May 20, 1933, Johnson notes [Johnson, 1935, p. 251]:

> Mobilization of public opinion becomes important. If it is commonly understood that those who are cooperating are soldiers against the enemy within and those who omit to act are on the other side, there will be little hanging back. The insignia of government approval on doorways, letterheads, and invoices will become a necessity in business. This method was a success in 1918. It is a short cut to action and to public support without which no such plan can succeed. By this method a large part of the emergency job can be accomplished in short order.

In no uncertain terms, Johnson notes that the fate of the NIRA was inextricably tied to the Blue Eagle. Its role was to serve as an identifier of those loyal to the tenets of the NIRA, a necessary part of bringing pressure to bear on them to conform with the new market structure proposed by the New Deal, as well as to identify the individuals and companies who refused to fall in line with the new social rule regime.

The importance, and purposiveness, of this pressure is revealed in Johnson's own words [Johnson, 1935, p. 253]: "when a change like NIRA comes along — raising wages, shortening hours, and inevitably increasing costs — one company in an industry cannot accept it unless practically all other companies in that industry accept it." Several pages later, Johnson notes [1935, p. 261]: "There was a political reason far deeper and more subtle.... The Blue Eagle put the enforcement of this law [the NIRA] in the hands of the whole people." Roosevelt, in his Fireside Chat of July 24, 1933, reinforces this view of the role of the Blue Eagle, stating:

> There are adequate penalties in the law, but I am asking the cooperation that comes from opinion and from conscience. *These are the only instruments we shall use* [emphasis added] in the great summer offensive against unemployment. But we shall use them to the limit to protect the willing from the laggard and to make the plan succeed.

It seems that the Blue Eagle appears to have been a very vital part of the mobilization of public opinion to support the NIRA and its directives, as once again suggested by Johnson's own words [1935, p. 263]:

> Men might argue about how many business angels could stand for the point of an economic needle — and let the chance go by, but a woman in support of her home is about as safe for triflers as a Royal Bengal Tigress at the door of a den full of cubs. When every American housewife understands that the Blue Eagle on everything that she permits to come into her home is a symbol of its restoration to security, mercy on the man or group of men who attempt to trifle with this bird.

In its intent and functioning, the role of the Blue Eagle within the development of the NIRA was to clearly identify "recalcitrants," the enemy in the battle to restore prosperity [Johnson, 1935, pp. 155, 251]. The Blue Eagle was designed and used to generate the change in social rules required to reshape the competitive market structure of the United States, and to provide a means for society to punish those who refused to adopt this revised view of the social and economic structure of the United States. Reflecting the essence of Burns and Flam's social rule systems theory, the NIRA and the Blue Eagle, were part of the intense media campaign used by Roosevelt to create public support for the tenets of the New Deal.

While the NIRA was dismantled, then, its influence remained as a driving force embodied in the Blue Eagle. It is hard to argue, though, that a simple symbol would in itself be enough to reinforce, or create, the major shift in the economic markets desired by the New Deal proponents. To succeed, big business had to be brought into the arena of influence.

4.2 Business and New Deal Economics

> While no doubt many industrialists had a greater or lesser degree of hope, if not faith, that increases in wages might be conducive to recovery, and while there is no doubt that many individuals were moved to take what they regarded as the added risks of wage increases, it is equally without a doubt that for the most part codes of fair competition would not have been "voluntarily" brought forward and would not have been voluntarily agreed to unless they contained what the industrial groups regarded as a quid pro quo. This quid pro quo was in many cases permission to do as a group what was at least of questionable legality before the passage of the Recovery Act.... [Lyon, *et al.*, 1935, p. 563]

Pulling the threads of the argument together, it appears that the Blue Eagle provides a mechanism for the continued influence of the NIRA beyond 1935, including its pursuit of uniform costing methods as embodied in full cost recovery. To gain acceptance from business, though, the increased costs of doing business inherent in the New Deal legislation had to be passed through to the public in the form of price increases that effectively moved prices above the competitive market level. In order to create acceptance of the NIRA by business, companies were allowed to pursue a "reasonable profit" based on full cost recovery of both "earned" and "unearned" costs [Lyon, *et al.*, 1935]. In other words, in agreeing to abide by the NIRA, and to signal this adherence through display of the Blue Eagle, business was awarded with a guaranteed profit, or return, on all of its costs, whether value-adding or not.

The implicit agreement to overturn the market as the basis for price setting, replacing it with a full cost recovery plus "reasonable profit" mode of operation, is the essential element of the NIRA and its impact on the extant market economy of pre-1933 America. As noted throughout the texts of the period, the goal of the NIRA was to define the concept of "fair" competition, and to weed out the predators who were charged with the destruction of the economy. In essence, the businesses who subscribed to the NIRA, and its symbol (the Blue Eagle) agreed to disengage from the market-based pricing mechanisms that formed the basis of the neoclassical, laissez faire form of market competition, replacing it with a "full cost plus reasonable profit" price mechanism. Cost accounting practices played a constituent role in shaping the New Deal economy and its pseudo-competitive market structure.

The NIRA targeted market trade policies, or the basic structure of rules and norms guiding market transactions, in its efforts to redefine the American economy, and used a uniform definition of "cost" to stabilize these changes. The importance of this argument cannot be left unstated. Specifically, if this logic were to be found to hold, it would suggest that the free market system, and its inherent *customer-defined price pressure* on businesses to control costs and pursue the optimal mix of productive resources (e.g., equipment, people, and capital) was purposely and effectively destroyed within the American economy by the NIRA. By tacitly agreeing to compete on a cost-based definition of market value, or price, business was creating a safety net for itself that would effectively remove it from the harsh realities of the free market system. The redefinition of price to reflect full cost recovery plus "reasonable profit" on the basis of full cost provided business with a means to stabilize and improve its financial performance. In its early phases, then, the NIRA was supported by business because business itself stood to benefit.

4.3 The "Recalcitrants"

Not all business could be argued to benefit from the NIRA. In fact, those businesses that were thriving under the free market were likely to lose, if not profitability, at least control over their destiny should the NIRA succeed. These successful businessmen formed the core of the "recalcitrants" that the Blue Eagle, and subsequent government sanctions, sought to identify, and through public boycotts, put pressure on to accept the newly defined market structure.

Of all of the recalcitrants who brought on the pressure, and ire, of the NIRA and its proponents, Henry Ford is perhaps the most well known. Clearly Schechter's challenges led to the undoing of the formal body called the NIRA, but it was Henry Ford who ultimately bore the brunt of the pressures — on whom the Blue Eagle truly landed. Ford would not adhere to the rules created under the NIRA, for reasons stated so eloquently by his spokesman, William J. Cameron [Fine, 1963, pp. 76–78]:

> There can be no doubt ... that proposals are being made in the name of recovery that have nothing to do with recovery, and that seriously affect the fundamental American idea. We doubt that it is necessary to scrap America in order to achieve recovery.

As Brand goes on to describe, Ford adhered to his convictions that the free market, or "American idea" was the best, and only, economic system viable within the United States. He refused, in spite of increasing pressures and the economic risks they represented to his own firm, to sign the codes that attempted to place cost and price controls on the automobile industry, an act that "*prevented him from displaying the Blue Eagle on his products*" [Brand, 1988, p. 171; Johnson, 1935, p. 237]. To continue quoting from Brand [1988, p. 171], "Without the Blue Eagle, the government initially refused to purchase Ford cars, and there was considerable uncertainty whether the public would buy them either. Hugh Johnson's appeals to individual consumers to boycott products that did not display the Blue Eagle had been relatively effective at the time Ford was refusing to place the emblem on his vehicles."

It appears that the Blue Eagle was purposely used as a mode of identifying, and hence punishing recalcitrants through the withholding of vital government contracts for business. The Blue Eagle also provided the basis for government-supported public boycotts of products, individuals and companies that refused to join the "Gentleman's Club," as suggested by the following: "Non-compliance! Dereliction of statutory duties — it is not just a misdemeanor — it is failure to *play the game in a great national crisis*" [Johnson, 1935, p. 362]. There is no need to create or assume this intent regarding the Blue Eagle and its use; it is freely and openly stated by Johnson in his autobiography, and by Roosevelt in his speeches and actions. Hence, while the NIRA proved to be an aborted attempt at altering the free market system in the United States, through the Blue Eagle its intent and power remained a constant force, integral to the social rule system that defined the post-Depression economy.

4.4 The Blue Eagle, Full Costing, and its Implications

The key to the reforms driven by the NIRA was the intense desire to get people back to work [Slichter, 1934; Richberg, 1934; Johnson, 1935]. This can hardly be faulted as a reasonable goal given the dire straits in which the American economy found itself. Hooked to the various efforts to increase both employment and wages (e.g., WPA, or Works Progress Administration], the creation of the Securities and Exchange Commission, and a large number of public works, the New Deal's attack on the free market system was consistently driven by the belief that the essence of a fair, and sustainable, market economy lay in the full employment of all citizens. People were desperate for work, and businesses were desperate for consumers with the funds necessary to purchase their goods. It was not a time for lofty ideals, it was a time for action [Johnson, 1935; Richberg, 1934].

However, the Blue Eagle, and the cost-based, pseudo-competitive market structure that emerges from this period, had several troubling implications. The first of these is most effectively captured by simply reprinting a cartoon found in Johnson's autobiography [Johnson, 1935, p. 229; see Exhibit 2]. As can be seen, Hugh Johnson is depicted as removing feathers from the American Eagle in order to create the Blue Eagle. There is no more striking evidence of the underlying intent of these self-appointed architects of the New Deal economy.

Exhibit 2
Working on the Eagle, Again

Source: H. Johnson, *The Blue Eagle from Egg to Earth*, 1935, p. 228

Reading through Johnson's text, one is constantly brought face-to-face with the ties between the NIRA and the fascist policies of Mussolini. Mussolini, as an ideal to which the American system could aspire, is specifically cited in Johnson's work, not once in passing, but at length. Ledeen [1972] details this influence as follows [p. 104]: "For many of the alarmed statesmen and intellectuals in the centers of power, Mussolini's Italy seemed to offer the possibility of a new model for Western nations, and Roosevelt's request for a study of the Italian Corporate State is symptomatic of this state of mind in 1933. In the whirlpool of Western society, many seemed willing to grasp at the apparent straw of fascism."

Herein, then, lies the primary issue and concern represented by the NIRA and its "enforcer," the Blue Eagle: They appear to have sought to undo the democratic state. This may seem like an overstatement of the facts presented so far, but the juxtaposition of the NIRA, the concept of "rugged individualism," and laissez faire capitalism, the dominant social rule system of the United States preceding the New Deal, was consciously made by Johnson. A cost-based and governmentally-defined economic structure was the solution sought, and effectively implemented, through the NIRA and the Blue Eagle.

In response to various forms of attack on his efforts at the NIRA, Johnson constantly refers to the need to subvert existing social and economic ideals to attain the benefits of a balanced economy [Johnson, 1935, pp. 158–171]. As referred to in an earlier quotation, Johnson felt strongly about the need to abandon all ties to the laissez faire system [Johnson, 1935, p. 160]: "But no prophet crying in the wilderness could then have convinced the country. Old slogans would have killed new thoughts. 'Let nature take its course' — 'rugged individualism' — 'competition is the life of trade' — 'combinations to restrain it are unlawful' — 'liberty of contract' — etc., etc., ad nauseam." To enact these major changes in the social rule system shaping the American economy required a complete abandonment of existing ideals by the public.

Full cost recovery accounting methods played a major role in this quest to reshape the overall nature of American social and economic structures [Lyon, *et al.*, 1935; Johnson, 1935]. This non-market based costing model became the basis for competition, for the definition of "market price," and the definition of value-added, and waste, within the post-Depression economy. As long as all industrialists agreed to adhere to this costing ideal, which in fact it was in their self-interest to do, the economic order would be restored and all would benefit. This was the underlying logic that drove the New Deal proponents. As Roosevelt stated, "the NIRA was to restructure the economy for all time." And perhaps it might have, had the United States been able to avoid, or defend itself, against the onslaught of the global marketplace.

5.0 THE FALL OF MANAGEMENT ACCOUNTING

> For forty years accounting systems have provided the critical management information that determines goals and actions in American companies. Most companies today use accounting information to motivate actions that are intended to achieve a common accounting goal, usually return on investment. But this goal misleads managers into chasing false imperatives. When management accounting information directs businesses, invariably two imperatives of competition emerge: always sustain output at a level to cover all costs, and always persuade customers to buy output at prices high enough to earn the market's required rate of return .... Companies need management information that will help them capitalize on their two most important resources — people and time. [H. Thomas Johnson, *Relevance Regained*, 1992, pp. 10–11]

The NIRA and the Blue Eagle have been argued to represent an intentional form of restructuring of the American economic system away from laissez faire, or free market capitalism, to a more general political economic model [Burns and Flam, 1987a,b] premised on government interference in markets. Reinforcing these formal policies was the adoption of informal norms that suggested that full cost recovery become the basis for setting "fair" market prices [Lyon, *et al.*, 1935; Johnson, 1935]. In this process, the rich history of economics-based costing, which argued that the market equilibrium price would not accommodate excessive levels of cost or waste, appears to have fallen into disuse. And, as suggested by Johnson above, it may have resulted in an almost religious adherence to full cost recovery-based pricing and its assurance that a company will earn a reasonable profit. As such, the NIRA and the Blue Eagle appear to result in a major market fracturing and reconstruction of the guiding social rule system within the United States' economy.

This argument suggests a logical explanation for the apparent mass amnesia that surrounds management accounting today. Specifically, the rich history of dialogue surrounding the economics of cost that defined the pre-1933 world of accounting would appear to have no ultimate demand, or purpose, in a market system that defines *competitive price* as what a company spends plus a fair return. Such a mass amnesia, or ignorance argument, though, is normally troubling. What is missing in a mass ignorance argument is motive and force. In exploring the accounting literature in the twentieth century, the marked fissure in the literature is striking. It is clear that the existence of some powerful, all-encompassing force is necessary to explain why the wisdom of writers such as Church [1930], Gantt [1915] and Clark [1923] falls into disuse, and ultimately, disappears from modern management accounting literature.

Many have argued that the SEC Acts of 1933 and 1934 were responsible for this decline in management accounting [Johnson and Kaplan, 1987], yet a careful reading of these Acts betrays no global prescription for "full cost recovery." Only the NIRA, which specifically promoted and relied upon the logic of full cost recovery in its framing and operation appears to provide a reasonable explanation for this major change in the role and definition of relevant management accounting data. In redefining the set of social rules that defined the market economy in the United States, Roosevelt, with intent, employed full cost accounting methods to define and stabilize the pseudo-competitive market structure. In linking cost to a new social rule system, Roosevelt created the platform for a blind adherence to full cost recovery method, yet, as Johnson [1992] suggests above, this apparent "blind adherence" to full cost recovery logic is proving to be a handicap in the global marketplace. It is this final issue to which this paper will now turn.

5.1 The Re-emergence of the Invisible Hand

Non-market based pricing appears to have been relied upon for almost 40 years within the United States as a basis for defining market behaviour that would ensure the prosperity of business and labour alike [Johnson, 1992]. This pseudo-competitive market structure appears to have served everyone's interest in the end, providing consumers with the jobs and prosperity necessary to purchase goods and support their families. There was, indeed, little motivation for anyone to undo this "civilized" structure [Johnson, 1935]. While consumers might pay a slightly higher price for their goods, at least they could buy them. In addition, over time, the mechanisms that had created the distortions in the market economy faded from memory, as World War II, the recovery, the Korean War, the Cold War, and related events occupied center stage [Brand, 1988].

The prosperity arising from being a global market power appears to come to an abrupt halt in the United States in the early 1970s. As suggested by Exhibit 3, the impact of the developing global market, and the return to laissez faire capitalism on the global scale that it represents, is argued to represent a second major displacement within the American economy. In the wake of this displacement of the cost-based, pseudo-competitive market economic system, the United States abandons the gold standard, and the steel industry topples, triggering an economic crisis and the re-enactment of price controls by Nixon's government in 1974.

Exhibit 3

Fragmentation of the US Economy

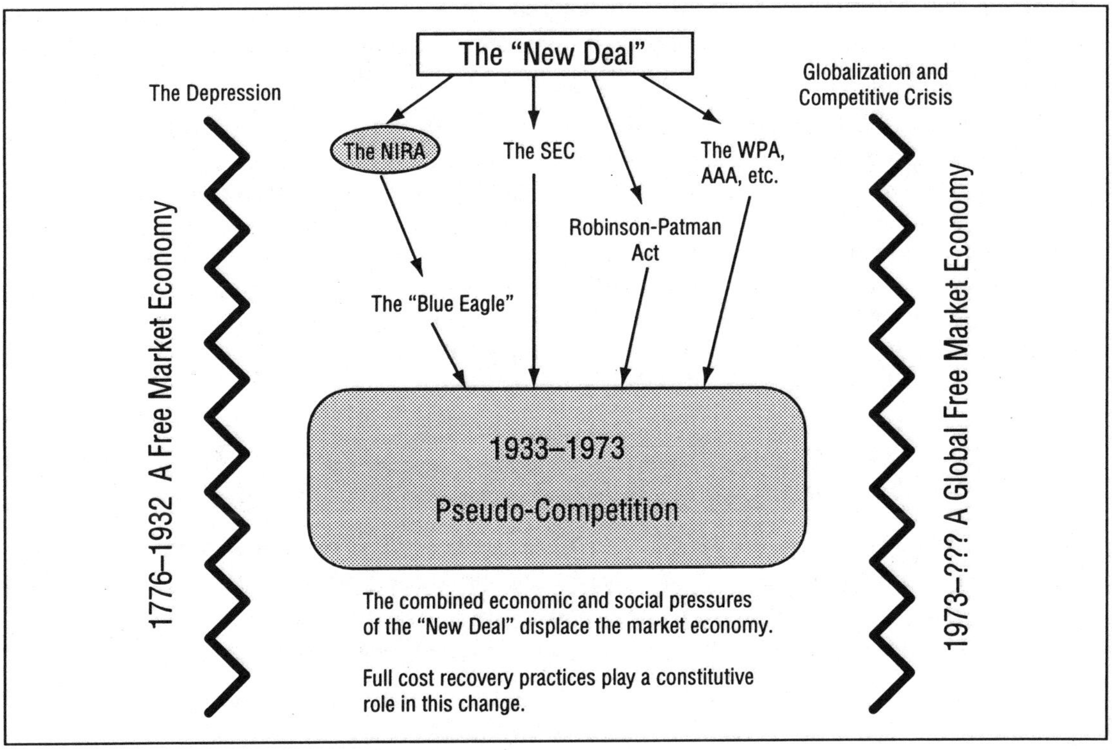

A potential explanation for this displacement can be found by returning to Burns and Flam [1987a, b], who describe different means for enforcement of market rule systems depending on the degree of homogeneity in moral or ideological commitments. First, in talking about communities with strong moral and ideological commitments, they note [1987b, pp. 158–59]:

> Strong ideological or moral sentiments in a community will increase the likelihood that market participants will adhere to market rules.... For example, social rules arrived at through democratic, religious, and legal institutions to which members of the community are committed would also be experienced as legitimate and felt to be binding.... Other things being equal, the supply and demand curves arising under the market exclusion rules would be more or less predictable.... Members of the community are predisposed to react with universal condemnation of those who breach the rules.... The treatment of such deviants would serve as an example to any others with weak moral fibre.

This description appears to be applied aptly to the pseudo-competitive market structure which is argued to have been the outcome of the NIRA and its continued enforcement by the Blue Eagle. Specifically, it is possible that as these "social rules" became an ingrained part of the market structure of the United States, they assumed the role of moral principles, which might be argued to have been codified by the accounting "high priests" through generally accepted accounting principles (GAAP) and the mantra, "we must full cost" that appears to be surviving even the most rigorous and logical attacks of the new accountants.

The opposite of a market based on common moral sentiments, as has been suggested to be the dominant structure of the American market system from 1933–1973, are "communities with weak moral or ideological commitments and administrative regulation of market behavior" [Burns and Flam, p. 159]. One of the causes for this type of market structure to emerge is noted to be, "the community has undergone rapid changes, in terms of social mobility, changes in technology ...." This statement appears to be a reasonable description of the global marketplace, with its diverse participants who build their competitive models on very diverse beliefs and moral commitments. Burns and Flam go on to note [1987b, pp. 159–60]:

> In the absence of moral or administrative controls enforcing market rule systems, market participants and potential participants are likely to break the rules.... *Supply and demand curves as socially generated relations would be unstable and subject to unpredictable shifts* [emphasis added] as actors would conceal information from one another and find ways to take advantage of one another. Many markets would disappear altogether, because the validity and reliability of transactions could not be guaranteed. Not only would uncertainty and opportunism be maximized, but the risks of escalating conflict and a struggle of all against all, including the widespread use of non-market weapons, would be increased.
>
> Of course, few societies — or markets within them — are so "normless". But the "thought experiment" points up the economic risks that are involved once the social regulation of transactions and market participation have broken down....

This lengthy quotation is reproduced here because it provides a strong potential explanation for the current economic crisis facing the United States. Since the early 1970s, entire industries have been felled by the onslaught of foreign competition that was once described as "predatory" and as using "dumping" to conquer markets.

A different explanation is suggested here. Specifically, it appears that the globalization of the world economy serves to undo the cost-based, pseudo-competitive market which defined the competitive structure of the United States between 1933 and 1973. Over this 40-year period, business came to believe that full cost recovery-based pricing, as defined, calculated, and reported by the accounting profession, was the equivalent of the free market price as set under laissez faire economic practices. Lulled into a belief that they were competing in a free market, business defined success on the very profits it was guaranteed under the social rule system structure created by the NIRA. The economic risks this position, or "myth" represents for the United States is evidenced in countless articles and books in the trade press detailing the death of the steel industry, the imminent collapse of General Motors, and the continuous struggle of many American companies to rediscover the "golden key" (e.g., management fad) that will return them to prosperity.

5.2 Redefining Management Accounting: A Free Market Perspective

Is it not possible that the combination of these events, and the 40 years of history over which they transpired, may have led to the apparent loss of knowledge that significant and valuable alternatives to full cost recovery methods of costing might be usefully applied in various business settings [Johnson and Kaplan, 1987]? This series of arguments might be seen as a set of unfounded claims, yet it is a common theme that runs throughout current management accounting literature [for instance, Johnson and Kaplan, 1987; Cooper, 1989; Johnson, 1992; Shank and Govindarajan, 1993]. Johnson and Kaplan [1987] appear to have made this logic, the perceived "fall" of management accounting, the basis for a rebirth of the economic theory of cost.

Trends within the United States suggest that economic theories of cost appear to be undergoing rebirth as one basis for the effective management of competitive business in a global market. For instance, "target costing" [Sakurai, 1989] is an economic model that suggests that companies should work from the market in establishing their price, profit, and hence allowable cost expectations for a product even before it is launched. Target costing is simply one way a company can begin to focus on cost, not as a naturally recoverable expense of doing business, but rather as a constraint, or cap, on the perceived value of goods and services. In this model, cost is what is sacrificed to gain the market price; when such "cost" exceeds the market-determined value of the good or service, a loss is sustained. Target costing, then, appears to start from the belief in a free market economy with supply and demand curves set by perceived product value, or consumer utility functions, rather than from the current "cost" of the resources consumed to create that good or service.

A related recent "innovation" in management accounting, *strategic cost management* [Shank, 1989; Shank and Govindarajan, 1988, 1992, 1993] suggests that competitive advantage can be gained by redefining the *structure* of an industry's value chain. Once again, this popular approach appears to build from the belief that predatory practices that actually seek to disrupt the structure, or existing rule system, of a market represent acceptable, and in fact desirable, competitive actions. The entire logic of strategic cost management adheres to the description of behaviour that would occur in a market characterized by having weak moral commitments [Burns and Flam, 1987].

It is difficult to make the same argument about *activity-based costing* [Cooper, 1990; Kaplan, 1988], not because its proponents are not equally committed to identifying an economic theory of cost that is viable within the free market economy of the global marketplace, but because this model does not as directly divorce itself from the logic of full cost recovery. Activity-based approaches reconnect costing theory to the tenets of causality, effectively attacking the notion that companies can, and should, recover "unearned costs" [Lyon, 1935] in established market prices, yet in the end, they suggest that all costs are still to be charged to ongoing production (e.g., full cost recovery). This may, in the final analysis, be the critical flaw in activity-based costing.

As each of the major innovations in management accounting take hold, whether they are truly "new" or simply "old wine in new bottles" that date back to pre-Depression theories of the economics of cost, they appear to augment the attack on the status quo (e.g., full cost recovery approaches). These new methods, consequently, appear likely to meet with significant resistance from the existing "enforcers" of the old order, in much the same way that the shapers of the NIRA faced bitter attacks from major industrialists and economists. It seems that in a "winners take all" battle for the power to dictate the social rule system guiding the American economy, either the old or the new model of calculative practice must dominate. The only question that remains is, which one?

5.3 An Eye Toward the Future

The objective of this paper has been to trace the historical development of the market economy within the United States, suggesting that it has undergone two radical upheavals that have effectively redefined the basis for competition. First, the Depression and its key act, the NIRA, were suggested to represent a deliberate restructuring of the laissez faire market in a manner consistent with social rule system theory [Burns and Flam, 1987a, b]. This period is described as a pseudo-competitive market where fair competition is defined by full cost recovery with a built-in expectation for a "reasonable profit." It is an economic model that is driven, not by the iron laws of the marketplace, but rather by tacit agreement on a prescribed set of market rules and norms.

The second disruption in the American economy is then argued to be driven by the re-emergence of laissez faire capitalism in the guise of the global market. As suggested by Burns and Flam [1987a,b], this second disruption appears to have the power to put the United States at severe economic risk, as its accepted modes of doing business, and defining market practices, fall in the face of competitors who do not abide by these market rules.

In recasting economic history in this light, the constitutive role played by accounting-based theories of cost become evident. Specifically, it is argued that full cost recovery, which is not an economically sound basis for competition in a laissez faire free market, serves as a primary tool for enforcing the rules of the New Deal, or pseudo-competitive, market. Ultimately, this very tool of market structuration appears to hinder the responsiveness of the American economy to the changing rule structures embedded in the global economy. It is this disabling influence that may account for the increasingly heated attacks on accounting as the basis for the competitive decline of American industry [Johnson, 1992; Goldratt and Cox, 1986].

The paths forward for business, and the accounting systems which support them, appear to lie in rediscovering the essence of the economic theory of costs which drove Henry Ford to constantly search for ways to eliminate waste, and that motivated Church [1930] to discuss capacity as the productive capability of an organization to create value in the marketplace. This economically-motivated approach to costing theory appears to be the basis for such innovations as target costing, product life cycle costing, and strategic cost management. As such, there appears to be a logic for, and demand for, the rebirth of management accounting theory, a rebirth that reattaches the accounting profession to the logic of the market.

The ideas presented in this paper suggest many fruitful paths forward for research, including the re-examination of the development of the management accounting field in light of social rule system theory and its implications, the exploration and redefinition of economics-based theories of cost, the exploration of emerging practices in business today to determine the extent to which they reflect a return to laissez faire practices, and a historical analysis of the constitutive role of the standardization of costing practices (e.g., full cost recovery). In addition, it is likely that the development of the accounting profession itself may, in the end, be traceable to the shift away from markets-enforced to rule-enforced competition.

In the end, this paper will have accomplished its purpose if it merely moves the dialogue surrounding costing to one that more accurately places accounting developments within their historical and social contexts. In a search for the "root cause" for the decline of management accounting, this paper, then, represents one potential explanation for the mass amnesia that appears to be at the heart of the fall of management accounting.

> Contemporary trends in competition, in technology, and in management demand major changes in the way organizations measure and manage costs and in the way they measure and manage short- and long-term performance. Failure to make the modifications will inhibit the ability of firms to be effective and efficient global competitors. [Johnson and Kaplan, *Relevance Lost*, 1987, p. 262]

ACKNOWLEDGEMENTS

The authors would like to thank the participants of the 3rd Management Control Conference for their helpful comments in the development of this paper. In addition, the support and advice of Barbara Merino, David Barton, and the anonymous reviewers of the paper are recognized. The authors retain all responsibility for the arguments presented and their potential errors.

REFERENCES

Baker, W. "The Social Structure of a National Securities Market," *American Journal of Sociology*, Vol. 89 (1984), pp. 775–811.

Brand, Donald R. *Corporatism and the Rule of the Law: A Study of the National Recovery Administration* (Ithaca, NY: Cornell University Press, 1988).

Buhite, Russel D. and David W. Levy (Eds.). *FDR's Fireside Chats* (Norman, OK: University of Oklahoma Press, 1992).

Burns, T. R. "Actors, Transactions, and Social Structure: An Introduction to Social Rule System Theory," in *Sociology: The Aftermath of Crisis*, U. Himmelstrand, Ed. (London: Sage Publications, 1986).

———. "The Structuring of Markets and Other Distributive Systems," in *The Shaping of Social Organization: Social Rule System Theory with Applications* (London: Sage Ltd., 1987a) pp. 123–151.

Burns, T. R. and H. Flam, Eds. "Market Organization and Performance Properties," in *The Shaping of Social Organization: Social Rule System Theory with Applications* (London: Sage Publications Ltd., 1987b), pp. 152–175.

Church, A. Hamilton. *Overhead Expense in Relation to Cost, Sales and Profits* (New York: McGraw–Hill, 1930).

Clark, J. M. *Studies in the Economics of Overhead Costs* (Chicago: The University of Chicago Press, 1923).

Cooper, R. "You Need a New Cost System When...," *Harvard Business Review* (January-February, 1989), pp. 77–82.

———. "Implementing an Activity-Based Cost System," *Journal of Cost Management*, Vol. 4, No. 1 (1990), pp. 33–42.

Fine, Sidney. *The Automobile Under the Blue Eagle: Labor, Management and the Automobile Manufacturing Code* (Ann Arbor, MI: University of Michigan Press, 1963).

Gantt, H. L. "The Relation Between Production and Costs," *American Machinist* (June 17, 1915), pp. 1055–1062.

Goldratt, Eliyahu M. and Jeff Cox. *The Goal: Excellence in Manufacturing* (Milford, CT: North River Press, Inc., 1986).

Himmelberg, Robert F. *The Origins of the National Recovery Administration* (New York: Fordham University Press, 1976).

Hubbard, J. B., Ed. *Current Economic Policies: Selected Discussions* (New York: Henry Holt and Company, 1934).

Johnson, H. Thomas. *Relevance Regained* (New York: The Free Press, 1992).

Johnson, H. Thomas and R. Kaplan. *Relevance Lost: The Rise and Fall of Management Accounting* (Boston: Harvard Business School Press, 1987).

Johnson, Hugh S. *The Blue Eagle from Egg to Earth* (Garden City, NY: Doubleday, Doran and Company, 1935).

Kaplan, R. S. "One Cost System Is Not Enough," *Harvard Business Review* (January–February, 1988), pp. 61–66.

Ledeen, M. A. *Universal Fascism: The Theory and Practice of the Fascist International, 1928–1936* (New York: Howard Fertig, 1972).

Lowi, Theodore J. *The Politics of Disorder* (New York: Basic Books, 1971).

Lyon, L., P. Homan, L. Lorwin, G. Terborgh, C. Dearing and L. Marshall. *The National Recovery Administration: An Analysis and Appraisal* (Washington, DC: The Brookings Institution, 1935).

Lyon, L. and V. Abramson. *The Economics of Open Price Systems* (Washington, DC: The Brookings Institution, 1936).

McBain, Ed. *Killer's Payoff: An 87th Precinct Mystery* (New York: New American Library, 1974).

Newcomb, Robinson. *How the NRA Worked* (New York: American Council Institute of Pacific Relations, 1936).

Prothro, J. *The Dollar Decade: Business Ideas in the 1920s* (Baton Rouge: Louisiana State University Press, 1954).

Richberg, D. R. "N.R.A. Ideals: A Reply to Critics," reprinted from the *New York Times Magazine* (February. 25, 1934), p. 1.

Roos, Charles F. *NRA: Economic Planning* (New York: Da Capo Press, 1971).

Sakurai, M. "Target Costing and How To Use It," *Journal of Cost Management*, Vol 3., No. 2 (1989), pp. 39–50.

Shank, John K. "Strategic Cost Management: New Wine or Just New Bottles?" *Journal of Management Accounting Research* (Fall, 1989), pp. 47–65.

Shank, John K. and V. Govindarajan. "Strategic Cost Management and the Value Chain," *The Handbook of Cost Management*, B. Brinker, Ed. (New York: Warren, Gorham and Lamont, 1991).

———. "What 'Drives' Cost? A Strategic Cost Management Perspective," in *Advances in Management Accounting*, Vol. 2 (1993), pp. 27–46.

Slichter, S. "Labor Aspects of the National Recovery Administration," in *Current Economic Policies: Selected Discussions*, J. Hubbard, Ed. (New York: Henry Holt and Company, 1934).

Harrington Emerson's Standard Costing Reconsidered:

His Critical Viewpoints on Cost Accounting[1]

Hiroshi Okano
Osaka City University

1.0 ABSTRACT

As is well known, Emerson, a pioneer in standard costing, has been studied in a number of historical papers on management accounting. His theories were later revised by his followers, including G. C. Harrison, into standard cost systems. Critics agree that it was only after this stage that standard costing was established as a "control device."

While being acclaimed as the first to present standard costing theory by those who favour this evolutionary process, Emerson encountered criticism by D. Solomons (for the inconsistency of his concept of standard costing and for the inaccuracy of his analysis on the variance between standard costs and actual costs) whose view is generally followed by most critics both in and outside Japan.

This paper considers standard costing as a part of the efficiency improvement system proposed by Emerson. His main idea was that "efficiency may be converted to cost but cost cannot be converted to efficiency." This means that even if the efficiency of finished operations may be quantified by costing, it is impossible to improve efficiency by varying costs: efficiency can only be improved through "preliminary surveys" (task management). Accordingly, Emerson's standard costing theory should be regarded as a means of measuring *a priori* the degree of improved efficiency attained through task management. Emerson's standard costing may appear similar to "standard costing as a control device," systematized by his followers, but the former is in fact different from the latter. Thus, criticism of Emerson in D. Solomons [1952], and others[2] requires reevaluation. Such misunderstanding is caused by paying too much attention to the computational aspects of standard costing without putting it into perspective within Emerson's efficiency theory.

2.0 INTRODUCTION

Harrington Emerson (1853–1931) was a leading efficiency engineer and pioneer of standard costing.[3] Some critical views on Emerson's standard costing, however, can be seen. D. Solomons points out that:

> There are two great weaknesses in Emerson's system, or at least in his account of it. First, his idea of what constitutes a standard is confusing and confused. In one place he talks of it as being "always elusively ahead of the actual" and again, "The worker is limited by conditions for the worker." Yet later he says that "predetermined standard costs can be attained through the direct and indirect assistance given to the line by the staff." Thus he seems to vacillate between an ideal and an attainable standard. A second weakness in his work is that he makes no attempt to arrive at anything more detailed than an overall variance between actual and standard costs. [1952, p. 43]

Solomons' criticism has been supported by many historians, including M. Chatfield [1977, p. 171], R. L. Brummet [1957, p. 13], M. Matsumoto [1961, p. 52], K. Okamoto [1969, p. 24] and M. J. Epstein [1978, pp. 101–102].[4]

This paper tries to reexamine Emerson's works through efficiency and *task management* which is expressed by physical measures. It shows that the above critical views are due to a misunderstanding of his true intentions by some critics who failed to examine his three cost concepts: *efficiency cost, allotted cost* and *standard cost,* and who fail to distinguish his use of *standard* from *standard cost.* In other words, while he had critical viewpoints toward cost accounting for improving efficiency, many critics did not grasp his real intentions. Emerson did try to discover cost accounting's "lost relevance"[5] and advocated a "new" method of cost accounting, but it was efficiency of which he made much.

3.0 EFFICIENCY AND TASK CONTROL

In 1904 Emerson was called to the Atchison, Topeka and Santa Fe Railroad Co. at the time of its machinists' strike. Vice-president J. W. Kendrick assigned Emerson [1912 [1972], p. 85] these four duties:

- to continue the repair and renewals of the rolling stock and the motive power of the road, in spite of the strike
- to take care of a 40 percent increase in business without securing new shops or new equipment, because the business came suddenly, and to secure the new equipment
- to restore amicable relations between the employer and the employee, relations that had been disturbed for a long number of years and had finally culminated in this very bitter strike
- to lessen the unit cost — although this was incidental, it did not make much difference to the railroad whether its shop expenses were a little higher or a little lower, so long as it was able to fulfill its duty to the public and take care of the traffic.

However, Emerson stated that the fourth point, to lessen the unit cost, had no relation to the change of factory cost, so it was an incidental problem. This was due to the peculiarities of railroad industries.

Since he published well-known papers in *Engineering Magazine* between 1908–1909 when he was working as a railroad consultant, he assimilated the managerial practices of the railroad industry.[6] In order to understand his efficiency theory and standard costing, the position of Emerson should be made clear in the historical development of management practices in the railroad industry.

Differences between Emerson's efficiency methods and F. W. Taylor's scientific management movement must also be recognized. While Emerson was on good terms with Taylor, he called himself an "efficiency engineer" and established the line-and-staff organization[7] as an alternative to Taylor's functional foremanship.

C.B. Thompson [1917, pp. 49–62] emphasizes their differences rather than their similarities. Deniel Nelson [1975, pp. 63–64] also states that "Although essentially the same problems interested Taylor and Emerson, they differed radically in their approaches and solutions." Indeed, while Taylor insisted on the interrelatedness of his innovations, Emerson concentrated on the "principles of efficiency" and said relatively little about specific measures.

Notably, Samuel Haber [1964, pp. 55–56] insists that the most important link between scientific management and efficiency is Harrington Emerson. The linkage between them is cost accounting.

Researchers should not overlook the similarities between Taylor and Emerson. Emerson [1911, p. 41, 1912, p. 6] also states that:

> It is scientific swimming, not the method of entering the water, that is important. ... Scientific management recognizes that there are many, many ways of accomplishing a result but that one of them is best.

One of Emerson's and Taylor's similarities is that both lay great emphasis on *task control*. A task is a standard quantity of work expressed by physical measures (time and quantity). *Task control* is regarded as individual, objective, and physical control — that is, the direct way of management.

On the contrary, *accounting control* (e.g., standard costing or budgeting) is considered as a general, periodical, and financial control — that is, an indirect way of management [Tsuji, 1987, p. 9].[8] This point is reinforced in Exhibit 1.

Exhibit 1

Task Control and Accounting Control

TASK CONTROL	⟶	Physical measure (time and quantity)
ACCOUNTING CONTROL	⟶	Monetary measure (cost)

Another point is essential to our understanding the nature of Emerson's standard costing. Emerson [1911, p. 41] insists that:

> the test of comparative cost is so fallacious, so unscientific. Because costs depend on many variables, but an efficiency percentage is absolute like the reading of a thermometer. Efficiencies can always be converted into costs, but costs can very rarely be converted into efficiencies and perhaps a dozen efficiencies will enter into a single cost.[9]

In general, Emerson [1928, p. 714] defines efficiency as the industrial relationship between what is and what ought to be; between the actual and standard,[10] or, to carry out standard performance in the standard time, at the standard place, for the *standard cost*. In other words, efficiency means that the right things are done in the right manner by the right people, at the right place, in the right time [Emerson, 1914, p. 254].

Furthermore, his [Emerson, 1909, pp. 166–171; 1914, p. 254; 1928, pp. 437–439] notion of efficiency includes improving workers' conditions, which is not only for workers but also for managers and various interests, and ultimately for nations.

Emerson's efficiency theory encompasses three levels:[11]

1. physical or engineering efficiency
2. business efficiency
3. social or human efficiency.

Physical or engineering efficiency is the relation between physical goods consumed and quantities produced, input and output.

Business efficiency is the relation between money consumed (cost) and money gained (profit) — that is, monetary efficiency.

Social or human efficiency is the relation between human expenses required (labour expenses) and benefit (individual and social).

Of the three levels, physical or engineering efficiency is the most important for reexamining Emerson's standard cost concept. Most reviewers of Emerson's standard costing pay much attention to the second concept of efficiency as a device for measuring business efficiency at the monetary level, while criticizing its deficiency from this viewpoint. As a result, Emerson's real intention that his standard costing was used as a measure of efficiency and promotion of efficiency has been overlooked by previous critics.

Tsuji [1987, pp. 5–6] also states that:

> the projection of task in which was found here and there in Emerson's arguments on standard costing have vanished, then, the function of control inhered in task management system has changed its nature into another one, being absorbed in the financial accounts. It should be noteworthy to state that the lack of cognition of this "change" has resulted in misunderstandings or faults in the investigation for the modern standard costs system, and the confusion in relation to the interpretations on the difference of standard costing from budgeting is the example.

It is to be noted that Emerson's efficiency concept is based on the five pre-surveys, which are also the foundations of task control or task management.

1. to ascertain whether materials are being properly handled and checked
2. to cover the condition of the machine and tools
3. to assay the relation between what men are actually doing and what they should do
4. to show as to a few operations the relation between current costs and standard costs
5. to measure the speed of movement of work through the shop.

These pre-surveys are very important to our reexamination of Emerson's standard costing [Emerson, 1908, p. 172].

4.0 STANDARD COST, EFFICIENCY COST AND ALLOTTED COST

Emerson states that there are two radically different methods of ascertaining costs. The first method is to ascertain them after the work is completed, while the second method is to ascertain them before the work is undertaken. The objection to the first method is not only that it delays information of comparative value, but that it is wholly and absolutely incorrect, mixing up unrelated costs. For example, Emerson [1908, p. 336] argues that the analysis of cost statements as to repair cost per locomotive mile does not lead to an elimination of waste.[12]

However, the advantages of the second method are not only that costs must be ascertained before the work is begun, but that the costs are divided as to each unit, whether a single element or aggregated (1) into standard expense and (2) into avoidable loss, both of which are the *real costs*. An analysis of costs so stated, facilitates an almost inexorable elimination of inefficient conditions of all kinds, standard expenses being constantly standardized at new levels — wastes, as to standards, being constantly removed [Emerson, 1908, p. 336].[13]

This assertion of Emerson's implies a critical view of "Accountants' Accounting" by which only actual costs are used.[14]

Emerson [1909 (VII), p. 676] shows the four cost concepts:

1. actual cost
2. efficiency cost
3. allotted cost
4. standard cost.

These were illustrated by Emerson as shown in Exhibits 2, 3, and 4.

Many researchers, however, have overlooked Emerson's changing of his four cost concepts. The changes described later can be seen clearly not only between Emerson [1908–9] and Emerson [1909] which is the revised edition of [1908–9], but also between Chapter 7 (January, 1909) and Chapter 8 (February, 1909) of Emerson [1908–9]. Tracing these changes in his cost concepts enables us to understand the nature of his standard cost concepts. Exhibit 5 summarizes these changes.

One of these changes is as follows: in Emerson [1908–9, p. 676] Chapter 7, *efficiency cost* was the sum of wastes (or saving) in the previous time period and *actual cost* in current time period, but in Chapter 8 [1909 (VIII), p. 816], not using the concept of *efficiency cost*, the sum of wastes (or saving) in the previous period and those of this year were carried to the next time period by "efficiency account." It is to be noted that Emerson used *efficiency cost* as a synonym for *standard cost* in Emerson [1909, p. 127].

Also, while the sums of (allotted) *standard cost* and allotted waste (or current waste) was (total) allotted cost in Chapter 7 [1908–9 (VII), p. 676], Emerson changed *allotted cost* into allotted total cost in Chapter 8. Moreover, in Emerson [1908] the concept of allotted cost was transformed, using "predetermined", which is an antithesis of "actual", in place of "allotted", and the sums of predetermined standard cost and predetermined waste were called predetermined total cost [Emerson, 1909, pp. 120–127].

Thus, he considers *efficiency cost* as a synonym for *standard cost* and carried the sums of wastes (or saving) in the past to efficiency account. Inefficiency is transferred out and the efficiency account can indicate the performance since his efficiency system is introduced.

Moreover, by doing so, his *standard cost* concept is made clearer. Emerson's *standard cost* is only a measure of efficiency improvement. His insistence [1908–9 (VI), p. 343] that "It is, however, not the cost per mile but the efficiency which is important" is an important concept. As for Emerson, the supreme imperative is to accomplish tasks expressed by physical measures.

This is also apparent from his perception of cost components. Though he states that all operating costs and all manufacturing costs are derived from material, labour and fixed cost, Emerson [1912, p. 86] emphasizes the physical measures — that is, the quantity of material and time that it takes to do the work of all the components.

Seen in this light, Solomons' criticism of Emerson is not entirely convincing. Although the conceptual changes of efficiency cost and allotted cost can be seen in Emerson [1908–9, 1909, 1914], the *standard cost* concept is unchanged. He stresses not *standard cost per se*, but efficient accomplishment of the individual task, which is expressed by physical measures — that it, time and quantity.

Exhibit 2
Allotted Costs, Actual Expenses and Efficiency Expenses

	1903–4	1904–5	1905–6	1906–7
Total units	4,725,000	4,785,400	5,776,000	6,462,800
Allotted standard costs	$283,000	$287,124	$346,560	$323,140
Allotted wastes	189,000	191,416	57,760	–
Total alloted cost	$472,500	$478,540	$404,320	$323,140
Discrepancy between record and actual				
Increase	14,671	8,080	–	7,296
Decrease	–	–	28,214	7,296
Actual total expense as it appears in President's report	$487,171	$486,620	$376,106	$315,841
Amount forward				
Debit	–	14,671	22,751	–
Credit	–	–	–	5,483
Efficiency expense	$487,171	$501,291	$398,857	$310,381
Allotted cost	–	$478,540	$404,320	$323,140
Debit forward	–	14,671	22,751	-5,463
Current deficit	–	8,080	–	–
Current credit	–	–	$427,071	$317,677
Current credit	–	–	28,214	7,296
Efficiency expense statement	–	$501,291	$398,857	$310,381

Source: Emerson, H., "Efficiency as a Basis for Operation and Wages," (VII), *Engineering Magazine*, Vol. 36 (January, 1909), p. 679. (Some mistakes in figures by Emerson have been corrected.)

Exhibit 3
Allotted and Actual Costs and Their Reconciliation

	1903–4	1904–5	1905–6	1906–7
Total units	4,725,000	4,785,400	5,776,000	6,462,800
Allotted unit standard costs	$0.06	$0.06	$0.06	$0.05
Allotted unit wastes	0.04	0.04	0.01	–
Allotted total unit cost	$0.10	$0.10	$0.07	$0.05
Actual unit costs	0.1031	0.1017	0.065	0.048
Allotted standard costs	$283,500	$287,124	$346,560	$323,140
Allotted wastes	189,000	191,416	57,760	–
Allotted total costs	$472,500	$478,540	$404,320	$323,140
Actual costs from President's annual report	487,171	486,620	376,106	315,844
Credit to Efficiency account	–	–	$28,214	$7,206
Debit to Efficiency account	$14,671	$8,080	–	–
Credit carried from preceding year	–	–	–	$5,463
Debit carried from preceding year	–	$14,671	$22,751	–
Credit to carry following year	–	–	$5,463	$12,759
Debit to carry to following year	$14,671	$22,751		

Source: Emerson, H., "Efficiency as a Basis for Operation and Wages," (VIII), *Engineering Magazine*, Vol. 36 (February, 1909), p. 816.

Therefore, for Emerson, accounting procedures, especially standard costing, is only an index to show the results since his efficiency system was introduced.[15] This can be proved by the fact that Emerson introduced his efficiency system into many companies as a consulting engineer. His standard cost system was the basis of calculating savings. Emerson's famous testimony ["Testimony," 1910] before the Interstate Commerce Commission (ICC) that "the railroad companies could save 'a million dollars a day' on their operating costs" should be remembered.

It is to be understood that he never denied the first ("old") method of ascertaining costs based on actual costs, but intended to be dependent on them. Therefore he has no alternative idea about which cost is the *"true"* cost.

Many researchers, however, conclude that Emerson's standard cost concept [attainable (expected) *standard cost*] includes avoidable loss, so that it can not be useful for control. Okamoto [1969, p. 24] and Tsuji [1971, p. 136] believe that he does not regard *standard cost* as a *"true"* cost, considering allotted cost (standard expenses plus avoidable loss) which Emerson called *"real"* cost as *"true"* cost.

Nevertheless, referring to Emerson's viewpoints on cost accounting described earlier and the development of the four cost concepts, these opinions should be reexamined. If the word *"real"* costs is regarded as *"true"*, even an unavoidable loss should be included in the "*true*" costs, and the inefficiency factor would be included in *standard costs* as "a measure of efficiency". This is not his genuine intention. As described earlier, remembering the fact that *allotted cost* (which is composed by standard expenses and avoidable loss, and printed in italic letters) is changed into predetermined cost (which is printed in roman letters), "*real* means not what is true or ideal, but only what is actually expected. '*Real* cost' should be understood as *actual* or *factual* cost". This interpretation is supported by A.H. Church's word "ascertained" or actual (i.e., real) cost. Church [1910, p. 37] also uses the word "real" as a synonym of "actual."

Emerson did not consider allotted cost which is the sum of standard expense and allotted waste, and did not intend to regard his four cost concepts as true or ideal. The misunderstanding of these points results in the critical view of Emerson's standard cost concept. Standard cost in his system is always revised at the new level, by eliminating the inefficient factors through pre-surveys. By doing so, standard cost can be utilized as an index of efficiency. The total of every year's variances between actual cost and determined total cost (total allotted cost in Chapter 7, allotted total cost in Chapter 8) is not a tool of control, but an index which shows the savings by the introduction of his efficiency system.

Exhibit 4

Predetermined Costs and Actual Costs and Their Reconciliation

	1903–4	1904–5	1905–6	1906–7
Total units	4,725,000	4,785,400	5,776,000	6,462,800
Predetermined unit standard costs	$0.06	$0.06	$0.06	$0.05
Predetermined unit wastes	0.04	0.04	0.01	–
Predetermined total unit cost	$0.10	$0.10	$0.07	$0.05
Actual unit costs	0.1031	0.1017	0.065	0.049
Predetermined standard costs	$283,500	$287,124	$346,560	$323,140
Predetermined wastes	189,000	191,416	57,760	–
Predetermined total costs	$472,500	$478,540	$404,320	$323,140
Actual costs from President's annual report	487,171	486,620	376,106	315,844
Credit to Efficiency account	–	–	$28,214	$7,296
Debit to Efficiency account	$14,671	$8,080	–	–
Credit carried from preceding year	–	–	–	$5,463
Debit carried from preceding year	–	$14,671	$22,751	–
Credit to carry following year	–	–	$5,463	$12,759
Debit to carry to following year	$14,671	$22,751		

Source: Emerson, H., *Efficiency as a Basis for Operation and Wages*, First Edition (New York: The Engineering Magazine, 1909), p. 127.

5.0 CONCLUSION

Solomons' first critical view of Emerson's standard costing would be clearer if Emerson's real intentions were recognized — that he tried to distinguish *standard task control* (expressed by physical measures) — from *standard cost* (expressed by monetary measures — *accounting control*). Indeed, Emerson's standard cost concept is unchanged.

Exhibit 5
Standard Cost, Allotted Cost and Efficiency Cost

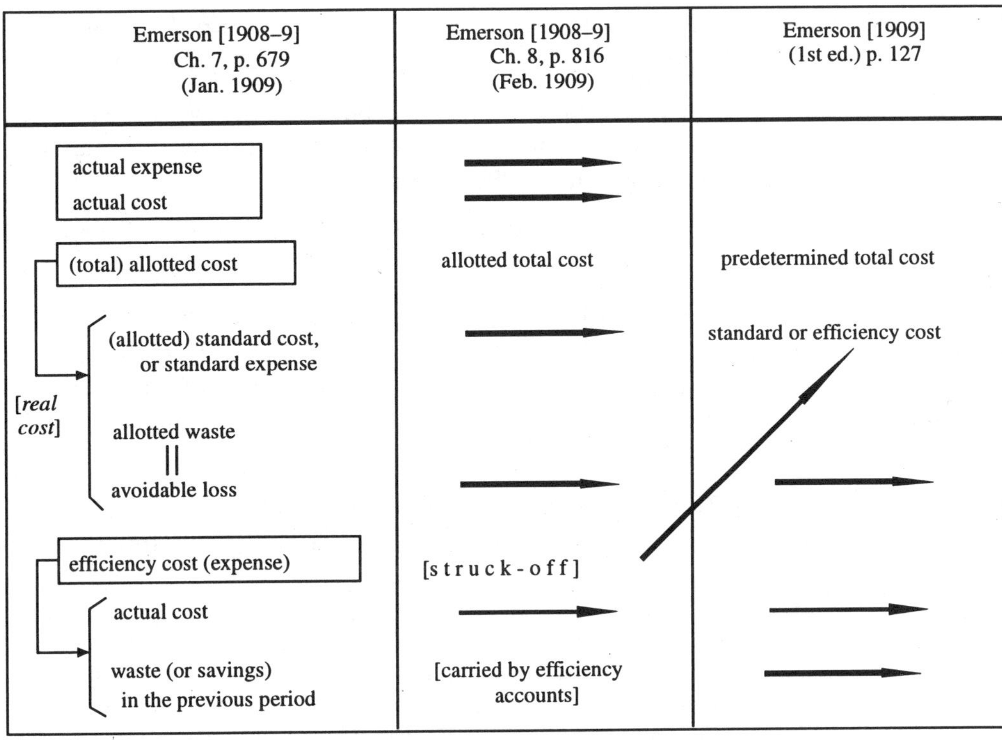

Also, Solomons' second critical view that Emerson made no attempt to arrive at anything more detailed than an overall variance between actual and standard cost is not significant, because as Emerson [1911, p. 41] himself insisted, "the test of comparative cost is so fallacious, so unscientific."[16]

Therefore, M. Chatfield's [1977, p. 171] assertion that "He [Emerson] failed to locate the exact sources of inefficiencies because he attempted nothing more detailed than an overall variance between actual and standard results" is also inaccurate. On the contrary, in order to locate the exact sources of inefficiencies, Emerson attempted nothing more detailed than an analysis of overall variance between actual and standard results.

This paper tries to show that critical views of the Emerson's standard costing are due to a misunderstanding of his real intentions. His standard costing is only an index to measure the savings after his efficiency system is introduced. It is from this perspective that the specialities in Emerson's standard cost system[17] become apparent. He prefers efficiency (or *task* control) to cost accounting (or *accounting control* through variance analysis). Accordingly, Emerson's idea and his standard cost system are now calling attention to modern cost accounting and management accounting. The gap between theory and practice could always exist [Scapens, 1988, pp. 26–28], and we should examine the continuous process of their interaction. The significance of historical study must be emphasized.[18]

ENDNOTES

1 This is an enlarged version of my paper in Japanese "H. Emerson's Standard Cost Theory." I gratefully acknowledge the helpful comments of S. Paul Garner, H. Thomas Johnson, Lee D. Parker, R. W. Scapens and James Quigel.

2 Other critics include Matsumoto [1961], Okamoto [1969] and Tsuji {1971, 1988].

3 For example, E.M. Sowell [1944, p. 206] describes that: "As a forerunner of standard costs, perhaps the greatest significance should be given to the expositions of Harrington Emerson." See also Garner [1954, p. 135], Epstein [1978 (1974), pp. 100–104, 109–112], Kranowski [1979, pp. 214–215], Wren [1987, p. 150], Johnson and Kaplan [1987, p. 51].

4 On the other hand, A. Tsuji [1988, pp. 137–142] had some doubts about these criticisms. This is the first work which investigates the historical development of management accounting including budgetary control in the United States.

5 Emerson's intention is very similar to that of H. Thomas Johnson [1987, 1988] and Robert Kaplan [1987].

6 For example, Emerson introduced his Efficiency System into various factories in about 200 companies [Drury, 1915, p. 145]. On Emerson's careers in detail, see Urwick [1956] and Quigel [1986]. On the relations of engineers and the foundation of *American Society of Mechanical Engineers* (ASME), see Calvert [1967], Layton [1971], Sinclair [1980] and Meiksins [pp. 219–246].

7 Emerson [1908, pp. 915–920] classifies staff into these four groups: (1) staff as to men, (2) staff as to equipment, (3) staff as to materials, and (4) staff as to methods and conditions.

8 Tsuji states [1987, pp. 5–6]:

> Judging from the viewpoint of task system, it may be said that standard costs is a converted measurement system in relation to monetary measures instead of physical ones. In this connection, such conversion was not necessarily so difficult in case of direct costs such as material and labor cost, because task data measured with physical dimensions were more easily recognized or changed into monetary unit in comparison with burden. While the way to solve standardization of overhead costs was hard because of the continual fluctuations of capacity level and the difficulties in allocation to each department, process and product. Anyway, the decisive importance to be noteworthy is that throughout the converting from physical base to monetary one the saturation of some arbitrary valuation was unavoidable and that the development of such conversion intending to contrive standard costs by Emerson and his successor was nothing but the dissolution of the relationships with task.

L.D. Parker [1986a, pp. 71–92, 1986b] examines the evolution of control concepts clearly.

9 This critical viewpoint of cost accounting is just the same as that of M.C. Wells [1978].

10 See also Durell [1914] and Brisco [1913, 1914].

11 See Slichter [1931, pp. 437–439]. M.E. Dimock [1951, pp. 125–148] values Emerson's efficiency notion highly, especially the social aspect of efficiency.

12 Emerson's insistence is critical reviews of cost accounting practice in railroad industries, for example, by A. Fink. See Okana [1985, pp. 103–125] and Chandler [1977]. However, A.H. Church [1910, p. 37] stated that:

> I venture to think there is a confusion in nomenclature here. One cannot "ascertain" a cost in advance, although it may be perfectly feasible to "estimate" it more or less closely.

This clearly reveals their difference of viewpoints on the relation between factory management and cost accounting. While Emerson regards cost accounting as only an index or device to measure the promotion of efficiency, Church seeks to attach objectivity to cost accounting *per se*. R. Vangermeersch [1988, pp. 1, 14, 63, 85] shows that Church was greatly influenced by the writings of Emerson.

13 However, the meaning of "real" cost is questionable for reviewing Emerson's concept of standard cost system, but further details will be discussed later.

14 Tsuji [1971, 1972, pp. 1–18, 1975, pp. 23–29, 1987, 1988] studies the historical development of management accounting by examining the interrelation between "Engineers' Accountancy" and "Accountants' Accountancy."

15 P. Sutcliffe [1982, p. 120] also suggests the same conclusion.

16 See Emerson's assertion "Cost records are only one of many forms of efficiency records." in Keely [1913, p. 992].

17 Wells [1978, pp. 132–134] also criticises standard costing from the view of factuality.

18 Tsuji states [1987, p. 17]:

> Thus, in order to solve those disorders, circuitous way as it may be, it should be essential to investigate the process of germination and evolution of the "engineers's accountancy" as well as the process of absorption or assimilation by the "accountants' accountancy", recurring to the starting point of management accounting. In this sense, the valuable significance of analytical viewpoints with historical and logical methodology may be emphasized .

The following is E.H. Carr's assertion [1987, p. 30]:

> My first answer therefore to the question "What is history" is that it is a continuous process of interaction between the historian and his facts, an unending dialogue between the present and the past, is greatly suggestive.

REFERENCES

Brisco, N. A. *Economics of Business* (New York: The Macmillan Co., 1913).

———. *Economics of Efficiency* (New York: The Macmillan Co., 1914).

Brummet, R. L. *Overhead Costing: The Costing of Manufactured Products* (Ann Arbor, MI: The University of Michigan, 1957).

Carr, E. H. *What is History?* Second Edition, by R.W. Davies [Harmondsworth, Middlesex: Penguin Books Ltd., 1987(1961)].

Calvert, M. A. *The Mechanical Engineer in America, 1830–1910: Professional Cultures in Conflict* (Baltimore, MD: The Johns Hopkins Press, 1967).

Chandler, A. D. Jr. *Visible Hand: The Managerial Revolution in American Business* (Cambridge, MA: The Belknap Press of Harvard University Press, 1977).

Chatfield, M. *A History of Accounting Thought,* Revised Edition (New York: Robert E. Kreiger Publishing Co., 1977).

Church, A. H. "Production Factors: in Cost Accounting and Works Management," *The Engineering Magazine*, New York, 1910.

Dimock, M. E. *Free Enterprise and the Administrative State* (University, AL: University of Alabama Press, 1951).

Durell, F. *Fundamental Sources of Efficiency* (Philadelphia, PA: J.B. Lippincott Co., 1914).

Drury, H. B. *Scientific Management: A History and Criticism* (New York: Columbia University, 1915).

Emerson, H. "Efficiency as a Basis for Operation and Wages," (III), *Engineering Magazine*, Vol. 35 (September 1908) pp. 915–920 (Emerson [1908–9]). [This paper is reprinted in *Management & Management Accounting* 1880–1920, A. Tsuji, and H. Sonoda, Eds., (Tokyo: Yushodo Booksellers Ltd., Vol. II 1975), pp. 480–564].

———. "Efficiency as a Basis for Operation and Wages," (V), *Engineering Magazine*, Vol. 35 (November, 1908).

———. "Efficiency as Basis for Operation and Wages," (VI), *Engineering Magazine*, Vol. 35 (December, 1908).

———. "Efficiency as Basis for Operation and Wages," (VII), *Engineering Magazine*, Vol. 36 (January, 1909).

———. "Efficiency as Basis for Operation and Wages," (VIII), *Engineering Magazine*, Vol. 36 (February, 1909).

———. *Efficiency as a Basis for Operation and Wages*, First Edition (New York: The Engineering Magazine Co., 1909).

———. "Efficiency: What the Term Means as Applied to Business Management," *System*, Vol. 19 (1911).

———. "Efficiency Methods" in *Scientific Management Course: A Landmark Series of Lectures Given at the YMCA*, F. Gilbreth *et al.*, Eds. [Worcester, MA: The Educational Dept. of the YMCA, 1912 (reprint ed., Easton: Hive Publishing Co., 1980)].

———. "The Opportunity of Labor under Scientific Management," in *Addresses and Discussion at the Conference on Scientific Management Held October 12–13–14 Nineteen Hundred and Eleven*, Dartmouth College, Amos Tuck School of Business Administration, 1912 (Easton: Hive Publishing Co., 1972).

———. *Efficiency as a Basis for Operation and Wages*, Fourth Edition (New York: The Engineering Magazine Co., 1914).

———. "Efficiency Engineering" in *The Encyclopedia Americana* (New York: Americana Corporation, 1928), p. 714.

———. "Efficiency Engineering" in *The Encyclopedia Americana* (New York: Americana Corporation), Vol. 7, (1928), pp. 437–439.

Epstein, M. J. *The Effect of Scientific Management on the Development of the Standard Cost System* [New York: Arno Press, 1978 (1974)].

Garner S. P. *Evolution of Cost Accounting to 1925* (University, AL: The University of Alabama Press, 1954).

Haber, S. *Efficiency and Uplift: Scientific Management in the Progressive Era 1890–1920* (Chicago: The University of Chicago Press, 1964).

Johnson, H. T. "Rediscovering Management Accounting's Lost Relevance," in *Collected Papers of the Fifth World Congress of Accounting Historians*, A.T. Craswell, Ed. (Sydney: Accounting and Finance Foundation within the University of Sydney, 1988).

Johnson, H. T. and R. S. Kaplan. *Relevance Lost: The Rise and Fall of Management Accounting* (Boston: Harvard Business School Press, 1987).

Keely, R. R. "Overhead Expense Distribution," *Journal of A.S.M.E.*, Vol. 35 (June, 1913).

Kranowski, N. "The Historical Development of Standard Costing System until 1920," in *The Academy of Accounting Historians Working Paper Series Vol. II*, E.N. Coffman, Ed., The Academy of Accounting Historians, 1979.

Layton, E. T. *The Revolt of the Engineers: Social Responsibility and the American Engineering Profession* (Cleveland, OH: The Press of Case Western University, 1971).

Matsumoto, M. *HYOJUN GENKA KEISANRON (Theory of Standard Costing: Its Nature and Development)* (Tokyo: Kunimoto-Shobo, 1961).

Meiksins, P. "The 'Revolt of the Engineers' Reconsidered," *Technology and Culture*, Vol. 29, No. 2 (1988), pp. 219–246.

Nelson, D. *Managers and Workers: Origins of the New Factory System in the United States, 1880–1920* (WI: The University of Wisconsin Press, 1975).

Okamoto, K. *BEIKOKU HYOJUN-GENKA-KEISAN HATTATSUSHI (Historical Development of Standard Costing in the United States)* (Tokyo: Hakuto-Shobo, 1969).

Okana, H. *Introduction of Management Accounting History.* Unpublished Master Thesis (Osaka City University, 1985).

———. "H. Emerson's Standard Cost Theory," the KEIEI KENKYU, *Business Review*, Vol. 36, No. 4 (November, 1985), pp. 85–104.

Parker, L. D. "The Classical Model of Control in the Accounting Literature," *The Accounting Historians Journal*, Vol. 13, No. 1 (Spring 1986a), pp. 71–92.

———. *Developing Control Concepts in the 20th Century* (New York: Garland Publishing, Inc., 1986b).

Quigel, J. P. "Harrington Emerson Papers Guide," Historical Collections and Labor Archives, Pattee Library, The Pennsylvania State University, 1986.

Scapens, R. W. "Research into Management Accounting Practice," *Management Accounting* (UK) (December, 1988), pp. 26–28.

Sinclair, B. *A Centennial History of the American Society of Mechanical Engineers 1880–1980* (Toronto, ON: ASME, 1980).

Slichter, S. H. "Efficiency," *The Encyclopedia of the Social Science* (New York: The Macmillan Co., 1931) Vol. 5, pp. 437–439.

Solomons, D. "The Historical Development of Costing," in *Studies in Costing*, D. Solomons, Ed. (London: Sweet & Maxwell, Ltd., 1952).

Sowell, E. M. *The Evolution of the Theories and Techniques of Standard Costs* [University AL: The University of Alabama Press, 1973 (1944)].

Sutcliffe, P. "The Role of Labour Variances in Harrington Emerson's 'New Gospel of Efficiency'," *Accounting and Business Research*, Vol. 12, No. 46 (Spring, 1982).

"Testimony of Harrington Emerson" in *Evidence Taken by the Interstate Commerce Commission in the Matter of Proposed Advances in Freight Rates by Carriers*, 61st Cong., 3d Sess., 1910.

Thompson, C. B. *The Theory and Practice of Scientific Management* (Cambridge, MA: The Riverside Press, 1917).

Tsuji, A. *KANRI-KAIKEI HATTATSUSHIRON (Historical Development of Management Accounting: 1800–1920)* [Tokyo: Yuhikaku, 1971, 1988 (Revised and Enlarged Edition)].

———. "Some Notes on the Early Development of Budgetary Control Concept in the United States: C.U. Carpenter, as a Pioneer in Business Budget," *The KEIEIKENKYU (Business Review, Osaka City University)* No. 121 (1972), pp. 1–18.

———. "Shade of the Past: Budgeting in the Early 1900," *Managerial Planning*, Vol. 23, (March–April, 1975), pp. 23–29.

———. "The Analytical Viewpoints to Studies in Management Accounting: A Verification on the Adequacy of Historical and Logical Methodology," *Osaka City University Business Review*, No. 1 (1987).

Urwick, L. *The Golden Book of Management: A Historical Record of the Life and Work of Seventy Pioneers* (London: Newman Neame Ltd., 1956).

Vangermeersch, R. *Alexander Hamilton Church: A Man of Ideas for All Seasons* (New York: Garland Publishing, Inc., 1988).

Wells, M. C. *Accounting for Common Costs* (Arbana, IL: Center for International Education and Research in Accounting, 1978).

Wren, D. A. *The Evolution of Management Thought*, Third Edition (New York: John Wiley and Sons, 1987).

Part II: Education

Turn-of-the-Century CPAs and the Accounting Education Movement

Dale L. Flesher
University of Mississippi

Tonya K. Flesher
University of Mississippi

Gary John Previts
Case Western Reserve University
Ohio

1.0 ABSTRACT

The year 1996 marks the 100th anniversary of the Certified Public Accountant (CPA) examination in the United States. The first law establishing the CPA designation was passed in New York on April 17, 1896. The motivation for this study was to determine the role played by early CPAs in the accounting education movement. This paper outlines and analyzes the careers of the educators among the first group of CPAs — those who were certified in 1896 and 1897. Although the first CPAs were all practitioners, many academic types emerged from the first group of CPAs. Indeed, some of the first CPAs were the pioneers of academic accounting as it is known today. In fact, all of the academics at major schools were involved in the CPA exam movement.

2.0 INTRODUCTION

The passage of the first CPA law was the culmination of several years of efforts by practising accountants. As early as 1884, the first professional accounting organization in the United States, the Institute of Accounts (originally called the Institute of Accountants and Bookkeepers) issued certificates to its members who had passed an examination. Similarly, the American Association of Public Accountants admitted the more experienced members as "Fellows" beginning in 1887. However, this early certification was limited in that the organizations could not restrict practise by nonmembers. Legislation was needed to control the growing ranks of practitioners.

In 1894, a rough draft of a bill providing for a professional examination was circulated in Albany, New York, by Charles E. Sprague (a man who would later hold New York CPA certificate number 11). According to one source, Sprague's bill had actually been written by the president of the Institute of Accounts, Henry Harney (who eventually became CPA number 18, and in 1897 a founder of the New York State Society of CPAs) [Wilkinson, 1903, p. 3]. However, in a letter to the editor of *Business*, appearing in the July 1896 issue ["Letter to the editor," p. 320], Sprague stated that he had prepared the bill as a member of a committee of the Institute of Accounts. Sprague learned from his friend, Melville Dewey (the innovator who developed the Dewey Decimal System for libraries), that his best bet for passage was to put the enforcement of the CPA law under the jurisdiction of the Regents of the University of the State of New York. The bill was introduced before the New York State Legislature in February 1895, but failed to emerge from a House committee and was defeated in the Senate.

At the same time, another bill, similar in its provisions, was being circulated by the membership of the American Association of Public Accountants (AAPA), an organization with many British-born members. The AAPA had been established in 1887. That bill had been written by an AAPA member, Francis Gottsberger, who did not even notify the membership of his action until February 1895, after the bill had been sent to the legislature. Upon hearing of the bill, the AAPA immediately appointed Gottsberger as the head of the legislative committee ["The Incorporators ...," 1953, p. 219–220].

Several members of the AAPA and Institute of Accounts called a meeting in March 1895 to negotiate the differences between the two bills. Forty-five accountants attended and formed a group to decide exactly what terms should be in the bill to be supported by the accounting profession. This group was known as the "Committee of 14." Accountants representing the AAPA included James T. Anyon, W. Sanders Davies, James Yalden, and Francis Gottsberger, the chairman of the Committee of 14. Harney and Charles Dutton were among those representing the Institute, as was the renowned educator Silas S. Packard ["The Incorporators ...," 1953, p. 219]. The Committee quickly decided that the Institute's bill proposing a title should be pushed over the Association's bill which proposed a licence. Despite the efforts of the Committee of 14 and its lobbyist, neither bill passed.

A bill with similar provisions was introduced in 1896, and passed by almost unanimous vote on April 7; it was signed by the governor on April 17, 1896. The AAPA, under the leadership of Frank Broaker, took charge of the 1896 lobbying campaign. One reason for the ease of passage in 1896, as opposed to the difficulties of 1895, was the fact that the earlier bill limited the CPA designation only to US citizens. The 1896 version made the designation available to citizens and to any individual who had duly declared his intention to become such a citizen. This amendment opened the way for British chartered accountants and other non-Americans who had not yet secured their citizenship papers [Previts and Merino, 1979, pp. 97–98]. Alternatively, it has been said that Senator Albert Wray, who introduced the 1896 bill into the Senate, supported the bill because he wanted American companies to have an alternative to hiring British chartered accountants for their audits ["Albert Wray," 1896, p. 409].

The CPA law provided for a "grandfathering" provision which allowed experienced practitioners to become CPAs without taking an examination. To qualify, a practitioner had to prove that he had been in reputable practice as a public accountant since January 1, 1890. According to one secondary source, during 1896 and 1897, a total of 108 certificates were granted under the grandfathering clause. In addition, four people passed the first examination. That first CPA examination was administered in December 1896. The three who passed that first exam are known; they were Edward C. Charles (Certificate No. 119), Joseph

Hardcastle (Certificate No. 104), and William H. Jasper (Certificate No. 105) [Wilkinson, 1903, p. 9]. The remainder of this paper is about some of those individuals who were the first to hold CPA certificates, and who also went on to become university teachers. These were all New York residents at the time they became CPAs because the earliest certificates were all granted under New York law. Pennsylvania passed its CPA law in 1899, followed by Maryland in 1900 and California in 1901. Washington and Illinois followed in 1903.

As Henry R. M. Cook (CPA Certificate No. 107) wrote in a discussion of the new CPA law and the role of university education for accountants:

> Concerning legislation of this kind, I have some doubts as to its scope. I believe it to be only partly creative, while in a sense stimulative. All professions of importance have an educational foundation upon which to rest; mere legislation does not change individuals or enhance their knowledge; it only provides ways, means and facilities whereby professions may be benefitted. The unit of strength is the actual knowledge of the individual members of the profession. [Cook, 1901, p. 2]

Thus, the law merely provided an opportunity for public accountants to become professionals; it was the later development of an educational base that consummated the true development of accountancy as a modern profession in the new industrial environment of the early 20th century. This paper explores the individuals who formed that educational base.

3.0 WHO WERE THE FIRST ACADEMIC CPAs?

The June 1898 issue of *Accountics: The Office Magazine* ["Certified ...," pp. 72–73] published a listing of New York CPAs and their addresses and certificate numbers. An analysis of that listing turned up several individuals who later went into academia. Profiles of these individuals follow. A brief conclusion analyzes and summarizes the important facets of these individuals and their lives. The first group of certificates awarded, consisting of 14 in number, were issued in alphabetical order. Thus, Frank Broaker, by virtue of his surname initial, became the first CPA in America. Sixteen additional certificates were granted at a second meeting and 25 more at a third meeting. An additional 31 (through number 86) were granted at the fourth meeting and 17 more at a fifth meeting. Ten more were issued at a sixth meeting (through Number 113) and eleven at a seventh meeting (through 124). An additional five certificates were apparently granted at another meeting in early 1898. However, this alphabetical analysis conflicts with a published statement that "75 certificates were issued in 1896" ["The New York State ...," 1949, p. 327]. Another article notes that Frederick S. Tipson was issued certificate number 84 in 1896, which concurs with the above analysis indicating that the end of one block of certificates (issued at the last meeting in 1896) was number 86.

4.0 PROFILES OF ACADEMICS AMONG THE FIRST 129 CPAs

4.1 Frank Broaker (Certificate No. 1)

It is perhaps appropriate that Frank Broaker was the first CPA; he was the person most instrumental in getting the initial law passed in New York State. In fact, despite being a New York City practitioner, he spent much of his time during early 1896 in Albany lobbying for passage of the act. Broaker had started his career with a Scottish accountant, John Roundey, and practiced on his own account after 1887 ["Pace Institute," 1950, p. 530].

Frank Broaker was born in Millerstown, PA on March 16, 1863; his father died a year later. The family moved to New York City in 1870, where he received a grammar school education and went on to New York University. In 1878, Broaker commenced as a junior in an East Indian importing and shipping business, remaining with the company for eight years, by which time he held the position of chief accountant. In 1886, Broaker joined the accounting firm of John Roundey, a well-known Scottish accountant and auditor. Roundey died the following year, leaving the business to Broaker. He moved his office to 150 Nassau Street in 1889 and became a partner with R. M. Chapman. A biography in *The Banking Law Journal* ["Frank Broaker," 1892, pp. 298–299] stated that Broaker acted as a professional adviser and auditor for British and other European bankers and financiers.

Broaker became the first secretary of the New York Board of CPA Examiners. He had taught accounting at the (first) New York School of Accounts during its only year of operation (1893–1894) and later established his own school to help aspiring accountants prepare for the CPA examination. Broaker was criticized for publishing a book in 1897 entitled *The American Accountants Manual,* which contained questions and answers from the first CPA exam. He kept the proceeds from the sale of the book. He also was charged with forming a society of accountants with himself as president. It was alleged that Broaker had led prospective members of the society to believe that the Board of Regents might be willing to waive the CPA examination for those who were members. The Board of Regents responded to these complaints by appointing James T. Anyon to replace Broaker on the Board of CPA Examiners ["Regulation ...," 1897, p. 38]. Broaker subsequently sued for reinstatement to his position.

Broaker was again criticized in 1897 when a Wall Street broker used the firm name of Broaker and Chapman in advertising circulars which promised investors high returns in a short period of time. The circular, which had the CPAs' names in large type, stated that all deposits would be audited by the firm; it was even noted that Broaker was the president of the American Association of Public Accountants and secretary of the State Board of Examiners. The circular stated that investors would receive weekly statements, each of which would be certified by the auditors. The editor of *Accountics* asked:

> In the name of all that is honorable and respectable, I ask: Has it come to this that stock gambling concerns can command the services of Certified Public Accountants for advertising purposes and as a means of roping in the inexperienced? I most frankly admit that accountants as well as all other business men have the right of choice of clientage. No one can quarrel with the firm of accountants here named in this regard. At the same time, I deplore their manifestation of bad taste, and their apparent willingness to be used for advertising purposes, even though the profession is disgraced thereby. In this latter particular all accountants, I take it, have a peculiar interest. ["The Free Lance," April 1897, p. 26]

The firm was apparently influenced by the editorial as the next issue reported that Broaker and Chapman had severed the questionable relationship and had published an announcement in *The Financial Record* to explain the relationship. The editor of the latter journal, however, castigated the editor of *Accountics* for criticizing the CPAs in an "uncalled-for manner". ["The Free Lance," May 1897, pp. 50–51]

Frank Broaker was indeed a major contributor to the professionalization of accountancy in America through his work in achieving passage of the 1896 act. However, given the preceding two paragraphs, he may have also made a contribution, albeit both positive and negative, to the ethics of accountancy. Nevertheless, *The Financial Record* aptly concluded:

"the profession could not have a better watch dog to guard their interests" ["Frank Broaker, C.P.A.," 1897, p. 78]. Broaker died on November 12, 1941, at the age of 78.

4.2 Charles Waldo Haskins (Certificate No. 6)

Perhaps the most famous name among the early CPAs was that of Charles Waldo Haskins. Besides being the senior partner of what was to become a major international accounting firm, Haskins was the first president of the Board of Examiners, the founding president of the New York State Society of CPAs (1897 until his death in 1903), and the first dean of the New York University (NYU) School of Commerce, Accounts and Finance. At NYU, he held the title of Professor of Auditing and of the History of Accountancy. He took an active part in the work of several patriotic societies including the National Society of the Sons of the American Revolution for whom he served as Secretary-General, the Society of Mayflower Descendants, the Society of Colonial Wars, and several yacht clubs. He was a prolific author and lecturer [Haskins, 1904].

Haskins was born in Brooklyn on January 11, 1852. He was educated in the Brooklyn Polytechnic Institute, and subsequently completed his studies in Paris. He came from a wealthy family; one of his obituaries alluded to this wealth with the following:

> Mr. Haskins occupied a position singular and unique in relation to his fellows in the profession; removed from all the petty jealousies engendered by the battle for a livelihood; possessing means more than ample for the requirements of himself and his personal family, he gave freely in time, money and influence to every movement designed to place the certified public accountant on a par in the eyes of the world with the professions of law and of medicine. ("The Late … C.P.A.," 1903, p. 78]

Perhaps indicative of Haskins' admiration in the profession, his pallbearers included the presidents of the state societies of accountants in Illinois, Pennsylvania, Massachusetts, Maryland, and New York.

At the time of Haskins' death from pneumonia on January 9, 1903, the firm of Haskins & Sells was perhaps the most respected firm in the country. This firm had been entrusted with some of the most important work that it could fall upon an accountant to perform, including: the revision of the accounting system of the United States Government, the examination of the accounts of the City of Brooklyn prior to the consolidation with New York, the investigation of the accounts and finances of the Island of Cuba, and the revision of the assessment accounting system of the City of Chicago ["The Late …," 1903, p. 18].

4.3 Charles Ezra Sprague (Certificate No. 11)

Much has been written about the life of Colonel Charles E. Sprague, including a 67-page biography authored by Helen Scott Mann and published in 1931. Thus, this paper will not go into great detail about the man. Sprague was born in Nassau, NY on October 9, 1842. He graduated from Schenectady's Union College in 1860, where he was a Phi Beta Kappa; he received a master's degree from the same school in 1862. Also in 1862, Sprague enlisted in the Union Army. He was wounded at Gettysburg, a wound that was to plague him throughout his life, and was discharged as a colonel in March 1864. Following the war, Sprague became a teacher at military academies in Yonkers, Peekskill, and Poughkeepsie, New York. He then joined the Union Dime Savings Bank in New York in 1870 where he was to spend 41 years as accountant, secretary, and president. He received an honorary Ph.D.

from Union College in 1893. Late in life, he joined the faculty of the School of Commerce, Accounts and Finance at New York University. In 1910, he was awarded an honorary doctorate by Olivet College in Michigan. Following the Civil War, he became active in the Grand Army of the Republic.

Despite his career at the bank, Sprague apparently also worked part-time as a public accountant. This is evidenced by his advertisements which appeared in *The Bookkeeper* between 1880 and 1884. In October 1880, his office address was given as the Union Dime Savings Institution, Broadway and 32nd Streets ["Charles ...," 1952, p. 431].

Sprague was active in professional organizations, including the Institute of Accounts, which he joined in its initial year, 1882. He served that organization as president in 1886 and again in 1897 [Accountants ...," 1897, p. 14]. Because of his efforts in getting the first accountancy law passed, he was named to the first State Board of Examiners.

Sprague was a prolific writer, publishing articles in such journals as *Business* and *The Office*, and serving as associate editor of *The Bookkeeper* (from 1880 to June 19, 1883) and *Journal of Accountancy* (although this fact is mentioned only in his biography; there is no indication of such an affiliation in the *Journal*). *The Bookkeeper* was first published July 20, 1880, and to that first issue Sprague contributed the first of four installments of his epic saga, "The Algebra of Accounts." Following that, there was a series of 25 articles on "Bank Bookkeeping." The magazine changed its name to *American Counting-Room* in mid-1883, and in early 1884 the publisher incorporated, with Sprague as president.

Sprague's publication activities were also vented in his work with artificial languages. Although he spoke 16 languages, he was interested in developing a universal language. In 1902, he authored a volume entitled *Handbook of Volapuk*, a language that he had created. The term "accountics," which was popularized for a time, between 1897 and 1900, by an accounting journal of that name was a product of the Volapuk language. In the first issue of Accountics ["Editorial Notes," 1897, p. 19], Sprague stated that he had coined the word because there was no single expression in the English language which connoted the "Science and art of accounts." Subsequently, the word accountancy was to replace the short-lived "accountics."

Today, it is probably one book, *The Philosophy of Accounts*, published in 1908, for which Sprague is most remembered. The book went through five editions by 1923. Prior to Sprague, books on accounting were purely practical with little in the way of theoretical explanations. However, in *The Philosophy of Accounts*, Sprague was more concerned with principles than with mechanics. The "why" was more important than the "how" of accounting. Sprague's book is truly a classic in accounting literature.

In summary, Charles Sprague was an accounting practitioner, educator, author, theoretician, and the man who carried the legislative bill to Albany. Both because of his education, his writings, and his contacts in educational circles, he added scholarly credibility to the infant profession. He died in 1912 as a result of pneumonia.

4.4 Ferdinand William Lafrentz (Certificate No. 20)

The longest surviving of the early CPAs was Ferdinand Lafrentz who was born in 1859, of German parents, on a small island off the Jutland Peninsula, then under the dominion of Denmark. He came to Chicago in 1873 where he attended the Bryant and Stratton Business College. He later taught at the same school. At the invitation of a Chicago banking firm,

Lafrentz joined the headquarters of a cattle company in Wyoming where he was responsible for the organization's financial affairs. After a few years, he was elected to the territorial legislature where he introduced the resolution that the territory be admitted into the Union. In 1889, he moved to Ogden, Utah, where he established himself as a public accountant. He moved to New York in 1893 when he accepted a position with the American Surety Company. By 1899, he was practicing with the American Audit Company, a firm devoted to the independent practice of public accounting. The firm's name was changed in 1923 to F. W. Lafrentz & Co.

Lafrentz was active in the American Association of Public Accountants, including serving a term as president from 1901–1903. He was also one of the first members of the New York State Society of CPAs. He was a member of the New York State Board of CPA Examiners from 1903–1907 and again from 1917–1925. Upon the founding of the School of Commerce at New York University, Lafrentz became a professor of auditing. He authored at least one article for a professional journal. Lafrentz died on July 15, 1954, at the age of 95 [Horowitz, 1961, p. 274–275].

4.5 John R. Sparrow (Certificate No. 54)

John R. Sparrow was born in Brooklyn in 1859 and was educated in the public schools. He then attended the Sprague Law School in Michigan. He entered the office of Henry C. Wright, CPA, and eventually took over the business. Wright was the founder of the Long Island Business College, and Sparrow became a faculty member at that institution. For about 15 years, he was identified with the faculty of the Long Island Business College as a lecturer on the theory and practice of accounts. During that time, he directed the commercial education of nearly ten thousand men of all ages ["John R. Sparrow, CPA," 1916, p. 185].

His first offices in New York were at 99 Nassau Street. In 1897, he performed a job for the municipality of New York City, which gained him recognition among the city's financial officials. In March 1898, Comptroller Bird S. Coler formed a body of consulting accountants known as the Commission on Revision of City Bookkeeping, and named Sparrow as chairman. In 1900, Sparrow was named to the State Board of CPA Examiners and served until 1904. In 1902, he was appointed to the position of Superintending Accountant and Statistician of the New York City Department of Finance. He was a member of the New York State Society of CPAs and the Institute of Accounts ["Superintending ...," 1902, p. 60]. He served as president of the New York State Society from May 1917 to May 1919. He was a strong believer in the value of professional societies to individual accountants; he even authored an article to that effect in 1903 [Sparrow, 1903, p. 88]. In a 1916 biography, it was stated:

> The Accountancy firm of Sparrow, Harvey & Company is well known not only in New York City where it has an extensive general practice, but generally throughout the United States and in Latin America as well. For several years the firm's branch office at San Juan, Puerto Rico, has audited most of the municipal, transportation, public utility, banking, tobacco, and sugar accounts of the entire island of Santo Domingo, besides having a growing business in the installation of accounting systems. ["John R. Sparrow, CPA," 1916, p. 179]

4.6 Theodore G. C. F. Koehler (Certificate No. 76)

Theodore G. Koehler, who had a practice at 1215 Broadway, was a member of the New York State Senate from 1896–1898 when a bill was presented to extend the certification waiver requirements to any individual who had practiced as a public accountant for one year prior to the April 17, 1896, passage of the CPA law. Koehler strongly supported the bill, which passed the Senate, but was defeated in the Assembly. He was a member of the AAPA, the New York State Society, and the National Society of CPAs.

Koehler was born in Ahrensboeck, Denmark on July 30, 1856. He was the bookkeeper for the East River Gas Co. of Long Island City from 1885 to 1895. By 1872, he was teaching bookkeeping in Long Island City, New York. Koehler may be best remembered as an educator. He was the proprietor of the second New York School of Accounts, which operated from 1897 to 1929 ["Pace Institute, 1950, p. 530]. He authored several accountancy textbooks. Koehler died in New York on March 19, 1929 [Webster, 1954, p. 358].

4.7 Frederick Samson Tipson (Certificate No. 84)

Tipson was born in Twickenham, England in 1858. He taught in British Guiana from 1881 to 1885. He then studied music at Cambridge University from 1885–1887. Tipson was the author of several accountancy books. He authored an article in the July 1904 issue of The *Business World* entitled "Hotel Auditing." A picture of Tipson, wearing an academic cap and gown, accompanied the article. The short biography of the author stated:

> Mr. Frederick S. Tipson, C.P.A., is too well-known to the readers of *The Business World* as the author of the two works, "Theory of Accounts" and "Commercial Law," to need further introduction at our hands further than to say that he has had upwards of twenty years' practice as a public accountant, a large part of which time has been spent in hotel accounting. [Tipson, 1904, p. 342]

Despite the man needing no introduction, these authors could find out little about him (apparently he did need an introduction). In 1898, Tipson was practicing at 441 Pearl Street, but had moved to 150 Nassau Street by 1904. He earlier practiced in London and arrived in New York about 1890. He apparently operated a CPA exam coaching course around 1900 to 1906 ["Pace Institute," 1950, p. 530]. A note in *Accountics* stated that every student of Tipson's CPA coaching course had passed the examination. Tipson died in New York in 1921 [Webster, 1954, p. 382].

4.8 Leon Brummer (Certificate No. 88)

Despite the fact that many published photos of Leon Brummer could be found, little in the way of personal information was uncovered. He was one of the first group of accounting faculty at New York University where he was professor of practical accounting and secretary of the faculty. He was a member of the group of New York Society of CPAs' officers (along with Haskins, Sells, Cook, Loomis, and Kittredge) who met with NYU chancellor McCracken to request the university to start a School of Commerce, Accounts and Finance [Brummer, 1911, p. 254]. Brummer was the Society's secretary. In 1898, he was with the firm of Bergtheil, Cook & Co., but moved to Horley, Brummer & Co. in 1900. By 1904, he was with Hertle, Cook, Brummer & Haag. A 1900 article called him one of the younger practitioners in the field of accounting; a contemporaneous photo showed him to be in his late 30s or early 40s, but a birthdate has not been found.

4.9 Joseph Hardcastle (Certificate No. 104)

Hardcastle, whose 1898 office was at 1198 Broadway, had the lowest numbered certificate for a person who passed the CPA examination. He may also have been one of the oldest persons, at the age of 69 years, eight months, to ever pass the CPA exam. One source states that Hardcastle was offered a waiver certificate, but declined so that he could attempt the exam ["Joseph Hardcastle," 1951, pp. 615–617].

Hardcastle's scores on the CPA exam were: 87 in theory, 80 in practical accounting, 85 in auditing, and 95 in law. These scores averaged 87, compared to 85 and 79 for the two other individuals who passed the exam at the same sitting ["Joseph Hardcastle," 1951, p. 615]. Thus, were awards given, Hardcastle would have been the first "gold medalist" on the CPA examination.

The exam that Hardcastle took consisted of four parts: theory of accounts, practical accounting, auditing, and commercial law. Each of the four sessions was three hours in duration. The CPA law provided that all four parts of the exam must be passed at one time; there was no provision for partial credit on fewer than four parts. The examination fee was $25 — the same amount that one would have to pay to obtain a waiver (grandfather) certificate. Applicants had to be high school graduates or the equivalent. Since he was a resident of the city, it is presumed that Hardcastle sat for the exam in New York City, although it was also offered in Buffalo.

To give an idea of the types of questions Hardcastle had to answer, the following examples from the first CPA exam are given [Broaker, 1897]. The first theory of accounts' question was:

> State the essential principles of double entry bookkeeping, and show wherein it differs from single entry bookkeeping.

The first practical accounting question gave a trial balance for a partnership which could not meet its obligations. The CPA candidate had to:

> Prepare a statement of affairs, showing the liabilities and the assets with respect to their realization and liquidation; also a deficiency account showing such of the above stated particulars as would account for the deficiency shown by the statement of affairs.

The initial auditing question asked for "a brief outline of the duties of an auditor, and of his responsibilities."

The first question in the commercial law section asked the candidates to

> Draw the following promissory notes and forms of indorsement:
> a. Not negotiable;
> b. Negotiable;
> c. Negotiable, requiring no indorsement.

The candidates then had to illustrate four different types of indorsement.

Joseph Hardcastle was born April 22, 1827, at Skipton in Craven, Yorkshire, England. He attended a free grammar school and then received a scholarship to York and Ripon Diocesan Training School. By 1858, he had moved to New York City where he passed the examination to become a New York public school teacher. He taught from 1847 to 1864, including three years at Belize in British Honduras, where he was also superintendent of schools, and six years at Grammar School No. 38 in New York.

Hardcastle quit teaching in 1864 to pursue accounting on a full-time basis. His first client may have been Peter Gilsey, for whom he acted as an accountant for 42 years (including the period as accountant for Gilsey's estate). While teaching at Grammar School No. 38, Hardcastle had charge of two of the sons of Peter Gilsey. Gilsey had an income tax problem involving sinking funds, which the boys' teacher was able to solve. His mathematical solution was accepted by the Income Tax Commissioners, much to the pleasure of Gilsey. The result was that Gilsey offered Hardcastle a job ["Prof.", 1906]. Hardcastle was active in early professional organizations, including the Institute of Accountants and Bookkeepers (later changed to Institute of Accounts), which he joined as a charter member in 1882. He joined the New York State Society of CPAs in 1897, shortly after that organization's founding, and the American Association of Public Accountants (the predecessor organization of the American Institute of CPAs) in 1905.

Despite the fact that Hardcastle left education in 1864, his educational abilities were recognized in 1882 when he was selected as the first Chief Examiner of the Institute of Accounts. He also chaired the Institute's Committee on Lectures for several years. He apparently was an excellent lecturer himself and was often invited to speak at professional meetings ["Joseph Hardcastle," 1951, p. 616]. He re-entered education when he taught at Koehler's New York School of Accounts. Finally, in 1901, he joined the faculty of the New York University School of Commerce, Accounts and Finance as a Professor of the Principles and Practice of Accounts, a position he held until his death in 1906. His obituary called him "senior professor of the School." His skills and abilities were recognized by New York University in 1905 when he was awarded an honorary master's degree. The citation accompanying the degree read as follows:

> He has taken a prominent part in the elevation of accounting to the rank of a profession. For many years a contributor to the periodicals of his profession and writer of text books recognized as authoritative in their field. Teacher, author and leader in his profession, he is recommended for the honorary degree of Master of Letters.

Joseph Hardcastle was a prolific author. The first edition of *The Accountants Index* lists 25 articles by the man, with the first published in 1890. Another source lists 61 titles dating back to 1882. Some of the articles were seemingly the material for what was intended to become a book. One book published by New York University was actually an accumulation of his lectures on accounts of executors and testamentary trustees. Hardcastle states in the Preface of that volume that it is "written primarily for the aid of students. It gives in substance the matter which I present in a course of lectures at the New York University School of Commerce, Accounts and Finance. For the students who hear these lectures it will serve as a syllabus." He goes on to state:

> The book, however, is more than a syllabus, and the general reader will, I trust, find it a source of independent help and guidance in his study of the subject. I have aimed to make it useful, not only to the teacher, but also to the professional accountant. [Hardcastle, 1903, p. 3]

The objectives of the book included bringing "the lawyer and the accountant into accord on the subject, so that they may profitably co-operate in their mutual work," and "to give the accountant such a knowledge of both the principles and practice of the law that he may do his work intelligently, leaving, however, the legal guidance, the procedure, and the forms to be attended to by the lawyer."

Altogether, Hardcastle's writings appeared in at least 137 issues of nine different journals, and the first of these did not appear until the man was 55 years old. Albeit, some of these articles were quite short, and others were longer papers published in installments, but Hardcastle was still, nevertheless, a prolific writer in the field of accountancy.

There are always critics; some thought Hardcastle's writings more prolific than beneficial. An 1897 editorial in the British *The Accountants' Magazine* commented on an article entitled "Logismography" appearing in the September issue of *Business*. It was first noted that "logismography" appeared to be a new title for bookkeeping:

> The revenue account is called "Economical Situation, Direct," and the balance Sheet "Specific Situation, with Development." There is a great deal more of this kind of thing, but one is glad to see that it all comes to the same in the end. Mr. Hardcastle's theories and absurd titles appear much more calculated to confuse than to simplify the art which we think most people will prefer still to call bookkeeping. ["American ...," 1897, p. 17]

Actually, logismography was a system for the ordination of accounts that was devised by Giuseppe Cerboni, Accountant-General of Italy. Hardcastle was merely trying to explain an Italian innovation.

Hardcastle's writing ran the gamut from purely theoretical to purely practical. His 1901 article in *Business*, "An Illustration of a Personal Theory of Accounts," was a theoretical discussion of a proprietary theory of accounts — a theory he contrasted with the "empiric school" [Hardcastle, 1901a, p. 225]. As a contrast, he also published in 1901 an article entitled "Balancing an Account at One Operation" [Hardcastle, 1901b, p. 428], in which he explains one of his experiments with "the mechanical parts of bookkeeping." That article claims to explain his innovative way of calculating the balance in an account with a balance column. Unfortunately, Hardcastle's explanation is beyond the minds of these authors, who have grown accustomed to ten-key adding machines and calculators.

Another example of Hardcastle's emphasis on both theory and practical application is his two-part article published in *American Counting-Room* in 1883. The October issue carried the first installment under the title "Equation of Payments Mathematically Considered," followed by a subtitle "First Theoretical" [Hardcastle, 1883a, p. 219]. The November issue of the same journal had an article with the same title, but the subtitle was "Second — Practical" [Hardcastle, 1883b, p. 281]. The theoretical article was basically a mathematical explanation of calculating present values without the use of present-value tables. The equations, which included logarithms, would have fit well into most of the present-day high-brow accounting journals. The "practical" article illustrated how to calculate interest on unpaid receivables balances. A nine-step "Order of Procedure" provided guidance for practicing accountants [Hardcastle, 1883b, p. 282].

Still another article with a theoretical discussion was Hardcastle's 1883 article in *The Book Keeper* [Hardcastle, 1883c, pp. 17–20], entitled "On the Theory of Life Insurance." Hardcastle showed his facility with math as he used both actuarial tables and present values to explain how life insurance worked. The article would be a good introduction to the field even today.

Hardcastle's article "Depreciation in Its Application" [Hardcastle, 1901c, p. 470] explained the basics of depreciation accounting, including both theoretical and practical considerations. It must be remembered that depreciation was not commonly recorded in that era; thus, Hardcastle was on the "cutting edge" in recommending such use. He stated that there were three common methods of depreciation: the straight-line method, a declining-balance method, and an annuity method. Given his love for math, Hardcastle gave a thorough illustration of the annuity, or sinking fund, method of depreciation.

As the citation accompanying his honorary degree indicated, Joseph Hardcastle played a prominent role in the growth of accountancy as a profession. Furthermore, he was an outstanding teacher; a student publication at New York University included the following quotation about Hardcastle: "Beloved by every student and most highly respected by members of his profession" ["Joseph Hardcastle," 1951, p. 617]. He died on June 16, 1906, at his Brooklyn home (92 Monroe Street) following an accident on June 8 in which he was knocked down by a horse ["Prof ...," 1906]. He was 79 years of age at the time of his death.

Joseph Hardcastle was not only a CPA practitioner, but also a noted educator and author. He was a contributor to accounting as a field of practice and as a profession. His mathematical background was evident as he incorporated higher math into most of his articles. He was a theoretician at a time when accountancy needed theories. Perhaps he was even ahead of his time; alternatively, many of his contributions have been overridden by bookkeeping machines, calculators, and computers. Thus, in this respect, his timing was perfect. All of this came from a man in the twilight of his life; were accountancy to have emerged earlier, who knows what Joseph Hardcastle might have had to offer.

4.10 Henry R. M. Cook (Certificate No. 107)

Cook, a British-born (1853) one-time sea captain, practiced at 7 Pine Street in 1898, along with Leon Brummer. While in England, he had never worked in a chartered accountant's office, but instead had achieved his experience in an industrial setting. Cook was a member and president of the American Association of Public Accountants and a supporter in 1892 of the AAPA's College of Accounts. He served as president of the New York State Society of CPAs from 1909 to 1912. For many years, he served as Auditor of the Board of Education of the City of New York. When the School of Commerce, Accounts and Finance was established at NYU in 1900, Cook was named as professor of public accounting. At the time, he was apparently working as auditor of the New York Board of Education ["A New ...," 1900, p. 2]. Cook was also the individual who made the formal motion that the New York Society should approach NYU [Brummer, 1911, p. 252]. Cook was also involved in the ill-fated attempt of the AAPA to start a New York School of Accounts in 1893. It was Cook who presented the state charter which had been obtained by the AAPA to the first trustees of the new school ["An Educational ...," 1901, p. 2]. He died in 1932.

4.11 Thomas B. Dean (Certificate No. 116)

Dean was born in Blackburn, England, and educated at Liverpool. His father was a practising accountant. Thomas B. Dean received his accounting education at the Lancashire & Yorkshire Institute in Manchester, England, where his teacher was a chartered accountant. He came to the United States in 1888, where he first practised in the west with his father's firm. He moved to New York in 1892. He served two years in the firm of Broaker & Chapman. Later, he was with the firms of Patterson, Teele & Dennis and Haskins & Sells. He taught an auditing class for at least three years at New York University when that school began its accounting program. This latter position arose because of his employment in the firm of Haskins & Sells and his familiarity to Charles Waldo Haskins. Judging from a 1903 photo, Dean was probably born in the late 1860s or early 1870s. Unlike the other NYU faculty members, Dean held the title of instructor instead of professor — an indication that he was probably younger and less experienced than the senior faculty ["Archer and ...," 1903, p. 1].

4.12 Anson O. Kittredge (Certificate No. 121)

Kittredge was born in Dayton, Ohio, on February 19, 1848. He began his business career as a bookkeeper in the stove foundry of Greer & King in Dayton. While there, he originated and constructed what was probably the first card ledger ever used. He was involved in several other businesses over the years before he turned to public accounting. At one point while still in Ohio, he authored a book entitled "The Manual of Sheet Metal Architectural Work." From 1874–78, he published *The Sheet Metal Builder*, a journal circulated among manufacturers and dealers in sheet metal work. Kittredge moved to New York in 1878 where he became editor of *Carpentry and Building*. In 1886, he began publication of *The Office*, a monthly journal related to accounting and bookkeeping. While serving as editor of several publications in the 1880s, he also found time to patent several inventions constructed of sheet metal. In 1892, he severed his other publishing connections and established The Kittredge Company, Publishers. He was also involved in some accounting work at this time. His obituary credits him with being one of the prime movers in securing the passage of the law in New York State. In 1898, he established the Account, Audit and Assurance Company. In 1900, he became a faculty member at New York University where he held the title of Professor of the Theory and Practice of Accounts. Also, in 1900, he became secretary of the American Institute of Bank Clerks, an education enterprise sponsored by the American Bankers' Association.

Kittredge, whose office was at 1003 Wool Exchange Building (260 West Broadway), was the editor of *Accountics* from at least as early as its second issue in May, 1897. In addition to authoring an editorial column, he wrote articles of a practical nature for most issues during his tenure as editor. Kittredge also authored accounting-related articles for other journals, such as *Banker's Magazine* [Kittredge, 1898, p. 113]. He was also the proprietor of the Self-Proving Account-Book Company, Publishers. He had an advertisement in the January 1898 issue of Accountics with the headline "I WRITE BOOKS," followed by:

> On accounting — Merchandising, Manufacturing, Publishing, Transportation, Banking and other lines. What are you looking for? Pamphlet and other particulars for stamp. A. O. Kittredge, F.I.A., 407b Wool Exchange Building, New York. [p. 99]

Kittredge also sold books from his office that had been published by others; these sales were conducted under the business name of Accountics Association.

Kittredge died on March 23, 1903, while on a business trip to Boston ["Anson O. Kittredge," 1903, pp. 9–10]. Interestingly, little is recorded of Kittredge's accounting career or how he might have qualified for a CPA certificate. He was a charter member of the Institute of Accounts [Sparrow, 1903, p. 88]. Although he had worked in industrial accounting early in his career, his only association with accounting after 1890 seemingly was as a publisher and professional organization executive. Thus, Kittredge appears to be an anomaly in the early history of the accountancy profession.

5.0 CONCLUSION

This paper has outlined the careers of the first academic CPAs. One profile omitted from this article is that of Silas S. Packard, who was a noted educator and active in the passage of the first CPA law. Unfortunately, Mr. Packard was not a public accountant, and was thus not eligible to become a CPA. Also, he died in 1898 at the age of 72. Given his contributions to the profession, both as an academician and as a key player in the passing of the first law, it is indeed unfortunate that professional educators were not able to take the CPA exam in the early days. At a surprise party on the occasion of Packard's 70th birthday, Colonel Charles E. Sprague rose before the assemblage of more than 200 and lauded Packard's contributions to accounting, including the following lines:

> Early in the history of this institute [Institute of Accounts] Prof. Packard, entering, as all of us did, upon a test of his qualifications, became a member and has always taken the greatest interest. He is one of the few in that division of our profession, occupying the position of a teacher of accounts, who has associated himself with us and has given us the benefit of his knowledge and has endeavored to rub up against the men who are in the practical work of which he is teaching so admirably the theory; and he is at present the president of our organization. He has done us noble service in that capacity. Only a few days ago the Governor signed a bill which will tend to elevate the position of accountants in the State of New York and which will confer, upon examination by the Regents of the University and proper tests of qualifications and experience, the degree of Certified Public Accountant. Packard has been largely instrumental in getting this for the benefit of the accountants of the State of New York. [*Testimonial* ..., 1896, p. 49]

In some respects, this paper is incomplete in that it includes only those individuals who taught accounting, and not those non-teachers who were avid supporters of organized accountancy education. Such men as Elijah Watt Sells (Certificate No. 10), John R. Loomis (Certificate No. 51), and William J. Gunnell (Certificate No. 118) come to mind. Indeed, this latter group made major contributions by supporting accountancy education in general, and at specific institutions in particular. However, it was men like Broaker, Haskins, Sprague, Lafrentz, Sparrow, Koehler, Tipson, Hardcastle, Brummer, Cook, Dean, and Kittredge who entered the classroom and inaugurated accounting education as it is known today. These twelve made a difference in the lives of thousands of early 20th century accountants. For the most part, these were all older men — individuals who had made successful careers and were perhaps looking for a change when they decided to enter the teaching profession. Thus, the first academic accountants were not only experienced accountants, but were also respected. All were published gentlemen and active in a number of professional organizations. The older gentlemen also may have had the resources that would allow them to take time away from their regular jobs to undertake a teaching assignment at low pay.

In conclusion, the pioneer public accountants were also the pioneer academic accountants. This is not meant to dismiss the contributions of the business colleges of the 19th century — this was how many of the early CPAs acquired their educations, but academic accounting in its modern form was the product of the post-CPA-law era, and it was CPAs who inaugurated the modern era in accounting education.

REFERENCES

"A Successful Certified Public Accountant," *The Business World* (October, 1902), p. 455.

"Accountants," *Accountics* (September, 1897), pp. 14, 129.

"Albert Wray," *Banking Law Journal* (June, 1896), p. 409.

"American Accounting Literature From a British Point of View," *Accountics* (October, 1897), p. 17.

"A New Departure," *The Financial Record* (September 12, 1900), p. 2.

"An Educational Basis," *The Financial Record* (August 14, 1901), pp. 2–3.

"Anson O. Kittredge," *Commerce, Accounts and Finance* (April, 1903), pp. 9–10.

"Archer & Dean," *The Financial Record* (July 8, 1903), p. 1.

Broaker, Frank, and Richard M. Chapman. *The American Accounts' Manual* (New York: Broaker & Chapman, 1897).

Brummer, Leon. "The Inception and Foundation of the School of Commerce, Accounts, and Finance," *Journal of Accountancy* (February, 1911), pp. 252–255.

"Certified Public Accountants," *Accountics* (June, 1898), pp. 72–73.

"Charles Ezra Sprague — Public Accountant," *The New York Certified Public Accountant* (July, 1952), pp. 430–432.

Cook, Henry R. M. "An Educational Basis," *The Financial Record* (August 14, 1901), p. 2.

"Editorial Notes," *Accountics* (April, 1897), pp. 16–20.

"Frank Broaker," *The Banking Law Journal* (April, 1892), pp. 298–299.

"Frank Broaker, C.P.A.," *Accountics* (June, 1897), p. 78.

Hardcastle, Joseph. *Accounts of Executors and Testamentary Trustees: Lectures Before the New York University School of Commerce, Accounts and Finance* (New York: New York University School of Commerce, Accounts and Finance, 1903).

———. "An Illustration of a Personal Theory of Accounts," *Business* (June, 1901a), pp. 224–226.

———. "Balancing an Account at One Operation," *Business* (November, 1901b), pp. 428–429.

———. "Depreciation in Its Application," *Business* (December, 1901c), pp. 471–472.

———. "Equation of Payments Mathematically Considered — First Theoretical," *American Counting-Room* (October, 1883a), pp. 219–222.

———. "Equation of Payments Mathematically Considered — Second — Practical," *American Counting-Room* (November, 1883b), pp. 281–286.

———. "On the Theory of Life Insurance," *The Book Keeper* (January 16, 1883c), pp. 17–20.

———. *Science and Practice of Installments* (New York: Business, 1901).

Haskins, Charles Waldo. *Business Education and Accountancy* Frederick A. Cleveland, Ed. (New York: Harper and Brothers Publishers, 1904).

Horne, Henry A. "The History and Administration of Our Society," *New York State Society of Certified Public Accountants Fiftieth Anniversary*, 1947, pp. 5–14.

Horowitz, Abraham. "Ferdinand William Lafrentz (1859–1954)," *The New York Certified Public Accountant* (April, 1961), pp. 274–275.

"John R. Sparrow, CPA," *Pace Student* (October, 1916), pp. 179.

"Joseph Hardcastle," *The New York Certified Public Accountant* (September, 1951), pp. 615–618.

Kittredge, Anson, O. "Improvements in the Boston Ledger," *Accountics* (February, 1898), pp. 113–121.

"Letter to the Editor," by Charles E. Sprague, *Business* (July, 1896), p. 320.

Mann, Helen Scott. *Charles Ezra Sprague* (New York: New York University, 1931).

"Pace Institute," *New York Certified Public Accountant* (September, 1950), pp. 530–534.

Previts, Gary J. and Barbara D. Merino. *A History of Accounting in America* (New York: John Wiley & Sons, 1979).

"Prof. Hardcastle Dead," *New York Times* (June 18, 1906).

"Regulation of the Accountants' Examining Board," *Accountics* (November, 1897), p. 38.

Slocum, Elliott L. and Alfred R. Roberts,."The New York School of Accounts — A Beginning," *The Accounting Historians Journal* (Fall, 1980), pp. 63–70.

Sparrow, John E. "Advantages of Societies for Accountants and Bookkeepers," *The Business World* (February, 1903), p. 88.

"Superintending Accountant and Statistician," *The Business World* (February, 1902), p. 60.

Testimonial Banquet to S. S. Packard. New York: April 28, 1896.

"The Free Lance," *Accountics* (April, 1897), pp. 25–26.

"The Free Lance," *Accountics* (May, 1897), pp. 50–51.

"The Incorporators of the New York State Society of Certified Public Accountants," *The New York Certified Public Accountant* (March, 1953), pp. 217–221.

"The Late Charles Waldo Haskins," *The Book Keeper* (February, 1903), p. 18.

"The Late Charles Waldo Haskins, C.P.A.," *The Business World* (February, 1903), p. 78.

"The New York State Society of Certified Public Accountants: Its Genesis," *The New York CPA* (May, 1949), pp. 327–329.

Tipson, Frederick S. "Hotel Auditing," *The Business World* (July, 1904), pp. 342–343.

"W. Sanders Davies," *The Banking Law Journal* (June, 1896), p. 410.

Webster, Norman E. *The American Association of Public Accountants 1886–1906* (New York: American Institute of Accountants, 1954).

Wilkinson, George. *The C.P.A. Movement* (New York: Wilkinson, Reckitt, Williams & Co., 1903).

The CPA Examination in the United States:

Its Beginnings

Mary Ellen Oliverio
Pace University
New York

Bernard H. Newman
Pace University
New York

1.0 ABSTRACT

The first examination for accountants was scheduled to be administered in New York State in Buffalo and New York City in December 1896. That first examination reflected the efforts of a szmall group of practitioners in accounting to gain professional status in one state. Efforts followed in other states in the United States; within a decade seven states had passed legislation and had granted certificates based on examinations or waivers.

The objectives of this historical review are to:

- identify conditions for the first CPA examination administered in the United States
- describe briefly the business society at the time of emerging professionalism in accounting
- discuss and assess the nature of the first examination administered in New York State
- discuss criticism of the first examination
- identify some implications for further historical investigations.

There are limitations to this effort. The review is based primarily on publications of the American Institute of Certified Public Accountants and its predecessor organizations. This review, therefore, is based primarily on the documentation as developed by the professional associations. The period for consideration is generally from the early 1890s to approximately 1905.

2.0 INTRODUCTION

A small group of accountants in New York State was successful in getting the New York State Legislature to enact a law. Their efforts initiated certification of accountants in the United States. By the end of 1905, 118 persons in New York and 126 in other states had earned certificates on the basis of examination. Additionally, a total of 373 persons were granted certificates by waiver, for a total of 617 CPAs in a society with 23,000 persons classified as accountants and auditors in the United States' census of 1900.

Those who provided leadership saw opportunity for professional public accountants in a society where businesses were growing larger and more complex and outside experts were invaluable. While accountants discussed the role of the accountant, examiners in the several states were preparing examinations based primarily on their experience. Criticism of the examination in the first issues of *The Journal of Accountancy* highlighted the elementary nature of the examination as well as its limited scope. However, the examination was accepted as a prerequisite to professional standing.

The first examination for accountants was scheduled for administration in New York State in Buffalo and New York City in December 1896. That first examination reflected the efforts of a small group of practitioners in accounting to gain professional status in one state. Efforts followed in other states in the United States; within a decade seven states had passed legislation and had granted certificates based on examinations or waivers.

Since approximately the mid-1980s considerable attention has been given to the adequacy of the CPA examination and to the educational requirements appropriate for persons wishing to enter the field of public accounting. Now that a hundred years have transpired since the administration of the first examination, it seems appropriate to reconsider what motivated those who provided leadership for an examination, what the examination actually provided, and how this initial examination requirement was assessed.

3.0 THE SCOPE OF THIS HISTORICAL REVIEW

The objectives of this historical review are to:

- identify conditions for the first CPA examination administered in the United States
- describe briefly the business society at the time of emerging professionalism in accounting
- discuss and assess the nature of the first examination administered in New York State
- discuss criticism of the first examination
- identify some implications for further historical investigations.

There are limitations to this effort. The review is based primarily on publications of the American Institute of Certified Public Accountants and its predecessor organizations. This review, therefore, is based primarily on the documentation as developed by the professional associations. The period considered is generally from the early 1890s to approximately 1905 and only the experience in New York State is reviewed. Circumstances that immediately preceded the examination and the aftermath of the administration of the first examination are reviewed in general rather than in detail. The influence of the experience in the United Kingdom and the influence of individuals are aspects that deserve attention but were considered outside the scope of this investigation.

4.0 THE LAW ESTABLISHING THE FIRST EXAMINATION

In April 1896, the New York State Legislature enacted the law that established the requirement that any person assuming the title "Certified Public Accountant" or who made any use of the letters "CPA" within the State of New York, must possess a certificate issued to him by the Regents of the University. The Regents of the University were empowered to make rules for the examination of persons applying for certificates under the article, and were to appoint a board of three examiners for the purpose, which board shall be composed of certified public accountants [American Institute of Accountants, *Yearbook*, 1916, pp. 196–197].

Shortly thereafter the Regents of the University of the State of New York issued their rules in connection with the examination. *The Accountant* reported excerpts of these rules:

> section 2 of this Act leaves it for the Regents to make rules for the examination of persons applying for certificates thereunder, and that section 3 provides further that the Regents "may" in their discretion waive the examination test in certain cases. At one time it appeared probable that the Regents would not exercise the permissive discretion allowed them under section 3, but the rules which are now before us state that the examinations may be waived on unanimous recommendation of the examiners in the case of candidates well known to them as meeting the professional requirements, and as having been in reputable practice as Public Accountants since the 1st of January 1890, upon payment of the same fee as that which has to be paid by candidates for the examination, namely $25. ["Accountancy ...[a]," p. 951]

4.1 Implementation of the Law

Shortly after the approval of the C.P.A. Act in April 1896, the three examiners who constituted the first board were named. They were: C. W. Haskins, President; Frank Broaker, Secretary; and Charles E. Sprague. These three, along with an additional eleven accountants, were granted certificates based on the waiver provision that allowed for certification based on appropriate experience at the third meeting of the Board. Haskins was granted Certificate No. 6; Sprague, No. 11 and Broaker, No. 1.[1] In the history of Haskins and Sells, Haskins' participation at the State level is described in these words:

> He took an active interest in the passage, by the New York Legislature in 1896, of an Act to regulate the Profession of Public Accountancy which was the first legislation in the Country to create the professional designation "Certified Public Accountant." Mr. Haskins qualified under the terms of the Act and was chosen the first President of the Board of State Examiners of Public Accountants instituted thereunder. [Brief, 1970, p. 4]

The historical account of the activities of these first years by Previts and Merino included a brief discussion of a "minor scandal" on the part of Broaker who published a book a year after the first examination based on the examination questions with recommended solutions with the proceeds going to his personal account. The authors stated that a published comment noted the summary dismissal "was severe and perhaps unwarranted" [Previts and Merino, 1979, p. 101]. Broaker's book was available early in 1897 and was favourably reviewed in *The Accountant* in March 1897. (The review is discussed later in this paper.)

Broaker was replaced on the State Board of Examiners in 1897 by James T. Anyon. (The minutes of the Board are silent as to the reason Broaker was no longer a member since his term was to expire in 1898.) Broaker had been active in the American Association of Public Accountants, having served as vice president from 1893–1896 and as president from 1896–1897. He does not appear in the rosters of officers after 1896–1897 [American Institute of Accountants, *Yearbook*, 1916]. However, at the 18th anniversary banquet of the American

Association of Public Accountants in 1905, Broaker was asked to deliver a salutation on behalf of the American Association (his earlier penalty had been forgotten or forgiven). Broaker's salutation highlighted the value of suitable laws, which began in New York State:

> Leading representatives of the financial and business world, members of the bar, educators, and legislators by their endorsement, have aided the various state societies of public accountants in accomplishing the enactment of suitable laws which now recognize and regulate the profession, and by their presence tonight again offer assurance, support and esteem, the memory of which shall be the incentive for honest efforts that will in the future command the respect and confidence of the courts, national, state and city governments and the business community. The aim has been for fair government and the encouragement of progression, distinguished by a stern insistence on integrity, honor, and morality, ... [Broaker, 1905, p. 86]

Charles E. Sprague was a recognized leader in the movement toward professionalism [Previts, Merino, pp. 100–102, 139–140]. When Haskins declined the presidency of the Board for the 1897–1898 year, Sprague was elected president and served for the year in that capacity [New York State Board of Examiners, Minutes, November 15, 1897].

4.2 Nature and Timing of the Examination

The examinations were to be held twice each year, in June and December, and were to consist of four sessions of three hours each. The subjects were to include theory of accounts, practical accounting, auditing, and commercial law. Candidates would have to pass in all four subjects at the same examination. (This latter requirement was later changed.)

4.3 Granting of Certification

The full certificate was to be granted to those who successfully completed the examination and who were at least 25 years of age and had completed five years of "satisfactory experience" in the study or practice of accountancy. Those who were otherwise qualified, except with regard to age, would be certified as "junior accountants," provided they were not less than 21 years of age [American Institute of Accountants, *Yearbook*, 1916, p. 198].

Before the first examination was administered, the Regents had considered the rules to be applied if a candidate was unsuccessful on parts of the examination. At the Board's sixth meeting in December 1896, there was acceptance of the Regents' proposal, which stated:

> A candidate failing in one topic only, whose general average in the other three topics is at last 80%, may be admitted to the next examination only in the subject topic in which he failed. A candidate who fails in more than one topic, or who fails in one topic only, and whose average in the other three topics is below 80% must either wait one full year or pay an additional fee for admission to the next subsequent examination. [New York State Board of Examiners, Minutes, December 11, 1896]

5.0 OVERVIEW OF THE UNITED STATES FROM 1880 TO 1900

The United States was growing at an impressive rate during the final decades of the nineteenth century. That growth was especially evident in New York, where many leaders in banking, railroading, and major manufacturing industries maintained headquarters. Leroy-Beaulieu, a Frenchman, noted in his preface to a study of the United States which was based on the twelfth census report (1890) of the United States:

> The true causes of the progress of the United States ... may be summed up in the statement that the natural resources of the country are immense and its inhabitants the most energetic of people, their innate energy increasing under the influence of the environment of a new land where everything grows quickly and where labor and intelligent enterprise can rapidly earn a far greater recompense than would be possible in Europe.... One is particularly impressed by the ease and rapidity with which American manufacture adjusts itself to new conditions; by the way in which commerce and transportation are organized; by the absence, among the working-class, of the routine spirit and of prejudices against the employment of machinery; by the boldness of the capitalists, and by the enterprise of the captains of industry and the higher employees, who are always on the lookout for technical improvements and for capable assistants. [Leroy-Beaulieu, 1907, p. xxiv]

American business development in the final years of the nineteenth century significantly influenced the role of accounting. Have, for example, noted:

> Commerce and industry were speedily reacting to information concerning market situations; world markets and world market prices developed, industries competed on a world wide basis. [Have, 1976, p. 80]

By 1892, as an illustration, Wall describes the status of the newly created Carnegie Steel Company within the industrial world:

> Carnegie held a majority interest in a company capitalized at $25M, with annual earnings of $4M. It was the largest and most profitable steel business in the world.... in a period of 5 years (in the 1890s) Carnegie's annual profits increased over 500 percent. [Wall, 1970, pp. 583, 584, 638]

Banking was being transformed too. Brown Brothers (later to be Brown Brothers Harriman & Co.) made changes in their way of handling business:

> During the final decades of the nineteenth century, while E. H. Harriman was building his railroad empire, John Crosby Brown and his partners were presiding over the modernization of the old banking firm .... In 1885 the old methods of longhand bookkeeping and accounting were abandoned and "printed forms with blanks to be filled" were substituted. The departments in the office were divided and subdivided, each with its respective head, and the records of original entries were kept by these departments.... [Kouwenhoven, 1968, p. 163]

Leroy-Beaulieu summarized in words what he had read in the census figures. The United States had experienced a population increase of approximately 25 percent between 1880 and 1890 and an increase of almost 21 percent during the decade from 1890 to 1900. At the same time professional services were employing increasingly larger numbers of people. While there were 603,202 persons so classified in 1880, there were 944,323 so classified in 1890 (an increase of 56.6 percent). By 1900 there were 1,234,000 professional, technical and kindred workers in a work force of more than 29 million. However, the percentage of the total work force that was classified as professional, technical and kindred workers in 1900 was only 4.25 percent of the total work force. There were 23,000 persons identified as accountants and auditors in 1900 [*Statistical Abstract of the United States*, 1900].

The educational levels of United States citizens were increasing, also. In 1880, 24,000 persons graduated from high school (this represented 2.5 percent of persons 17 years old); in 1890, there were 44,000 graduates (3.5 percent of persons 17 years old). By 1900, the number had increased to 95,000, representing 6.3 percent of 17-year-olds. The rate of increase in high school graduation was greater than the overall increase in population. The change from 1880 to 1900, for example, was a 296 percent increase. A bachelor's degree was also becoming more common during this period. While there were 12,896 bachelor's or first professional degrees conferred in 1880, there were 15,539 conferred in 1890 and 27,410 in 1900. The increase from 1880 to 1900 was 112.5 percent [*Historical Statistics of the United States, Colonial Times to 1970*].

The demand for skilled employees was beyond the supply. The leaders in the developing accounting profession did not feel that they could require a high school degree for entrance into the field or require an unpaid apprenticeship. Too few citizens had earned high school diplomas and too many opportunities existed for industrious young people which precluded a requirement of an apprenticeship without remuneration, because such a requirement would fail to attract young people with ambition.

6.0 COMMERCIALIZATION VS PROFESSIONALIZATION

The nineteenth century was a time of considerable growth of professional occupations. As Parker, writing about the British experience noted:

> At the beginning of the nineteenth century only the church, the law and medicine were recognized as professional occupations. By the end of the century there had been added not only accountancy but also engineering, architecture, pharmacy, veterinary surgery, dentistry and actuarial science and the older professions had been reorganized. [Parker, 1986, p. 13]

Two factors driving the movement toward professionalism in accounting were an awareness of the need for competence and self interest to protect those who could provide accounting service that was high quality. These factors were evident in both the United Kingdom and in the United States. Anyon, an Englishman who wrote and privately printed his recollections of the early days of American accountancy reflected on his early impressions when he arrived in New York in 1883:

> Public accounting in this country as a profession, I have reason to believe, had its birth some time between the years 1880 and 1883 ... Mr. Edwin Guthrie, acting in the capacity of receiver in the case of a certain bankrupt financial concern in England...(1883) found it necessary to proceed to this country to enquire into the value and status of certain property and assets .... On arriving here his first thought was to find a good accounting firm whom he might employ to assist him in his investigations. He made enquiries in this direction and discovered that not only was the profession of accounting as it was understood and practiced on this side practically unknown in this country, but there was no such thing as a responsible accounting firm upon whom he could rely for any assistance he may require in his work. His attorneys in New York informed him that he did not need accountants, and that they would attend to all matters, both legal and accounting, in connection with the case. [Anyon, 1925, pp. 9, 10]

The growth and consolidation of businesses in the United States is generally perceived to be an important factor in making evident the need for specialists in accounting. Haskins, as noted previously, was a leader in the profession who seems to have learned much from living abroad.

Haskins, born in 1852, began working in the accounting department of an importing firm as a youth. Later he spent two years in Paris where he studied art. During this period in Paris, he became acquainted with what was happening in accounting in Great Britain. On moving back to the United States, he returned to accounting, establishing a public practice in 1886. In a discussion of Haskins, identified as an American pioneer in accountancy, the reviewer stated:

> At the time accountancy in America was a poor, weak, struggling thing, with its possibilities unrecognized even by those within its ranks. It was not a profession; it was but a business adjunct, and not much of one at that. The accountant was little more than a bookkeeper and the line of demarcation between the two was slight indeed. Accountancy had no ideals, no organization, no inspiration and influence. It required a man of big vision ... Mr. Haskins had this vision. With the imagination of a poet and the intuition of a prophet, he realized what accountancy could become.... [Sells, "Foreward," 1923, p. 11]

In a discussion of the CPA movement and the future of the profession at the 1904 Congress of Accountants, Wilkinson discussed the importance of professional status when he stated:

> It is not contended that a mantle of wisdom is conferred with the diploma; but in receiving a certificate from the State an accountant becomes a member of a legally recognized profession, and is amenable to control of the properly constituted authorities. [Wilkinson, 1904, p. 96]

Wilkinson also discussed the role of the accountant within a broad context, noting that the most valuable "service that the accountant can render to his client lies along the lines of giving sound business advice." Further, Wilkinson noted the commercialization of accounting services through audit companies that had been incorporated in the largest US cities. His perception of the influence of such companies was:

> The influence of incorporated audit companies is to commercialize the business and reduce it to the common level of trades and manufactures, while our influence exercised through the societies we belong to must ever be in the opposite direction, to lift it up, establish high ideals and secure its recognition as a learned profession. [Wilkinson, 1904, p.102]

7.0 THE CONTENT OF THE FIRST EXAMINATION

The content of the first examination reflected what practitioners felt was important for those aspiring to be public accountants. The three Board members at their second meeting had as an agenda item the "Preparation and formulation of questions for regents' examinations." At that meeting, the questions were prepared, enclosed in an envelope, sealed with wax, "the president impressing thereon his private seal" and the secretary instructed to forward the envelope to the Regents by first registered mail [New York State Board of Examiners, Minutes, November 12, 1896].

There was no written body of organized standards and rules for practitioners of accounting. There were few published materials. Littleton, in his discussion of early professional literature, noted that a literature was slow to develop in England, especially in auditing. His opinion was that the principal source of information concerning opinions and activities of accountants, prior to the establishment of the Institute of Chartered Accountants in England and Wales in 1880, was *The Accountant* which began publication in late 1874 in London [Littleton, 1933, p. 315].

Approximately fifteen years after the first examination in New York State, there were still few accounting publications available to American accountants. For example, a listing of books suggested to the State Board of Accountancy had only 12 books, mostly English, plus another 28 items, including pamphlets from the Interstate Commerce Commission and the Public Service Commission of New York [unpublished correspondence between Homer Pace of Pace Institute, now University, New York City and Samuel D. Patterson, Secretary, New York State Board of CPA Examinations 1910]. Those who were preparing examinations were functioning within a sparsely documented arena and relying on their experiences and observations.

The copy of the examination that is discussed herein is based on the copy that Broaker and Chapman published in early 1897. These authors included all the questions. However, candidates did not answer all questions. The examination provided in *The Accountant* in January 1897 included the directions for candidates.

7.1 Theory of Accounts

Fifteen comprehensive essay-type questions constituted this three-hour examination. However, candidates were required to answer only 1, 2, 4, 8, and 13. They were to answer an additional five, but no more. In Exhibit 1 these fifteen questions are displayed by type of question. Those required are noted. Only one explicitly asks the candidate to state

Exhibit 1

Nature and Summary Content of Theory of Accounts Questions

Stating principles (one question):

- of double entry bookkeeping and showing difference from single entry bookkeeping (Q. 1, **required**)

Describe or define (four questions):

- accounts: personal, real, current, impersonal, nominal, summary (Q. 11)
- funds: sinking, reserve, redemption, depreciation, contingent, investment (Q. 13, **required**)
- equity: stock, capital, surplus, deficiency, capital stock, preferred stock, common stock, share capital, loan capital (Q. 14)
- accounts: merchandise, construction, consignment, joint, subscription, expense, maintenance, venture, suspense, dividend (Q. 15)

Describe and show differences (five questions):

- trial balance, balance sheet, statement of affairs and realization and liquidation account (Q. 2, **required**)
- the accounts of revenue, trading, profit and loss and deficiency (Q. 4, **required**)
- statement of income and expenditures and statement of receipts and payments (Q. 6)
- capital and revenue, capital receipts and revenue receipts, capital expenditure and revenue expenditure (Q. 8, **required**)
- fixed assets and cash assets, fixed liability and floating indebtedness, fixed charges and operating expenses (Q. 10)

Explanation of practical application and/or purpose (five questions):

- considerations in devising a system of accounts (Q. 3)
- purpose of perpendicular columns in books of original entry when several ledgers are planned (Q. 5)
- method of keeping accounts related to due from customers and due to creditors (Q. 7)
- arrangement of accounts in a trial balance to facilitate preparing financial statements (Q. 9)
- describe process and some of the purposes of analyzing a ledger (Q. 12)

principles. There were four questions that required description or definition of components of financial statements or statements themselves. Five questions asked for description and explanation of differences among the components named. Another five questions required a basic, practical application of the knowledge of accounting. None of the practical application questions were required. There is little evidence of theory in this examination.

7.2 Practical Accounting

The accounting tasks for the candidate were indeed practical. There were six problems of which the first two were required and two additional ones were to be answered. The subject matter of these practical problems ranged from preparing journal entries to opening the company's books to properly accounting for transactions between a company in New York and one in London. The tasks of the six questions are shown in Exhibit 2.

Exhibit 2

Content of the Practical Accounting Examination

Prepare a statement of affairs, and a deficiency account. (Q. 1, **required**)

Prepare for a partnership, a trading account, a profit and loss account and a balance sheet, as well as partners' capital accounts. (Q. 2, **required**)

Prepare entries to open the company's books, showing the capital stock and fixed assets on the face of the ledger, also prepare a balance sheet. (Q. 3)

Prepare partners' accounts showing the amounts payable monthly to each without prejudice to the rights or individual interests of others. (Q. 4)

Prepare account current as rendered by A to B also the accounts of B and C as they appear in A's ledger (Provided with details re: payment of A of New York to B of London.

Prepare an account of a joint venture account. (Provided with details of A, B and C agreeing to purchase and sell coffee for their joint account.) (Q. 6)

7.3 Auditing

The fifteen questions of the auditing examination range from identifying duties and responsibilities of auditors to the specific procedures an auditor would employ to audit a particular account or type of account. Questions 1, 8, 10, 14, and 15 were required. An additional five were to be answered. Two of the required questions are general, two relate to evidence required, and one relates to procedures. It is interesting to note the extent to which the questions deal with matters that continue to be of concern to auditors. The questions are summarized in Exhibit 3.

7.4 Commercial Law

The fifteen essay/short answer questions cover a broad range of subject matter. The majority of the questions required straightforward knowledge about meaning and basic laws. As Exhibit 4 shows, the candidate responded to 12 questions that required the drawing up of forms, to descriptions of forms of business, to the commercial law applied to contracts, debtors, and partnerships, which were common concerns of the early accountants. Only three questions required an understanding of the law applied to specific circumstances.

Exhibit 3
Nature and Scope of Auditing Examination Questions

General:
- responsibility of auditor (Q. 1, **required**)
- responsibility for correctness of inventories, payrolls, depreciation, and discounts (Q. 14, **required**)
- what a company must provide for an audit of its books (Q. 6)
- points to which an auditor should direct attention (Q. 2)
- books required for a first-time audit (Q. 11)

Specific procedures:
- verification of cash at a date later than the date of the balance sheet (Q. 3)
- detection of wilful omission of sales or cash (Q. 5)
- necessary steps in auditing cash payments to prevent the reproduction and passing of vouchers a second time (Q. 8, **required**)
- what examination must be done of the receivable book to ascertain which accounts, if any, should be written off (Q. 9)

Evidence needed:
- correctness of values of assets (other than accounts receivable) (Q. 7)
- determination of whether certain expenditures are maintenance or repairs or actual betterment. (Q. 10, **required**)
- proper vouchers (evidence) related to purchases, sales, cash receipts, returned purchases, returned sales, cash payments, and journal entries (Q. 14, **required**)
- valuation of assets including manufactured goods, partially manufactured goods, raw materials, open book accounts receivable, stocks, bonds, other investments, and bills receivable (Q. 15)

Nature of audit:
- requirements in an audit that does not stipulate an exhaustive detailed examination (Q. 4)
- requirements beyond the ordinary books and subjects of an audit when auditing accounts at the conclusion of the first fiscal year of a corporation (Q. 12)

Exhibit 4
The Nature of Content of the First Commercial Law Examination

Require either drawing of forms, explanations, or descriptions:
- promissory notes and endorsements (Q. 1)
- bills of exchange (Q. 3)
- corporations (Q. 5, 6)
- contract (Q. 7, 8)
- debt (Q. 9)
- partnerships (Q. 10, 11, 12, 13)
- sale and consignment (Q. 14)

Explanations of what should be done:
- when an endorsed promissory note is not paid at maturity (Q. 2)
- when a drawee of a draft or bill of exchange refuses to accept the same on presentation (Q. 4)
- what kind of action a consignor can maintain against a consignee who converts to his own use the proceeds of the sale of consignor's goods (Q. 15)

It is interesting to note that it is likely that some accountants were still drawing up forms. However, at least a decade earlier they had begun to use printed forms with blanks to be filled in, as described in the changes at Brown Brothers Harriman & Co. made in 1885 [Kouwenhoven, 1968, p. 163].

8.0 THE RESULTS OF THE FIRST TWO EXAMINATIONS

The results of the first examination were included in the minutes of the tenth meeting of the Board of Examiners of Public Accountants which was held on April 23 and 24, 1897. Although earlier minutes indicated that the first examination would be administered in New York City and Buffalo, there is no discussion in the minutes about the Buffalo results.

Papers for five candidates who sat for the examination at Cooper Union, New York City, were marked by the Board of Examiners. A notation explains that "30 counts" were allowed on the practical accounting examination "for lack of conveniences" at Cooper Union. Three of the candidates passed; one failed commercial law; the fifth candidate failed in all subjects. The average scores were [New York State Board of Examiners, Minutes, April 23, 24, 1897]:

- theory of accountants: 75.6
- practical accounting: 72.6
- auditing: 77.2
- commercial law: 74.8.

There is no information in the minutes identifying specifically the candidates who earned certificates based on successful completion of the examination. Previts and Merino [p. 98] noted "three of the four who passed this examination are known" and they referenced Wilkinson. The minutes, however, do not indicate that a fourth person passed the first examination. The fourth candidate passed three of the four examinations. Possibly, the fourth candidate was later deemed to have passed, although, there is no such comment in the minutes. However, at a later meeting [New York State Board of Examiners, Minutes, April 22, 1899] a candidate's grade on the fourth examination was raised to 75 from 65 because the candidate had passed successfully on all other subjects. Previts and Merino did not indicate when the certificates were actually granted to those who successfully passed the examination in 1896.

The Board of Examiners reported the marks of the second examination given in June 1897 in August. There were nine candidates (no indication of where these candidates sat for the examination was provided). Two candidates passed all four parts; three candidates passed all parts except practical accounting; four candidates failed the examination. The average scores were [New York State Board of Examiners, Minutes, August 19, 1897]:

- theory of accounts: 85.8
- practical accounting: 51.8
- auditing: 80.9
- commercial law: 75.2 .

The average scores on the auditing and commercial law for the two examinations were not significantly different. However, the average for theory of accounts was approximately ten points higher in June 1897 when compared with December 1986; the average for practical accounting, approximately 21 points lower in June. If the actual average for the practical accounting examination in December (without the added 30 points) is compared with the June examination, the average for the June examination is only 9 points lower. (With so few candidates, such analysis is not meaningful.)

No candidate was certified based on the examination during the first two years according to Edwards [*History*, 1978, p. 352].This conclusion is understandable since, as already noted, there was no indication of certificates being granted based on the examination in the minutes of the Board of Regents.

9.0 MONITORING BY *THE ACCOUNTANT*

The Accountant was monitoring what was happening in New York. In reviewing the preliminary information, it was noted:

> an absence of any scheme by which (in the future at all events) it will become necessary for candidates for accountancy to embark upon any exclusive course of study, such as articles would pre-suppose; while, further, the subjects of the examination do not strike us as being all that could be desired. Upon this latter point, however, it is impossible to express any decided opinion until at least one examination has been held, and the questions set thereat are available for discussion. ["Accountancy ...[a]," p. 952]

The next reference to the New York examination in *The Accountant* was in January which noted when the first examination was given and there was a brief note that stated "that 56 certificates have been issued as the result of the first examination held in New York" ("Accountancy ...[b]," p. 99]. This statement about the success on the first examination is not correct. All 56 certificates were issued based on the waiver. In fact, all certificates granted during the first two years appear to have been based on waivers. While *The Accountant* had noted the waiver provision in a November 1896 story, they seemingly did not receive complete information about what the results of the December examination were [Edwards, 1978, pp. 74, 352].

Early in 1897, *The Accountant* published a favorable review of The American Accountants' Manual by Broaker and Chapman. (This was the publication referred to earlier.) Among the comments made in the review were the following:

> A technical work on accountancy, written by an American author (the first we remember having seen — there are newspapers, of course, in existence) has just made its appearance ... and this alone is sufficient to make it an interesting publication. Apart, however, from this merely historical interest, the volume appears to be possessed of considerable value, and will, no doubt, be found useful both to British and American accountants. The first 80 pages are devoted to the questions set at the recent examination ... to which are added very full answers thoroughly dealing with the various points raised in the questions. These questions seem to us to have been well designed to test the general capacity and experience of candidates at the examination, which is approximately upon the same lines as that of the English Institute, upon which it is doubtless founded.... The remaining portion of the book contains essays upon Balance Sheets, Statements of Affairs, and Trading and Profit and Loss Accounts.... We have no hesitation in saying that this work will be found of the greatest utility to all connected with accounts, both in America and here. ["Accountancy ...[c]," p. 338]

There was a brief comment about the second examination, which was administered in June 1897, in an August issue of *The Accountant*, as well as the reproduction of the June examination. The second examination was similar to the first examination in scope and nature of questions. The brief comment included:

> to secure a pass, candidates had to obtain 75 percent of full marks; but they were only required to answer about two-thirds of the questions set at each paper, and the time limit is very ample for this purpose. The papers, however, are not without interest, as showing what is the standard exacted in New York before a man is entitled to hold himself out as a certified public accountant. ["Accountancy ... New York," p. 771]

Later, *The Accountant* reported on the progress being made in New York State in these words:

> that only 115 New York accountants have qualified under the recent legislation required that all practising [*sic*] accountants should pass an examination ... at the last examination only two out of eleven candidates passed. These figures seem to show that there must have been a considerable number of incompetent accountants in New York, and consequently the very greatest necessity for the Act in question. ["Accountancy ...[e]," p. 1011]

10.0 CRITICISM OF THE EXAMINATION

Wilkinson, Secretary of the Federation of Societies of Public Accountants in the United States of America gave an address on the CPA movement and the future of the profession at a significant meeting of accountants, the Congress of Accountants, held at the World's Fair in St. Louis in 1904. He prefaced his comments about the examination with the statement that "it has been suggested that this paper contain a recommendation" re: the examination. In attendance were 91 public accountants, with sixteen states represented. Ten were from outside the United States, seven from Canada, two from England, and one from Holland.

Wilkinson stated that the four subjects of the original examination in New York were appropriate. He commented that recent questions in practical accounting "would defy the best accountants in practice to answer within the time limit." He suggested that if examiners drew on their professional experience, they shouldn't draw too deep. Furthermore, he had had a suggestion that questions being used by the examiners might be scrutinized by "some central bureau, to be conducted by a professor whose training and study should fit him for the difficult task and whose standing should place him beyond the reach of distrust, to the end that a uniform standard might obtain" [Wilkinson, 1904, p. 101].

Wilkinson's comments about the examination did not elicit any discussion in the period following his presentation. Matters of organization and national visibility were of far more interest to the group present in St. Louis.

In the first issue of *The Journal of Accountancy*, Sterrett noted that "the public accountants of America have devoted far more attention to the problem of securing legislation than they have to the training of candidates." (Sterrett played an important role in the Saint Louis sessions in 1904.) His assessment of the examination was:

> The nature of the examination leaves much to be desired. The classification of questions under the different subjects is far from uniform, particularly as between the theory of accounts and practical accounting .... Questions which at one time and place are given under theory of accounts have their equivalents stated elsewhere under practical accounting. The lines are more clearly drawn in regard to auditing, which may be considered the analytical as practical accounting is the constructive branch of the subject. Commercial law occupies a field by itself, but it cannot be denied that a much more comprehensive knowledge of this subject is indispensable to the accountant. [Sterrett, 1905, p. 6]

Among other criticisms noted by Sterrett were the following [Sterrett, 1905, pp. 6, 7]:

- examination questions were of a narrow and technical nature
- questions do not test ability of student to understand and interpret the accounting needs of business
- questions poorly stated so that satisfactory interpretation of meaning is practically unattainable
- subject matter draws on problems arising in the course of the examiner's own experience.

In turning to what was needed, Sterrett noted:

> Where the entrance gate to a profession is guarded by a single examination, it is most desirable that this examination should be as comprehensive as possible, and that it should demonstrate the ability of the candidate, not only as a manipulator of figures under assumed conditions but also as the possessor of the faculty of sound judgment with the power of analysis, and the ability to originate solutions of difficult problems. Arithmetical gymnastics have their proper place but they should not be found among the requirements for entrance to the accounting profession. [Sterrett, 1905, p. 7]

Sterrett acknowledged that it would not have been wise to have insisted upon higher standards earlier. He believed that a final certificate granted upon the passing of a single examination was a serious mistake. He felt that an intermediate as well as a final examination should be required as well as a period of practical training in the office of a certified public accountant before the full certificate was issued. He also felt that candidates should have a high school education, as was required for admission to the bar. Furthermore, he believed that in addition to accounting, auditing, and law, candidates should be required to pass examinations in such subjects as political economy, commercial geography, banking, finance, industrial history, and industrial management [Sterrett, p. 10].

An editorial in 1906 noted the candidates' discontentment with the examinations for admission into the profession in these words:

> It has long been a reproach to the accountancy profession in the United States that the examinations proposed for admission ... were exceedingly elementary and in no way comparable with the examinations for admission into the other learned professions .... The questions in commercial law can readily be answered after a few days "cramming" from some elementary text books, ... The auditing questions require a mastery of Dicksee's Auditing and little more. The theory of accounts examination usually asks of the candidate a number of elementary definitions .... These are questions in bookkeeping, and their answers demand no very high order of intellectual attainment. The questions in practical accounting are of a different nature. These are almost without exception problems of simple arithmetic which the student is required to express in "technical form." The problems themselves ordinarily present not the slightest difficulty, provided the meaning of the examiners can be clearly determined. [*The Journal of Accountancy* (July, 1906) pp. 216–218]

At a symposium on accountancy education headed by E. W. Sells, who was the president of the American Association of Public Accountants, Sterrett, who was then serving as secretary of the Pennsylvania State Board of Examiners of Public Accountants, made many of the same points that were noted in his November 1905 article in *The Journal of Accountancy*. Another speaker, Meade, quoted at length from the July 1906 editorial earlier cited. Meade also stated:

> The present situation is far from satisfactory. There is little uniformity in the requirements of the various boards; and in no way, so far as my observation has gone, do the CPA examinations, either in extent or in method deserve to take rank along with examinations in law or medicine. As a matter of fact, with no exception, so far as I know, the examination for certified public accountant in every state in the United States can be passed by a young man who has a fair knowledge of bookkeeping, supplemented with an experience in an accountant's office and who has the persistence to cram on certain textbooks on the subject of accountancy .... This situation should be speedily remedied if accountancy is to be recognized as a learned profession. It certainly does not deserve or receive such recognition at the present time ... not because there are not many accountants who, by their intellectual attainments and the character of work they do, are not entitled to be called professional men, but because of the indifferent equipment of the rank and file of the profession, most of whom have entered it under the waiver clause and because the examinations for admission into the profession are not of a character to make sure that none but high class men can enter. [Meade, 1907, pp. 193, 194]

It appears from a review of the second New York State examination and an examination from Pennsylvania published in *The Journal of Accountancy* in 1905, there was no significant change in the content or nature of questions during the first decade of the examination.

Ten years after the first examination there appeared to be much to be done to raise the level of the examination. Training programs geared to preparing candidates for sitting for the examination were underway in a number of cities and practitioners were being encouraged to participate as lecturers.

11.0 THE EXTENT OF CERTIFICATION FROM 1896 THROUGH 1905

The group pressuring for professionalism was small. Anyon described the membership at the time of incorporation of the American Association of Public Accountants in 1887 as composed of 31 members, of whom only a few were in "full professional practice" [Anyon, 1925, p. 34]. For the first two years no candidates were certified on the basis of the examination. All certificates granted were based on the waiver provided. As can be noted in Exhibit 5, during the first ten years of the administration of the new Act in the State of New York, there were 118 accountants who were certified by examination while 185 were certified by waiver [Edwards, p. 352].

Exhibit 5
CPA Certificates Issued in New York State, 1896–1905*

Year	By Examination	By Waiver	Total
1896	0	56	56
1897	0	70	70
1898	6	1	7
1899	9	2	11
1900	6	0	6
1901	13	49	62
1902	30	1	31
1903	15	2	17
1904	15	2	17
1905	24	2	26
Totals	**118**	**185**	**303**

* as provided in Edwards [1978, p. 352].

In the United States by the end of 1905, a total of 617 certificates had been issued. Of these 244 (39.5 percent) were by examination; 373 (60.5 percent) by waiver. New York issued 118 based on examinations while four other states — California, Illinois, Maryland, and Pennsylvania — issued 126. Therefore, approximately half (48.4 percent) of all certificates issued on the basis of examinations were issued by New York State. With a total of 23,000 accountants and auditors in the United States (the 1900 census figure), the 617 who had certificates represented 2.7 percent of the group. (This percentage is likely to overstate the ratio, since this category had 39,000 persons in the 1910 census!)

Membership in the American Institute of Accountants [*The Journal of Accountancy* (November, 1905) pp. 94–98] included 601 persons, who were affiliated with a state society, members at large, associates, and honorary members. Both CPAs and non-CPAs were members, with some members participating in more than one group. Names of state associations varied slightly but all included the title of Certified Public Accountants.

The numbers of CPAs in the several state societies (as of November, 1905) by states as well as at large, associate and honorary are shown in Exhibit 6.

Exhibit 6

Numbers of CPAs by State, 1905

California	20
Illinois	45
Maryland	21
Michigan	9
Missouri	4
New Jersey	43
New York	101
Ohio	6
Pennsylvania	37
Washington	8
Members at Large	76
Associates	11
Honorary members	1
Total	**382**

Of the 382 members who were CPAs, there were 48 whose names appeared in more than one listing, which means that the total membership had only 334 CPAs. Of the accountants (617) who had been granted certificates through 1905, slightly over 54 percent were members of professional societies. In the public accountants' associations in Colorado, Georgia, Massachusetts, Minnesota, and Tennessee, there were no certified public accountants [*Journal of Accountancy* (November, 1905) pp. 94–98].

The first certificates granted on the basis of examination in New York State appear to have been granted in 1898, when six such certificates were issued. In that year only one certificate was granted by waiver, according to the information provided by Edwards [1978, p. 352].

The first examination was a significant initial step in defining what competency might be for the infant profession. The examination highlighted the inadequacies of the educational preparation for accounting and seems to have motivated a number of educational initiatives in several states. Accountants across the country were active in the passage of state legislation, but it would be approximately another decade (1916) before 40 states had enacted a law requiring certification of accountants.

12.0 SUMMARY AND CONCLUSIONS

Accountants, along with other groups in American society, began to realize the value of establishing professional status in the final decades of the 1900s. A small group of accountants in New York State was successful in getting the New York State Legislature to enact the first law in the United States to regulate the profession of public accountants in April 1896. Shortly thereafter, the requirements for the examination were issued. The first CPA examination was administered in December 1896.

By the end of 1905, 118 persons had earned certificates in New York State on the basis of an examination, while 185 were granted certificates by waiver, for a total of 303. (New York's number represents approximately 49 percent of all certificates granted through 1905 in the United States.) Following New York State, accountants in other states undertook efforts to establish laws and introduce an examination. By the end of 1905 an additional four states — California, Illinois, Maryland, and Pennsylvania — had granted 126 certificates based on examinations and 118 based on waivers. Another two states — New Jersey and Washington — had issued, by waiver only, 70 certificates. Therefore, these six other states issued a total of 314 certificates, or 50.9 percent of the 617 issued.

Those who provided leadership saw opportunity for public accountants in a society where businesses were growing larger and more complex. While accountants discussed the role of the accountant, examiners in the several states were preparing examinations based primarily on their experience. The criticism of the examination which appeared in the first issues of *The Journal of Accountancy* highlighted the elementary nature of the examination as well as its limited scope.

The history of the profession of accounting in the United States has many aspects that deserve far fuller treatment than has been provided to date. There are very few thorough historical studies available that probe in depth what appear to have been astute and visionary strategies in the story of the public accounting profession.

The significance of the examination in relation to the development of the profession and its adequacy for determining entry to the profession might well be fruitfully studied historically. Among other topics for further exploration are the following:

- the nature and content of the examination over time
- analysis of the changes in the nature of questions included
- historical analysis of criticism of CPA examination
- analysis of the responsiveness of the examination to the extension of accounting pronouncements
- analysis of the adequacy of examinations at times of changing demands on the professional accountant
- historical trends in the work of accountants and the responsiveness of the examination's content and nature
- the role and nature of educational programs supporting preparation for the examination through the years

- an analysis of the success in establishing a single examination and the failure in establishing single certification requirements throughout the United States
- an analysis of the progress of women and minorities in the accounting profession as reflected in performance on the examination.

The current era is perceived to be one of marked change — in fact discontinuous change — where wise judgments are needed to assure a viable profession in the next century. There have been times of change in the past. However, there have been marked social developments in the last several decades that have significantly influenced American society, including the accounting profession. The environment in which the accounting profession got underway was far different from today's. For example, a review of the language of the law in 1896 and a reading of the list of CPAs in 1905 reveal the limited group participating in the profession. The references were always to "he" and "men." The surnames of the men do not reflect the diversity of a roster of names in 1995!

The CPA examination in the United States has been significantly changed in recent years. It becomes a nondisclosed examination in 1996. Further exploration of the judgments of the initial group that established the profession — and the examination — might be enlightening to those who assess the current effectiveness of the examination and determine its direction in the future within the framework of a society that strives to be sensitive to limiting all types of unwarranted barriers to entry.

ENDNOTE

1 The handwritten minutes of the Board of Examiners has Haskins with Certificate No. 1, Sprague No. 3 and Broaker No. 6 [New York State Board Examiners, Minutes, November 24, 1896]. However, the Board of Examiners was overruled by the Board of Regents of the University System of New York which changed the numbering. The head of the Board of Regents was Melville Dewey (of Dewey Decimal system fame) who liked structure in organization. As a result, he changed the numbering to an alphabetical system, which meant that Frank Broaker got Certificate No. 1. This is discussed in the 1954 book by Norman E. Webster, *The American Association of Public Accountants 1886–1906* (New York: American Institute of Accountants, 1954).

REFERENCES

"Accountancy in New York," *The Accountant* (August 7, 1897), p. 771.

"Accountancy in the States [a]," *The Accountant* (November 21, 1896), pp. 951–952.

"Accountancy in the States [b]," *The Accountant* (January 23, 1897), p. 99.

"Accountancy in the States [c]," *The Accountant* (March 27, 1897), p. 338.

"Accountancy in the States [d]," *The Accountant* (September 11, 1897), p. 857.

"Accountancy in the States [e]," *The Accountant* (October 30, 1897), p. 1011.

American Institute of Accountants. American Society of Public Accountants *Yearbook*. 1916, pp. 196, 197.

Anyon, James T. *Recollections of the Early Days of American Accountancy* (Privately printed, 1925).

Brief, Richard P., Ed. *Haskins & Sells. Our First Seventy-Five Years* [New York and London: Garland Publishing, Inc., 1970 (Facsimile Series, 1984)].

Broaker, Frank. *The American Accountants' Manual*, Vol. 1 (New York: Broaker & Chapman, 1897).

———. "A Salutation on Behalf of the American Association," *The Journal of Accountancy* (November, 1905), p. 86.

Edwards, James Don. *History of Public Accounting in the United States*, Accounting History Classics Series (University, AL: The University of Alabama Press, 1978).

Have, O. *The History of Accountancy* (Palo Alto, CA: Bay Books, 1976).

Historical Statistics of the United States, Colonial Times to 1970. United States Government.

The Journal of Accountancy. Membership (November, 1905), pp. 94–98.

The Journal of Accountancy. Editorial (July, 1906), pp. 216–218.

Kouwenhoven, John A. *Partners in Banking: An Historical Portrait of a Great Private Bank Brown Brothers Harriman & Co. 1818 – 1968* (New York: Doubleday and Company, Inc., 1968).

Leroy-Beaulieu, Pierre. *The United States in the Twentieth Century* (New York and London: Funk & Wagnalls, 1907).

Littleton, A. C. *Accounting Evolution to 1900* [New York: Russell & Russell, 1933 (Reissued edition, 1966)].

Meade, Edward Sherwood. "Establish Preliminary Examinations in Law and Economics," *The Journal of Accountancy* (January, 1907) pp. 193–195.

New York State Board of Examiners of Public Accountants. Unpublished Minutes. State Board Archives. (November 12, 1896)

New York State Board of Examiners of Public Accountants. Unpublished Minutes. (November 24, 1896).

———. Unpublished Minutes. (December 11, 1896).

———. Unpublished Minutes. (April 23, 24, 1897).

———. Unpublished Minutes. (August 19, 1897).

———. Unpublished Minutes. (November 15, 1897).

———. Unpublished Minutes. (April 22, 1899).

Pace, Homer and Samuel D. Patterson. Unpublished Correspondence. Pace University Archives, 1910.

Parker, R. H. *The Development of the Accountancy Profession in Britain to the Early Twentieth Century*, Monograph Five (Exeter, England: The Academy of Accounting Historians, 1986).

Previts, Gary John and Barbara Dubis Merino. *A History of Accounting in America* (New York: John Wiley & Sons, 1979).

Sells, Elijah W. Foreward in Charles Waldo Haskins. *An American Pioneer in Accountancy* (New York: Prentice Hall, 1923).

Statistical Abstract of the United States, 1900. United States Government.

Sterrett, J. E. "Education and Training of a Certified Public Accountant," *The Journal of Accountancy* (November, 1905).

Wall, Joseph Frazier. *Andrew Carnegie* (New York: Oxford University Press, 1970).

Wilkinson, George. "The C.P.A. Movement and the Future of Profession of the Public Accountant in the United States of America." Official Record of the Proceedings of the Congress of Accountants. Federation of Societies of Public Accounts in the United States of America. Saint Louis, Missouri, 1904, pp. 91–103.

Part III:

Financial Accounting and Auditing

An Historical Perspective on Fraudulent Financial Reporting in the United States

Mohammad J. Abdolmohammadi
Bentley College, MA

Paul J. McMann
Boston University

Mai E. Iskandar
Finance Research Associates
Waltham, MA

1.0 ABSTRACT

Detection of fraudulent financial reporting (FFR) was part of the responsibility of auditors in early years of audit practice in the United States. However, as the complexity of the business entities increased through mergers and acquisitions and as auditing formally became a profession, detection of FFR was pushed to the periphery of the auditors' responsibility. This phenomenon has cost the profession dearly in terms of reduced credibility and heavy monetary losses in a number of scandalous audit failure cases involving FFR in the last three decades. This paper provides an historical perspective on FFR by critically reviewing the literature. In addition, several strategies are suggested for consideration in dealing with FFR.

2.0 INTRODUCTION

The auditing profession in the United States has been criticized by the public, the courts, and lawmakers on the basis that, historically, auditors have neglected their responsibility for uncovering fraudulent financial reporting (FFR) by public companies. Well-known companies such as Penn Square National Bank, Continental Illinois National Bank, United American Bank, Home State Savings, Baldwin United, and many others have failed, some having received clean, unqualified opinions shortly before their demise [Klott, 1984]. Although most FFRs are detected through internal controls or internal reviews by internal auditors and others, only about one percent of them result in false financial statements [Pincus, 1994], but the magnitude of the loss potential from this small portion of cases against auditors is immense. For example, by the end of 1992, the Big Six accounting firms faced litigation claims exceeding $30 billion, more than 20 times their combined permanent capital ["Big Six Litigation ...," 1993]. While litigation against auditors stems from many different causes, the FFR cases are a significant portion of the litigation.

The effects of such litigation on auditors has been significant and humbling. In some audits involving management fraud, the auditors had to return their fees for failure to detect fraud and in other cases they were even found criminally liable and were sentenced to prison. For example, while in the case of McKesson & Robbins, where the auditors returned their hefty audit fees of over $500,000 in 1938 [Edwards, 1968 p. 207], the audit partners in charge of the case of National Student Marketing Corporation were fined and jailed in 1974 for blinding themselves to the facts about which they should have inquired [Tinker, 1985, p. 58].

Factors that have contributed to such litigation against auditors include [AICPA, 1976; Olson, 1982]:

- the judiciary system that has taken an active role in defining and expanding auditors' liability to third parties for the detection of fraud in financial statements
- technical legal developments have made legal remedies more available to third parties
- social and consumer changes have influenced the public's expectations of auditors as insurers of the accuracy of a company's financial statements.

The problem became so severe in the 1970s and 1980s that a commission called the National Commission on Fraudulent Financial Reporting, also known as the Treadway Commission [NCFFR, 1987], was established to address this issue as well as a number of other issues resulting from the differences between what the auditors were doing and what the public expected from them.[1] In 1988, the Auditing Standards Board issued nine new *Statements on Auditing Standards* (dubbed the "expectation gap" Statements) to deal with these issues, one of which, *SAS No. 53*, "The Auditor's Responsibility to Detect and Report Errors and Irregularities" [AICPA, 1988] deals with the auditors' responsibility for FFR.

No other problem has caused as much damage to the profession's credibility as the cases where irregularities and fraud transpired without auditor detection [St. Pierre, 1983]. The purpose of this paper is to present historical evidence that detection of FFR was part of the auditor's responsibility in the early days of the audit in the United States, but that it was abandoned in the early 1900s when the profession was formally organized. It is argued that from an historical perspective, the abandonment of the responsibility to detect FFR was a mistake and that the steps that the profession has taken to assign responsibility for detection of FFR do not go far enough. Several strategies are presented for future consideration. Since the literature on this issue is quite extensive, only FFR as defined in the Treadway Commission is considered. The Commission defined FFR as intentional or reckless conduct, whether by act or omission, that results in materially misleading financial statements [NCFFR, 1987, p. 2].

The remainder of the paper is organized as follows. The historical background regarding FFR is discussed in the next section. The auditing profession's differing attitudes toward FFR are presented next, followed by a section on the forces that have effected changes in the profession's attitudes. A number of conclusions and recommendations are presented in the final section of the paper.

3.0 HISTORICAL BACKGROUND

Traditionally, auditors have had an implied duty to provide a reasonable level of care in performing their contractual services. The issue is whether detection of FFR falls under reasonable care. In early years of audit practice, such a detection was implied as the auditor's duty. Moyer [1968, p. 190] reports that the sixteen-page *Auditor's Guide* by H.J. Mettenheim that was published in 1869 gave suggestions for detecting and preventing fraud. However, as accountants formed their professional organization,[2] references to detection of fraud disappeared from the professional literature for three decades. The only reference found on the issue of fraud detection by the profession is a book by George E. Bennett called *Fraud, Its Control Through Accounts*, published in 1931 [Carey, 1969, p. 305].

Thus, as St. Pierre [1983] has argued, auditors have abdicated the responsibility to detect FFR through statements in the professional literature or audit-client agreements. Even when the profession tried to acknowledge the issue in 1972, it stated that:

> the ordinary examination directed to the expression of an opinion on financial statements is not primarily or specifically designed, and cannot be relied upon, to disclose defalcations and other similar irregularities, although their discovery may result .... The responsibility of the independent auditor for failure to detect fraud ... arises only when such failure clearly results from failure to comply with generally accepted auditing standards. [AICPA, 1977, section 110.05]

As will be discussed later, it was only under heavy pressure from Congress, the courts, and private commissions that the AICPA finally issued *SAS No. 53* [AICPA, 1988] requiring auditors to design auditing procedures to detect material errors and irregularities.

It is not clear why auditors implicitly accepted the responsibility for detection of FFR in the early years of their practice but abandoned it in later years. Possible reasons include the following:

1. Given the collusive nature of many management fraud cases, the auditors may have found detection of FFR to be very difficult and risky, particularly in light of the many corporate mergers during the last decade of the nineteenth century which increased the complexity of business operations and gave impetus to the accounting profession [Moyer, 1968]. The profession reasons that if it accepts further responsibility, audit risk would increase by increasing auditors' exposure to third parties, and hence, greater legal liability would occur [St. Pierre, 1983].

2. Detection of fraud may have been viewed as putting the auditors in an adversarial position with their clients. However, although it may be unreasonable to expect auditors to detect collusive fraud, detection of irregularities is within the reasonable domain. St. Pierre [1983] finds that in many of the cases brought against auditors for not detecting irregularities, the inability of auditors to properly interpret accounting principles or auditing standards and auditors' failure to properly implement auditing procedures were the major reasons behind not detecting fraud.

3. The nature of the investigation changed from "detailed" to "test" audits [Moyer, 1968, p. 194], thus making detection of fraud more difficult, especially if collusion is involved between members of the client's management.

4. There was a lack of court ruling on auditors' legal liability in general and FFR detection in particular [Carey, 1969, p. 81].

5. The profession has systematically understated its social responsibility, Tinker [1985] has argued. An editorial in the *Journal of Accountancy* in May 1912 stated that, "The great majority of American accountants today regard the moral liability for their work as equally imperative with any legal liability, but it must be admitted that there are members of the profession — happily their numbers are small — who require to have some sort of legal obligation in order to stimulate their sense of honor and their respect for integrity …." [in Carey, 1969, p. 81]. This statement indicates that the issue of lack of moral liability has been an issue of concern from early days of the professional practice of auditing.

Of the reasons listed, the last two are particularly plausible in light of anecdotal evidence from the literature. Under common law, an auditor's responsibility to clients was based on the direct contractual relationship with the paying client. The duty of care owed to a third-party non-client was limited to situations where the third party was known and intended to be a beneficiary of the performed service [Arens and Loebbecke, 1988]. In such circumstances where due care was required but lacking, only those with privity or a primary beneficiary relationship could sue an accountant for ordinary negligence under common law. The most prominent case in support of the common law in auditing is Judge Cordozo's confirmation of the law in the case of *Ultramares Corporation* v. *Touche et al.* in 1931 [Edwards, 1968, p. 207]. Generally, the auditor argues for the reasonableness of the generally accepted auditing standards (GAAS) as a means of due care under common law.

In recent years, however, technical, social, and consumer changes have resulted in a shift in auditor liability and, subsequently, an increase in the number of lawsuits filed against accountants. A 1985 *Wall Street Journal* article reported that "More lawsuits have been filed against accountants in the past 15 years than in the entire previous history of the profession" [Berton, 1985]. The public, the courts, and the legislature are quick to register disappointment when auditors fail to meet their expectations. The disappointment quickly translates into lawsuits, damage awards, and Congressional hearings. For example, in 1968, Judge Walter Mansfield ruled in the case of *Continental Vending* v. *Arthur Andersen* that adherence to GAAS does not exempt an auditor from liability if the court finds there was a need for further disclosure [Louis, 1970, p. 97]. The extent of the damages expected or awarded is so significant as to cause large accounting firms to cease existence. For example, the seventh largest accounting firm, Laventhol and Horwath, filed for protection under Chapter 11 of the US Bankruptcy Code due in part to several law suits against it [*Wall Street Journal,* 1990]. Today, auditors are seen as the public's watchdog and are charged with the responsibility of supplying the public with accurate decision-making financial information which serves to facilitate the smooth and continued operation of the nation's capital markets [Ostling, 1986].

The above discussion indicates the accumulation of court rulings over the last four decades broadening the extent of auditors' legal liability. Thus, the fourth reason enumerated earlier (i.e., lack of court rulings) for lack of accepting responsibility for detection of FFR is no longer valid. However, a few cases provide anecdotal evidence indicating that even under the pressure from courts, the profession has not voluntarily accepted social responsibility in FFR detection unless and until it has confronted a crisis situation. For example, the McKesson and Robbins scandal in 1939 resulted in the professional requirement of confirmation of receivables and observation of inventories to reduce the likelihood of clients intentionally overstating these assets, but still no responsibility for detection of FFR was accepted by the profession.

Other cases (e.g., the National Student Marketing Corporation in 1974) in which auditors were given criminal penalties for lack of sufficient care in fraudulent financial reports of their clients also pointed to serious problems regarding lack of response to FFR. The Congressional hearings of the 1970s and 1980s provided the pressure for the profession that resulted in nine "expectation gap" *Statements on Auditing Standards* [AICPA, 1988]. For example, in a 1977 Congressional hearing, Senator Metcalf stated that, "The staff study of the accounting establishment reflects the concern of many of us in Congress that the present system has been incapable of developing effective accounting practices which will adequately protect and inform the public. It seems as though nearly every day we read in the *Washington Post* or the *Wall Street Journal* some newly discovered fraud, slush fund, or unsuspected financial difficulty concerning a major corporation" [US Senate, 1977, p. 3]. Thus, only after the profession has confronted these types of criticism from the Congress, has it responded with doing something about its social responsibility of detecting irregularities. These developments are further discussed at a later point in the paper.

4.0 PROFESSION'S DIFFERING ATTITUDES TOWARD FFR

The accounting profession has responded slowly to the long-standing gap between public expectations and the profession's attitudes. Carey [1969] reports that an editorial appeared in the *Journal of Accountancy* in the May 1912 issue stating that "It is well to have clearly in mind that the function of the auditor is primarily to safeguard the interests of the creditor and stockholder. ... Unfortunately some accountants, and we fear their number is distressingly large, do not take their work with a sufficient degree of seriousness, and give audit certificates that deserve less confidence than they inspire" [Carey, 1969, p. 80]. Although not directly related to FFR, this editorial indicates that the profession has been struggling with the issue of expectation gap from its first decade as an organized national profession (1904, the National Congress, being the beginning of the national profession).

Speaking at the Seaview Symposium on Corporate Financial Reporting in November 1971, A. A. Sommer, Jr., former Securities Exchange Commissioner, asserted that "If a professional group fails to sufficiently articulate its identity, its duties, the identity of those to whom it owes a duty, and the manner in which the duty is to be acquitted, and if society assigns it a role which, despite its professional standards, it does not fulfill adequately, the courts, vested by society with the responsibility to define and enforce duties, will undertake to do it" [Miller, 1986].

In the two decades since his statement, Mr. Sommer's prophecy appears to have been fulfilled. By failing to adequately identify its duties, the profession has suffered, and the number of lawsuits filed against auditors by third parties has significantly increased. Nevertheless, there is no single attitude among professional auditors with regard to FFR. One attitude is that a major problem with regard to FFR does not really exist. This is because the profession's self-regulatory process that has been endorsed by both the Public Oversight Board and the Securities and Exchange Commission [Zick, 1985] has adequately responded to FFR. This group also argues that when viewed as a percentage of all professional engagements, the number of lawsuits brought against accountants is extremely small; therefore, no corrective action is required. Maintenance of the status quo, in their opinion, is the appropriate response because regulatory pressure intended to force auditors to detect FFR may not even be pareto optimal [Buckley and Weston, 1980, p. 156]. An argument against this attitude is that reported audit failures usually occur only with bankrupt companies and there are many audit failures out there that have gone undetected because of a company's continuing solvency [Kaplan, 1987].[3]

A second type of attitude is that some auditors recognize the problem with FFR, but disclaim responsibility for detecting it. This attitude stems from the belief among auditors that it is the responsibility of the public to understand the auditor's true function.[4] This attitude, generally shared by international accounting firms, contends that third-party users do not comprehend the difference between an audit and police work. This group promotes an agenda of educating third-party user groups regarding to what the audited financial statements actually attest. A faction has even put forth a proposal for a series of televised public service announcements as part of a comprehensive public educational campaign [Minow, 1984]. Further regulation is not necessary, the group contends, because the solution lies in voluntary initiatives.

Finally, a group of auditors acknowledges the increasing number and scope of lawsuits against auditors as a serious problem that must be proactively addressed. Holstrum [1991, p. 1] states that "the issuance of *SAS No. 53*, "The Auditor's Responsibility to Detect and Report Errors and Irregularities" [AICPA, 1988], served to eliminate the auditor's false sense of immunity from responsibility for detecting material fraud." As a result of this lack of immunity, there is significant interest among auditors to learn about how to guard against fraud. Training videos prepared by interviews of management fraud convicts are also hot sellers [Pae, 1991]. This attitude is a legalistic one and is concerned with the rising cost of accountants' malpractice insurance which has been estimated at $50 million annually for the nation's largest 20 firms in the 1980s [Miller, 1986]. This group offers solutions which attempt to realistically address the problem's true foundations.

5.0 FORCES EFFECTING CHANGE IN THE PROFESSION'S ATTITUDE

As stated earlier, in the past, the profession's reaction to problems was not forthcoming until the difficulty reached crisis proportions. Furthermore, the profession has typically responded by limiting obligations and changing the audit report. Occasionally, changes were the result of litigation losses or the threat of government intervention. For example, the audit failure and "cooked books" scandal which ensued from the McKesson & Robbins case in 1939 resulted in the *Statement on Auditing Standards No. 1* [AICPA, 1977, section 330] which required observation and testing of physical inventory and confirmation of receivables [Kell, Boynton and Zeigler, 1990]. We now turn to the major forces that have put pressure on the profession to institute change in its attitude. These forces include legislation, court decisions, Congressional hearings, and private commission investigations.

5.1 Legislation

The federal statutes affecting auditors are the Securities Act of 1933 and Securities Exchange Act of 1934. The former act, which regulates by disclosure, "makes the auditor liable for losses to third parties resulting from ordinary negligence, as well as from fraud and gross negligence, to the effective date of the registration statement ...." [Kell, Boynton, and Zeigler, 1990]. The Act served to increase an auditor's potential liability to third parties regardless of the fact that they are not clients with a privity relationship or known third parties with a primary beneficiary relationship. Additionally, under both 1933 and 1934 acts, auditors are exposed to criminal penalties; however, because of absence of personal gain motivation, there have been few criminal suits against auditors.

It is interesting to note that when Congress was considering the 1933 Securities Act, thought was given to a proposal that financial statements covered in the act be reviewed by government auditors instead of independent public accountants. The profession was able to convince the Congress that auditors would be able to make the required examinations more quickly and economically than an army of government accountants [Miller, 1986]. Carey [1969, pp. 182–192] provides an historical account indicating that the profession influenced the legislature by hiring the highly respected, knowledgeable, and influential Washington judge, J. Harry Covington, to represent it at the Congressional hearings. Furthermore, Colonel Arthur H. Carter (a senior partner with Haskins and Sells and the then-president of the New York Society of CPAs) testified at the hearings before the Senate Committee on Banking and Currency and argued that the Committee include a provision in the securities bill to give the function of auditing to CPAs. "The house bill, which was finally enacted into law, contained an audit provision and additional provisions of vital interest to the accounting profession" [Carey, 1969, p. 190].[5]

Few cases have been tried under the 1933 Act, but those that have confirm the auditor's expanded responsibility to third parties. The first and most significant where a favourable judgment was rendered for third-party plaintiffs is *Escott* v. *Bar Chris Construction Corporation* [Escott ..., 1968]. The action was brought under the portion of the act covering false statements and material omissions in the registration statement. As a consequence of Bar Chris, the profession made two significant changes in its auditing methods:

- *Statement on Auditing Standards (SAS) No. 1* was changed to require greater emphasis on procedures the auditor must perform regarding subsequent events
- a greater emphasis began to be placed on the importance of the audit staff understanding the client's business and industry.

The most significant outcome from the case, however, was that the courts demonstrated that they were willing to choose between alternative accounting principles if they believed the application of a specific pronouncement did not result in fair statements [Defliese *et al.*, 1984, Kell *et al.*, 1990].

Under the 1934 act, an auditor's liability centres on the audited financial statements submitted to the SEC as a part of annual 10-K reports. The principal focus on CPA liability litigation has been Rule 10b-5 (referred to as "anti-fraud provision"). For many years, it was unclear whether auditors were liable under Rule 10b-5 for misrepresentations or omissions that were negligent but not fraudulent. In 1976, in *Hochfelder* v. *Ernst & Ernst*, the US Supreme Court ruled that some knowledge and intent to deceive are required before CPAs could be held liable for violation of Rule 10b-5. The case involved the auditor's responsibility for detecting fraud perpetrated by the president of the client firm, First Securities Co. of Chicago. As a result of this case, it is more difficult for third parties to successfully sue using Rule 10b-5, unless more than simple negligence can be proved [Arens and Loebbecke, 1988].

5.2 Court Decisions

The explosion of litigation against auditors began in the latter part of the 1960s. Prior to the 1960s, lawsuits brought against auditors by third parties claiming audit negligence were mostly unsuccessful. The various judicial decisions in the three decades hence resulted in an extension of the concepts of auditors' liability for negligence to third parties. The courts allowed recovery by third parties by introducing the concept of "foreseen" and "foreseeable" users and by changing, bypassing or otherwise attempting to reduce the effects of the privity doctrine [Defliese *et al.*, 1984].

For example, in *Rusch Factors, Inc.* v. *Levin* [*Rusch* ..., 1968], the courts extended the foreseen party concept to common law ordinary negligence cases, thus widening the number of third party groups that could sue auditors for ordinary negligence under common law. In *Ryan* v. *Kanne* [*Ryan* ..., 1969], the Iowa Supreme Court used the verdict from Rusch Factors in its decision which served to further weaken the concept of privity and increase an accountant's potential liability to third parties. In *Rosenblum* v. *Adler* [*Rosenblum* ..., 1983], the plaintiff charged the auditors with negligence by failing to detect the fictitious assets and omitted liabilities. The court ruled that the auditors were liable even though the plaintiff was only a foreseeable party. Because of auditors' "deep pockets" arising from liability insurance, the Rosenblum decision had the effect of making auditors guarantors against an audited company's financial failure. In addition, the decision served to extend an auditor's liability to reasonably foreseeable third parties [Kell *et al.*, 1990].

As it currently stands, an auditor generally is liable for ordinary negligence to parties the auditor specifically knows may rely on an audit opinion (primary beneficiary), as well as to any reasonably limited and reasonably definable class of persons the auditor may reasonably expect to rely on the opinion (foreseen third parties) and in some cases to reasonably foreseeable parties as well. Liability for gross negligence and fraud extends to all third parties, including merely foreseeable third parties.

5.3 Congressional Hearings

Meanwhile, Congress has been irritated by auditors' failure to assume greater responsibility and initiated hearings to examine audit deficiencies. One of the first examples of hearings by Congress which involved the accounting profession was in the mid-1970s with the Senate Subcommittee on Government Operations, chaired by Senator Metcalf, and the House Subcommittee on Oversight and Investigation, chaired by Congressman Moss.

Another series of hearings concerning the adequacy of operations of the accounting profession commenced in the 1980s. This time it was the House Subcommittee on Legislation and National Security, chaired by Congressman Brooks, and the House Subcommittee on Oversight and Investigation, chaired by Congressman Dingell. The Brooks Committee addressed assertions by the General Accounting Office that there were widespread deficiencies in the audits of federal grant funds by CPAs. It issued a report stating that CPAs performing these audits frequently did not comply with professional auditing standards. In addition, the report contained recommendations for the profession to remedy the problem and promised Congressional action if the quality of these audits did not improve. Both the American Institute of Certified Public Accountants (AICPA) and the National Association of State Boards of Accountancy appeared before the committee to respond to the report and promised to take action.

The Dingell hearings, sparked by business failure of Penn Square National Bank and Continental Illinois Bank, took a more antagonistic approach in its quest to protect the public. The most recent of the Congressional hearings, this two-year investigation has been described as unsympathetic and openly hostile [Kaplan, 1987]. In a speech given prior to the commencement of the subcommittee's hearings, Dingell expressed the opinion that quality control within the accounting profession is inadequate. He stated that:

> the work product of the large firms is evaluated through a peer review system that they [the big firms] have set up. This system is overseen by the Public Oversight Board — selected and paid for by the major firms themselves. The firms review

> each other's work, congratulate each other after noting a few minor errors, perform the whole process in the dark — and then destroy the work papers so nobody can later check into or question their judgment. The "clean" review opinions they give each other are similar to the "clean" audit opinions they have given many of their clients shortly before those businesses have gone bankrupt or experience serious losses. Those failures have had devastating effects on shareholders, depositors, customers, suppliers, communities and, often, the federal government, when it has had to pick up the tab at the end. ["Dingell Voices Concerns ...," 1985]

The primary focus of the commission's report was examining the issues of fraud detection and various "failures." The subcommittee proposed ways to improve the performance of independent auditors in detecting and disclosing financial fraud. Occurring concurrently with the Dingell hearings was the introduction of a bill (H.R. 4886), The Financial Fraud Detection and Disclosure Act, which was sometimes referred to as the "Whistle-Blower's Bill," proposed by Congressman Wyden. The bill would have required independent auditors to use every reasonable effort to detect and disclose to the SEC illegal and fraudulent activities at publicly held corporations. Also, the bill would have amended the Securities Exchange Act to set audit standards to implement the new bill's provisions. Under the influence of the AICPA and the major national accounting firms, the Wyden Bill did not pass [Holstrum, 1991]; however, again, it served to indicate how serious Congress perceived the situation to be.

5.4 Private Commissions

As a result of these Congressional hearings and pressures, private commissions were set up with co-sponsorship of the AICPA to study the problems and to recommend appropriate courses of action. We discuss two such commissions: the Cohen Commission and the Treadway Commission.

Dubbed the Cohen Commission for its chairman, Manuel Cohen, former SEC chairman, this AICPA-sponsored commission investigated auditors' responsibilities [AICPA, 1976]. The commission's published report served as a basis for restructuring various existing auditing standards. With respect to the standard auditor's report, the commission stated that:

> evidence abounds that communication between the auditor and users of his work — especially through the auditor's standard report — is unsatisfactory. The present report has remained essentially unchanged since 1948 and its shortcomings have often been discussed .... Users are unaware of the limitations of the audit function and are confused about the distinction between the responsibilities of management and those of the auditor. [AICPA, 1976]

The Cohen Report also provided for the evaluation and reporting of internal accounting controls as well as a reassessment of the entire self-regulatory process. The commission pointed out that the courts are increasingly holding auditors accountable for material misrepresentations in the financial statements, and it concluded that failure in detecting fraud is an indication of failure to apply the standard due care that society demands.

Few of the changes that resulted from the Cohen Commission Report, however, were considered lasting [Sager, 1986]. As a result, the threat of Congressional legislative action became more apparent in the early 1980s. Consequently, in 1985 the National Commission on Fraudulent Financial Reporting (NCFFR for short, also known as the Treadway Commission, after its chairman's name, James Treadway, a former SEC commissioner) was created and funded by the AICPA and a number of other interested accounting organizations [Miller, 1986]. The commission's stated objectives were threefold:

- to consider the extent to which acts of fraudulent financial reporting undermine the integrity of financial reporting, and what forces may have contributed to these acts
- to consider the role of the independent public accountant in detecting fraud and especially whether changes in auditing standards or procedures might reduce the extent of fraudulent financial reporting
- to identify attributes of corporate structure that may contribute to acts of fraudulent financial reporting or the failure to detect such acts promptly.

While the Cohen Commission Report looked strictly at the auditor's role and had only one chapter devoted to fraud detection, the Treadway Commission probed the entire financial reporting process and looked beyond the auditor to a number of other groups involved in the preparation of financial statements. The commission attempted to take an open-minded view of the situation, realizing that the problem of fraudulent financial reporting would not lend itself to a simple or easy answer. In characterizing fraud, Chairman Treadway has stated, "the activity is as complex as human nature itself, with all its quirks and eccentricities" [Treadway, 1986]. The commission examined actual fraud cases to identify and catalogue common characteristics of FFR [Liebtag, 1986]. The compiled catalogue could then provide an "early warning system" checklist which might help red flag trouble areas.

The commission's final report on FFR stated that four groups (management, the audit committee, the internal auditors, and the independent auditors) could assist in reducing fraud. Regulatory agencies and universities were also mentioned as capable of contributing to fraud reduction. The following recommendations were the most significant with regards to FFR [NCFFR, 1987]:

1. Change auditing standards to better recognize the independent public accountant's responsibility for detecting fraudulent financial reporting. For example, mandate the greater use of key fraud ratios in analytical procedures to uncover misstatements [Grove, Lee, and Hanbery, 1988].

2. Change the standard audit report to better communicate to the users of financial statements the role of the audit and its limitations. For example, the report should include a statement that the audit provides reasonable but not absolute assurance that the financial statements are free from material misstatements caused by fraud or error. The statement should also describe the extent to which the accountant has reviewed and evaluated the system of internal accounting control.

3. Require public companies to establish and involve strong audit committees and internal audit departments in the financial reporting process. In examining actual fraud cases between 1981 and 1986, the commission found that in the majority of fraud cases, top management was the perpetrator. This finding emphasized the need to separate monitoring duties and elevate the internal auditors' reporting responsibility to the audit committee, not to management [Grove, Lee, and Hanbery, 1988].

4. Have the state boards of accountancy, coupled with SEC sanction, adopt more "positive enforcement programs that periodically ... review the quality of services" provided by their licensees.

In 1988, the AICPA responded to Congressional hearings and private commission recommendations by issuing nine new *Statements on Auditing Standards* (*SAS*) which incorporate some of the major recommendations from the Treadway report. Two SASs which specifically address fraudulent financial reporting include *SAS No. 53*, "The Auditor's Responsibility to Detect and Report Errors and Irregularities," and *SAS No. 54*, "Illegal Acts by Clients."

SAS No. 53 requires auditors to design auditing procedures to detect material errors and irregularities. It includes a requirement for a preliminary assessment of the risk of material irregularities and the likelihood of management misrepresentation. Moreover, it requires the use of analytical procedures at the planning and review stages of an audit. *SAS No. 54* reemphasizes the nature and extent of an auditor's consideration of the possibility of illegal acts. Another *Statement, SAS No. 58*, "Reports on Audited Financial Statements," modified the auditor's standard report. The report requires the auditors to state whether they have any doubts the company being audited will continue as a "going concern." Also, the auditors are expected to use new language which clarifies how an audit is conducted.

These new audit standards are a good start. The formation of the Governance & Structure Committee by the AICPA to recommend appropriate changes in the structure and governance of the AICPA and the profession to meet the needs and expectations of the members and the public [Chenok, 1990] is another recent, positive step. Finally, the plan approved by the membership of the profession to restructure professional standards in January 1989 [Chenok, 1990] has created a sense that the profession is serious about doing something to respond to societal demands. However, other initiatives can also be undertaken to respond further to the calls from public to deal better with FFR as presented in the next section.

6.0 CONCLUSIONS AND RECOMMENDATIONS

The profession's actions, while responding to the criticism that many auditors either are confused or simply do not want to accept their responsibility under new *SAS No. 53.6*,[6] are not sufficiently adequate to warrant credibility in the eyes of the public. More needs to be done to meet the legitimate needs of the public and to respond adequately to the profession's social responsibility. Since auditors are judged liable in some cases of business financial failure, the profession should take a proactive stance and maintain its professional credibility. Among actions that might assist in correcting the profession's current perceived deficiencies are the following:

6.1 Adopt the Treadway Recommendations

The profession should take steps to see that all of the Treadway Commission recommendations regarding public companies and their auditors are implemented. So far, the profession has only chosen to adopt a select number of the Treadway Commission's recommendations and even for those selected, the profession has failed to respond satisfactorily. For example, *SAS No. 55*, "Consideration of the Internal Control Structure in Financial Statement Audit" [AICPA 1988] was designed by the Auditing Standards Board to partly respond to the Treadway Commission recommendations. However, despite the Auditing Standards Board's efforts to make *SAS No. 55* more understandable through the issuance of a guide, it has come under heavy criticism for obscure reasoning, imprecise language, and confusing discussions regarding the assessment of control risk [Morton and Felix, 1991]. The extent of the problems with *SAS No. 55* is such that some critics have recommended a thorough revision of the standard, one that would incorporate a foundation of logic and consistent theory into the statement [Morton and Felix, 1991, p. 10]. Furthermore, in an apparent dissatisfaction with *SAS No. 55*, the organizations that sponsored the Treadway Commission have issued a report defining internal control and how public companies can judge the effectiveness of their internal control systems [the Committee of Sponsoring Organizations of the Treadway Commission, 1991].

The profession must adopt and implement all major recommendations of the Treadway Commission. Once adopted, the recommendations should be monitored and evaluated for their effectiveness. For example, auditors can exercise some control by working with their clients to enhance the functioning of audit committees and internal auditors; these groups constitute the first stages of fraud prevention and detection. It is not sufficient that auditors' clients have just the internal audit function and/or audit committees. The auditors should work with their clients to make these functions competent and effective. Abdolmohammadi and Levy [1992] report that although over 85% of public companies have formed audit committees, a substantial number of the members in these committees do not have the necessary auditing knowledge and one third of all audit committee members surveyed did not even believe that knowledge of auditing (even at the elementary level) was necessary to serve on audit committees. It is clear that auditors must take some initiative to educate the audit committees of their clients on major issues such as FFR.

6.2 Expand *Statements on Auditing Standards*

Part of the adoption of the Treadway Commission recommendations includes expanding the auditing standards. Fraud investigation has generally been regarded by the profession as a by-product, not a primary function of the audit. Existing professional auditing standards should be expanded to require the auditor to:

- Identify potential symptoms (red flags) existing within the company's business environment that would indicate a higher risk of intentional misstatement of the financial statements. The auditor should be required to consider performing certain audit procedures if such symptoms are present [Connor, 1986]
- Add supplementary disclosure on more items. The more that is divulged by the auditor, the more informed the user will be and the less likely that a fraud claim can be made against them by the user
- Require all public companies over a certain size to audit for fraud. An example of the effectiveness of such a requirement is audits for companies at the initial public offering (IPO) stage. The process leading to IPO is governed by the 1933 Securities Act which sets forth standards and liability. Since the Act's inception, there has been little reported fraud in the proxies leading to IPOs.

6.3 Provide a More Discretionary Audit Report

Auditors should seek new methods to communicate their findings to third-party users more clearly and fully. Such added communication should reduce the expectation gap. Prior to 1933, auditors had considerable discretion in wording the audit report. Perhaps, by allowing the auditor more discretion in the report, more informative material would be disclosed. Added disclosure would also force investors to read the report, something which is not always done by financial statement readers. When an individual becomes familiar with the words, as most are with a standard audit report, they tend to not read it and, hence, attempts to communicate become less successful.

If discretion in the standard report is not a viable option, then the addition of a narrative highlighting findings and disclosures that the auditor considers significant might be a feasible alternative. The disclosures in the narrative might provide information such as:

- additional analysis of the meaning of the data in the financial statements
- forecasts and projections or other future-oriented statistics
- factors on which the company's future success is most dependent (e.g., the ability to develop new products, find new sources of raw materials, retain a major customer, product market share, etc.)
- the unique business and industry risks facing the company in the foreseeable future [Mednick, 1986].

Another option for those who prefer more of a free-market approach would be to offer a menu of audit reports and let the company purchasing the audit select what type of report they want. If a company wants an extra paragraph on fraud detection or anything that management or users deem important, let them buy it for an additional cost. If an organization does not consider the fraud detection paragraph worthwhile, it can get a standard audit report. This report, however, would contain a disclaimer, similar to that of a product disclaimer on merchantability or fitness for a particular purpose, that would tell all interested parties that no guarantee is made regarding the existence of fraud. Just as with product warranties, the implied warranty provided in the audit statement could be excluded or modified by agreement between the parties.

6.4 Redesign Financial Statements

Many users find that audited financial statements lack information that is vital to their decision making. Net income figures and earnings per share are not enough. Some have called for the development of "consumer-oriented financial statements" that would provide additional information and greater utility to a third-party user's decision making [Schmidt and Sanborn, 1987]. These statements might be tied in with the auditor narrative discussed earlier where a brief interpretation of the statements is given. With additional information available, a user is less likely to cry foul and sue when a company goes under. If no fraud or negligence exists, an auditor can argue that the investor had been supplied with enough information to determine the company's fate. With the information revolution that is occurring and the abundance of data that is now available, new means should be examined to harness information, both financial and nonfinancial, and distribute it in a meaningful manner to interested parties. Financial statement presentation has not changed significantly since the turn of the century, yet information technology has. There may be a better method to provide third parties with information. While messengers of bad news usually get shot, auditors who do not inform often wind up with higher insurance premiums.

6.5 Seek Equity in Civil Liability

The huge damage awards or settlements in recent years have had a devastating impact on the profession. Major accounting firms (e.g., the seventh largest, Laventhol and Horwath) have ceased to operate under pressure of lawsuits at the expense of healthy competition in the profession. The profession should explore options for reforms that would provide a more equitable approach to determining liability at both the state and federal levels. Options at the state level include establishing a uniform professional corporation statute and modifying the apportionment of liability. On the federal level, legislating a ceiling on auditor liability and more clearly defining the standards and scope of transactions that give rise to liability would be beneficial. The accounting firms have already succeeded in attaining permission to organize as LLP (limited liability partnership) in many states and have mounted a campaign to pass federal legislation on limiting damage awards.

The Treadway Commission Report clearly states that FFR involves a number of players beyond the auditors. By bringing in other groups (internal auditors, the audit committee, board of directors) to the fraud detection arena, liability could be spread. In fact, internal auditors are already required by the *Standards for the Professional Practice of Internal Auditing* (IIA, 1978, Sect. 280.01) to "be alert to the possibility of intentional wrongdoing" and "to those conditions and activities where irregularities are most likely to occur." Recent surveys indicate that in fact, 47% of frauds in the United States and 32% of those in Canada were uncovered by internal auditors while only three percent of frauds in the United States and two percent in Canada were uncovered by external auditors [KPMG Peat Marwick, 1993 and KPMG Peat Marwick Thorne, 1993]. Thus, internal auditors are in a position to uncover fraud and should be held responsible to do so in court of law.

Distributing the liability, however, will not happen by itself. Lobbying should be mounted to have legislation drawn which would force the other groups identified in the Treadway Commission Report to accept their share of responsibility and liability for deceptive statements. For example, if board members on an audit committee were held liable for third-party losses sustained due to fraudulent management reporting, the audit committee members would be more zealous in insisting that the auditors look for fraud.

6.6 Institute Tougher Rules to Discourage Opinion Shopping

The profession should take a tougher stance to discourage opinion shopping. Commissioner Treadway cited opinion shopping as "an especially insidious pressure on the accounting function" [Treadway, 1986]. To deter this activity, a firm changing auditors should be required to have a paragraph inserted in its audit report for a period of time (e.g., two years) following the change stating that a new auditor has been retained. Such disclosure should give notice to users that there may have been a reporting problem with the former auditor. The stigma of having such a paragraph inserted in the opinion and broadcast to all third-party users should go a long way toward reducing the amount and frequency of opinion shopping. Only those with legitimate motives will be inclined to change.

6.7 Establish Regulated Fees

The current opinion shopping phenomenon is also contributing to the FFR dilemma by putting downward pressure on auditor fees. This cost pressure requires that an auditor do more for less, thus eroding the profit margin. Obviously, such competitive practices are good for price efficiency, yet they raise questions as to the quality of the service. Of special concern are intangible products that require judgment, such as that of an audit. Furthermore, can we economically justify price competition when users of audit reports find it hard to judge the quality of the service because of asymmetric information?

The following suggestion might be heresy to some, but perhaps a regulated fee structure such as in a "No Fault" insurance program with mandated levels of service is more appropriate. Such a program would better ensure that proper fraud protection and service is rendered in an audit. The fee could be based on a number of criteria such as the type of industry, the dollar value of sales, the size of the firm, or management's history. The concept might be similarly compared to and thought of as that of automobile insurance. When a driver insures his/her car, the premium is based on the cost of the car, where it is garaged and driven, how old it is, and who is driving it.

Quality of audit, service level and the firm's reputation would become the distinguishing factors for selecting an audit firm. This standard audit fee might add inefficiencies to the process and serve to raise the cost of an audit, but it would provide the safety and quality of service the public, the courts, and the legislature are asking for. The question remains as to whether the cost is worth the benefit.

6.8 Conduct Random Fraud Audits

If the cost to society of conducting fraud detection audits by every firm is too high, it may very well be in the best interest of all if the SEC require informational audits similar to those required by the Internal Revenue Service by randomly requiring a certain percentage of clients each year to have fraud detection audits. Thus, only a small number of clients will incur the extra cost of a fraud detection audit in any one year. It is hoped that such a requirement will result in a chilling effect on management considering fraudulent methods, and reduce audit costs.

In summary, the public's demand for accurate financial information has grown, while the public auditor is increasingly viewed as the provider of the accuracy assurance of the reported statements. In concert with their social responsibility, auditors must begin providing audits that more accurately reflect the popular understanding of their mission. A prompt attempt to enhance the quality of audits and their scope is needed. The profession has been gifted with self-regulation, yet, its hesitancy to address problematic issues has resulted in others — the courts and the Congress — chipping away at its positive public image and its power to govern itself.

ENDNOTES

1 Similar bodies were set up in other countries to deal essentially with the same issues. For example, the Canadian Institute of Chartered Accountants created the Commission to Study the Public's Expectations of Auditors, also known as the McDonald Commission [1988].

2 Although small accounting firms existed as early as 1866 (e.g., Veysey & Veysey was established in New York City in 1866 per Edwards [1968]) auditing as a profession was not recognized until 1896 when the State of New York passed a CPA law followed by the establishment of the New York Society of Certified Public Accountants in 1897 [Carey, 1969, p. 50]. By 1904, many states had state societies but no national professional organization existed. In 1904, 150 accountants met in the first accounting congress in St. Louis to establish the pillars of a federation that later became the American Institute of Certified Public Accountants.

3 The General Accounting Office issued a report in 1986 stating that CPAs did not satisfactorily comply with standards on 34% of the governmental audits they performed, and more than half of the unsatisfactory audits had severe violations of standards

[General Accounting Office, 1986]. Two prominent problems identified were insufficient audit work in testing compliance with governmental laws and regulations and the evaluation of internal accounting controls.

4 This denial of responsibility is not limited to the accounting profession in the United States. A recent article in the *Australian Accountant* states that keeping the auditor responsible is like blaming the fire brigade for arson. The article further states that (1) there is a confusion of the roles of directors and auditors; (2) there is a misunderstanding of the nature and inherent limitations of accounting and audits,"It is not widely appreciated that such material errors and irregularities can be very difficult to detect...." [Godsell, 1991, p. 26]; (3) there is a misconception that business failure in some way implies audit failure [Godsell, 1991].

5 Similar pressures were put on governmental actions in the early 1900s. For example, when the vice-chairman of the Federal Trade Commission, Edwin N. Hurley, advocated a standard system of bookkeeping and cost accounting in 1915, the then American Association of Public Accountants (AAPA) took a strong stand against it. After a lengthy discussion and lobbying, the AAPA suggested a reorganization and renaming of the Association to the American Institute of Accountants in 1917. The new organization then successfully argued for self-discipline and came up with detailed audit procedures that received endorsement from both the Federal Trade Commission and the Federal Reserve Board [see Carey, 1969, pp. 130–135].

6 Many questions were raised by the professional auditors at the AICPA National Conference on "Current SEC Developments," (Washington DC, January 11–12, 1994) that the author attended related to *SAS No. 53*. The extent of the questions were apparently to the point that John Sullivan, the then Chairman of the Auditing Standards Board, emphasized to his colleagues in public accounting that *SAS No. 53* was issued in 1988 requiring that auditors plan the audit for detection of fraud. Similarly, while the May 1993 issue of *The CPA Letter* had discussed the auditor's responsibility to detect fraud, a later issue revealed that "it is clear some members are still confused about their responsibility — and some commentators have objected to the position of the AICPA Board of Directors on the Matter," ["The Auditor's Responsibility ...," 1993, p. 5].

REFERENCES

Abdolmohammadi, M. J. and E. S. Levy. "Availability and Cost of Audit Committee Members," *Research in Accounting Regulation*, Vol. 6 (1992), pp. 149–162.

American Institute of Certified Public Accountants. *Cohen Commission Study on Cases Involving Audit Failures* (New York, NY: AICPA, 1976).

———. *Statements on Auditing Standards Nos. 53–58* (New York: AICPA, 1988).

———. *Codification of Statements on Auditing Standards, Numbers 1 to 15* (New York: AICPA, 1977).

Arens, Alvin A., and James K. Loebbecke. *Auditing: An Integrated Approach* (Englewood Cliffs, NJ: Prentice Hall, 1988).

Bates, H. L., J. V. Garbacik and J. E. McEldowney. "The Dingell Hearings: Accounting on Trial," *Business* (Jan–Mar 1986), pp. 55–59.

Berton, L., "Investors Call CPAs to Account," *The Wall Street Journal* (January 28, 1985), p. 30.

"Big Six Litigation Costs Skyrocket," *Public Accounting Report* (July, 1993), pp. 1, 4.

Buckley, J. W. and J. F. Weston. *Regulation and the Accounting Profession* (Belmont, CA: Lifetime Learning Publications, 1980).

Carey, J. L. *The Rise of the Accounting Profession: From Technical to Professional, 1896–1936* (New York: American Institute of Certified Public Accountants, 1969).

Chenok, P. "Outline of Presentation at the Auditing Luncheon in Toronto," *The Auditor's Report*, Vol. 14, No. 1 (Fall 1990), pp. 16–17.

Committee of Sponsoring Organizations of the Treadway Commission. *Internal Control: Integrated Framework* (New York: Committee of Sponsoring Organizations of the Treadway Commission, March 1991).

Connor, J. E. "Strengthening Public Confidence in the Accounting Profession," *Price Waterhouse Review*, Vol. 30, No. 1 (1986), pp. 2–8.

Defliese, P. L., H. R. Jaenicke, J. D. Sullivan and R. A. Gnospelius. *Montgomery's Auditing* (New York: Wiley, 1984).

"Dingell Voices Concerns on Accounting Profession at D.C. Meeting" *WG&L Accounting News* (Summer 1985), p. 10.

Edwards, J. D. "Some Significant Developments of Public Accounting in the United States," in *Contemporary Studies in the Evolution of Accounting Thought*, M. Chatfield, Ed. (Belmont, CA: Dickinson Publishing, 1968), pp. 196–209.

Elliot, R. K. and P. D. Jacobson. "The Treadway Report—Its Potential Impact," *The CPA Journal* (November, 1987), pp. 20–32.

Escott v. *Bar Chris Construction Corporation* (283 F. Supp. 643, 701 [S.D.N.Y., 1968]).

Gavin, T. A. "Discussant's Response to 'Under the Spreading Chestnut Tree' Accountants' Legal Liability — A Historical Perspective." Auditing Symposium VIII: Proceedings of the 1986 Touche Ross/University of Kansas Symposium on Auditing Problems (1986), pp. 24–30.

General Accounting Office. *CPA Audit Quality: Many Government Audits Do Not Comply with Professional Standards* (Washington, DC: General Accounting Office, GAO/AFMD-86–33, March 19, 1986).

Godsell, D. "Auditors' Legal Liability and the Expectation Gap," *Australian Accountant* (February 1991), pp. 22–28.

Grove, H., P. Lee,and G. Hanbery. "The Internal Auditor: Key Agent for Reduction of Fraudulent Financial Reporting," *Internal Auditing* (Summer, 1988), pp. 12–22.

Holstrum, G. L. "ASB Actions Concerning Fraud," *The Auditor's Report*, Vol. 14, No. 1 (Winter, 1991), pp. 1–3.

Institute of Internal Auditors. *Standards for the Professional Practice of Internal Auditing* (Altamonte Springs, FL: The Institute of Internal Auditors, 1978).

Kaplan, R. L. "Accountants' Liability and Audit Failures: When the Umpire Strikes Out," *Journal of Accounting and Public Policy*, Vol. 6, No. 1 (1987), pp. 1–8.

Kell, W. G., W. C. Boynton and R. E. Ziegler. *Modern Auditing* (New York: Wiley, 1986 [1990]).

Klott, G. "Auditors Feel The Heat of a New Scrutiny, *The New York Times* (May 13, 1984), p. 1F.

KPMG Peat Marwick, *Fraud Survey Results* (New York: KPMG Peat Marwick, 1993).

KPMG Peat Marwick Thorne, *Fraud Survey Results* (Kitchener, ON: KPMG Peat Marwick Thorne, 1993).

"Late Developments," *Journal of Accountancy* (April, 1985), p. 3.

Liebtag, B. "Profile: James C. Treadway, Jr." *Journal of Accountancy* (September, 1986), pp. 78–82.

Louis, A. M. "A Fat Maverick Stirs up the Accounting Profession," *Fortune* (December, 1970), pp. 96–99, 122–125.

Mednick, R. "The Auditor's Role in Society: A New Approach to Solving the Perception Gap," *Journal of Accountancy* (February, 1986), pp. 70–74.

Miller, R. D. "Governmental Oversight of the Role of Auditors," *The CPA Journal* (September, 1986), pp. 20–31.

Minow, N. "Accountants' Liability and the Litigation Explosion," *Journal of Accountancy* (September, 1984), pp. 70–86.

Morton, J. E. and W. L. Felix, Jr. "A Critique of Statement on Auditing Standards No. 55," *Accounting Horizons*, Vol. 5, No. 1 (March, 1991), pp. 1–10.

Moyer, C. A. "Early Developments in American Auditing" in *Contemporary Studies in the Evolution of Accounting Thought*, M. Chatfield, Ed. (Belmont, CA: Dickinson Publishing, 1968), pp. 188–195.

Muczyk, J. P., Smith, E. P. and G. Davis. "Holding Accountants Accountable: Why Audits Fail, How They Can Succeed?" *Business Horizons* (November–December, 1986), pp. 22–28.

National Commission for Fraudulent Financial Reporting, *Report of the National Commission of Fraudulent Financial Reporting* (NCFFR, 1987).

Olson, W. E. *The Accounting Profession: Years of Trial, 1969–1980* (New York: AICPA, 1982).

Ostling, P. J. "'Under the Spreading Chestnut Tree' Accountants' Legal Liability — A Historical Perspective." Auditing Symposium VIII: Proceedings of the 1986 Touche Ross/University of Kansas Symposium on Auditing Problems (1986), pp. 1–23.

Pae, P. "Do You Know Me? I Stole Millions — and Here's How," *The Wall Street Journal* (April 1, 1991), pp. A1, A6.

Pincus, K. V. "Discussion of Fraud Detection: The Effect of Client Integrity and Competence and Auditor Cognitive Style," *Auditing: A Journal of Practice and Theory*, Vol. 13 (Supplement, 1994), pp. 90–96.

Previts, G. J. and B. D. Merino. *A History of Accounting in America: An Historical Interpretation of the Cultural Significance of Accounting* (New York: Ronald Press, 1979).

Rosenblum v. *Adler* (461 A.D.D. 2d 138 [N.J. 1983]).

Rusch Factors, Inc. v. *Levin* (284 F. Supp. 85 [D.R.I. 1968]).

Ryan v. *Kanne* (170 N.W.2d 395 [1969]).

Sager, W. H. "Detecting and Reporting Financial Fraud—Fallout From the Dingell Hearings," *The National Public Accountant* (August, 1986), pp. 6–9.

St. Pierre, K. E. *Auditor Risk and Legal Liability* (Ann Arbor, MI: UMI Research Press, 1983).

"Should Auditors be Policemen Too?" *International Accounting Bulletin* (November 8, 1993), p. 6.

Schmidt, S. L. and R. H. Sanborn. "Consumer-Oriented Financial Statements: The Changing Role of the CPA," *Journal of Professional Services Marketing*, Vol. 3 (1987), pp. 247–256.

Taylor, D. H. and G. W. Glezen. *Auditing: Integrated Concepts and Procedures* (New York: Wiley, 1988).

"The Auditor's Responsibility to Detect Fraud," *The CPA Letter* (January 1994), pp. 5–6.

Tinker, T. *Paper Prophets: A Social Critique of Accounting* (New York, NY: Preager, 1985).

Treadway, J. C. "The National Commission on Fraudulent Financial Reporting: An Update," *Management Accounting* (September, 1986), pp. 24–27.

United States Senate: Committee on Governmental Affairs, Subcommittee on Reports, Accounting and Management. *Accounting and Auditing Practices and Procedures* (Washington, DC: US Senate, 1977).

Wall Street Journal, "Laventhol Says it Plans to File for Chapter 11," (November, 21, 1990).

Zick, J. W. "Self-Regulation of the Accounting Profession: It Works," *Vital Speeches* (May 1, 1985), pp. 429–431.

The Origin and Development of Survivors' Pensions in the Spanish Army: The First Military Pension Fund

M. Pilar Pérez
University of Valladolid
Spain

1.0 ABSTRACT

The Ordinances of April 20, 1761 determine the beginning of the first military pension fund with official character founded in Spain and that was going to be extended immediately to its American colonies. It is also the first system of compulsory social foresight which recognizes the right to a pension for military widows and orphans, and which served as a model for other similar associations created during the eighteenth century.

With our present work, we develop an introductory analysis of the reality of the Military Pension Fund: its organization, the most relevant tasks it had and the funds which it had to administer. We have chosen the first 30 years of its history because it coincides with the period during which *Diego Jose de Cosa* was facing the Treasury; he was in charge of presenting the annual countable information about the movement of the funds which would serve to demonstrate the progress of the institution. We also have some of the documents elaborated by *Antonio de la Portilla*, Accountant of the Military Pension Fund, whose mission was now reduced to supervising the accounts presented by the treasurer. However, he had a definite part in the analysis and control of the development of the Military Pension Fund by justifying reasonably and via documents the need for and movements of resources which took place since the opening of the institution.

2.0 INTRODUCTION

Social foresight, understood as a means of protecting workers and their families from poverty, has been subject to different regulations throughout history. In the concrete scope of the Spanish Army, we can find references to institutionalized aids for the so-called "Invalid" since the sixteenth century. On many occasions, the royal benevolence provided the necessities, not only for the wounded and aged military men but also for family members in case of the death of the former. However, these forms of assistance were received sporadically, conceived of more as alms than the beneficiary's right [Moles, 1962, p. 103].

As time passed, the systems of social foresight in the army became more objective. Therefore, we can contemplate the birth of a series of pension funds in the eighteenth century which has as its main purpose the protection of the widows and orphans of public servants and members of the armed forces.

Dating from April 20, 1761, Charles III ratified the Ordinances which determined the beginning of the first official Military Pension Fund founded in Spain and which would spread immediately to his Indian domains. This institution is also considered to be the first system of obligatory social foresight which recognizes the right to a pension fund for the widows and orphans of military men. Before this, a royal disposition had noted the annual delivery of a total of 6,000 doubloons (Spanish gold coin) among the widows of the officers. This is important because it does not cover all military personnel, but only the officers' widows who proved their poverty [A.G.S., S.G., leg 4465].[1] It was also prepared to give the equivalent of two months' "hood salary" to the widows to pay all the expenses of the funeral and two other honour salaries at Christmas to those who had no other kind of pension [A.G.S., S.G., leg 4467], etc.

The idea of constituting a fund to pay the future pensions seems to have emerged from a Neapolitan experience and about which the Marquis of La Mina knew when he was in those lands.[2] From there he took out a model for Rules which, after a long process of revision and adaptation, was presented for royal consent. The nearly ten years which had passed from the proposition presented by the Marquis until the beginning of the functioning of the Military Pension Fund are justified if we consider the following: although the creation of the institution seemed profitable for the Royal Treasury,[3] it was just going to be so insofar as it would achieve its aims with funds that were self-generated. Thus, the question to be asked was if the Military Pension Fund was capable of financing itself. Studying if the contributions of members were going to pay the future pensions, was a definite subject for debate. As in every awkward discussion, there were people who bet strongly on the Military Pension Fund while others clearly saw the inconveniences which this would bring. Among the people who opposed the proposition were the ones who did not want to reduce the already low salaries of the officers to widen the funds of the new institution,[4] while others thought that it was a comparative offense to create a Military Pension Fund for future widows and orphans, leaving aside those who had suffered this fate already. There were also alternative propositions to the Fund which had the same attendant character, for example, the creation of a school for military orphans.

Alternatively, the defendants of the Military Pension Fund supported their view because of the successful Neapolitan experience which was based principally on "reduction of eight *maravedis* by *escudo* (Spanish coin) which every one of the officers of the army, from the captain general to the ensign had deducted from their salary every month." To these expenses were added other rents which came from the investment of the funds of the Military Pension Fund in the banks and Neapolitan trade houses [A.G.S., S.G., leg 4421].

As we have noted in the preceding paragraphs, the idea of creating the Military Pension Fund prevailed and, at last, on April 20, 1761 the first "Regulation of the foundation and establishment of the Military Pension Fund" was approved. Furthermore, and due to the faulty application of it in American lands, the king would delimit again the "method and observance" to follow in his Royal Declaration of June 17, 1773 [National Library 3-68680]. With the passing of time and the accumulated experience in the management of the institution, the Regulation of 1761 began getting old and that is why, before the end of the century, on January 1, 1796, Charles IV would approve the "New Regulation for the Government of the Military Pension Fund in Spain and in the Indies" [General Archives of Argentina, 25-2-4, ff.310–336].

Our primary focus here is the activity of the Military Pension Fund from its beginning until the 1790s. The reason for choosing this period of time is simply our desire to show an appreciation for those who managed the accounts of the Military Pension Fund, the first accountant and first treasurer. Because of many documents that await analysis and some which remain to be found, this study is introductory in nature. We are, however, still able to determine how the institution was developed.

We are going to follow the steps of Diego de la Cosa through the "Wealth States" that he elaborated during the years he was in charge of the Treasury of the Military Pension Fund: from its inception until 1791. The accountant, Antonio de la Portilla, a particularly relevant person in the life of the institution, was responsible for many things: checking the treasurer's accounts; controlling the activity; budgeting the necessities of the funds; advising reasonably of the dangers to the Military Pension Fund and also of defending its rights. On many occasions, we can see through the analyzed documents, how the treasurer and the accountant jointly kept up with the Military Pension Fund, having been supported many times by the Government Council.

It is also easy to see from the documents Antonio de la Portilla's worries when he realized that the money received in the Military Pension Fund was insufficient to pay all the pensions. On many occasions and with well calculated accounts, he tried to make the persons in charge of the Government of the Military Pension see that the discounted quantities of the salaries of the officers, for as long as they lived, could never cover the funds of the pensions of the widows. In this way he would justify the many petitions for extraordinary aid to combat the compromises faced by the Military Fund which were increasing through time and attending many royal regulations.

Neither the treasurer nor the accountant of the Military Fund were going to achieve recognition for the job they were doing for the institution. In spite of their numerous petitions, they never had the nomination of "War Commissars" which is the professional category they thought fair, due to the tasks for which they were responsible.[5]

3.0 THE FIRST STEPS

When the creation of the Military Fund was set, it was a proposal by the Marquis of La Mina. It was clear that a first and inevitable step before its inception should be the correct establishment of regulations for the licences given to the officers to get married, considering that "not limiting the marriages ... it would be better not to establish the Military Fund or otherwise it would only serve for multiplying them to infinite." Although we are not going to consider the problems of the marriage licences, it is necessary to consider the importance that this subject had in the life of the Military Fund, because such licences were really the key to obtaining the benefits of the coming pensions. It was determined, generally, that the licences should only be given to marry "officers' daughters or noble parents' daughters either by origin or by privilege" or something similar. Still, except for those who were officers' daughters, they should all have brought a dowry which would guarantee their financial future.

> Every single woman whose parents or immediate grandparents have or have had bad or mean jobs were excluded from all licences, and among these particularly the artists' daughters or granddaughters, also those who are maids in any house and all kinds of merchants, unless he is a moneychanger or an account merchant; in the latter, the woman had to bring at least one thousand ducats to the dowry. [A.G.S., S.G., leg 4421]

Although the regulation was approved in 1761 this proposition was not sound. In the model presented by the Marquis of La Mina there was a point where the possibility of substituting the quantity of dowry as practiced in some Military Funds in Naples to compensate for the woman's low social ranking. The price which had to be paid "to prescind" from the origin of the woman was a dowry of at least eight thousand ducats.

Chapter IV in the Regulation of 1761 says that, except for specific questions, the officers will do what the Ordinance of October 30, 1760 demands regarding the prohibition of marrying the military officers who did not have royal permission. Apart from clearly explaining the process to follow in the request for the licence, the Regulation specifies the precise conditions that the woman has to fulfil in case she wants to marry an officer. Basically they coincide with the ones mentioned above in the Neapolitan Regulation although the endowment, consisting of either money or goods, that those who are not officers' daughters have to bring vary only slightly. It also established how to deal with the endowment brought as the dowry, which would not have been used by them without the Military Fund's permission.

If the King's authority was not requested, even if the woman fit the guidelines, the officer who got married would lose his job. Correspondingly, the widow would not have any right to the benefits of the Military Fund. In practice, there were married officers without a licence who later got the royal forgiveness in order to keep their jobs but this forgiveness would not be extended to their relationships with the Military Fund; therefore, the widows would not get the pensions.

4.0 GOVERNMENT AND ADMINISTRATION OF THE MILITARY PENSION FUND

The people in charge of the institution, under the Regulation of 1761, would be its director and two governors; there would also be an accountant with three officials, a treasurer with an official and the secretary of the Military Pension Fund.

The director would be the dean of the Supreme War Council, the two governors would be elected by the king among the rest of the members and the secretary would be the major official of the secretary of the mentioned Council. As far as the accountant and the treasurer were concerned, the Regulation says that they should be nominated by the king and "be practical people with the papers and accounts" ["Regulation ...," Chap. I, Art. 2]. The nomination of the previously mentioned accountant and treasurer would be executed for a limited time, in a different way than the two governors who were changed every year.

At least every week there was an Assembly with the director, the governors, the accountant, the treasurer and the secretary to deal with the subject of the Military Pension

Fund. In addition, every month there would be a "General Assembly" where apart from all the above mentioned people, all ministers and advisers of the War Council were present. In both cases the accountant, the treasurer and the secretary could speak but not vote ["Regulation ...," Chap. I, Art. 7].

In these assemblies they discussed the regular events of the institution knowing that "all the matters related to the economic and administrative aspects of the debits — *Cargo* — and credits — *Data* — of the Military Pension Fund will be for sole inspection by the director and governors of the Fund, but all the rest of the matters under discussion will be examined by the whole Council jointly with the Director and the Governors, and then their decisions transmitted to the Secretary of State and the War Department, so that We may determine what is most appropriate" ["Regulation ...," Chap. I, Art. 6]. The Assemblies had as an objective "finding out and promoting all the advantages which led to a greater conservation and increase of the Military Fund by all fair and regular means" ["Regulation ...," Chap. I, Art. 9]. If in the particular ones there was any doubt or quarrelsome point it would be brought to the first General Assembly so that the whole Council could be briefed, and the secretary of the Military Fund would have to write down in a book all the agreements. Besides that book, the secretary had three others: one to gather all the questions made to the king by the Government of the Military Fund, by itself or within the Council and another one to take note of all the royal resolutions destined to the Military Fund and a third one where the private letters were kept ["Regulation ...," Chap. I, Art. 10].

As far as the register of the executed operations of the Military Fund were concerned, the traditional system of the *Cargo and Data* was followed, giving the books to the different ministries; for example, the governor at that moment had the entry book and another with the exits, and once the six months of his dedication to the institution were finished, he had to show these books to the accountant so as to have the same criteria ["Regulation ...," Chap. I, Art. 11].

In the Regulation of 1761 the books that the accountant had to keep are not mentioned, although we can imagine that he had this task because of what is said in the third chapter about the control of wealth, articles one to six.

4.1 Entry of Funds

All these funds were received by the treasurer, who took charge of them "in the name of the Military Fund, giving receipts for the amounts, explaining where they came from, keeping copies and entering every detail in a book so as to acquire himself fully and correctly of his task."

The quantities of money owing to the Military Fund "have to go directly to the Treasurer with the precise intervention of the Accountant; He will have to keep a copy in his books of every receipt given by the Treasurer, and also he will have to write down all the items in a different book from the one that the Treasurer has to write down or register which will be the same as those notes of the Governor's ...."

4.2 Expenditure of Funds

No payment should be made

> without the particular permission, either of the whole Government of the Military Fund or of the Governor; but in both cases it has to be approved by the Accountant, without which condition it will not serve ....

> All the expenditures have to go through the Treasurer, who, the Governor of the moment and the Accountant having notice of them, obtains the receipts of the people he has paid money to, and then he can justify the amount of the expenditure with the approval of the Accountant and the Governor.
>
> All the expenditures which are made have to be written down by the Treasurer, with details in his Cashbook or "general Data book," and the Accountant will do the same — with even more detail — and will specify the persons who have made such expenditures or who have received the money.

There was, as was usual, a coffer with three keys: one for the director, the other for the governor and the third one for the treasurer. There they guard the wealth and nothing could be done without the three persons who had the keys and also the accountant who had to write everything down ["Regulation ...," Chap. I, Art. 12]. The information registered in the different books which the governors, the treasurer and the accountant had, had a precise moment for its verification: the one which showed the end of the command of the two governors of the institution. Every year, the governors with the accountant and the treasurer had to leave all the accounts of the Military Pension Fund resolved. They had a month to do so and also to elaborate a "General State which will gather with every detail the quantities which have been received and given during that year, and the money left in the Cash for the next year" ["Regulation ...," Chap. I, Art. 13]. This document would also have some notes clarifying everything so that the incoming governors knew the situation and the amount of money in the Military Fund. There would be three copies of it: one to be sent to the king, another for the director and the other for the new governors.

Besides the general revision, and beforehand, "the Government of the Military Fund with the War Council" asked the treasurer about the accounts once a year and they gave him the correspondent settlement of accounts which had already gone through the Accountant. ["Regulation ...," Chap. III, Art. 7].

5.0 ABOUT THE FUNDS OF THE MILITARY PENSION AND THEIR ORGANIZATION: THE REDUCTIONS

It would be very interesting to compare the funds foreseen to maintain the Military Pension Fund in what we could call the pre-regulation presented by the Marquis of La Mina with the ones which were approved afterwards for its establishment in 1761. So as not to go too far with this exposition, a high number of endowments which were the responsibility of the officers who got married were eliminated. This money represented a large sum and without it the Military Fund would have faced different circumstances.

If we limit ourselves to the Regulation approved ["Regulation ...," Chap. II, Art. 1 and 2], the wealths stipulated for the functioning of the Military Pension Fund were of two kinds: royal contribution and funds coming from the members. In the first group we can specify the following:

1. Six thousand annual doubloons (360,000 reals — Spanish silver coin). This royal assignment given as "fixed and perpetual contribution" was not to benefit the Military Fund immediately, because in this contribution there were some pensions given by the king to other military widows. In this way, those funds would go gradually to the Military Fund as the "old widow" members would die, and this did not happen until the nineteenth century [A.G.S., S.G., leg 6587].

2. Also as a fixed contribution it was given 20% of the "Spolium of the Episcopates of our Domains in Spain, Majorca and Prisons in Africa."
3. The reduction of eight maravedis by escudo on every pension given by royal privilege.
4. The sum of two payments, named until then "hood," to the military widows when these died. At the beginning only the widows with the right to a pension received funds, but from 1765, all would receive some, because that very Military Fund would be in charge of paying these widows [A.G.S., S.G., leg 4498].

According to the normal funds which would broaden the wealth of the Military Fund, the Regulation indicated ["Regulation ...," Chap. II, Art. 3 to 5]:

1. The half payment which would be reduced from their salaries "to all the General Officers and particulars from the Major States of our Sea and Land Army; to those from Castles and to their Aggregated; to those from Infantry, Gunnery and Navy; to those from Cavalry and Dragons; to those from the General Body of Gunnery; War and Ordering Commissioners, and to the Officers of our Royal House ...." This reduction would take place in six equal periods "a twelfth part of the payment every month." The invalid officers would not have this reduction because of their small salaries [A.G.S., S.G., leg 4473]. According to the Regulation, the Officers from the *Engineering Body* would also be excluded from this reduction "because they have their own Military Fund," but this privilege would soon disappear because they would join the General Military Pension Fund in October 1761 [A.G.S., S.G., leg 4466].
2. Reduction of eight *maravedis* by *escudo* on the salary of the above mentioned officers, began at the same time as those of the half payment, in May 1761. These would be taken away from the salary after having subtracted the reduction for the "Invalid."
3. The differences produced in the salaries in case of promotion: they would get the deduction in one period and this would happen every time there was a promotion.
4. The previous dispositions — first and third — were applicable to those who were serving the king at the date of the approving of the Regulation. Those who came in later would get a whole payment deducted, the one corresponding to the first month. In this way they would not have to pay the half payment and also the difference of salary foreseen in the third disposition, but only the one referred to in the first change of employment.

It was not easy to carry through the prescriptions related to the reductions. In fact, in practice many varied interpretations were given to the legal text. Because of this, and to settle definitely the method to be followed, the Royal Declaration of December 3, 1763 was issued, which not only had the written text but also practical examples of how to carry out the reductions in each particular case — making a distinction among those who were in the Military Fund since its creation and those who came after May 1, 1761, those who came from another Military Fund and finally, those who were called the Invalid [A.G.S., S.G., leg 4477].

In addition to the normal funds mentioned and those assigned by the king, the Regulation specified that the inheritances of all the military members who died without having made a will and without having left heirs should be given to the Military Fund. The only established restriction by royal will to this inheritance was made to the feudal wealth that "because of their origin should go to the Royal Crown" ["Regulation ...," Chap. II, Art. 11]. In fact, the Military Fund only had entrances of this kind twice, in 1798 and 1794 (at least this data only appears twice in the treasurer's accounts) [A.G.S., S.G., leg 6579 and 6584].

As time went by, and because of the difficult periods through which the institution passed, the king would ask for other contributions, as something perpetual or eventual, situated as contributions as Temporalities (1769), Vacant of Indias (1779), Taxes paid by the church (1784), etc.[6] In Exhibit 1, we can see that 60% of the total of the funds collected by the Military Fund between 1761 and 1794 came from the members; 40% came from the Royal Wealth as other resources of the Military Fund.

Exhibit 1

Origin of the Resources Received by the Military Fund (1761–94)

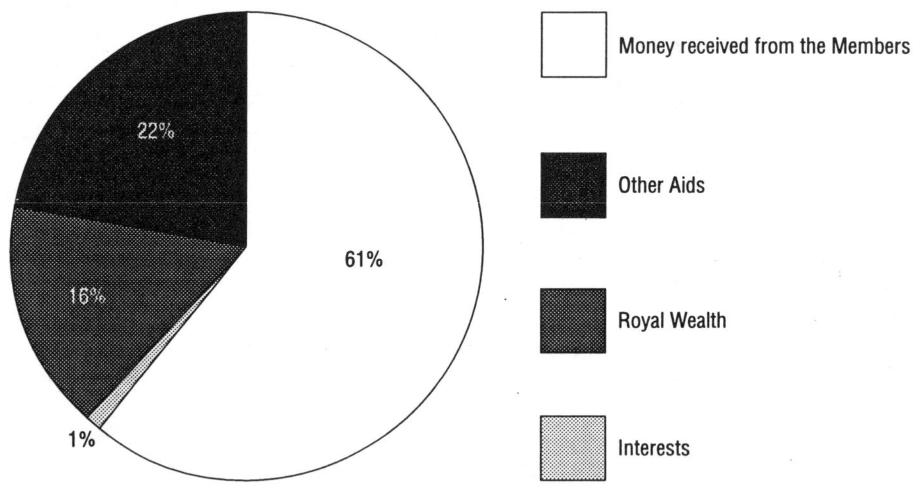

A very interesting aspect which is contemplated in the Regulation of 1761 is the necessity "to give time to the Military Fund so that it can collect the funds and can be organized so as to execute its obligations." Although they started to receive money from May 1761, the pensions and benefits "would start and be current from the first of January in 1762 ...." ["Regulation ...," Chap. IV, Art. 1]. This waiting period had its origin in the pre-regulation of the Marquis of La Mina, where the stipulated time to begin to pay the pensions was established as being four years, which would have been a more advantageous period of time in which to start correctly.

The payments of the pensions which were contemplated in the Regulations referred only to those who had become widows after May 1, 1761. The rest of the widows had no right to the benefits of the Military Fund as their husbands had not had any reduction in salary. Still, so as not to forget them, the king proposed to give them 250,000 reals, which would become 375,000, a year, "pro rata division depending on the husband's rank." This would not be given to those who had received 6,000 doubloons or of any other kind [A.G.S., S.G., leg 4467].[7]

The above mentioned 250,000 reals had to be taken from the 20% that the Military Fund had received from the Spolium and Vacants of the Episcopates and also from the reduction of eight *maravedis* by *escudo* imposed on every member, "ever since the rest of the funds of the Cash are sufficient to satisfy the pensions to the modern widows" ["Regulation ...," Chap. IV, Art. 2]. When the amount was increased to 375,000 reals, the king suggested getting the difference — 125,000 annual reals — from the remaining quantity of 6,000 doubloons [A.G.S., S.G., leg 4462].

Until 1773, as we can see in Exhibit 2, the Military Pension Fund gave the pensions to the old widows using other resources apart from those assigned to them. From this date, the whole of the resources coming from reductions to pensioners, from the remainder of the 6,000 doubloons and, especially, from 20% of Vacants, were much more than were needed to pay the old widows and so they could be destined to cover other necessities of the institution. These needs were basically those derived from the payment of the modern pensions since, as it can be deduced from Exhibit 3, the resources coming from the members were highly insufficient.

Exhibit 2
Pensions Paid toOld Widows 1761–94

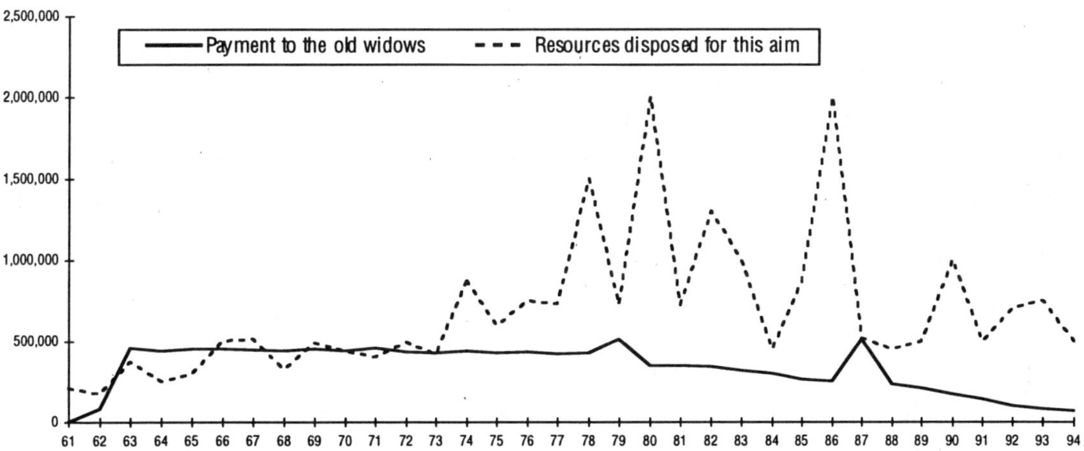

Exhibit 3
Evolution of Pension Funds and Payments 1761–94

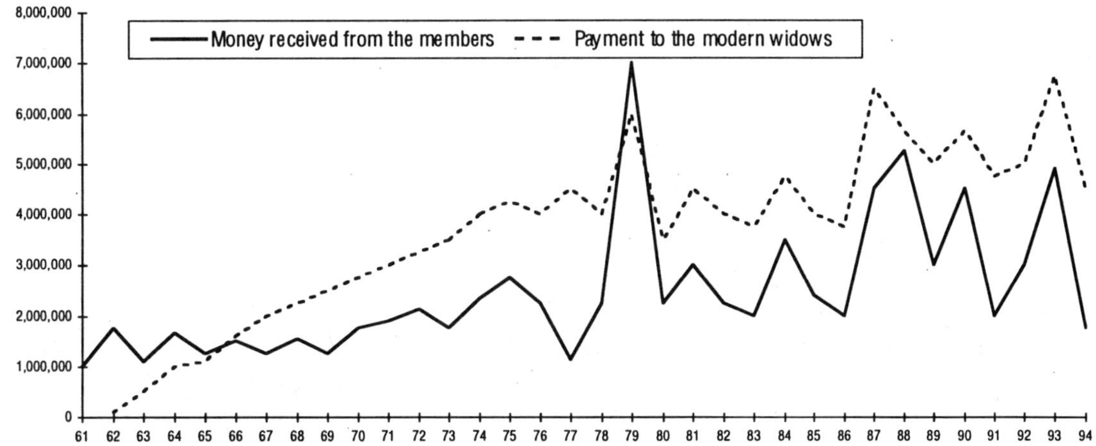

In the Regulation of 1761, everything related to the quality of the widows who were to receive a pension and the corresponding amounts were discussed. The quantities received were always the same, depending on the position occupied by the husband at his death, independent of the number of children or relatives the widow had to maintain. It is also ruled in detail when the pension had to go to the children or to the deceased military man's mother. In the case of the children, it was determined that they should receive the pension up until the age of 18 for sons and for the daughters, the date at which they changed their marital status. With regard to the latter, and due to the economic difficulties experienced by the Military Fund, there was a time when the limit at which to receive the pension was the age of 25. When daughters passed that age they did not receive anything further. Also, during some years the Military Fund thought that it could reduce the pensions paid to the widows if the Fund arranged a new marriage, in which case they would get just half of the pension.[8] As this did not achieve the results they were expecting, they suspended total payment of the pensions to the widows who remarried [A.G.S., S.G., leg 4497].[9] However, the casuistry related to the widows who received the pensions from the Military Fund was very extensive and too difficult to summarize in a few pages.

6.0 ABOUT THE SPECULATION WITH THE WEALTH OF THE MILITARY PENSION FUND

A chapter of great importance in the life of the Military Fund, if we consider the Regulation, was going to be the management of the remaining wealth which, as it is said in the ninth article of the second chapter, there should not be "any death in the Cash." The legal text insisted upon the necessity of multiplying the wealth of the Military Fund so that it could make all the necessary payments. Due to this, "its Government within the War Council, were gathered to think and propose without wasting time, by certain advantageous means to use the money in the Cash of the Military Pension Fund."

The set conditions to guarantee the security of the funds were "not to put the benefit in hands of private businessmen if they do not have or do not give as mortgage the goods corresponding to the whole of the pay-back of the capital and its interests, and no portion of the money should be used in sea trade of any kind, unless it is executed through an insurance company by which any danger towards the funds could be avoided" ["Regulation ...," Chap. II, Art. 9].

The information given in the account document that we have used is very limited, although the Regulation foresees the existence of a key book where all public writings related to such operations should be copied, but we have not found it.

There were not many opportunities for the Military Fund to invest the funds because it needed the help of others to stay in existence, but it could not find them even by paying an interest premium [A.G.S., S.G., leg 4497]. There is evidence of the imposition in the *Five Gremios* in Madrid at the beginning of the Military Fund: in 1767 it had 3,300,000 reals with a rent of 3% a year.[10] This experience was not going to last long, because in 1770 part of the money was needed to pay all the current expenses, and it continued spending this money until it was all spent in 1775. Since then, there would be no occasion to invest until the end of the 1780s when the situation of the Military Fund allows for the precise permission to acquire "*royal vales*," which would produce a good benefit. After this, they diversify the portfolio and they buy shares of the "*Royal Loan*," "*vales of the Channel*" are bought, etc. [A.G.S., S.G., leg 6585].

Up to this moment, we have not been able to find enough information to determine the model followed by the Military Pension Fund to control its investments, especially those carried out from the 1790s. Everything aims at, as in the case on the imposition of the *Five Gremios,* simple notes of entries and exits of money: charges and credits. When they invested funds it was considered to be an exit in the *Data* and when the interests were received they registered as a cause of the *Cargo* the money received. What is never going to appear as registered is the whole of the investment accumulated at every moment. It is true that if we consider all complete series of charges and credits, as in the summaries of the treasurer, it does not initially seem difficult to sum up the investments of each period of time to obtain the total, but the reality is far too complex, especially when the financial assets acquired by the Military Fund start to diversify.

7.0 CONCLUSION

As we have already said in our introduction, there is still a lot to do in the analysis of the activity of the Military Pension Fund. It is not only a question of investigating the criteria followed in the counting of its financial investments, but also of explaining in detail the accounting order conceived by Antonio de la Portilla to register all the operations of the Military Fund. It does not show the detailed evolution of the *cargos* and *datas,* and the problems brought by the use of the criterion of coffer instead of that of earnings when they had to see the *cargos* and *datas* of each period.

In other respects, it will be interesting to know not only the impression created by the Military Fund in America, but also what the Indian contribution meant to the maintenance of the institution in Spain, because in many situations the foreign funds were the resources that avoided decay.

There is a lot to do in the future and we will surely discover apart from all the data mentioned before, the figures of some people who worked hard and contributed to the progress of the accounting discipline.

ENDNOTES

1 Archivo General de Simancas (A.G.S.), Secretaría de Guerra (S.G.), legajo (leg) 4465. From this document it is understood that on May 5, 1721, 6,000 doubloons were deposited in the Major Treasury for widows of officers who had died from 1717 onwards.

2 This hypothesis is actually being studied intensively by Professor Martínez Casado, of the University of Buenos Aires, who is the person who introduced this topic, and supported me in the study of the economic and accounting aspects of the Military Pension Fund.

3 As an example, just consider May 1, 1761, when the Royal Treasury was paying the pensions for 323 widows [A.G.S., S.G., leg 4467], this without considering the ones who had other kind of aids.

4 In fact, they were already suffering from deductions of eight *maravedis* — Spanish copper coin — for the "invalid" people and a three percent for other expenses. (A.G.S., S.G., leg. 4465).

5 The document which points out the refusal of the first petition is dated on September 13, 1766. Later they would ask for the nomination of Accountant and Treasurer of the Army, receiving another negative answer. Only Antonio de la Portilla, at the end of his

professional life, obtained the title of Accountant of the Army, but not in gratitude for his contributions but because it was established under general rule "for everyone who from now onwards would get those kinds of jobs." [A.G.S., S.G. leg 6582]

6 The dates in parentheses do not mean the moment of the concession of aids but the date the first money is received by the Military Fund.

7 They justified the right of 864 old widows to have some of the 375,000 reals.

8 Royal Declaration of December 2, 1768.

9 The previous Royal Declaration of May 17, 1777 is drawn back.

10 Curiously, in compliance with the data gathered, the interests received from the *Five Gremios* increase when part of the money is taken away to be invested. For example, in 1769 when the investment reaches the quantity of 3,300,000 reals, the counted interest was of 9.000 reals; in 1770, 300,000 reals are obtained from the *Gremios* and the interest goes up to 100,500; in 1771, 500,000 reals are obtained and the interest was 132,473.

REFERENCES

Archivo General de Simancas, Secretaria de Guerra, legajo [A.G.S., S.G., leg] — General Archives of Simancas), Valladolid, Spain.

General Archives of Argentina. Colonial Government IX, Buenos Aires, Argentina.

Moles, Ricardo, R., "Historia de la prevision social en Hispanoamerica," Depalma, Buenos Aires, 1962.

National Library, Madrid, Spain.

"Regulation of the Foundation and the Establishment of the Military Pension Fund (1761)." National Library (Madrid, Spain), 2-65906.

The Royal Exchequer's Book of Current Accounts with the Capital Proceeding from Pepper that Sunda Paid in the Year 1743[1]

Manuel Rodrigues Benavente
Associaçao Portuguesa de Tecnicos de Contas
Lisbon, Portugal

1.0 ABSTRACT

This small book written by hand and not even bound, is catalogued with the number 47—*Casa dos Contos* (House of Accounts), in the Historical Archives of the Audit Department of the Exchequer in Lisbon.

It is a book of accounts that covers a period between 1743 and 1760 and it tells us, in a remarkable way, not only how commercial exchanges were made, but also gives us an idea about the unusual way in which accounts were kept at the time.

The Portuguese State in India had ancient matters of contention with its neighbours—the Indian leaders—who were either allies or enemies. They were fighting over several issues; however, almost all these issues were a consequence of a clash of cultures and mentalities between the European colonists and the east natives.

In this context and after a long war with the King of Sunda—a territory near Goa—which would continue for many years, the Portuguese defeated the Sunda—as he was known—and he was obliged to make the necessary investment required to reconstruct the two provinces, Ponda and Zambaulim. The Portuguese mediated that payment which consisted of 40,000 *xelins* (shillings), the Goa's local currency.

This book describes precisely the accountancy of these 40,000 *xelins*.

The accountancy and other things ...

2.0 INTRODUCTION

The document that, as we have already said, is stored in the Historical Archives of the Audit Department of the Exchequer in Lisbon, is a copy from an original document which was properly attested in 1771. This document refers to the period between 1743 and 1760 and everything indicates that it was kept in Goa, the Portuguese State of India.

Why is it a copy? This copy was carried to Lisbon probably because the accounts had to be examined by the Royal Exchequer, which was the supervising body of the Public Accountancy in Portugal from December 22, 1761 onwards.

The document is divided in two parts: the first is epistolary, the other is a current account. The epistolary section may also be divided into three parts:

- a table of contents
- a piece of news reporting the existence of the 40,000 *xelins* (shillings)
- a letter sent from the Secretary of the Reign, Diogo de Mendonca Corte Real, who was in Lisbon, to the Exchequer's Inspector of the State of India.

The part that deals with the accountancy has a very interesting feature, which is that the information is given in double-entry and it goes back to a period—from 1743 to 1760—where it was not compulsory. In fact, it was the *Erario Regio*, the supervising body of the Public Accountancy in Portugal created in December 1761, that imposed the method of double-entry bookkeeping on the Public Accountancy.

The book may be easily read, though it is in a deplorable state, and it consists of twenty pages which are not bound. The registrar's handwriting is excellent.

3.0 ABOUT THE 40,000 *XELINS*

The Portuguese State of India was formed by three territories: Goa, Damao and Diu. Goa, the biggest territory, had established its capital city in Pangim.

As we have already mentioned, the King of Sunda paid 40,000 *xelins* (shillings) to the Portuguese for the expenses made by the State of India in the reconstruction of the Ponda and Zambaulim provinces.

King John V of Portugal ordered that this capital should be kept separately and should circulate in the ships of the reign. The payment made by Sunda was mixed: 10,000 *xelins* in cash and 30,000 in candins (an ancient dry measure) of pepper, considering that each *candil* (the ancient measure) corresponds to 200 *xelins.*

Before we go any further, Exhibit 1 explains the coins and units of weight that were used at the time in the Portuguese State of India.

In the middle of the eighteenth century, a Goan shilling was worth about 180 Portuguese *reis*. With 2,000 shillings, one could buy about a kilo of gold. We may say that a ton (2,240 lb) of pepper was roughly equivalent to about half a kilo of gold.

So we have divided the allotment of the debt into two parts. First, we shall see how they justify the 10,000 *xelins* (shillings) in cash.

From the 10,000 *xelins* (shillings) sent by the Sunda, 1861 *xelins* and 48 *reis* were spent on the transport of the pepper by a certain Goinda Naique. We do not have any information about the existence of the 8,131 *xelins*, 4 *tangas* and 12 *reis* so the Exchequer of Goa does not have any choice, except to wisely assume that they were spent with the State's expenses... (See Document 1.)

Exhibit 1

Units of Weight and Currency in use in the Portugese State of India

Units of Weight

1 *candil*	=	4 hundredweight	=	235.037 kg
1 *quintal* (1 hundredweight)	=	4 *arrobas* (each *arroba* = 32 pounds)	=	58.758 kg
1 *arroba*	=	32 *arrateis*	=	14.680 kg
1 *arratel* (sometimes used like 1 pound)	=	16 *oncas* (ounces)	=	459.058 g
1 *onca* (ounce)	=	28.691 g		

Units of Weight (Precious Metals)

1 *marco*	=	8 *oncas* (ounces)	=	64 *oitavas*	=	4,608 *graos*	=	229.504 g
1 *onca* (ounce)	=	8 *oitavas*	=	576 *graos*	=	28.691 g		
1 *oitava*	=	72 *graos*	=	3.586 g				
1 *grao*	=	0.048 g						

Goa's Currency

1 *xelin* (shilling)	=	5 *tangas*	=	300 *reis*
1 *tanga*	=	60 *reis*		

Document 1

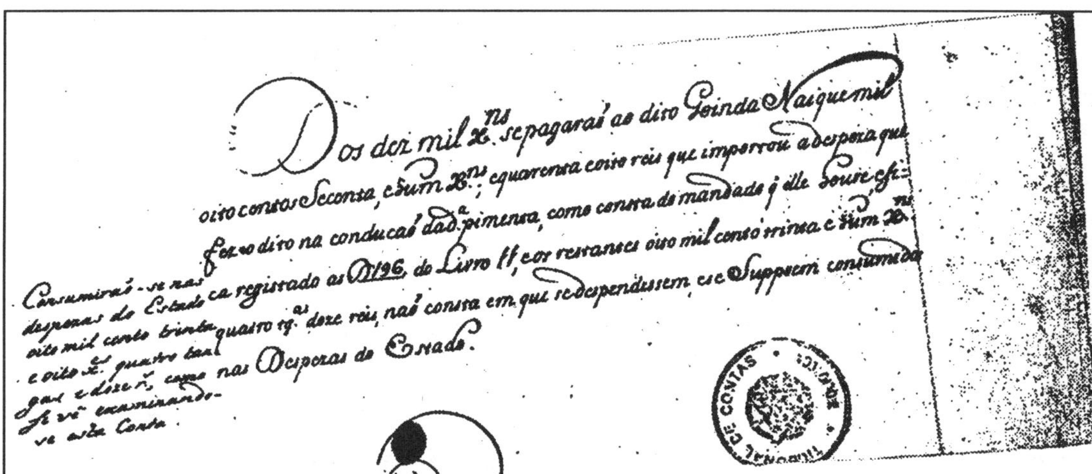

We shall now examine the pepper accounts.

The 150 *candins* from the Sunda's kingdom that came from the above mentioned pepper, were reduced to only 133 *candins*, 2 *quintais*, 3 *arrobas* and 31 *arrateis* according to Goa's unit of weight. Comparing these values with the current units of weight we have about 31 tonnes and 435 kg, which were charged to the steward Manuel Carvalho da Silva. The reason why there is a difference of 16 *candins*, 1 *arroba* and 1 *arratel*—more than 3,700 kg—is explained in the margin of the document as a "loss."

From the 133 *candins* of pepper, that is to say 534 *quintais*, 100 *quintais* were sent to the "Trustee of Her Royal Highness the Queen Our Ladyship's Treasury," which consisted of an account of what the State's Treasury had taken from the Queen's capital, to face the wars in the North, that occurred in the Portuguese State of India.

So, there are 434 *quintais,* 3 *arrobas* and 31 *arrateis* of pepper remaining, which finally went to Lisbon in January's monsoon of the year 1743. There were two shiploads: one of 148 *quintais* and 3 *arrateis* in the ship *S. Francisco Xavier;* the other of 286 *quintais,* 3 *arrobas* and 18 *arrateis* in the ship *Nossa Senhora da Conceicao.*

Now we shall start with the Goa's Royal Exchequer's current accounts. With the capital proceeding from the pepper that Sunda paid in the year of 1743 which was sent subsequently to Lisbon in January's monsoon of the same year, it was His Majesty who was served by sending His product to India. He commanded that this capital should be kept separate and should circulate in the trade in the ships of the Kingdom.

Before analyzing the current accounts, we shall see what the letter of April 2, 1751 says. This letter was sent to the Exchequer of the State of India's Inspector by the Secretaty of State Diogo de Mendonca.

It starts by saying that it was very strange that since 1743 nobody rendered accounts about the capital that was circulating. The letter also mentions that the Marquis Viceroy and the Exchequer's Inspector—to whom the letter is addressed—did not notice the reasons why the circulation of the capital was interrupted.

The viceroy to whom the letter refers is still the Marquis of Alorna, though, by that time, there was another viceroy, the Marquis of Tavora. Diogo de Mendonca is surprised as he did not get any information about the gold and *patacas* valuing 10,350$134 *reis,* that had been sent from Lisbon during the monsoon in 1747.

He finishes the letter demanding, in the name of the king, that the accounts should be rendered.

Notably, this letter, which is registered in Goa in November 1751, will be instituted from 1752 on. It explains why all the accounts between 1744 and 1751 were not kept up to date and why nobody cared to make the proper entries later, in the appropriate dates.

The current account starts in 1744 with two payments that are used to discharge the pepper loads which arrived in Lisbon in 1743, as follows:

- 2,568 packets of glass beads were shipped in the *Madre Deus* in Lisbon, in April, and they made a sale in Mozambique, where they were exchanged in September for 152 ivory tusks. In October of the same year, this ivory was sold in Diu for 25,958 *xelins,* 2 *tangas* and 30 *reis*. With this money, horses were bought to serve in Goa's army.
- 2,568 packets of glass beads were shipped in the *Nossa Senhora da Caridade,* in the same monsoon of April 1744. They arrived in Goa in September where they were sold to the Mozambique's Board of Commerce for 17,976 *xelins.*

As it is Goa's Exchequer who is responsible for the transport, it charges 35% as an assurance against damages in the value of 6,291 *xelins* and 3 *tangas,* (17,976 x 35%).

Goa's Exchequer also charges interest of about 10% a year for the delay of the debt after the expiration of the term and the interest was calculated in an amount of 12,583 *xelins* and 1 *tanga* from 1745 to 1752 (17,976 x 10% x 7 years).

Now we comment on this:

1. The high term rate of the insurance—35% of the value of the shipload—really shows the fragility of the ships and also the risk of sea robbery that existed on the sea routes.

2. The expiration date of the term only occurs when the ship *Barroquinha* arrives in Goa in September without any means of payment. In fact, the ship left Goa for Mozambique in January 1745 and only nine months later, when it returned, the date of the term starts.

3. The accuracy used to calculate the expiration of the term. In fact the ship *Barroquinha* returns to Goa on September 21, 1745 and the 10% interest per year is calculated from 22 October, 1745 on, which means exactly 30 days after the date of the arrival, just as we do presently in a normal procedure with any bill.

4. The debt of seven years' worth of interest—from 1745 to 1752—and with the date of 1744 is created all at once. Therefore, it is a consequence of the letter from the Secretary of State Diogo de Mendonca that we have mentioned already. So the "administration of the capital proceeding from pepper," which is the responsibility of Goa's Exchequer, did not have any accounting support during all this time.

Then comes another entry as follows, no less curious, with the date of 1747:

- 10,350$134 *reis* in *patacas* that came from Lisbon, which pays for a previous shipload of pepper in 1745. This shipload of pepper is not registered and is not even counted. That pepper whose value also is not registered should pay 838 silver *marcos* (an ancient coin) in *patacas* coming from Goa in 1744 in the ships *Madre de Deus* and *Caridade*. Goa's Exchequer promises at once to investigate the amount of money produced by the selling of the silver in Goa's currency and how much pepper was sent to Lisbon in exchange ....

It is important to say that *pataca* is a Brazilian silver coin which was worth 320 Portuguese *reis*. This Brazilian *pataca,* which was known also as Portuguese *pataco,* corresponded to 8 *cobres,* and one *cobres* had the value of 40 *reis*.

In 1755—eight years later—an entry appears indicating a difference in a purchase of pepper of 1,396 *xelins,* 1 *tanga* and 30 *reis,* which is related to the previous entry because of a note in the margin of the folio which says the following:

- The 838 silver *marcos* in *patacas* from 1744, produced, by Goa's measure, only 818 *marcos,* 1 *onca* and 5 *oitavas,* which by Goa's currency is 31,582 *xelins,* 3 *tangas* and 12 *reis*.

Goa's Exchequer explains that in 1745 it sent to Lisbon 510 *quintais,* 1 *arroba* and 8 *arrateis* of pepper, at 258 *xelins* each *candil,* which makes 32,978 *xelins,* 4 *tangas* and 43 *reis*. The difference between the two values is exactly the entry made in 1755, which is to say 1,396 *xelins,* 1 *tanga* and 30 *reis*.

Curiously, the formal control exercised by the Royal Exchequer detects and records an error of half a "real," so the exact value would be 1,396 *xelins,* 1 *tanga* and 30 *reis* and a half ... (See Documents 2 and 3.)

From 1752 onwards, the accountancy starts to match more or less with the respective dates. It is also curious that, perhaps because of the change in policy—the King is now Joseph I, his Minister is Carvalho e Melo and administrative centralism is at its inception—or perhaps because some doubts were cast upon Goa's Royal Exchequer, or perhaps because of both of the aforesaid reasons, only two types of registers will exist: by debit, the interests of the debt of the Mozambique Administration; by credit, the sales of pepper to Lisbon. It seems that someone wants the administration of the capital made by Goa's Exchequer to end; that is to say, by exhausting the circulating assets. Let us now see the evolution of the balance of the accounts of the administration of the capital proceeding from pepper:

- January 1753: 98,072 *xelins*
- January 1756: 65,013 *xelins*
- January 1757: 42,158 *xelins*
- January 1758: 24,089 *xelins*

Document 2

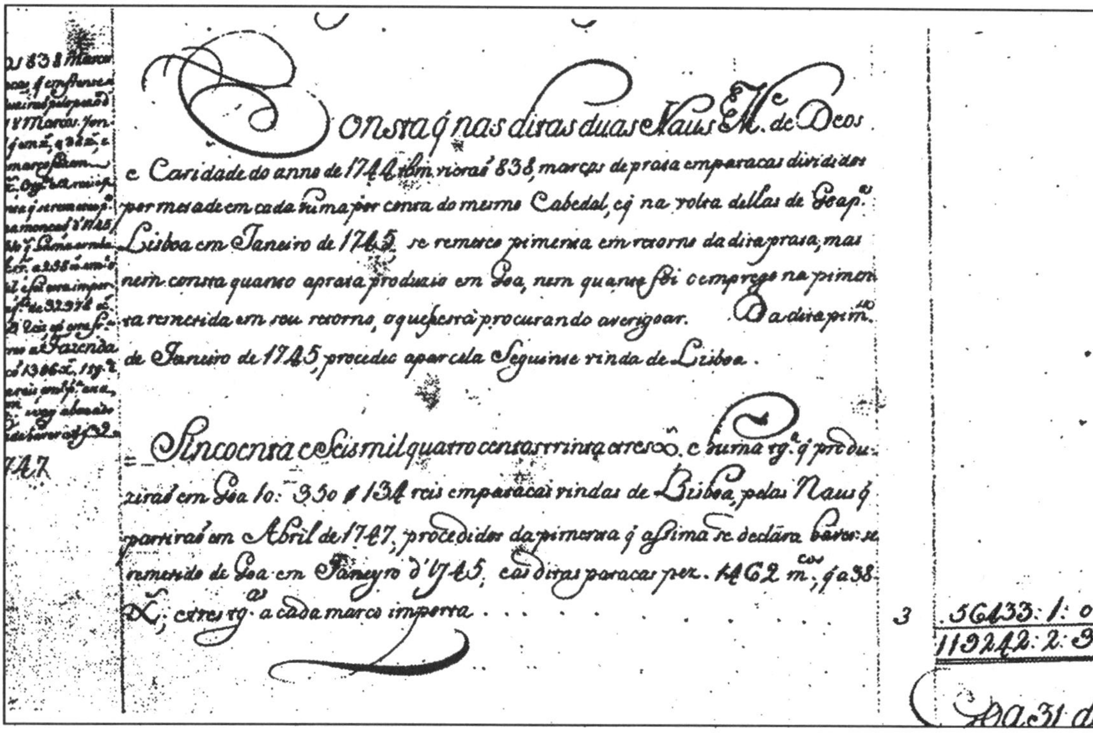

Consta q. nas ditas duas Naus N. S. M.e de Deos e Caridade do anno de 1744 vieraõ 838 marcos de prata em patacas divididos por metade em cada huma por conta do mesmo Cabedal, e q. na volta dellas de Goa p.a Lisboa em Janeiro de 1745 se remeteo pimenta em retorno da dita prata, mas nem consta quanto a prata produzio em Goa, nem quanto foi o emprego na pimenta remetida em seu retorno, o que se estará procurando averiguar. Da dita pim.ta de Janeiro de 1745 procedeo a parcela seguinte vinda de Lisboa.

Sincoenta e seis mil quatro centos trinta e tres x.s e huma tg.a q. produziraõ em Goa 10:350$134 reis em patacas vindas de Lisboa pelas Naus q. partiraõ em Abril de 1747, procedidos da pimenta q. assima se declara haver-se remetido de Goa em Janeyro d' 1745, cujas ditas patacas pez. 1462 m.cos q a 38 x.s e tres tg.as a cada marco importa . . . . . 3 | 56433:1:00

119242:2:30

Goa 31 de

Document 3

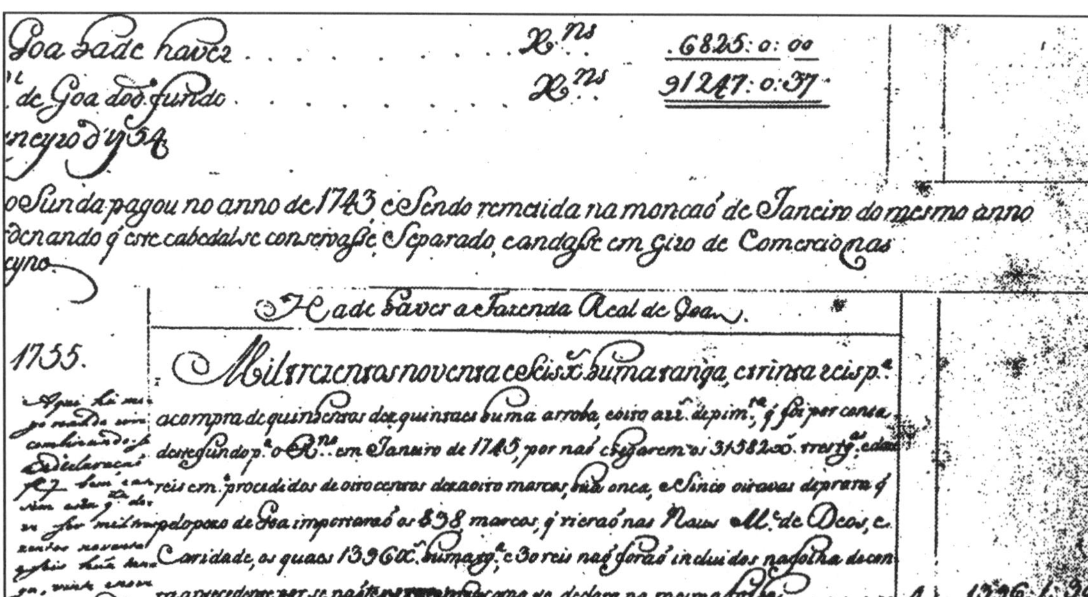

Goa ha de haver . . . . X.ns .6825:0:00

de Goa do d.o fundo . . . . . . X.ns 91247:0:37

neyro d' 1754

o fundo pagou no anno de 1743 e sendo remetida na monçaõ de Janeiro do mesmo anno ordenando q. este cabedal se conservasse separado, andasse em giro de Comercio nas eyno.

Ha de haver a Fazenda Real de Goa.

1755. Mil trezentos noventa e seis x.s huma tanga, e trinta reis p.a a compra de quinhentos dezaquinsaes huma arroba, e oito arr.s de pim.ta q. foi per conta deste fundo p.a o R.no em Janeiro de 1745, por naõ chegarem os 31582 reis em procedidos de oito centos dezaoito marcos, huã onça, e sinco oitavas de prata q. do peso de Goa importaraõ os 838 marcos, q. vieraõ nas Naus N. M.e de Deos, e Caridade, os quaes 1396 x.s huma tg.a e 30 reis naõ foraõ incluidos na folha decen ta antecedente por se naõ [redacted] como se declara na mesma folha . . . . 4 | 1396:1:30

In the second half of the 1750s the entries are more synthetic and scarce in information and they do not describe the quantities of pepper nor even the respective costs per unit.

In the year 1756, a sale of 23,841 *xelins*, 3 *tangas* and 47 *reis* is mentioned, which constitutes the difference between the sales of pepper—1752–53 and 1756—and the entry of half doubloons (ancient gold coins) in 1754–55.

In 1757, the inspection of the Royal Exchequer reveals the absence of 797 *xelins* and 3 *tangas* from a balance that has been transcribed. (See Documents 4 and 5.)

Until 1760, the debts of interest owed to the Administration of the Trade of Mozambique continue to mount and also the credits for the pepper shiploads to Lisbon.

Document 4

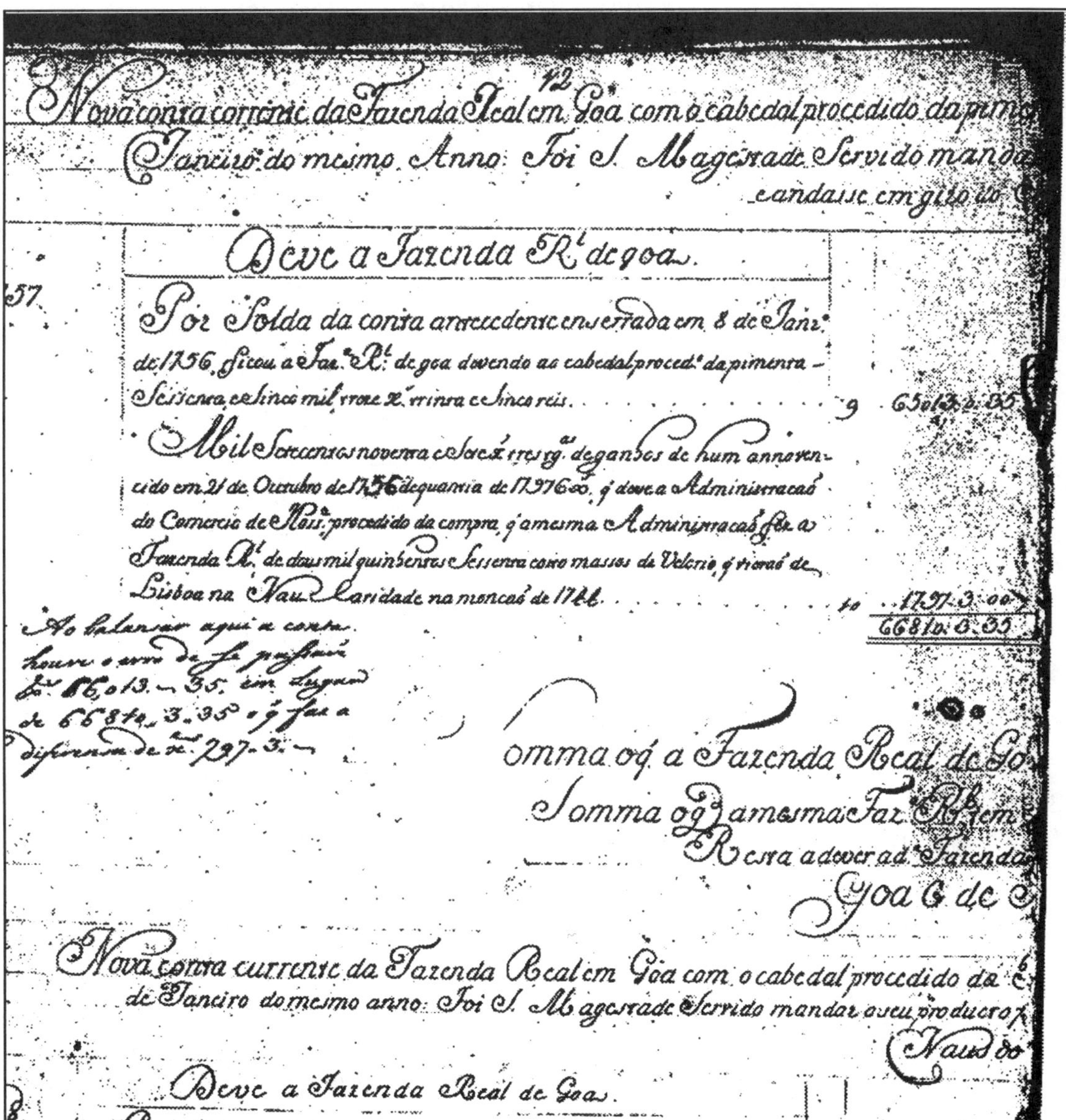
Nova conta corrente da Fazenda Real em Goa com o cabedal procedido da pim
Janeiro do mesmo Anno: Foi S. Magestade Servido manda
Deve a Fazenda Rl de goa.
Por Solda da conta antecedente enserrada em 8 de Janro de 1756, ficou a Faza Rl de goa devendo ao cabedal procedo da pimenta Sessenta e sinco mil treze xs trinta e sinco reis ... 65013.2.35
Somma o q a Fazenda Real de Go
Somma o q a mesma Faz Rl
Nova conta corrente da Fazenda Real em Goa com o cabedal procedido da
de Janeiro do mesmo anno: Foi S. Magestade Servido mandar o seu producto
Deve a Fazenda Real de Goa.

Document 5

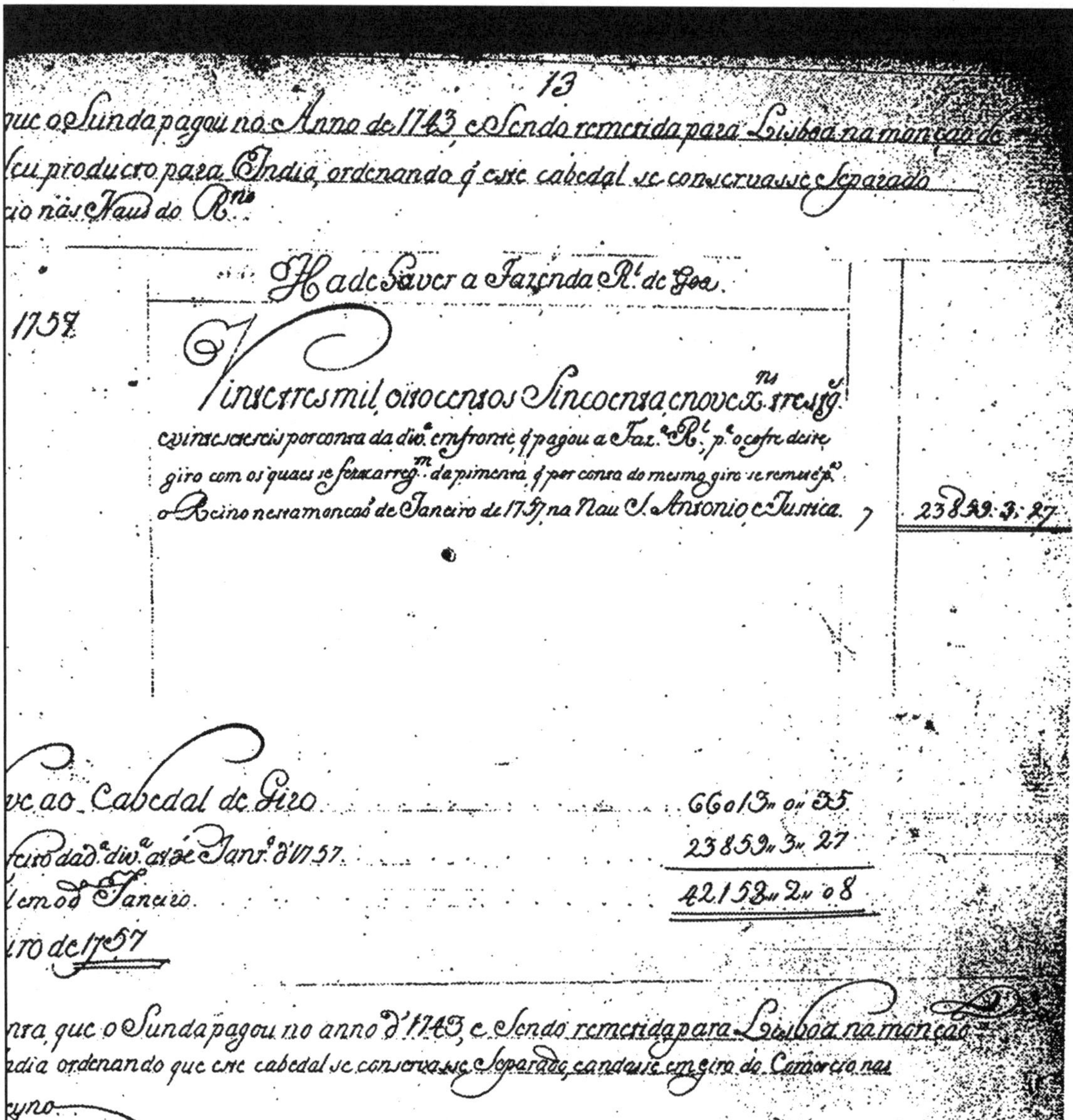
13
que o Sunda pagou no Anno de 1743, e Sendo remetida para Lisboa na monção de
seu producto para India, ordenando q este cabedal se conservasse Separado
rio nas Naus do Rno.
Ha de Saver a Fazenda Rl. de Goa.
1757
Vinte e tres mil oito centos Sincoenta e nove x. tres tg.
quinze e seis reis por conta da dita em fronte q pagou a Faz. Rl. p. o cofre deste
giro com os quaes se fez a carregm. da pimenta q por conta do mesmo giro se remeteo p.
o Reino nesta monção de Janeiro de 1757 na Nau S. Antonio e Justiça. 23859: 3: 27
ve ao Cabedal de Giro ... 66013 " 0 " 35
feito dad. dit. até Janr. de 1757 ... 23859 " 3 " 27
em o de Janeiro ... 42153 " 2 " 08
ro de 1757
nta, que o Sunda pagou no anno de 1743, e Sendo remetida para Lisboa na monção
dia ordenando que este cabedal se conservasse Separado, e andasse em giro do Commercio nas
yno

Before *Erario Regio*—the new Royal Exchequer—started to work and with the dictatorship of Carvalho e Melo showing its bloody face, Goa's Royal Exchequer wisely decided to pay the debt of 23,202 *xelins*, 3 *tangas* and 53 *reis*, to the Administration of the Capital ….

Meanwhile, it is a pity that we could not find out if the Administrator of Mozambique's Commerce had always paid his interest, the damages of transportation and the glass beads ….

4.0 HISTORICAL BACKGROUND

The Reign of King John V, the Magnificent, was the most luxurious and ostentatious of all Portuguese history as a result of the gold and diamonds that came from Brazil.

As we have already seen, by the end of the reign, this story of the bills "from the capital proceeding from the pepper" has its inception.

Actually, in 1743, King John is lying in his bed, paralyzed with the disease that will kill him in 1750. The mediocre government of the last years of his reign has Friar Gaspar da Encarnacao, a Jesuit, as prime minister. All the corruption and negligence that this book of accounts shows, is, actually, a sign of the economic and financial laissez faire attitude established in the country.

As we have also mentioned, by this time, the accountancy in Portugal used single entries and it was the *Casa dos Contos* (House of Accounts) that checked the public accounts. This situation went back to the fourteenth century.

When King Joseph I succeeded his father in 1750, he chose Sebastiao Jose de Carvalho e Melo to be his secretary of state. Carvalho e Melo—later Count of Oeiras and Marquis of Pombal—will be remembered along with his reforms as the leading figure of the bloodiest dictatorship in all Portuguese history.

In Portugal it was usual for the government to be formed by three secretaries. Soon Carvalho e Melo surpassed the other two, thanks to his ability for work, willingness to volunteer and persistence. One of the secretaries was Diogo de Mendonca Corte Real who wrote the letter we mentioned in this text addressed to the Inspector of the Royal Exchequer of the State of India.

So, we may guess that when Diogo de Mendonca wrote the letter to the inspector, he was inspired by the spirit of discipline that Carvalho imposed upon his government.

The criticism that we find in this letter is addressed more to the previous viceroy, Pedro Miguel de Almeida Portugal, Marquis of Alorna, than to the viceroy who was in charge by that time, Francisco de Assis, Marquis of Tavora. We can deduce this because the letter is dated from April 1751 and the Marquis of Tavora only arrived in India in September 1750. Therefore, he had been in charge for only six months and the negligence in the accounts came from the 1740s, as we know.

It is interesting to see what happened to these men, when facing Carvalho e Melo during the 1750s: the Marquis of Alorna died in 1756 but his son Joao de Almeida Portugal, the second Marquis of Alorna, son-in-law of Francisco de Assis, Marquis of Tavora, was sent to prison by command of the Minister, as a consequence of the attempt on the king's life in 1758. He was only released in 1777. Diogo de Mendonca was deported in 1756 to Mazagao, by command of Carvalho e Melo as a consequence of a failed substitution of the minister. Francisco de Assis, Marquis of Tavora, was executed in 1759, also by the command of Carvalho as he had been involved in the attempt on the king's life. It is important to explain that now history has already rehabilitated the Marquis of Tavora and the second Marquis of Alorna and absolved them of all their supposed wrongdoing. The same fate was shared by many others; that is why the attempt on the king's life was an excuse for Carvalho e Melo to "produce" the guilty parties who were useful to him. Finally, the earthquake in 1755 destroyed all the facilities of the *Casa dos Contos* (House of Accounts) in Lisbon. In that disaster, we lost an enormous and historically significant property. So, the "all mighty" Minister of King Joseph I thought about the foundation of a new body entitled the Inspection of Accounts—*Erario Regio* (the new Royal Exchequer)—and decided to impose the double-entry system of accountancy upon Public Accountancy. This measure turned out to be a courageous one for Portugal at the time and was officially decreed in an Act of Law on December 22, 1761.

On the one hand, Goa's Royal Exchequer is confronted by the debt of 1744 created by negligence (coming from the Administration of the Commerce of Mozambique) and which is not collected until the end of the decade of 1750; on the other hand, this new administrator also has to face the arrival of the Royal Exchequer, the new regulatory body, which will inspect and control the State's accounts.

To make things worse, in 1758 Manuel de Saldanha e Albuquerque, the first count of Ega, brother of Cardinal Saldanha who was a man in the confidence of Carvalho e Melo, was made viceroy of India. It is enough to say that when the Minister ordered the deportation of the Jesuits in 1759, this viceroy strictly followed the orders received from Carvalho and no less than 221 Jesuit priests who were living in the State of India were sent to prison in Lisbon. It was natural then, that the presence of this viceroy didn't give any tranquility to Goa's Royal Exchequer ...

Goa's Royal Exchequer wisely decided to settle the accounts of the Administration of the Capital, in 1760, before the *Erario Regio* started functioning and could demand information about these accounts.

Making an effort to show them clearly, Goa's Royal Exchequer rendered the accounts using double entries, when it was not obliged to do so. This attitude may be understood as an attempt to curry favour on the part of Goa's Royal Exchequer who wanted to be in the new body of inspection of the State's Accounts.

As far as the adoption of double-entry bookkeeping is concerned, considering the negligence and the disorganization of that time, we can speculate that this bookkeeping may only have been done after 1762, when the *Erario Regio* started to work.

5.0 CONCLUSION

From all the issues that have been explored, we may conclude the following:

1. The accounting was not completed between 1744 and 1751. It only started in 1752, though they had used earlier dates.
2. We do not know where the 8,131 *xelins*, 4 *tangas* and 12 *reis*, which are part of the money sent by the king of Sunda, were spent.
3. The 150 *candins* of pepper also sent by the King of Sunda had a loss of 16 *candins*, 1 *arroba* and 1 *arratel* when compared with Goa's weight.
4. Displacement of dates: there are entries of interest from 1745 to 1751 but with the date of...1744.
5. a) The 838 silver *marcos* in *patacas* which were sent from Lisbon in 1744 also had a loss of 19 *marcos*, 6 *onças* and 3 *oitavas* compared with Goa's weight.

   b) The 818 silver *marcos*, 1 *onca* and 5 *oitavas*, which were obtained by the Goa's weight, had a return of 31,582 *xelins*, 3 *tangas* and 12 *reis*. The 150 *quintais* and 1 *arroba* of pepper which were sent to Lisbon in 1745, were converted into 32,978 *xelins*, 4 *tangas* and 43 *reis*.

   It is worth noticing that these two operations—5 (a) and 5 (b)—were not rendered in the book of accounts. There is only an entry of the difference—1,396 *xelins*, 1 *tanga* and 30 *reis*.

6. The inspection carried out by the Royal Exchequer found an error of half a real (...) in an entry of 1755.
7. In 1756 it only mentioned a difference of 23,841 *xelins*, 3 *tangas* and 47 *reis*. An entry of a half doubloon and two shiploads of pepper are missing. These missing entries are not even quantified.
8. In 1757 there is an error in transcribing a balance of 797 *xelins* and 3 *tangas*, which was detected by the inspection of the Royal Exchequer.
9. In 1759 a small difference of 20 *reis* is still detected by the Royal Exchequer.
10. The inspection conducted by the Royal Exchequer took place after January 1771, which was the date when the public authentication of this copy was made in Pangim. Even the handwriting is quite different from the one that belonged to the registrar.
11. The Goa's Royal Exchequer rendered accounts of the Capital's Administration, in March 1760, probably because it was aware of the replacement of the *Casa dos Contos* (House of Accounts) by the *Erario Regio* the new Royal Exchequer, which would impose a greater strictness as far as the rendering of accounts was concerned. Also the ambiance of terror that was felt in Lisbon—with the executions in 1759 and the corresponding persecutions—led Goa's Royal Exchequer to assume such a position.

    (We must bear in mind that all the orders given by Carvalho were to be strictly followed in the State of India, by the viceroy of that time, Manuel Saldanha e Albuquerque, who, as we have already mentioned, was Cardinal Saldanha's brother and Carvalho e Melo's man of confidence in the deadly fight with the Jesuits.)
12. The presentation of the double-entry accounts in March 1760, when that procedure would only have been compulsory in December 1761, may show one of two things: either the wish to please the Royal Exchequer, inferring from this attitude an appeal to its goodwill when judging past errors; alternatively, the original book of pepper's current accounts referring to the period between 1743 and 1760, was only made between 1762 and 1771, immediately after the appearance of the above mentioned Royal Exchequer. By that time this copy was made, which we have been analyzing.

    Among all the negligence and corruption which were common at the time, anything would have been possible ...

ENDNOTE

1 English version by Manuela Pinheiro.

REFERENCES

Azevedo, J. Lucio. *O Marques de Pombal e a sua Epoca* (Lisboa: Classica Editora, 1990).

Branco, Camilo Castelo. *Perfil do Marques de Pombal* (Porto: Lello & Irmao Editora, 1990).

Domingues, Mario. *O Marques de Pombal* (Lisboa: Romano Torres, 1970).

Livro 47—Casa dos Contos—"Livro de conta corrente da Fazenda Real com o cabedal procedido da pimenta que o Sunda pagou no ano de 1743"—Arquivo Historico do Tribunal de Contas, Lisboa.

Machado, Jose Pedro. Grande Dicionario de Lingua Portuguesa. Lisoba: Amigos do Livro Editores , 1981.

Martins, Oliveira. *Historia de Portugal* (Lisboa: Guimaraes Editores, 1968).

Mattoso, Jose. *Historia de Portugal* (Lisboa: Circulo de Leitores, 1993).

Tavora, D. Luis de Lancastre. *D.Leonor de Tavora—o tempo da ira* (Lisboa: Circulo de Leitores, 1994).

Zuquete, Afonso Eduardo Martins. *Tratado de todos os Vice Reis e Governadores da India* (Lisboa-Rio de Janeiro: Editorial Enciclopedia, 1962).

———. *Nobreza de Portugal e do Brasil* (Lisboa: Editorial Enciclopedia, 1989).

Part IV:

Professional Organizations

The Demise of the Cost Accounting Profession in Australasia

Ray H. Anderson
Victoria University of Technology
Australia

1.0 ABSTRACT

This paper traces the history of the Australasian Institute of Cost Accountants. This body was formed in 1921, following establishment of similar bodies overseas. Its formation reflected a desire by practising cost accountants in Australia and New Zealand to have a professional body catering exclusively for their interests.

Its early years were difficult, with lack of recognition within the profession and industry. Following reorganization, an active promotion program was undertaken, although the professional accountancy bodies refused to grant it equal status. By the mid 1930s the Institute faced threats of a competing body being created by the Commonwealth Institute of Accountants, a reflection of disharmony within the profession.

The outbreak of World War II and associated growth in manufacturing heralded an era of growth in membership for the Institute and the formation of a New Zealand body reflecting the emerging national identity within that country and greater professional standing. In Australia, professional disharmony still existed, and ultimately under the guise of unification of the profession, the Cost Institute was affiliated and then integrated into the Society of Accountants. A similar process occurred in New Zealand on the grounds of enhancing services provided to members. The actions taken in each country are believed to have been detrimental to the cost (management) accounting branch of the profession and each respective country.

2.0 INTRODUCTION

The institutionalization of cost accounting in Australia and New Zealand occurred in 1921 with the foundation of the Australasian Institute of Cost Accountants. The term Australasia was one used to describe Australia, New Zealand and other countries located in the Pacific Ocean.

Although the origins of each country were different, their union led to the formation of the Institute. Australia had originated as the colony of New South Wales under British jurisdiction with first settlement in 1788. Over subsequent years another five colonies were formed and together voluntarily formed the Commonwealth of Australia in 1901.

Unlike Australia, New Zealand had not been subject to deliberate colonization. In 1838, the New Zealand Colonisation company was formed with the intention of establishing a self-governing colony in New Zealand. Following initial settlement by the first emigrants, within one year the British government had decided to claim New Zealand. The treaty of Waitangi signed with Maori chiefs gave Britain sovereignty in return for the maintenance of law and order. Self-government was granted in 1852 and by 1856 a central government with an elected parliament and cabinet had been established [Morrell and Hall, 1957]. In the 1880s and 1890s federation with the Australian colonies was discussed but little enthusiasm on the part of its government or people meant New Zealand kept its own identity [Oliver and Williams, 1981, p. 308].

Economic development in both countries was predominantly based on agriculture, forestries and fishing [Butlin, 1964, Condliffe, 1959, Condliffe and Airey, 1960]. In Australia, primary industry was dominant until 1939 after which major growth occurred in the manufacturing sector until the 1960s. In New Zealand, the economy is still heavily reliant on primary industry for continued economic stability and prosperity .

Exhibit 1 provides select statistics on manufacturing activity in Australia (Commonwealth) and New Zealand [Bloomfield, 1984]. From this it can be seen that Australia was more advanced in manufacturing activity, reflecting its earlier settlement, larger population and larger land size.

Exhibit 1
Manufacturing Activity in Australia and New Zealand

Year	Australia			New Zealand		
	No. of Factories	No. of Employees	Gross Value £'000	No. of Factories	No. of Employees	Gross Value £'000
1901	11,143	197,783	292,536	3,188	41,257	17,527
1920	16,291	376,734	324,586	3,619	58,475	78,836
1935	24,211	460,367	364,912	5,391	78,701	83,766
1945	28,930	750,579	867,647	6,847	118,886	205,649
1960	57,782	1,115,100	5,023,696	8,550	171,973	705,617

3.0 ORIGINS

The establishment of a professional cost accountancy body covering Australasia can be traced to two meetings of practising cost accountants held in 1920. The first meeting of interested men was held on October 26, 1920 at the Hardware Club, Melbourne; subsequently, a further meeting took place on December 15, 1920, when it was recorded that J.N. Shackleton, L.W. Duncan, R.G. Fishwick, N.W. Morey, J. Weir, E.A. Claringbold and W.W. Farmer were subscribers to the Memorandum and Articles of Association. All present at that meeting described themselves as cost accountants and designated the industry in which they practised. On January 4, 1921, The Australasian Institute of Cost Accountants was incorporated as a company limited by guarantee under the Victorian Companies Act. The Institute, when incorporated, had 31 foundation members, all of whom were granted membership on the basis that they were actively engaged accountants and held responsible positions in business as cost accountants. At the time of its foundation in Australia, there were two main accountancy bodies, the Incorporated Institute of Accountants (later the Commonwealth Institute of Accountants, CIA) and the Federal Institute of Accountants (FIA) together with a number of smaller state-based institutes. In New Zealand, three bodies existed: the Incorporated Institute of Accountants of New Zealand was formed in 1894, the New Zealand Accountants and Auditors Association in 1898 and the New Zealand Society of Accountans in 1908 [Strickett, 1952]. These bodies had their own examination syllabi with subjects taught by private accountancy colleges and they provided professional qualifications in accountancy.

The foundation of the Institute reflected a developing interest in cost accounting and the practical aspects of cost determination as well as a desire by practising cost accountants to form a professional body devoted solely to this branch of accounting. This developing interest can be identified with a number of factors including the advent of World War I, anticipated post-war developments in Australia, establishment of cost accountancy bodies overseas and the lack of interest of existing accountancy bodies in promoting cost accounting.

Prior to World War I, some growth in manufacturing had occurred with the removal of customs barriers following Federation [Boehm, 1993, p. 181]. With the outbreak of war, new industries were created to meet the demand for products no longer available as imports. A further stimulus to growth in manufacturing activity was the need to produce war-related equipment and this also spawned the establishment and growth of related industries [Schedvin, 1970]. These developments, together with the need for existing manufacturing concerns to become more efficient, resulted in cost accounting becoming recognized as a means of aiding manufacturers in the control of their operations and the establishment of prices for their output.

Following the war, a revival in the level of exports created a demand for increased protection of the Australian manufacturing industry which led to the passing of the 1921 Tariff Board Act [Mills, 1927, p. 5]. Forster [1964, p. 7] observes that the census in that year showed a higher proportion of the population engaged in manufacturing than primary industries. The passing of the Tariff legislation together with the growing population provided a stimulus for the establishment of manufacturing concerns in the textile, rubber and other industries [Forster, 1964]. The establishment of new factories and the likelihood of protective tariff legislation had, in the previous year, led a writer [Anonymous, 1920, p. 154] to observe that costing would assume greater importance and enable new and existing firms to compete successfully against the output of other countries. It was also pointed out that costing requirements could be imposed on firms given the recent decision to implement a uniform system of costing for principal industries. Furthermore, the likelihood of legislation against "profiteering," that is, abuse of the protective tariff, would require that firms have a proper costing system that could demonstrate any such accusation as unjust. The necessity for more accurate costing and the adoption by Australian manufacturers of costing systems was advocated by Adamson [1921] as the basis for their future prosperity, given the fact that Australia was entering an era of great industrial activity.

Another important factor which led to its formation was the establishment overseas of professional cost accounting bodies. In March 1919, the Institute of Cost and Works Accountants was formed in England and later that year the National Association of Cost Accountants was created in the United States of America. The establishment of the English Institute was a response to the recently concluded war which had established the need for costing; finally, practitioners decided to join together to further its development [Stacey, 1954, p. 98]. Loft [1990] identified government regulations imposed in World War I as raising awareness of cost accounting in the United Kingdom. In contrast, the formation of the American National Association of Cost Accountants was planned to meet the needs of business, but had been delayed by the outbreak of World War I in 1914, even though it was not until 1917 that the United States of America became involved [NACA, 1919, p. 3].

The formation of the Australasian body was perhaps more influenced by the establishment of a costing body in England, since the recent war experiences of practitioners in Australia were similar to those of English cost accountants. Government requirements imposed on Australian wartime contractors, like those in the United Kingdom, required them to have some form of proper costing system in place to justify payment of claims submitted. The formation of these overseas bodies may have led Australian and New Zealand cost accountants to recognize the need for such a body in their countries. The joining together of members in the two countries reflected the close ties binding them through their membership in the British Empire, and as well a desire for international cooperation. The founders believed cost accounting to be of such importance that it warranted a separate body to ensure that it received the attention it deserved. At the same time it should be recognized that the formation of a separate body did enable founding members, who were qualified accountants at the time, the opportunity to gain additional professional qualifications without examination, based on active employment as a cost accountant.

4.0 THE FORMATIVE YEARS

The Institute's objectives laid down in the Memorandum of Association were to:

- raise the status and advance the profession of cost accountants
- improve the theoretical and general knowledge and efficiency of persons engaged in or about to engage in the profession
- provide for and regulate the training and education of students and test by examination
- represent the views and interests of the profession
- promote a higher sense of the importance of costing records and accounts.

In accordance with its objective of improving the knowledge of its members, a series of lectures to members on costing principles was given by Powell [1921]. At the end of its first year the Institute had 160 members, all of whom were admitted under Article 11 which permitted admission without examination, subject to applicants satisfying General Council with their knowledge and experience in cost accounting. Growth in the next two years was slow and in 1924 General Council recognized that inadequate progress was being made in respect to membership. It therefore decided to form study circles with a view to discussion of certain aspects of costing, but these were not formed because of lack of member interest. By 1925, membership had increased to 235 but the minutes of its 1925 meeting indicated that General Council considered that it had been unsuccessful in fulfilling its objectives.

Major reasons for this were the poor financial position of the Institute which precluded it from promoting itself in professional and business journals and the view held generally within the accountancy profession that cost accounting was lacking the intellectual rigour and value attached to other accounting practice.

5.0 REORGANIZATION, PROMOTION AND PROFESSIONAL RECOGNITION

Dissatisfaction with the progress of the Institute led to a new General Council being elected in 1926 and the aim was to raise the status of the profession. The purpose of this revision was to give wider autonomy to the State divisions and leave Federal Council to deal with overall policy and to adopt an organizational form similar to that of the Commonwealth Institute of Accountants and the Federal Institute of Accountants. Divisions were established in all States except Queensland and Tasmania which, because of their small membership, were attached to New South Wales and Victoria respectively. While divisions were established in Australia without difficulty, it appears the change was more difficult to implement in New Zealand. Subsequently, these members were advised that if they did not properly organize themselves they would be forced to relinquish their membership [AICA General Council Minutes, December 3, 1926, Folio 13]. This ultimatum did not resolve the matter, but the Australasian Council, conscious of the need to develop the Institute and fearful of other rival bodies being established, did not carry out its threat and from January 1, 1929, New Zealand members were attached to the Victorian division until divisional status was granted in 1936 [AICA General Council Minutes, June 14, 1929, Folio 55].

The new Council's primary goal was the promotion of the Institute, and in 1928 it arranged for a lecture series to be given in Victoria and invited manufacturers and staff to attend. It was hoped that this series and its publication would assist the Institute in gaining further recognition by the business world. In 1930, a series of lectures was held in New South Wales [AICA 1930, NSW Division] to focus on the usefulness of cost accounting in difficult trading conditions, with the underlying objectives of improving the standing of the Institute and increasing its membership. In the same year, Victorian members gave a series of lectures [AICA, 1931] to members of the Victorian Chamber of Manufacturers and these gained a wider audience through their publication in the following year.

These activities came at a time of severe economic depression evidenced by declining prices in major exports and reduced capital inflow. Throughout this depression and the subsequent recovery in the 1930s, activities conducted were designed to ensure business survival through more efficient operation [CRS, 1933 and AICA, 1934]. These lectures did much to enhance the status of the Institute in the business community, but also created the seeds of disharmony within the profession. Both of the main professional bodies in 1934 sought financial support from the Institute in planning for the first Australasian Congress to be held in 1936 [Australasian Congress of Accounting (ACA), 1936]. The Institute, which also provided two speakers on costing topics, was not one of the sponsoring bodies to the Congress. In the same year both the FIA and CIA indicated that they planned to extend their activities into the area of cost accounting. The FIA plan was to provide a cost accountancy course and award a special diploma, but while the General Council was aware of this plan, no action was taken by them on this matter [AICA General Council Minutes, August 2, 1934, Folio 81]. The CIA announced in 1934 its intention to introduce postgraduate studies and at its 1935 annual meeting, the presidential address [CIA, 1935, *Annual Report*, p. 12] indicated that courses in specialist subjects such as taxation, cost accounting, economics and finance would be conducted, given the continued progress of accountancy and the need for specialization in certain branches of the profession. In 1935, the Victorian Division of the Commonwealth Institute of Accountants conducted a series of lectures covering the general principles and practices of cost accounting. The following year a series of lectures under the title of *Accounting for Management Purposes* covering classification, using cost records for control purposes and accountants' reports was also given. Four years later the New South Wales' division conducted its first course on cost accounting [CIA, 1939]. The decision of the Council of the Commonwealth Institute of Accountants to conduct such courses indicated their recognition of the future importance of costing, yet their actions (i.e., not encouraging members to obtain the AICA qualification) hindered its development and recognition as a professional body in its own right.

Another reason for the Institute's difficulty in gaining recognition, not only by the profession but by business, was that it did not issue a journal promoting costing and its own activities. While this may have been due to financial constraints in 1927, General Council noted that it was premature to issue a journal, a practice which was at variance with those of the Institute of Cost and Works Accountants in the United Kingdom and the National Association of Cost Accountants in the United States of America, both of which commenced to publish their own journal or the equivalent shortly after their formation. General Council resolved that any articles on costing should be submitted to *The Australasian Accountant and Secretary* for publication, a journal published by the private coaching college, Hemingway and Robertson Ltd. While this resolution simply formalized past practice, given this journal had previously published articles on costing by members, General Council may have considered that the issue of a journal was unnecessary due to the existence of other journals. Apart from the Institute's own publications, usually of their own lectures and seminars, members had to rely for publication on journals of other professional accountancy and engineering bodies [Anderson, 1984b]. This practice limited the opportunity to promote cost accounting applications, particularly as financial accounting, taxation and company law developments were of more relevance to practitioners and dominated journal contents.

In analyzing the content of the articles published from 1910 to 1935 [Anderson, 1984a], it is evident that determination of historical product cost was the main function under cost accounting. A partial solution to not having its own journal was the Cost Institute's decision to become a member of the publishing company and joint publisher of *The Australian Accountant*, a journal which commenced in 1936 as a joint publication of the Commonwealth Institute of Accountants and the Federal Institute of Accountants. Under the terms of agreement, future issues of *The Australian Accountant*, were to have a separate section devoted to cost accounting and this practice continued for many years.

6.0 THE GOLDEN YEARS

The outbreak of World War II provided considerable stimulus to the growth of Australia's manufacturing industries since, because imports were not available, a switch to home produced products took place. Other relevant factors were war expenditure and Australia's importance as a source of supply for British countries east of Suez [Boehm, 1993, p. 187]. This resulted in an expansion of key industries and creation of new ones in munitions, aircraft equipment, machinery and textiles.

In 1937, well before the outbreak of World War II, it had been recognized that existing munitions productions in Australia were limited in size [Jensen, 1943]. Planning and development was initiated by the Munitions' Supply Board who with defence supply officers formed the Australian Principal Supply Officer's Committee. In 1939 the nucleus of this body was transferred to form the Department of Supply and Development which was to be responsible for the production of munitions in Australia.

Among the arrangements involved in its establishment was the appointment of the Accountancy Advisory Panel. The function of this Panel was to assist the government in its consideration of schemes of costing and profit control in connection with the production of munitions by private enterprise. The individuals appointed to the Panel were prominent accountants, namely E. V. Nixon, S. W. Griffith, T. D. Hadley, D. J. Nolan and L. A. Schumer.

Within the Department of Supply and Development, a costing section was set up under T. L. McNamara who had established costing systems at the Colonial Ammunition Factory in Footscray in the First World War. Cost investigators were employed to check that the cost charged by a firm contracting with the government could be accurately determined, as this was an essential ingredient to cost-plus pricing.

Under cost-plus pricing contracts, manufacturers were required to have a satisfactory costing system. Where there was no costing system, the cost investigators had to advise and arrange for the immediate installation of a suitable costing system. At the outbreak of war, costing systems were operated by very few manufacturers in Australia. By the end of the war, many thousands of Australian manufacturers had established costing systems and had obtained four or five years experience in operating them. A further boost to the wider application of costing techniques was the return of the cost investigators to industry, where they could use their experience and knowledge to assist other firms to adopt some form of cost accounting system [Webb, 1995].

The Second World War also led to an expansion in government munitions' production in Australia. Additional government factories were established, and in order to operate efficiently, they were required to install and operate proper costing systems [Jensen, 1943, p. 29].

In 1940, New Zealand established a Ministry of Supply and Munitions and commenced the manufacture of munitions. A committee was established by the government to monitor costing practice and pricing which was comprised of one cost expert and three accountants, together with an engineer, lawyer and army supply man [Pohlen, 1943].

However, while these imposed regulations could be perceived to assist in the wider application of cost accounting techniques and methods, writers in each country expressed reservations about the benefits derived. In Australia, Anderson [1946] and Fitzgerald [1946] both expressed reservations about its benefits. Anderson [1946, p. 7] wrote:

> This activity on defence work has brought to the study of cost accounting both benefits and rebuffs. On the one hand, the demand for costing data by Government authorities has required more attention to cost accountancy principles than ever before, and firms which had never installed a cost system were compelled to arrange for a system of costing to suit their requirements.
>
> On the other hand, it cannot be said that the expenditure of all this time and energy and money, including the setting up of special costing sections in the Ministry of Munitions and other Departments, has contributed anything to the theory of cost accounting. It may be said that the reverse was the case, because the greatest emphasis was placed on job costing.

Fitzgerald [1946, p. 432] also viewed wartime developments on cost accounting as "a serious interruption to progress in cost accounting techniques and to the growth of the practice of systematized cost accounting." These views are disputed by Webb [1948] who believes that Anderson is misinformed and that Fitzgerald's view is incorrect. In New Zealand, Kay [1949, p. 188] observed that "while such a ready-made system may provide the data required by the government department concerned, it is often only a travesty of a proper system of cost accounting."

While industrial development was proceeding at a quicker rate in Australia than New Zealand, events in the latter country were acting as an impetus to local members to become more active. In 1936, a Bureau of Industry was established to plan new industries and reorganize existing ones, and to encourage and protect local manufacturers from overseas competition [Sinclair, 1959, p. 275]. This scheme was intended to promote new industries and greater efficiency in existing ones [Condliffe and Airey, 1960], and through the introduction of import controls in 1938, to emphasize the need for the application of cost accounting techniques.

Until then, the New Zealand members had been inactive, reflecting the small membership base and the limited scope for the application of cost accounting practices [Roberts, 1953]. The pro-active stance of New Zealand members to form their own division in 1936, coincided with what Sinclair [1959, p. 282] observed as the establishment of its national identity through the arts and literature. This culminated in 1942 with their expressed desire that they wished to form a separate body to be titled, the New Zealand Institute of Cost Accountants. The justification for this request was manifold: it would protect the name; make it difficult to form another cost accountancy body to be established in New Zealand; it would achieve greater government recognition, and lead to increased interest on the part of qualified accountants seeking additional qualifications; and the use of the name New Zealand would lead to greater recognition in official circles [AICA General Council Minutes, June 8, 1942, Folio 132].

The Australasian Institute's General Council acceded to their request in the belief that it was in the best interests of the profession to discourage the formation of a professional body in direct competition with the Institute, although the original name was retained in Australia [AICA General Council Minutes, June 8, 1942, Folio 132].

In 1945, the Australian body commenced the issue of a biannual Cost Bulletin similar to that issued by the National Association of Cost Accountants in the United States. The purpose of issuing the bulletins was to provide members with information on latest developments in cost accounting thought and research in Australia. These bulletins were published regularly until they were ceased by the Society following integration.

In the post-war years both the Australian and the New Zealand bodies experienced membership growth and improved recognition in the business community. However, this prosperity brought with it the first seeds of their demise with the move to affiliation and later integration.

7.0 AFFILIATION AND INTEGRATION

7.1 Australia

In 1952, the Australian Society of Accountants was formed through the amalgamation of the Commonwealth and Federal Institutes of Accountants, and the subsequent joinder of the Association of Accountants. Its formation reflected the profession's desire to consolidate itself as a national body, to achieve unity and, through this, legal recognition [Kenley, 1962].

One immediate task identified by the new body was to provide specialized qualifications and activities to members. It was considered that such specialization in cost accounting could best be achieved by a closer affiliation with the Cost Institute. In 1953, unofficial discussions commenced as to the possibility of forming an affiliated relationship, and within the year a proposal was developed for affiliation between the two bodies. The Institute then prepared a document for distribution to members, listing the case for and against the affiliation proposal.

The argument for affiliation was based on the following points:

1. The objects of the Institute as set out in its Memorandum of Association include as the second objective "to unite the Members of the Profession of Accountants into one general body, etc ...." The founders of the Institute and those following them have always had in mind the unification of the accountancy profession. This has now been partly achieved by the formation of the Australian Society of Accountants and it is therefore felt opportune to pursue the object of unification.

2. The Australian Society of Accountants intends, in the pursuance of its "objects" as set out in its Memorandum of Association, to cover the entire field of accountancy, and proposes to examine in cost accountancy, and issue a postgraduate diploma. The Society, after negotiation, has offered the affiliation proposal to the Institute in order that the Institute will, in affiliation with the Society, conduct this postgraduate phase of the profession. Should the Institute reject the proposal, the Society plans to enter the cost accountancy field as a competitor with the Institute. It was considered that such action would not be in the best interests of this Institute.

3. The Institute has never been prepared to consider the loss of its identity and has been insistent on requiring the maintenance of the status of a Cost Accountant as postgraduate to the accountancy degree. This aspect has been achieved in the proposed affiliation now placed before members.

4. The Institute will retain its separate identity, present degrees, certificates, and designation of status of members.

5. Subject to the general directions of the Society, the Institute will retain complete control in the administration of its affairs, including the syllabus and standard of examinations and the admission of members. The examination policy of the Institute and the Society will be co-ordinated to the ultimate benefit of both bodies.

6. The Institute will retain its own funds for the development of its own activities and services to its own members, including the Cost Bulletin.

7. The Society will vacate the field of cost accounting both as to the present coverage in the Society's examination papers and the conduct of activities related to the cost accountancy field.

8. The Institute has some 420 members who are not members of the Society. Membership of the Society will be offered to all those members at the commencement of the affiliation, but the acceptance of such an offer is not compulsory under the terms of the proposal.

9. The Society will encourage candidates qualifying for admission to the Society to continue with postgraduate work and qualify as members of the Institute. This should result in greatly increased membership of the Institute.

10. The present Institute Libraries will be amalgamated with the excellent Libraries of the Society and this facility will be available to all members of the Institute.
11. By making admission to the Society a pre-requisite of membership of this Institute, the postgraduate status of this Institute's degree will be emphasised.
12. Administration of the Institute would be carried on by the Society's officers, some of whom are permanently employed. The Institute's Registrars have, in the past, been part-time officers in all States. The new arrangement should prove of considerable benefit in all services to members. Part-time service has been a considerable burden to our Registrars in the various States. Such service, with the level of the Institute's activities, has been unable to provide the attention our status warranted but which was beyond the financial resources of the Institute. There should be savings in administration costs and these would be available for additional services to members.
13. Should the Society enter the field of Cost Accountancy, a substantial reduction in our membership could result. The financial effect of any substantial reduction in this Institute's membership would compel the Institute either to curtail its services and activities or substantially increase its fees.
14. Affiliation with the Society will present greater opportunities for the extension of the Institute's activities in centres outside capital cities.
15. The affiliation will ensure the continuance of the inclusion of the Institute as a publisher of "The Australian Accountant."
16. The affiliation will constitute another important step in unifying the profession and, at the same time, preserve for our members full recognition of their specialist qualifications.
17. In the event of a vote not being recorded in favour of this suggested affiliation, the Institute will continue as hitherto. In order to provide adequate administrative arrangements it will be necessary to provide the Institute with its own office and to employ a full-time General Registrar. This departure from existing arrangements, which will be necessary in order to extend activities and maintain the Institute's position in competition with the Society, will involve members in increased fees.

The case against the affiliation proposal was documented as follows:

1. With the administration of the Institute's affairs being handled by the Society, there may be a tendency for Institute members at Divisional Council and General Council level to lose interest in the affairs of the Institute. Our Institute has progressed over the years due to a tremendous amount of work voluntarily given by many members.
2. The Society with its much greater size may attempt to dictate the policy of the Institute from the General Council level of the Society.
3. If any change is considered necessary, the Institute's interests may be better served by developing as an Institute of Comptrollers with specialisation in management accounting. The Institute of Cost and Works Accountants, England, does not follow the postgraduate policy but leans more towards factory accounting and management and has shown that it can exist as a purely specialist Institute alongside powerful accountancy bodies.

4. An affiliation with the Society will not completely unify the accountancy profession in Australia as the Institute of Chartered Accountants in Australia is not included and there appears no reason why one other independent specialist body such as our Institute should not remain outside the Society.

5. By resolution of its General Council, the Society can demand a poll in the General Council of the Institute and can then outvote Institute representatives. In the event of such a position arising, it could well mean the end of the affiliation and place the Institute in a position where it had to re-establish administrative facilities throughout Australia, at considerable difficulty and cost.

6. It is believed that failure to accept the present proposal will involve the entry of the society in the field of cost accountancy as an active and strong competitor. We believe the Institute has been the most active and progressive Institute in Australia and that the only factor in which the Society would be superior in any such competition would lie in the field of its financial resources.

7. In the event of the affiliation proposal failing and the Society entering the cost accounting field, the Society may fail to achieve success with the proposed issue of a separate diploma. Other accounting bodies in Australia achieved little success with postgraduate costing diplomas. It is believed that the degree of a specialist Institute will still be preferred.

8. Administration by the Society may not provide any saving in cost. The Institute work has always been carried out by part-time officers on low remuneration in conjunction with a vast amount of honorary work by councillors, editors, examiners and members of committees. A change to full-time Registrars may cause a diminution in this honorary work in conjunction with a relegation of the importance of the smaller Institute in the administrative office.

9. Future applicants for membership to the Institute will be required to pay membership fees to the Society if not already a member of that body. [AICA General Council Minutes, May 31-June 1, 1955, Folio 206–212].

The affiliation proposal was one that provoked disagreement among members of the state councils and across the national council [AICA General Council Minutes, May 25–26, 1953, Folio 139]. Despite this, by 1954 agreement between the councils of both bodies had been reached, and the proposal had been distributed to members to be voted on. Lack of response to the proposal, reflected in the insufficient number of Institute members who voted, meant that the first vote was aborted. An adjourned vote by Australian members led to the affiliation proposal being rejected as 75 percent vote in favour was required for approval, but only 70.2 percent voted in favour of affiliation. The failure to obtain the requisite majority was due to a fear by members that the proposal would diminish the Institute's standing in the business community and result eventually in its demise. The response of the Society was to develop proposals for a diploma in cost accounting, a move perceived as involving direct competition with the course of the Institute and one reflecting disharmony in the profession. It was further decided that a cost section be established within the Society and an examination syllabus be prepared. This decision was conveyed to the Cost Institute with the view that further negotiation was undesirable given that insufficient numbers of the Institute's members had voted in favour of the affiliation proposals [ASA General Council Minutes, April 30–May 2, 1956, pp. 2–5].

Following the Society's disclosure of its intentions, J.G. Morten lodged a requisition under Article 41, signed by 32 members, which called for another extraordinary meeting to put the case more clearly to members as it was believed the earlier material provided had lacked appropriate direction. The Institute Council convened a meeting and 91 percent of the 67 percent of members voting, voted in favour of the affiliation proposal. The vote in favour of affiliation was only achieved through proxy votes and the result could be viewed as not constituting a genuine vote by members. As the proposal was approved by the necessary majority, the Society, in light of this development, did not proceed with its proposals for the issue of a diploma in cost accounting.

With the affiliation proposal completed, the future implications of the event were not fully realized by members of the Cost Institute. H. M. Harrisson, State President of the Queensland Division, in a newsletter [1956] wrote, "affiliation does not mean any lessening of interest or incentive to continue our own activities ... and with all doubts about our future cleared away, we are ready to forge ahead."

However, this view overlooked the objective of prominent Society Council Members led by C. W. Andersen and G. E. Fitzgerald for unification of the profession. The latter's brother, Sir Alexander Fitzgerald [1962, p. 290], believed that lack of unity had restricted its progress and prevented government recognition. Educational policy changes planned by the Society also provided another impetus and justification for integration, and led to the demise of the AICA.

Following its formation in 1952, the Society's active members expressed concern about the standard of education for accountants and their low status relative to other professions. It was considered that accounting education was too narrow and neglected to provide a wider perspective of the responsibilities of accountants in commerce and industry. In 1960, it was resolved to carry out a survey of accountancy education in Australia, and subsequently a report was made by Vatter [1964] which recommended that the basic education for accountancy should be provided by appropriate courses at tertiary institutions. This recommendation coincided with a report by the federal government on tertiary education in Australia, which also recommended elevated status for courses, including accountancy taught at non-universities [Commonwealth Report, 1964]. Its implementation meant that the area of cost accounting was now part of undergraduate accounting programs, forming the basic training to be received by future accountants.

Such development further supported the desire for unification of the profession through integration of the Society and the Cost Institute. In Australia, integration proposals were developed between the councils of both the Society and Cost Institute. The proposal contained the following reasons as to why members should support the integration proposal:

1. The professional status of accountants has been advanced by recent changes in the educational policy of the Society. The integrated body will provide the structure for the development and recognition of post-qualification studies recommended in both the Vatter report on accountancy education and the Martin report on tertiary education.

2. Post-qualification studies for membership of the Institute have emphasised management accounting techniques essential for effective accounting in commerce, industry and government. The new syllabus of the Society is placing greater emphasis on this aspect of accounting and the integration of both bodies will facilitate and assist this trend.

3. Other areas of post-qualification study and recognition will be developed by the integrated body. Suggestions for these areas from interested groups within the Society will be welcomed by the General Council.

4. The integrated body is a logical development from the recognition of the need for greater unity in the accountancy profession expressed in the formation of the Society. It is in line with the pattern of the older professions.

5. Unity is strength. The status of each individual accountant is related to the status and strength of the profession as a whole. The integration will strengthen the voice with which the Society can speak on the affairs of the profession.

6. The integrated body will facilitate the interchange of ideas and experience between accountants with common interests. In addition, it will provide all members with greater opportunities to benefit from association with accountants in fields other than their own.

7. The proposed integration will facilitate the continued development of a constructive service to members with a simplified administration. [ASA-AICA, 1966]

The proposal, when published in *The Australian Accountant*, was accompanied by a piece advising that the profession in the United Kingdom was considering integration of six bodies into one, including the Institute of Cost and Works Accountants, presumably in an attempt to legitimize the proposal. This reference was designed to convince members that the planned unification was occurring elsewhere and to give further justification for the planned integration. The United Kingdom amalgamation was unsuccessful; while 80.2 percent of members of the Institute of Cost and Works Accountants approved it, as did members of four of the other bodies, it did not receive the requisite majority from the Institute of Chartered Accountants in England and Wales [Banyard, 1985, p. 155]. For members of the Cost Institute, the integration proposal meant they would lose their designated qualification of Associate/Fellow of the Institute. In return they were granted Senior Associate status, a new grade of membership created to recognize their additional academic qualifications. A benefit of integration was that Institute members could obtain advancement to Fellow status of the Society, with only five years of professional experience instead of fifteen years. A major change in policy was that membership at Senior Associate level could be obtained after integration on the basis of academic standing, whereas previously a prerequisite of membership was five years of practical experience. The Senior Associate level of membership was discontinued with the CPA professional schedule adopted by the Society, commencing July 1, 1984.

7.2 New Zealand

The affiliation agreement between the Australian bodies did not apply to New Zealand members but perhaps made both the New Zealand Society of Accountants and the New Zealand Institute of Cost Accountants conscious of the need to come together. While unification was less important, by now the New Zealand Society of Accountants was even more aware of the importance of cost accounting and that they should be more active in this field [Graham, 1960, p. 125]. However, some months elapsed before tentative discussions commenced in 1957 regarding the issue of affiliation between the New Zealand Society of Accountants and the New Zealand Institute of Cost Accountants. The underlying justification for affiliation was the Society's view that it had an obligation to deal with all areas of accounting, including specialist ones such as cost accounting. Affiliation was perceived as advantageous to both bodies as is evident from the Presidential remarks of the Society's president, R. G. Stark, who stated [Stark, 1960, p. 288]:

> In our view both organisations will gain much from the proposed affiliation. In common with most specialist groups, the Cost Institute's membership and resources limit the progress which can be made, and disproportionately increase administrative costs. The assumption by the Society of administrative control, with its ramifications in fields such as education, public relations and research should greatly enhance the prospects of progress in cost accounting.
>
> For its part, the Society will assume final responsibility for all the Institute's activities, thereby ensuring a co-ordinated policy for the entire profession.

Following affiliation on 1 December, 1960, J. H. Pickles, the new president of the Society, espoused the benefits of specialization in the profession. In his presidential address he stated [Pickles, 1961, p. 283]:

> It will be some years before the full impact of this affiliation is felt, but I am sure that its results cannot be other than most beneficial to all concerned. Freed from administrative problems, the Institute will be able to concentrate on research and education in the field of cost accounting—a segment of the profession which is becoming of still greater importance with the increasing industrial growth in New Zealand. For its part, the Society will gain from its assumption of full policy control over all matters affecting the profession as a whole. Unnecessary duplication of facilities will be avoided, and more effective direction provided over such matters as discipline, publicity, publications and library facilities.

Integration was achieved in 1966 when the Cost Institute was wound up and replaced by a Management Accounting division within the Society [Editorial, 1966]. As such, it became the first postgraduate division of the Society, a move designed to emphasize its specialist postgraduate status and to provide Society members with an interest in the subject with the opportunity to participate in management accounting activities [Editorial, 1966]. Following the Society's review of its future direction, the division was wound up as it was believed that its existing structure was inadequate for meeting the needs of members employed in industry [NZ Society, *Annual Report*, 1987, p. 17].

7.3 Australasia: Why Different?

Given the continued existence of similar bodies overseas, why is the Australian and New Zealand experience different? Clearly, Australia and New Zealand, with their later settlement, lacked the costing heritage that existed elsewhere [Edwards, 1937; Garner, 1954; Solomons, 1968; Johnson and Kaplan, 1987]. Furthermore, unlike its counterparts, the Australasian body had no permanent administrative headquarters or staff and had to rely on part-time administrative contributions from practising accountants. While these accountants made an outstanding contribution, it meant that the Institute lacked administrative support and employed no full-time person able to develop a future policy.

Another significant difference between the countries was size of membership. The Australian body was small relative to the overseas bodies, and entry barriers would continue to constrain membership growth. In 1957 the National Association of Cost Accountants in the United States became the National Association of Accountants. This change of name reflected the progress towards a more managerial role of members and did not restrict membership to any one particular role function. This was an approach the Australasian bodies could have adopted to widen their membership base. Such an approach could have contributed to the maintenance of a separate existence, but the push for unification would have overcome any such action.

Unification of the profession was used as the underlying rationale for the integration of the two bodies in Australia. The Society sought integration in order to strengthen its role as the major Australian accountancy body, while the issue reflected long-standing State rivalry, primarily between members domiciled in Melbourne and Sydney. The Society's administration and National Council were based in Melbourne and this irked Sydney members who viewed the whole integration proposal as a takeover and initially opposed it [Thomas, 1995].

In voting for integration, Cost Institute members believed they were acting in the best interests of the profession. This is reflected in the writing of H. F. Fox, the last president [1966, p. 347] who states "the profession must be grateful to all those members whose expert judgment assessed the time when the Institute was ready for even greater service, no longer as a separate body but, as part of that greater whole — the accountancy profession."

Integration was not a relevant consideration in New Zealand as only one body was in existence in that country. As well, government recognition had been achieved in 1958, but integration was seen as necessary to achieve control of the profession as a whole [NZSA, *Annual Report*, 1960].

8.0 SUMMARY AND CONCLUSION

This paper has traced the history of the AICA and its affiliated body, the NZICA. Early years were difficult due to lack of recognition by business and other accounting professional bodies. Following reorganization in 1926, the Institute's activities, over the next eight years, sought to better promote the benefits available from costing methods and systems, particularly in a period of economic depression.

Despite increasing business acceptance, the AICA experienced lack of acceptance by the major accountancy bodies who indicated their intention to also have their own cost accounting qualification. World War II, with its imposition of cost-plus pricing and growth in manufacturing, led to growth in the Institute's membership and acceptance as a desirable professional qualification. In 1944, the NZICA was formed to better promote cost accounting in that country, although it remained affiliated with the AICA.

The post-war decade was one of growth in membership and status within the business community. In 1956 affiliation with the Australian Society occurred, and in 1966 integration, as a means of achieving a unified profession. In New Zealand, affiliation occurred four years later and integration took place in the same year to achieve full policy control of the whole profession.

Despite the arguments presented, in Australia the objective of unifying the profession has not been achieved as there are at least five professional bodies in existence at present and the profession has still not achieved legal recognition of the term *accountant*. Consequently, the title can be used by any person whether or not they possess membership in a professional accountancy body. In New Zealand this was not an issue and integration was justified on the basis that the New Zealand Society could better fulfil its duty to ensure members were cognizant of advances in accountancy knowledge and practice. The impact of each Society's actions with respect to the future of cost (management) accounting requires further investigation.

REFERENCES

Adamson, R. "The Necessity for More Accurate Costing in Australian Factories," *The Accountant* (December 17, 1921), pp. 849–853.

Anderson, M. V. *Cost Accounting and Budgetary Control*, Technical Publication No.27, Department of Labour and National Service, Industrial Training Division, Commonwealth of Australia, March, 1946.

Anderson, R. H. "A Bibliography of Australian Writings on Cost Accounting 1910–35," *Accounting History Newsletter* (Winter, 1984a), pp. 9–15. Reprinted in *Accounting in Australia: Historical Essays*, R.H. Parker, Ed. (New York: Garland Publishing 1990), pp. 535–542.

———. "A History of the Australasian Institute of Cost Accountants, A Progress Report 1921–39," *Accounting Association of Australia and New Zealand Annual Conference*, University of Tasmania (1984b).

Anonymous. "Costing and Cost Accounting: Their Importance in the Coming Era," *The Australasian Accountant and Secretary* (June 1, 1920), pp. 153–155.

Australasian Congress of Accounting (ACA). *Proceedings* of the Australasian Congress on Accounting, Melbourne, March 16–20, 1936.

Australasian Institute of Cost Accountants. *Annual Report.* (various years)

———. *Examination Syllabus.* (various years)

———. *Minutes of General Council.* (various years)

———. New South Wales Division, *Lectures in Cost Accountancy*, 1930.

———. Victorian Division, *Cost Reduction by Cost Control*, Melbourne, 1931.

———. Victorian Division, *Aspects of Business Management*, Melbourne, 1934.

———. Victorian Division, Cost Bulletin Stock Inventory Policy Part 1, 15 October, 1945 / Part II, 15 December, 1945.

Australian Society of Accountants. *Annual Report.* (various years)

———. General Council Minutes. (various years)

Australian Society of Accountants and Australasian Institute of Cost Accountants. *Integration of Australian Society of Accountants and Australasian Institute of Cost Accountants*, 1966.

Banyard, Cyril. *The Institute of Cost and Management Accountants: A History* (London: Chartered Institute of Management Accountants, 1985).

Bloomfield, G. T. *New Zealand: A Handbook of Historical Statistics* (Boston, MA: G. K. Hall & Co., 1984).

Boehm, E. A. *Twentieth Century Economic Development in Australia*, Third Edition (Melbourne: Longman Cheshire, 1993).

Butlin, N. G. *Investment in Australian Economic Development* (London: Cambridge University Press, 1964).

Commonwealth Institute of Accountants. *Annual Report.* (various years)

———. *Minutes.* (various years)

———. *Accounting for Management Purposes*, Victorian Division, 1935.

Commonwealth of Australia, *Year Book*. (various years)

———. *Report of the Committee on the Future of Tertiary Education in Australia to the Australian Universities Commission*, (Canberra, 1964).

Condliffe, J. B. *New Zealand in the Making*, Second Edition (London: Allan and Unwin, 1959).

———. and W. T. G. Airey. *A Short History of New Zealand* (Christchurch: Whitcombe and Tombs, 1960).

Cost Research Society, Melbourne and Australasian Institute of Cost Accountants. *Reorganising of Business for Profit* (Melbourne, 1933).

Editorial. "New Development in Cost and Management Accounting," *Accountant's Journal* (1966), p. 373.

Edwards, Ronald S. "Some Notes on the Early Literature and Development of Cost Accounting in Great Britain," *Accountant* (August 7, 1937), pp. 193–195; (August 14, 1937), pp. 225–231; (August 21, 1937), pp. 253–255; (August 28, 1937), pp. 283–287; (September 4, 1937), pp. 313–316; (September 11, 1937), pp. 343–344.

Fitzgerald, A. A. "Accounting — In Retrospect," *The Australian Accountant* (June, 1946), pp. 289–295.

———. "Modern Cost Accounting Techniques and Industrial Efficiency," *The Australian Accountant* (October, 1946), pp. 430–438.

Forster, Colin. *Industrial Development in Australia 1920–1930* (Canberra: Australia National University, Canberra, 1964).

Fox H.F. "Valedictory to the Australasian Institute of Cost Accountants," *The Australian Accountant* (July, 1966), p. 347.

Garner, Paul S. *Evolution of Cost Accounting to 1925* (Alabama: University of Alabama Press, 1954).

Graham, A. W. *The First Fifty Years 1950–59* (Wellington: New Zealand Society of Accountants, 1960).

Harrisson, H. M. "State President's Newsletter to Queensland Members of the Australasian Institute of Cost Accountants" (June 15, 1956).

Jensen, J. K. *The Development of Munitions Production in Australia* (Melbourne: Institute of Industrial Management, 1943).

Johnson, Thomas H. and Robert S. Kaplan. *Relevance Lost: The Rise and Fall of Management Accounting* (Boston, MA: Harvard Business School Press, 1987).

Kay, R. M. "Where to From Here? Past Development and Future Trends in Cost Accounting," *The Accountant's Journal* (February 28, 1949), pp. 187–189.

Kenley, W. J. *History of the Australian Society of Accountants and Its Antecedent Bodies* (Melbourne: Australian Society of Accountants, 1962).

Loft, Anne. *Coming into the Light* (London: Chartered Institute of Management Accountants, 1990).

Mills, R. C. "The Tariff Board of Australia," *Economic Record*, Vol. 3 (May, 1927), pp. 52–81.

Morrell, W. p. and D. O. W. Hall. *A History of New Zealand Life* (Christchurch: Whitcombe and Tombs, 1957).

National Association of Cost Accountants. "Organization and Objectives," *Official Publications*, Vol. 1, No. 1 (December, 1919).

New Zealand Institute of Cost Accountants, *Minutes of General Council and Annual Reports*. (various years)

New Zealand Society of Accountants, *Annual Reports*. (various years)

Oliver, W. H. and B. R. Williams, Eds. *The Oxford History of New Zealand* (Wellington: Oxford University Press, 1981).

Pickles, J. H. "President's Address to the Annual General Meeting," *The Accountants' Journal* (April, 1961), pp. 278–284.

Pohlen, F. J. "The Inside Story of Cost-Plus Contracts," *The Accountants' Journal* (November 30, 1943), pp. 108–114.

Powell, P. W. "Costing Principles and Problems," *The Australasian Accountant and Secretary*, Vol. IV (June, 1921), pp. 183–187, 210–217, and (August, 1921), pp. 247–251.

Roberts, M. G. "A History of the New Zealand Institute of Cost Accountants." Unpublished paper, 1953.

Schedvin, C. B. *Australia and the Great Depression* (Sydney: Sydney University Press, 1970).

Schumer, L. A. "Cost Accounting in Australia in Retrospect," *The Australian Accountant* (June, 1962), pp. 322–325.

Sinclair, Keith. *A History of New Zealand* (Middlesex: Penguin, 1959).

Solomons, D. "The Historical Development of 'Costing'" in *Studies in Costing*, Second Edition, D. Solomons, Ed. (London: Sweet & Maxwell, 1968), pp. 3–49.

Stacey, H. A. *English Accountancy: A Study in Social and Economic History* (London: Gee and Company (Publishers) Ltd., 1954).

Stark, R. G. "President's Address to the Annual General Meeting," *The Accountants' Journal* (April, 1960), pp. 286–292.

Strickett, H. E. "The Development of Accountancy in New Zealand," *The Accountants' Journal* (December 1, 1952), pp. 130–138.

The Institute of Cost and Works Accountants. *A Scheme for the Development of the Accountancy Profession in Great Britain and Ireland*, 1968.

Thomas, H. "Letter to R. Anderson" (July 18, 1995).

Vatter, William J. *Survey of Accountancy Education in Australia* (Melbourne: Australian Society of Accountants, 1964).

Webb, G. T. "The Nature of Accounting and Cost Accounting Records In Use in Australia at the Present Time," *The Chartered Accountant in Australia* (July, 1948), pp. 65–71.

———. "Letter to R. H. Anderson" (July 10, 1995).

Wells, M. C. *Accounting for Common Costs* (Urbana IL: University of Illinois Center for International Education and Research in Accounting, 1978).

From Charlatan to Doyen: The Legitimization of Australian Accountancy

Kathie Cooper
University of Wollongong
Australia

1.0 ABSTRACT

It is one thing for an occupational group to designate itself a profession but quite another to attain public recognition of this status. Accomplishing publicly recognized professional status was a prime task of Australian accountancy during the course of this century.

This task was, perhaps, more difficult for Australian accountancy than, for example, their United Kingdom counterparts. One factor contributing to the difficulty of the task was that many of the unexpected corporate failures in the wake of the Victorian land boom of the late eighteenth century cast many members of the early Australian accountancy associations in the role of charlatan or rogue. This occurred because subsequent investigation revealed that the accounts of many of these companies were grossly misleading even though they had been prepared and audited by so-called "qualified" accountants. Despite this ignominious start, two Australian accountancy associations, the Institute of Chartered Accountants in Australia and the Australian Society of Certified Practising Accountants (formerly the Australian Society of Accountants), have achieved a dominant position in the regulation of external financial reporting through control of the setting of legally backed accounting standards.

In this paper, a translation model of power will be used to explain some of the professionalization activities of Australian accountancy associations. In particular, it will demonstrate that the accountancy associations used traditional professionalization activities such as education, examination and training requirements to exclude the "unqualified" from membership. However, non-traditional strategies were also employed when necessary.

Non-traditional professionalization strategies included the formation of alliances and agency relationships with others interested in the activities of accounting associations, for example, the financial press, business interests, federal and state governments and the United Kingdom government and chartered accountants. Dissidence within Australian accountancy also had to be overcome by alliance strategies.

The translation model of power shows that achieving a dominant position, or for Australian accountancy, the transition from charlatan to doyen, was not so much a matter of proving claims to specialized knowledge and skill used in the public interest but an ability to form alliances and create agency relationships: in other words, an ability to win friends and influence people.

2.0 INTRODUCTION

This paper will demonstrate some of the strategies used by the Australian accountancy profession to seize a position of both prestige and dominance within the regulation of corporate financial reporting. It will show that at the turn of this century, those who sought to achieve professional status for Australian accountants did not enjoy the esteem of either the public or the state. Even one of their own role models, the Institute of Chartered Accountants in England and Wales (ICAEW), expressed doubt as to the quality of Australian accountants. However, through what could be described as a consistent and determined public relations campaign, Australian accountants, in particular, the Institute of Chartered Accountants in Australia (ICAA) and the Australian Society of Certified Practising Accountants (ASCPA), have achieved professional status within the regulatory framework.

The processes used to attain this status will be explained within the context of a translation model of power. In a translation model of power, power is not something that is possessed. In addition, power is an outcome rather than a cause. In other words, power is not the means used to achieve a particular outcome but the outcome itself. Resources, including knowledge and skill, are the means by which power is achieved. These resources are used to create an environment conducive to domination of a given field by a group or organization. For example, a group or organization seeking domination of a particular field may use a claim to specialized knowledge or skill to form alliances and agency relationships with other interest groups. Alliances and agency relationships are used, in turn, as resources to enable that group or organization to achieve hegemonic domination of that field. Hegemonic domination facilitates the exercize of power.

This paper argues that the Australian accountancy profession used its claim to specialized knowledge and skill to form an agency relationship between itself and the general public. This relationship was predicated on the assertion that accounting was a means by which management would be accountable for the resources entrusted to it and that only the members of specified accountancy associations had the requisite knowledge and skill to ensure that financial statements, duly audited, fulfilled this function. Support for acceptance of this assertion required the formation of alliances with legislators, the press and the business community, in particular, those most likely to avail themselves of accounting services.

The format of the paper is as follows: evidence of the changing perception of accounting; outline of the moments of translation; historical evidence of the strategies; concluding comments.

3.0 CHANGING PERCEPTIONS OF ACCOUNTANTS

The economic collapse in the wake of the Victorian land boom gave rise to a number of scandals involving accountants, including members of the early accountancy associations, when it was revealed that accounting had been used to conceal impending failure. Cannon's [1972] study of the land boom, the major companies involved and the impact of the collapse of the boom on the population provides evidence of this:

> The falsifying of balance sheets, the payment of dividends from non-existent profits were among the shocking features of the crash .... At the annual meeting of the Real Estate Bank on 7 August 1891, James Munro said: "The properties of the bank are in splendid order." Four months later it collapsed. At the meeting of the Land Credit Bank on 31 October 1891, a 10 per cent dividend was declared, although by that date the bank had lost all its capital and reserves. On the same day, Sir Matthew Davies's Freehold Investment Co. Ltd. declared an 8 per cent dividend and went into liquidation exactly three months later. [p. 28]

Public resentment was evident in subsequent parliamentary debates and also the press. For example, in the course of debates dealing with the 1896 Victorian Companies Act, it is clear that some members of the legislature did not consider membership of the Incorporated Institute of Accountants or The Federal Institute of Accountants to be any guarantee of an ability to undertake an audit [Victoria, 1896, pp. 3606–3608]. The arguments in support of this view included the claim that some of the auditors whose work had been called into question at the time of the collapse of the boom were members of "one or other of these institutes" [p. 3608].

Further examples of an adverse public perception of accountants and members of early accountancy associations are available from the *Australasian Insurance and Banking Record (AIBR)*. In 1893, it was stated that

> a proportion of the public accountants practising in the colonial centres are such, not because they are the most fit but because other employments have failed them. [1893, p. 668]

Furthermore

> when it is reflected that, ... most of the balance sheets of the bogus and mushroom companies of Melbourne, the administration of which has frequently been marked by the utmost unscrupulousness, have been signed from time to time by Fs.I.A.V., the pretension of the institutes to a monopoly of accountancy work ought not to be encouraged. [1896, p. 717]

However, some fifteen years later, the *AIBR* apparently was prepared to modify its perception of at least one accountancy association. The September 1911 editorial of *The Public Accountant* carried the following quote from the *AIBR*:

> The Australasian Corporation of Public Accountants is the one that is most professional and therefore merits the confidence of the financial and mercantile world .... Our long experience in examining accounts and balance-sheets convinces us that the more the services of the responsible professionals, highly qualified by actual experience, are retained, the better. The Australasian Corporation of Public Accountants is gradually raising the status and utility of the profession. [Editorial, 1911a, p. 199]

Similar sentiments were expressed by the editor of *The Register* at the 1911 annual dinner of the Australasian Corporation of Public Accountants (ACPA):

> it should be an absolutely requisite requirement that no accounts of any public body which handles public money should be audited except by a thoroughly qualified man; and to the extent to which your association raises, and keeps raised, the standard of accountancy and insists upon the greatest care in the management generally, to that extent the public is undoubtedly its debtor. [ACPA, 1911b, p. 229]

There is evidence that members of Parliament were also changing their perception of accountants. For example, at the second annual dinner of the ACPA, a member of Parliament stated: "We look upon accountants as ... closely identified with the progress of the country" [ACPA, 1910b, p. 170]. In addition, members of the accountancy associations were beginning to be approached to give advice on matters of public interest. For, example, members of the ACPA were appointed to investigate the costing methods of Victoria's suburban railways. The Victorian branch of the ACPA's Parliamentary and Laws Committee was invited to make recommendations on the draft of proposed Victorian companies' legislation [ACPA, 1911a, p. 217].

In more recent times, a majority of the South Australian Government Committee to Inquire into the Registration and Conduct of Accountants considered membership in either the ICAA or the ASCPA to be the necessary qualification for registration. The reason for this being that the ICAA and the ASCPA constituted the accountancy profession [South Australia, 1979, p. 26].

The Committee of Inquiry into the Australian Financial System (the Campbell Committee) also indicated a perception that the ICAA and the ASCPA were the leading exponents of accounting practice in Australia. For example, the Committee considered that accounting standards should not be designed or developed by a government body because

> it is questionable whether the standards would be soundly based or as closely attuned to the needs of users of accounts as standards developed by those actively involved in accounting practice. [Australia, 1981, 21.55, p. 372]

Therefore, the Committee recommended that the ICAA and the ASCPA continue to take responsibility for the design and development of accounting standards [21.57, p. 372]. However, the Committee also recommended the establishment of an Accounting Standards Review Board (ASRB) to be vested with responsibility for the adoption of standards which were to have legislative support [21.57, p. 372]. Legislative backing was deemed necessary to facilitate enforcement of the standards. While these recommendations suggested government sanction of the autonomy of accountants and, thereby, indicated that accountancy had "arrived" at true professional status, recognition of the expertise and status of members of the accountancy bodies to determine appropriate accounting standards was not unequivocal. The Committee considered that accounting standards potentially affect the economy through investment behaviour and, therefore, should not be solely determined by the accountancy profession [21.46, p. 370]. In the Committee's opinion, there should be a balancing of interests [21.56, p. 372].

The establishment of an independent ASRB was also suggested by the New South Wales Attorney-General, Frank Walker [1981a, b] and the National Companies and Securities Commission [NCSC, 1982, p. 21]. Understandably, the accountancy bodies maintained that they alone should be responsible for the setting of accounting standards including those with legislative backing [Australian Accountancy Profession Joint Submission, 1982]. However, in spite of extensive opposition from the two accountancy bodies, the ASRB became a reality in January 1984. It appeared that what the State gave to the ICAA and the ASCPA with one hand, it took away with the other. However, while the accountancy bodies did not achieve absolute autonomy or monopoly over the setting of accountancy standards with legal backing (approved accounting standards), they maintained control over the setting of Australian accounting standards which were binding on members of the two accountancy bodies. In addition, they achieved a dominant position in the setting of statutory backed approved accounting standards in that the profession-sponsored Australian Accounting Research Foundation (AARF) was to provide technical support for the newly created ASRB.

The dominance of the AARF in the standard-setting process is an historical fact. The ASRB was empowered, to consider for approval, standards emanating from the AARF *and* other interested parties. However, Release 200 paragraphs 3 and 4 states that the Ministerial Council endorsed the view that proposed approved accounting standards (that is, those that were to have legal backing) would normally originate from the AARF. Proposed standards submitted by other interested parties were to be referred to the AARF for comment. Of three standards submitted to the ASRB from sources other than the AARF, only one ever attained approved accounting standard status and it has since been withdrawn.

The dominance of the accountancy bodies is also evident in a review of the composition of the ASRB. Most of its members had accounting backgrounds and some had been senior office bearers of either the ICAA, the ASCPA or other accountancy associations. For example, the affiliations and designations of some of the members of the ASRB in its first four years of operations included past presidents and vice-presidents of the Australasian Institute of Cost Accountants, the ASCPA, the ICAA and the International Congress of Accountants 1972; a past chairman and members of the International Committee of the Accountancy Profession; International Federation of Accountants and the AARF [ASRB, 1987, pp. 6–7; ASRB, 1987–88, pp. 5–7].

In 1988, the profession secured even tighter control of the standard-setting process. In its 1987–88 annual report, the ASRB announced that a call had been made during the year by the Joint Accounting Bodies for a merger of the ASRB and the Accounting Standards Board of the AARF [1987–1988, p. 1]. The annual report further stated that the ASRB and the Joint Accounting Bodies had worked together to formulate agreed terms of the merger for approval by the Ministerial Council [p. 1]. The merger was approved at the fortieth meeting of the Ministerial Council [NCSC, 1988–89, p. 65]. The newly reconstituted standards' board was given responsibility for the development and promulgation of both approved accounting standards and Australian accounting standards. As a result of the merger, the ASRB was to set all accounting standards for the private sector [p. 66]. The membership of the ASRB was increased from seven to nine. Four members of the ASRB were to be nominated by the accountancy associations. Technical support in the standard setting process was still to be provided by the AARF which continued to be funded by the accounting bodies [p. 66].

In 1991, the ASRB was replaced with the Australian Accounting Standards Board (AASB). Unlike the ASRB which was created by a memorandum of the Ministerial Council, the AASB was established by an Act of Parliament. Arguably, this gives even greater recognition to the two accountancy bodies in that even though the membership of the Board was increased to eleven, its functions, composition and research base remained essentially the same. The Board itself has statutory recognition whereas before, only approved accounting standards had this status.

While it cannot be said that the peak accountancy associations or their members are seen universally as the purveyors of outstanding accounting and accounting-related services, they do hold a dominant position within the field. As indicated earlier, the achievement of this position was not realized overnight and not without substantial effort on the part of the current accountancy associations and their predecessors. The balance of the paper will provide an explanation of the processes which facilitated the transition of accountancy from infamy to legitimacy as professional practitioners.

4.0 THE TRANSLATION MODEL OF POWER

In a translation model, power may be an outcome but it is not a cause and it cannot be possessed. Outcomes are shaped and usually changed or modified, that is transformed, by all those who have an interest in them and are prepared to act on that interest. Power, as an outcome, facilitates the domination of a given field, for example, accountancy. Latour describes the processes of achieving and maintaining domination as links in a chain whereby each link injects its own energy, shaping claims and instituting change over time [1986, pp. 267–268]. A more specific explanation and one consistent with the domination of the standard-setting process by the ICAA and the ASCPA is offered by Callon

> To translate is to displace ... allies ... to express in one's own language what others say and want, why they act in the way they do and how they associate with each other: it is to establish oneself as a spokesman. [1986, p. 223]

The process of translation is complex and comprises four moments or stages of translation, problematization, interessement, enrolment and mobilization. There is a fifth phase, dissidence, which may limit the achievements of each other stage.

4.1 Problematization

The process of problematization involves attempts by one group or organization to convince another group or organization that the latter has a problem and that the solution to that problem can be provided only by the former group or organization. In Callon's terms, problematization involves a group or organization making itself indispensable in the network of relationships it is seeking to create [1986, p. 204]. The purpose of this process is facilitation of a strategic agency relationship. To achieve this, the would-be agent must establish and control a "necessary nodal point" [p. 205] between itself and the other group. Clegg refers to a "necessary nodal point" as "a channel through which traffic between them occurs on terms which privilege the putative strategic agent" [1989, p. 199]. Callon further elaborates on the meaning of problematization which "describes a system of alliances, or associations, between entities, thereby defining the identity and what they 'want'." [1986, p. 206].

As part of the professionalization process, would be professional groups often use their claim to expert knowledge and skill as a strategy to establish themselves as an obligatory passage point between themselves, their clients and the general public. Lubell, drawing on the works of others, describes the process as follows:

> Because professional services are built upon esoteric knowledge, the public tends to regard members of a profession with a certain degree of mystique. It is felt that the professional practitioner is better prepared than the client ... to determine the client's needs and the nature of services appropriate for a given situation. The client does not tell the professional what services are required. Rather, the professional tells the client what services are necessary. [1978, pp. 62-63]

This paper will demonstrate that Australian accountancy associations used this strategy in their bid to achieve domination of the regulation of external financial reporting through control of the standard-setting process in this country.

4.2 Interessement

In the next stage in the translation process, interessement, a group or organization seeks to cement its position by "interesting," "enrolling" or "attracting" another group or organization to its own by coming between that group or organization and another [Clegg, 1989, p. 205]. Callon explains interessement as "[t]o be interested is to be in between (inter-esse), to be interposed" [1986, p. 208]. The purpose of interessement is to establish membership and meaning of certain categorization devices [Clegg, 1989, p. 205]. This paper adopts the view that categorization devices include professionalization processes such as the formation of professional associations with entry requirements including specified training and education. In this way, the profession determines its membership and establishes a distinction between non-professional accountants and professional accountants, public accountants as opposed to those working in industry. Groups or organizations seeking professional status often argue that the distinction is necessary in order to protect the public interest. That is, the public will be best served if only those with the requisite skill, knowledge and training, as recognized by specified professional associations, undertake work or provide services in a particular field. This is consistent with Callon's view whereby interessement is aimed at achieving a balance of power favourable to the enrolling agency by reducing competition within a particular field [1986, p. 211].

Interessement can be seen as a consolidation of the problematization process. Those seeking to achieve a dominant position in a given field attempt to strengthen their position or claim by forming agency relationships with other parties who could also be expected to have an interest in that field. Callon describes interessement as "how the allies are locked into place" [1986, p. 206]. According to Callon, this is necessary because the entities and relationships identified during the problematization process must be tested to determine the strength of problematization:

> Each entity enlisted by the problematization can submit to being integrated into the initial plan, or inversely, refuse the transaction by defining its identity, its goals, projects, orientations, motivations, or interests in another manner. [p. 207]

As the extracts cited from the *AIBR* and parliamentary debates late last century suggest, the aspirations of some Australian accountancy associations to seize for themselves a dominant position in the regulation of external financial reporting were initially rejected. It will be shown later in the paper that these associations had to demonstrate their claim rather than have their claims to be serving the public interest accepted on faith. The process of interessement can take many forms depending on the nature of the problem identified and those to be enrolled and what they want [p. 211]. One of the major strategies adopted by Australian accountancy associations was education.

4.3 Enrolment

The third phase in the translation process is enrolment [Clegg, 1989, p. 205] or definition and coordination of roles [Callon, 1986, p. 211]. In this phase of the process, agencies attempt to form "alliances and coalitions between memberships and meaning which they have sought to fix" [Clegg, 1989, p. 205]. While this phase appears similar to the interessement phase, there is a difference. Alliances and coalitions are not the same as an agency relationship and could be seen as a means of avoiding resistance from other groups that may wish to encroach on another's hold over a particular field of endeavour. Interessement attempts to form alliances but may not be successful. Enrolment is the achievement of alliances [Callon, 1986, p. 211]. Callon describes enrolment as "the group of multilateral negotiations, trials of strength and tricks that accompany the interessements and enable them to succeed" [p. 211].

The process of enrolment was evident in the bid by Australian public accountants to acquire a royal charter because their claim to specialized knowledge and skill was not sufficient. In the political climate of the time, it was necessary for them to negotiate not only with the United Kingdom Parliament but also Australian state and federal governments and other accountancy associations.

4.4 Mobilization

The final phase of the translation process, mobilization, is the means by which the enrolling agent ensures that it is not betrayed by the enrolled agencies, that is, the representations of interest remain fixed [Clegg, 1989, p. 205]. This final phase can be seen as the most critical in the process as it is effectively the culmination of the previous phases. Will the enrolling agency be accepted as the representative of the enrolled and will the enrolled follow their representative? In other words, what the enrolling agency is seeking is a transition from enrolment to active support [Callon, 1986, p. 218]. Formation of associations and statutory endorsement of domination of a particular area could be seen as forms of mobilization. For example, membership of the ICAA and ASCPA carried an obligation to comply with the standards promulgated by those bodies. Legislative backing for approved accounting standards extended this obligation to companies coming within the bounds of the Corporations Law. The creation of the AASB by an Act of Parliament and the subsequent negotiations giving the ICAA and the ASCPA effective domination of the standard setting are evidence of the active support of those bodies by the State.

4.5 Dissidence

Even if the process of translation is successful, it does not mean a dominant position will be maintained. Dissidence arising from various sources, including those sought to become a party to an agency relationship, may result in the translation process becoming treason. Callon explains this stage as follows:

> Dissidence ... brings into question some of the gains of the previous stages. The displacements and the spokesmen are challenged or refused .... New displacements take the place of the previous ones but these divert the actors from the obligatory passage points that had been imposed upon them. New spokesmen are heard that deny the representativity of the previous ones. Translation continues but the equilibrium has been modified. [1986, pp. 218–219]

Power and dissidence or resistance are inextricably linked (refer for example, Clegg [1989]; Barbalet [1985]) because power may be limited by dissidence or resistance. The primary example of dissidence or resistance and its impact on the search for domination that will be offered in this paper will be the opposition of some of the Victorian accountancy associations to the second and third applications for a Royal Charter by other practising public accountants in Australia.

The next section will provide evidence of some of the strategies used by selected accountancy associations to navigate their way through the translation process and achieve a position of status and prestige within the community and eventually, a dominant position in the standard-setting process.

5.0 PROFESSIONALIZATION — THE PATH TO DOMINATION

The major processes used by Australian accountancy to achieve a dominant position in the determination of appropriate accounting practices and standards included the formal organization of accountancy associations; education, examinations and training; and the establishment of research and accounting standard-setting bodies. Formal organization and the demonstration of technical ability were the starting point and are consistent with the concepts of problematization and interessement. Subsequent activities, including the acquisition of a Royal Charter, were consolidation strategies incorporating interessement, enrolment and mobilization. Developing binding accounting standards further contributed to the mobilization process. This section will consider these activities in turn.

5.1 Formal Organization

It appears the impetus to form professional accountancy associations in Australia was twofold. First, the "boom" of the 1880s had witnessed a rapid expansion in joint stock companies to take advantage of the growth of a wide range of industries including building and manufacturing. This economic boom and its concomitant increase in capital expenditure led, in turn, to a need for more sophisticated forms of bookkeeping [Graham, 1978, p. 1; Marshall, 1978, pp. 10–11]. A new area of knowledge was beginning to take on an important role in the country and the accountants of the time seized the opportunity of laying claim to it:

> if those who were holding themselves out as public practitioners were to gain the confidence and support of the public, there must be a standard fixed which would connote the possession of the necessary qualifications for this special work. [Brentnall, 1938, p. 64]

Second, there was an apparent desire to attain for Australian accountants the perceived status and prestige of their United Kingdom counterparts [p. 64], in particular, those who had been granted Royal Charters. Apart from the perceived status of a Royal Charter, it was considered that this would preclude the unqualified from undertaking accountancy work [ACPA, 1910a, pp. 133–134].

In a bid to preclude the "unqualified" from work of an accounting nature, the accountancy associations invariably adopted a "problematization" strategy. The "problem" identified was that any person who wished could designate themselves an accountant. This "problem" was not unique to Australia. In England, for example, not only could lawyers do work of an accounting nature but also "charlatans and rogues" and others without the appropriate training. It was argued that this was detrimental to society [Howitt, 1966, p. 4]. The "solution" was the formal establishment of professional associations, membership in which would be limited to those with the requisite training and experience. For example, the objects of the first Australian accountancy association, the Adelaide Society of Accountants, included

> (iv) to foster in commercial circles a higher sense of the importance of systematic and correct book-keeping, and to encourage a greater degree of efficiency in those engaged in accountancy and auditing. [Adelaide Society of Accountants List of Members, Constitution and Rules, Adelaide Society of Accountants, 1886, clause 2]

This is also an example of interessement. By forming accountancy associations with a view to improving accounting and audit practice, the founders of these groups were, firstly, trying to make a clear distinction between those with the appropriate skills and those without them. In other words, they sought to categorize those performing accounting and audit duties into the qualified and unqualified. By so doing, they also attempted to come between the unqualified and those who used and relied upon accounting and audit services. They were effectively attempting to establish an agency relationship with users of accounting and audit services as the principal and members of the accounting association as the agent.

However, declaring that members of the accountancy associations possessed specialized knowledge and skill was not sufficient. It had to be demonstrated. According to Marshall, the reason for the introduction of a system of entrance examinations was the "urgent need to regulate and raise the standards of public accountants" [1978, p. 11]. This appears to have been particularly necessary following the land boom and economic collapse of the late 1880s and early 1890s. As indicated earlier in the paper, a number of scandals involving accountants, including members of the early accountancy associations, came to light in the wake of the economic collapse. These revelations were exacerbated by the knowledge that foundation members of most of these associations had been admitted to membership without examination to attest to their abilities [Victoria, 1896, p. 3607]. However, new members were traditionally required to sit for examination.

5.2 Education, Examinations and Training

Initially, examinations included bookkeeping, commercial, mercantile and company law, bankruptcy, receivership, partnership, executorship contracts and auditing [Marshall, 1978, p. 11, Brentnall, 1938, p. 65]. It was later considered that accountants required a broad-based education including English, foreign languages (for example, French and German), and commercial geography [Royal Commission of the University of Melbourne, 1904, p. 70].

While the various professional associations required new members to take examinations, no educational facilities were provided for would-be examination candidates. The Society of Accountants appears to be an exception in that classes were conducted in accountancy, auditing and law [p. 319]. For other associations, private coaches provided what teaching was available [p. 315, Nixon, 1936, p. 270]. This situation was remedied to a certain extent by the formation of students' societies. In 1898, a students' society was established in Victoria by the Victorian Institute [Brentnall, 1938, p. 67]. Students' societies were later established in Sydney in 1910 and in Adelaide and Hobart in 1911 [Australian Society of Accountants, undated, p. 30]. In September, 1902, The Corporation of Accountants Students' Association held its first meeting [Brierley, 1902, p. 21]. The Federal Institute of Accountants formed a students' society in conjunction with the ACPA in 1913 [p. 53]. In addition to passing the necessary examinations, some accountancy associations, for example, the ACPA, required aspiring members to undergo a minimum training period [ACPA, 1911b, p. 232].

The success of the profession's education and training activities in raising the status of accountancy associations was evident from the early 1890s. For example, the *AIBR* while critical of the accountancy associations in some respects, considered their education and examination activities to be a step in the direction of overcoming some of the deficiencies of then practising accountants [1893, p. 668; 1896, p. 718]. By 1903, the *AIBR*, was quite glowing in its comments regarding the Incorporated Institute of Accountants, Victoria:

> They have taken a much wider view in making the Institute a great training body .... That so many have passed the examinations of the Institute is highly gratifying. The qualifications of accountants and book-keepers in private offices have certainly been raised by the Institute system of examinations. [1903, p. 475]

The problematization process helped create a boundary around accountancy in that it provided a means of identifying qualified accounting practitioners from the unqualified through membership in accountancy associations. Membership in accountancy associations gave members the right to use designated appellations, for example, "FASA" (being a Fellow of the Adelaide Society of Accountants) and "FIAV" of "AIAV" (being a Fellow or Associate of the Incorporated Institute of Accountants, Victoria). However, the formation of accountancy associations and the introduction of education, examination and training requirements were not sufficient to give these groups domination of accountancy. Anyone who wished could designate themselves "accountant" and no one accountancy association could lay claim to being a "nodal or obligatory passage point" in the determination of accounting practice. To achieve this, the problematization process had to be tested through the formation of alliances and agency relationships between accountancy associations and other interested parties.

5.3 Consolidation Activities

The accountancy associations used a number of methods to create an environment wherein they could achieve prestige and status both for the organizations and for their members. This included cultivating the goodwill of other interest groups. As Selander argues, occupational groups form alliances or cooperate with others in order to protect themselves and strengthen their own position [1990, p. 140]. Once a social and occupational demarcation of a boundary has been achieved, a closure of the area or field of knowledge is effected. In other words, other groups or their views are called upon and taken into consideration in planning professional activities until such time as the group considers it is strong enough to stand alone. Selander considers that an occupational group which has organized itself around a body of knowledge, but is still in a middle or subordinate position, will adopt an associative strategy to assimilate and neutralize other organized interests [p. 142]. Alternatively, even where an occupational group or profession has achieved closure but is weakened for some reason, an associative strategy may be used to reduce conflict and mobilize resources [p. 143]. This is in keeping with Callon's interpretation of interessement which is directed towards achieving a balance of power and curtailing competition within a given field [1986, p. 211].

One of the ways in which early accountancy associations forged alliances and created an environment conducive to domination of their field of endeavour was through social activities and their journals. For example, the ACPA used *The Public Accountant* to reproduce dinner speeches given not only by members of the accountancy associations but also by judges, members of Parliament, editors of journals and other public figures. These speeches invariably reflected a positive image of the ACPA and its members. Addresses to student societies and at annual general meetings were also published. Once again, these addresses appear to have been designed to convey an image of a highly professional organization dedicated to providing the public with well-trained and knowledgeable accountants. Editorials were also used extensively to publicize the viewpoints of the would-be profession on a number of matters including the long battle for a Royal Charter by accountants in public practice in Australia. The purpose appears to have been to create an accountancy discourse in favour of the accountancy association and which would attain hegemonic domination of accountancy practices in Australia.

The various Royal Charter bids provide clear evidence of the translation process. It was a battle that spanned almost a quarter of a century and raised issues of appropriate education and training, the use of specified designations, accountancy association rivalries and the pride of a newly created nation. The battle also demonstrates that altruistic motives and even the demonstration of specialized knowledge and skill through education and training were not enough to overcome dissidence between the various accountancy associations or resistance from Commonwealth and state governments to proposals to seek incorporation of Australian accountancy associations from a foreign government. It proved to be more of a test of the aspiring chartered accountants' skills to strike bargains and compromise than any other issue. As Thomas Brentnall, one of the foundation members of Australian accountancy, noted "before we finally got the Charter ... in 1928, we had to concede almost everything which had barred the way ..." [1938, p. 191].

The First Charter Bid

In 1905, a formal application for a Royal Charter was lodged by accountants in Victoria. While the petition was supported by the Victorian Government, it was doomed due to resistance from accountants both in other parts of Australia and in the United Kingdom [Graham, 1978, p. 7; Marshall, 1978, p. 12; Brentnall, 1938, p. 69]. The basis of the opposition from other Australian accountants was that granting a charter to Victorian accountants would be detrimental to accountants in other states. In particular, members of the Victorian accountancy associations seeking the Charter would be entitled to use the designation, Chartered Accountant, a recognized and respected appellation, even if they practised in another state [Editorial, 1905a, 1905b, Corporation of Accountants of Australia, 1906]. It was proposed in a counter-petition lodged by the Corporation of Accountants of Australia and the New South Wales Committee of the Society of Accountants and Auditors, England [Proposed Victorian Charter, 1905, paragraph 12] that a federal association be formed for the purpose, *inter alia,* of seeking a charter.

The resistance to the Victorian Charter bid was not confined to Australia. In June 1906, *The Public Accountant* reproduced correspondence between the Secretary of State for the Colonies and the Under Secretary for Finance and Trade [The Treasury, New South Wales] regarding the use of the title "Chartered Accountant". This correspondence, which included a letter to the Colonial Office from the Secretary of the Institute of Chartered Accountants, London, had been forwarded for comment to the Corporation of Accountants of Australia.

The view expressed by the Secretary of State for the Colonies did not bode well for the Victorian Charter application if its success meant members of the Australian chartered body were able to adopt the initials and titles used by the English Institute. It was considered such usage "would lead to inconvenience and misunderstanding both here and in Australia, and would give the members of the English Institute serious ground for complaint" [Letter from Lord Elgin reproduced in "Correspondence, ..." 1906, p. 72]. This inconvenience would arise from the "multiplication" of chartered accountants, a title respected in financial circles around the world [p. 73], particularly, when the chartered accountants of England had no knowledge of the adequacy of Australian accountancy examinations and standards.

It is possible, however, that there was another motive for the English opposition. This other motive being that British chartered accountants had an effective monopoly on auditing the books of UK companies operating in Australia. The English Institute not only opposed the charter but also colonial legislation which could confer the title "Chartered Accountant" on members of specified professional associations or could provide for registration of Australian accountants. This had already occurred in Canada and South Africa [pp. 72–73]. This issue was again raised when a private member's bill calling for the registration of accountants was introduced into the New South Wales' Parliament. Once again, the Secretary of the Institute protested via the Colonial Office arguing that the provisions of the bill could prevent members of the English Institute from undertaking audits of New South Wales' companies and from doing business for clients in that State ["Correspondence ...," 1907, p. 147]. This was claimed to disadvantage British investors who, having invested capital in the colonies, should be able to appoint the auditor of their choice [pp. 147–148]. The English Institute was using its own particular problematization strategy.

These fears provided the basis of an enrolment or alliance strategy undertaken by the Australian accountancy associations aimed at quashing the resistance of UK chartered accountants. For example, the letter referred to above was forwarded for comment to the Corporation of Accountants of Australia by the New South Wales Treasury Department. The response made it clear that the Corporation considered British chartered accountants should not be debarred from undertaking accountancy work in any Australian state. The Corporation vowed to monitor all legislation affecting the accountancy profession and do their utmost to protect the interests of accountants throughout the British Empire ["Correspondence ...," 1907, p. 149]. Similar sentiments were expressed in the May and June 1907 editorials of *The Public Accountant* [1907b, p. 140, 1907c, p. 157, respectively]. While some Australian accountants quite rightly took exception to perceived slurs on the abilities of members of the Australian professional associations [Editorial, 1907a], a conciliatory approach was necessary because the support of the UK Institutes was needed if a Royal Charter was to be secured.

However, the assurances from the Corporation were to no avail, and, even if they had persuaded the English Institute to withdraw its opposition, other sections of Australian accountancy continued to oppose the petition. The Royal Charter petition was officially refused on the basis that a charter should not be granted to individual associations but to one representative body [Marshall, 1978, p. 12, Corporation of Accountants of Australia, 1907, p. 96, ACPA, 1911a, p. 206]. It was further suggested by the Colonial Office that the Australian accountants should be regulated by local legislation. In the absence of such legislation, any charter application should have the support of the Australian federal government [Poullaos, 1992, pp. 79–80, 83–84]. The challenge was set and those who sought a charter were faced with forming alliances with other accountancy associations as well as state and federal governments.

The Second Charter Bid

The challenge was taken up in 1907 with the formation of the Australasian Corporation of Public Accountants (ACPA). As will be discussed later, the formation of the ACPA was not for the sole purpose of obtaining a Royal Charter. However, within two years of its creation, the ACPA lodged a petition for a Royal Charter through the Australian federal government [Graham, 1978, p. 7]. Once again, there was dissidence and resistance to the charter application which proved insurmountable. Resistance came from three main sources: the Commonwealth and Victorian governments, the public accountants of England and the Victorian Institutes, particularly those responsible for the first unsuccessful charter bid.

The support of the Commonwealth Government had been specified by the Colonial Office as a prerequisite to the granting of a charter when the Victorian charter application was refused [Poullaos, 1992, pp. 79–80, 83–84]. However, it would appear that claims to specialized knowledge and skill in accounting matters were not enough. At this time, it was quite obvious that those who sought the charter had not considered the necessity of forming alliances or cultivating the goodwill of others in order to achieve their purpose. The prelude to the third charter bid suggests that the petitioners finally had acquired the essential skills of successful negotiators. During the second charter bid it would appear, however, that they indulged in a tactless, if not vitriolic, campaign against their adversaries. Poullaos, for example, argues that the support of the Commonwealth Government was not forthcoming during the second charter bid because the ACPA had alienated it by its frequent references to the constitutional barriers to federal legislation [p. 84]. A review of *The Public Accountant* provides ample evidence of what could be seen as a total lack of tact on the part of the ACPA with regard to this issue.

Given that the Commonwealth was still in its infancy, it is not unlikely that the Commonwealth and various state governments would take exception to the casting of aspersions on their abilities to come to agreement on Australian-wide legislation providing for the incorporation of an accountants' association or the referral of such legislation to the Commonwealth. For example, Brentnall argued at the second annual dinner of the ACPA that a Royal Charter, as a means of incorporation, was sought because the Commonwealth Constitution made it impossible to achieve incorporation which would be effective throughout all the States [ACPA, 1910b, p. 175]. Similarly, Yarwood's presidential address to the fifth annual meeting of the ACPA made reference to state jealousies and expressed the view that "in the present condition of Australian politics, there is [not] the slightest hope of anything being referred by all the States to the Federal Parliament" [ACPA, 1912c, p. 236]. Worse still, it appears that even if such agreement could be reached, it was considered that local legislation would not give Australian chartered accountants the worldwide recognition and prestige that a Royal Charter would confer [ACPA, 1912c, p. 239, Editorial, *The Public Accountant*, 1913, p. 74].

In addition, the Victorian state government took particular exception to the idea of a Royal Charter maintaining that the process was "archaic" and therefore, Australian accountants should be regulated by local legislation rather than the "old country" [ACPA, 1910b, p. 176]. It appears that the source of the Victorian government's opposition may have been based on dissidence within and between accountancy associations. In particular, some members of the ACPA considered that the Victorian government's resistance to the charter was founded on support of the Incorporated Institute of Accountants, Victoria:

> The action of the Incorporated Institute was the dominant factor which led to our defeat, because through their political influence the Victorian Government were induced to withhold their consent. [ACPA, 1924a, p. 111]

The opposition of the Victorian Institute appears to have had two sources, the first being a retaliation for the opposition of other accountancy associations to their initial charter bid. The second was far more deep seated and thus harder to overcome, particularly as it was closely connected with the most basic principle of the ACPA, the exclusion from membership of non-practising accountants [Graham, 1978, p. 5; ASA, undated, p. 27–28; Marshall, 1978, p. 13].

The various Institutes already in existence in Australia had members who were not practising public accountants even though they had actually passed the requisite examinations. The fact that even these individuals were not in public practice meant they were second-rate citizens in the eyes of practising public accountants and were often described as "commercial book-keepers" and "clerks" [Editorial, 1911b, p. 245; ACPA, 1912c, p. 236]. By denying membership to non-practising accountants, the founders of the ACPA adopted problematization and interessement strategies and a means of mobilization. The public interest was said to be served by excluding non-practising accountants from membership of the ACPA because only those with practical experience should undertake such work [ACPA, 1912c, p. 226; ACPA, 1913, p. 203; Editorial, 1914, p. 66]. The "problem" identified was that the "general clerk" did not have the skills necessary to undertake the more complex tasks required in public practice [ACPA, 1910a, p. 133] and practitioners should not be given the opportunity to learn at the expense of their clients. Therefore, practice in the office of a public accountant was essential training for those aspiring to offer their services as qualified public accountants [ACPA, 1912c, p. 226; Editorial, 1914, p. 66]. In addition, an essential ingredient in the formation of an agency relationship is effective organization. Grouping all practising public accountants into one body was a means of organizing or mobilizing resources in order to achieve public recognition of their superior capabilities [ACPA, 1910b, pp. 174–175] and also a Royal Charter.

The exclusion of non-practising accountants was also an alliance or enrolment strategy aimed at overcoming resistance from the public accountants in the UK to granting Australian accountants a Royal Charter. For example, when the question of a further charter application was raised with members of the ICAEW, support was contingent on provisions being made for a clear distinction between Australian chartered accountants and those in the UK. In addition, a minimum of three years' training in a public accountant's office was to be mandatory [ACPA, 1911b, pp. 232–233]. The ICAEW had implied this stipulation as early as 1906 in an editorial from *The Accountant* (England) and reproduced in *The Public Accountant*:

> it would be desirable that throughout His Majesty's dominions the term "Chartered Accountant" should be recognised as being synonymous with "qualified accountant," but that its use should be limited to those who are really qualified to practice.... [*The Public Accountant*, 1906, p. 39]

The ACPA steadfastly adhered to this viewpoint, insisting that a charter would not be granted to Australian accountants unless the application was lodged by an association consisting entirely of "bona fide" practising public accountants [ACPA, 1911b, pp. 232–233; 1912c, p. 237; Editorials, 1912, p. 251; 1913, p. 74]. However, the ACPA also adopted a further enrolment strategy in that it did attempt to overcome the opposition to the charter of the Victorian Institutes [ACPA, 1912c, pp. 193–194] but it was apparently too late.

The ACPA offered a number of compromises including providing for commercial examinations to be open to "commercial book-keepers" who, if they passed, would be eligible for membership if they entered public practice or became clerks in the office of a public accountant [Editorial, 1911b, p. 245; ACPA, 1912a, p. 157]. Provision was also made for those who were members of "specified local" institutes to join the ACPA on commencing public practice [ACPA, 1912a, p. 157; ACPA, 1912c, p. 237–238]. This compromise was accepted by all the relevant institutes and societies except the Incorporated Institute of Accountants, Victoria [ACPA, 1912c, p. 238].

The failure of these compromises to quell resistence from the Victorian Institute and the ACPA's less than sensitive approach to Commonwealth and state government rivalries appear to have sealed the fate of the second charter bid. In April 1914, *The Public Accountant* stated "the opposition has been politically too strong, and ... it is not likely the matter will be pursued further" [Editorial, 1914, p. 66]. The outbreak of World War I and the necessary preoccupation of the British government with it ensured the matter was dropped for some years [ACPA, 1915, p. 85].

The Third Charter Bid

In 1923, a third and final movement was begun in the quest for a Royal Charter [Brentnall, 1938, p. 69]. This successful bid was characterized by a marked difference in the ACPA's approach to its traditional antagonists. One of the clearest indications of a change in the approach of the ACPA was the lack of mention of the third charter attempt in *The Public Accountant* and public addresses by senior members of the association. There also was not a return to the acerbity that had characterized reports on the previous attempt including reference to the "antagonistic spirit" and "dog-in-the-manger" tactics of the Victorian Institute being, as it was, a "less publicly important" organization [Editorials: 1912, p. 250; 1914, p. 66]. The few public references to the charter bid tended to have a conciliatory tone. For example, Brentnall referred to charter negotiations at the New South Wales Branch annual dinner in 1924 but only to say that so far no progress had been made but there was still hope [ACPA, 1924b, p. 178]. At the Seventeenth Ordinary Meeting of Members in October of that year, Brentnall had made more extensive comment regarding the charter application but made it clear that even though the Victorian opposition was painful "beyond words" he still had "nothing but the kindest feelings" for the Institute of which he had earlier held office as President and Vice-President [ACPA, 1924a, p. 112].

There was also a clear change in the approach to the ACPA of the Victorian Institute, which had amended its title in 1922 to the Commonwealth Institute of Accountants [Marshall, 1978, p. 13; Graham, 1978, p. 8]. In 1924, the ACPA lodged a formal charter application with the Privy Council. Predictably, the Commonwealth Institute lodged a counter-petition [Marshall, 1978, p. 13; ASA, undated, p. 28; ACPA, 1925, p. 114]. However, unlike the past, opposition was based on the granting of a charter to a specified accountancy association rather than the exclusion of non-practising accountants [Marshall, 1978, p. 14; ASA, undated, p. 28; ACPA, 1925, p. 114]. It would appear that both organizations realized that compromise would be necessary if their members were to receive the recognition and prestige suggested by a Royal Charter of incorporation.

At the 1925 annual general meeting of the ACPA, Brentnall reproduced the presidential address of the latest annual meeting of the Commonwealth Institute [ACPA, 1925, pp. 114–115]. The address suggested meetings of all practising accountants throughout the country with a view to renewing the charter application on behalf of "every reputable and genuine practising accountant throughout Australia" [p. 115]. Brentnall expressed the view there was "little or nothing to object" to in this proposal and informed the members that meetings had already been held in Melbourne to "reconcile long-standing differences of opinion" [p. 115].

Early in 1926, agreement was reached between the two bodies. The terms of the resolution included that members of the Commonwealth Institute who had passed the full examinations of that body prior to the date of the granting of the charter should be eligible for membership of the chartered body on entering public practice. This was similar to the provisions the ACPA had already included in its articles except that prospective members previously had been required to sit for ACPA examinations. The deletion of this requirement represented a clear compromise on the part of the ACPA. In addition, the ACPA and the Commonwealth Institute were to have equal representation on the first Council of the new chartered body. It was also agreed that all negotiations and correspondence relative to this agreement be kept strictly confidential being disclosed only to members of the General Councils of the two bodies until such time as the Victorian Attorney-General withdrew that state's objection to the charter application [Graham, 1978, pp. 8–9]. This perhaps explains the lack of public reference to the charter bid and also the scant, almost negligible, records of the negotiations [p. 8].

The other hurdle to be overcome in the quest for a charter was gaining the active support of the Commonwealth government. This had been a stipulation imposed by the Colonial Office since the time of the first charter application. Up to this time, such support was not forthcoming. In 1923, however, Stanley Melbourne Bruce became Australia's prime minister and lent active support to the charter bid [p. 11]. Bruce apparently had a desire to cultivate a close relationship between Australia and Britain and, according to Graham, "saw the Royal Charter as fitting evidence of the special nature of this relationship" [p. 11].

With all hurdles effectively removed, The Institute of Chartered Accountants in Australia came into existence with the granting of a Royal Charter on June 19, 1928 to Thomas Brentnall, George Mason Allard and Henry Joshua Wise on behalf of the public accountants of Australia [Editorial, 1928, p. 3]. The status and prestige of a Royal Charter were now available to all who qualified for membership of the ICAA. Incorporating the practising public accountants in Australia into one body politic was now possible.

The Advent of Accounting Standards

Commercial accountants, however, still tended to be a more disparate group with a large number of accountancy associations. In 1952, the Australian Society of Accountants (now the ACPA), was formed through the amalgamation of the Commonwealth Institute of Accountants, the Federal Institute of Accountants and the Association of Accountants of Australia [Zeff, 1973, p. 1; ASA, undated, p. ix; Fitzgerald, 1962, p. 290]. Fitzgerald termed the formation of the ASA "a marked return to sanity in the organization of a unified profession" [p. 290]. This turn of events was, in retrospect, essential to the achievement of domination of the standard-setting process by the ASCPA and the ICAA. Having two major accountancy associations representing two broad categories of qualified accountants ultimately facilitated the mobilization of resources to establish standard-setting and research bodies and, thereby, demonstrate an ability to determine appropriate accounting practices and standards.

Australian accounting standards are a fairly recent phenomenon arising, it would seem, not out of any pressing urgency on the part of the accountancy associations to protect the public interest but out of a desire to establish accountancy as a "major" profession such as medicine and law [ASA, 1966, p. 30] and also maintain autonomy. In other words, if the accountancy associations did not set them, someone else, possibly legislators, would [p. 29]. While this fear was clearly evident in an ASA report dealing with corporate failures in the 1960s, it was not new. For example, while discussing a paper dealing with accounting standards presented at the Australian Congress on Accounting in Sydney in 1949, C.W.M. Court, State Registrar of the Western Australian branch of the ICAA, stated that "[c]omplacency on the part of the profession will mean compulsion, regimentation and legislation" and, therefore, the profession should act and "give the legislators no excuse to legislate for improvement of our standards" [Fitzgerald, 1949, p. 40]. An alternative strategy of giving the appearance of being prepared and qualified to assume certain responsibilities had been suggested seventeen years earlier. In 1932, the then president of the ICAEW, H.L.H. Hill, stated that the accountancy associations should lead the way in the formulation of corporate legislation:

> There is always a lag, and legislation with which we are concerned is always framed upon the best accountancy practice. We must, therefore, take the lead so that, if and when fresh legislation is enacted, there may be by that time an established practice in accountancy in advance of the requirements of present-day legislation, and established practice that will assist and direct those who frame the law to institute further safeguards for investors and the public. [*The Accountant*, 1932, p. 45]

Fitzgerald saw the lack of "authoritatively expressed accounting standards" as an unsuspected weakness of the profession and highlighted the limitations of accounting practice based on convention. Both this weakness and these limitations were brought to light by abuses of the corporate form [pp. 17–18]. This is not to say that accountancy associations were not at this time issuing practice guidelines to their members. The Commonwealth Institute had established a Committee on Accounting Principles in 1938 [ASA, undated, p. 47; Zeff, 1973, p. 29] which issued a pronouncement on cash discounts allowable and receivable in 1940 [ASA, undated; p. 47; Zeff, 1973, pp. 29–30]. An Accounting Research Committee was established in 1948 [Zeff, 1973, p. 32]. The ICAA had by this time also issued seven Recommendations on Accounting Principles [p. 3]. However, little progress towards the setting of accounting standards was made during the 1950s and early 1960s. The 1960s brought another series of spectacular corporate failures and, as with the failures in the wake of the Victorian land boom, accountants were implicated in the unexpectedness of these failures. According to Birkett and Walker:

> Many of the failures followed hard on the heels of the publication of audited financial statements depicting a profitable past and an apparently sound present. The inspectors' reports later documented breakdowns in accountability. Many of the failed companies had been in a state of crisis for some considerable period prior to their ultimate collapse. Their financial statements had not only failed to inform investors—they had also been misleading. These financial statements had been prepared by accountants, signed by auditors. In the public's eye they were the responsibility of the accounting profession. [1971, p. 131]

In 1964, the General Council of the ASA expressed its concern at the publicity which inspectors' reports into failed companies was generating in the press and instituted a study of some of these reports [ASA, 1966, p. 4; Zeff, 1973, p. 37]. The results of the study were issued in 1966 under the title, *Accounting Principles and Practices Discussed in Reports on Company Failures* [ASA, 1966]. The General Council conceded that there may be "deficiencies in the accountancy profession" [p. 5] but that the major problem was the lack of legally enforceable accounting methods [p. 7] and disciplinary procedures to ensure adherence to the accounting principles and standards of conduct developed and prescribed by the professional bodies [pp. 31–32].

Given that the ASA had not at this time issued any statements dealing with recommended practice, the Accounting Research Committee of General Council was instructed to undertake research with a view to the formulation, promulgation and review of accounting principles for the guidance of members [p. 28]. However, apart from the issue of effective enforcement, there were two other problems with the proposal to issue statements of recommended practice. First was the cost involved in developing and promulgating such statements. Second, activities of this nature would put the ASA in direct competition with the ICAA which had already issued Recommendations to its members [Zeff, 1973, p. 37]. The alternative was to create a jointly sponsored standard setting body.

The first step in this direction had already been taken with the creation of a jointly sponsored research body, the Accountancy Research Foundation, in 1965 [p. 43]. The aim of the Foundation was "the consolidation and dissemination of extant accounting and auditing principles and unresolved problems of accounting and auditing ..." [Boehme and Braddock, 1965, p. 318]. However, both the ASA and the ICAA continued to formulate their own principle statements with a consequent duplication of effort [p. 44]. The futility of this exercise was identified in 1971 and moves were made to bring the standard-setting process under the umbrella of the Research Foundation [p. 21]. In 1973, the separate standard-setting activities of the ICAA and ASA were brought under the auspices of a restructured and renamed research foundation, the Australian Accounting Research Foundation (AARF). The following year, the Australian Accounting Standards Committee assumed, as part of the AARF, the responsibility for developing accounting standards [Balmford, 1977, p. 546].

While legal backing for accounting standards was still some ten years away, the two accountancy associations, or at least, the jointly sponsored research body, the AARF and its Accounting Standards Committee, had established the basis of their recognition as the most suitable candidate to develop and design accounting standards because they had the "necessary expertise" [Australia, 1981, 21.55, p. 372].

6.0 CONCLUDING COMMENTS

This paper used a translation model of power to demonstrate some of the professionalization activities or strategies of Australian accountancy associations. While the use of such strategies is not unique to Australian accountancy, it was indispensable for a number of reasons.

As the paper indicates, Australian accountants and some of their associations were discredited at the turn of the century. This was due to revelations that the accounts of many of the large and spectacular corporate failures in the wake of the Victorian land boom were misleading, even though they had been prepared and audited by individuals who styled themselves as practising public accountants. In an effort to overcome negativity of this nature, many of the then existing accountancy associations and their successors introduced mandatory education and examination membership requirements. Some also required a minimum period of service in the office of a practising public accountant.

While this strategy appears to have been responsible for a change in the public perception of the capabilities of members of some accountancy associations, it was not sufficient to give them the worldwide prestige and status desired for members of these associations. One of the perceived ways of achieving this prestige and status was to be granted a Royal Charter. What appeared to be a simple matter of lodging a petition proved to be an exercise in politics and diplomacy spanning some twenty-five years and three separate charter applications. Superior knowledge and skill in the accounting arena had to be supplemented with the ability to form alliances and counter dissidence and resistance from accounting groups both in Australia and overseas and also from Commonwealth and state governments.

Further activities which helped to consolidate the position of accountants in Australia included the grouping together of several other accountancy associations to form the ASA. This meant there were now two major accountancy associations in Australia rather than a unified group of chartered accountants and disparate group of others who either chose not to become members of the ICAA or who were not in public practice. This, in turn, facilitated the creation of a joint research body which later assumed responsibility for the formulation and promulgation of accounting standards. When legal backing for approved accounting standards was initiated, the two associations and their research body, the AARF, were in an ideal position to accomplish domination of the standard-setting process.

While members of accountancy associations had clearly seen themselves as professionals since before the formation of such associations, the victory in achieving statutory backing of approved accounting standards and effective domination of the process could well be seen as long awaited affirmation of this status. After the best part of a century, qualified accountants completed the transition from charlatans to doyens.

REFERENCES

Accounting Standards Review Board. ASRB Release 200: Procedures For The Approval of Accounting Standards, ASRB, February, 1985.

———. *Annual Report 1986–1987* (Canberra: Australian Government Publishing Service, 1987).

———. *Annual Report 1987–1988* (Canberra: Australian Government Publishing Service, 1987–88).

Adelaide Society of Accountants. *List of Members, Constitution and Rules* (Adelaide, 1886).

———. *List of Members, Constitution and Rules* (Adelaide: W. K. Thomas & Co., Printers, 1896).

Australia. *Committee of Inquiry into the Australian Financial System. Final Report* (Campbell Inquiry). (Canberra: Australian Government Publishing Service, 1981).

Australasian Corporation of Public Accountants. "Third Annual General Meeting," *The Public Accountant*, Vol. 9, No. 9 (September 26, 1910a), pp. 133–139.

———. "Second Annual Dinner," *The Public Accountant*, Vol. 9, No. 11 (November, 1910b), pp. 169–179.

———. "Fourth Annual General Meeting," *The Public Accountant*, Vol. 10, No. 9 (September 30, 1911a), pp. 201–219.

———. "Annual Dinner," *The Public Accountant*, Vol. 10, No. 10 (October 25, 1911b), pp. 227–239.

———. "Victoria," *The Public Accountant*, Vol. 11, No. 8 (August, 1912a), pp. 157–158.

———. "Annual Report for the Year ended June 30, 1912," *The Public Accountant*, Vol. 11, No. 9 (September 25, 1912b) pp. 188–195.

———. "Fifth Annual Meeting," *The Public Accountant*, Vol. 11, No. 10 (October, 1912c), pp. 223–242.

———. "Sixth Annual General Meeting," *The Public Accountant*, Vol. 12, No. 10 (October, 1913), pp. 202–218.

———. "Annual General Meeting," *The Public Accountant*, Vol. 15, No. 4 (October, 1915), pp. 81–92.

———. "Seventeenth Ordinary General Meeting of Members," *The Public Accountant*, Vol. 24, No. 4 (October, 1924a), pp. 101–114.

———. "New South Wales. Annual Dinner," *The Public Accountant*, Vol. 24, No. 6 (December, 1924b), pp. 171–180.

———. "Annual General Meeting," *The Public Accountant*, Vol. 25, No. 4 (October, 1925), pp. 106–118.

Australasian Insurance and Banking Record. "Institutes of Accountants," *Australasian Insurance and Banking Record* (July 19, 1893), pp. 668.

———. "Institutes of Accountants," *Australasian Insurance and Banking Record* (October 19, 1896), pp. 717–718.

———. "The Incorporated Institute of Accountants, Victoria," *Australasian Insurance and Banking Record* (June 20, 1903), pp. 475.

Australian Accountancy Profession Joint Submission. *Submission to Mr. Leigh Masel, Chairman, National Companies and Securities Commission Commenting on the NCSC's Media Release 21/1981 of 29 November 1981 recommending the establishment of an Accounting Standards Review Board*, 1982.

Australian Society of Accountants. *History of the Australian Society of Accountants and Its Antecedent Bodies 1887–1962* (Melbourne: Australian Society of Accountants, [undated]).

———. *Accounting Principles and Practices Discussed in Reports on Company Failures* (Melbourne: Australian Society of Accountants, 1966).

Balmford, J. D. "Accounting Standards—Developments and Prospects Since 1972," *The Australian Accountant*, (October, 1977), pp. 546–555.

Barbalet, J. M. "Power and Resistance," *The British Journal of Sociology*, Vol. XXXVI, No. 4 (1985), pp. 531–548.

Birkett, W. P. and R. G. Walker. "Response of the Australian Accounting Profession to Company Failure in the 1960's," *Abacus*, Vol. 7, No. 2 (December, 1971), pp. 97–136.

Boehme, T. C. and L. A. Braddock. "The Accountancy Research Foundation. Announcement by the President of the Institute of Chartered Accountants in Australia, Mr. T. C. Boehme, and the President, Australian Society of Accountants, Mr. L. A. Braddock," *Chartered Accountant in Australia* (November, 1965), pp. 318–319.

Brentnall, T. *My Memories* (Melbourne: Robertson and Mullens Limited, 1938).

Brierley, A. J. "The C.A.A. Students' Union. Presidential Address," *The Public Accountant*, Vol. 2, No. 2 (December, 1902), pp. 21–23.

Callon, M. "Some Elements of a Sociology of Translation: Domestication of the Scallops and the Fishermen of St. Brieuc Bay," in *Power, Action and Belief: A New Sociology of Knowledge*, J. Law, Ed. Sociological Review Monograph. (London: Routledge and Kegan Paul, 1986), pp. 196–233.

Cannon, M. *Land Boom and Bust* (Melbourne: Heritage Publications, 1972).

Clegg, S. R. *Frameworks of Power* (London: Sage Publications, 1989).

"Correspondence as to the use of the title 'Chartered Accountant,'" *The Public Accountant*, Vol. 5, No. 4 (June, 1906), pp. 72–75.

"Correspondence with Reference to a Bill for the Registration of Public Accountants in New South Wales," *The Public Accountant*, Vol. 6, No. 9 (May, 1907), pp. 147–149.

Corporation of Accountants of Australia. [1906] "Sixth Annual Report," *The Public Accountant*, Vol.5, No. 3 (March, 1906), pp. 53–55.

Editorial. "Seventh Annual Report," *The Public Accountant* (February, 1907), pp. 94–99.

———. *The Public Accountant*, Vol. 3, No. 2 (December, 1903), pp. 18–19.

———. *The Public Accountant*, Vol. 5, No. 1 (September, 1905a), pp. 4–5.

———. *The Public Accountant*, Vol. 5, No. 2 (December, 1905b), pp. 28–30.

———. *The Public Accountant*, Vol. 6, No. 6 (February, 1907a), pp. 90–91.

———. *The Public Accountant*, Vol. 6, No. 9 (May, 1907b), pp. 138–142.

———. *The Public Accountant*, Vol. 6, No. 10 (June, 1907c), pp. 154–158.

———. *The Public Accountant*, Vol. 10, No. 9 (September, 1911a), pp. 198–200.

———. *The Public Accountant*, Vol. 10, No. 11 (November, 1911b), pp. 244–246.

———. *The Public Accountant*, Vol. 11, No. 11 (November, 1912), pp. 250–251.

———. *The Public Accountant*, Vol. 12, No. 5 (May, 1913), pp. 73–74.

———. *The Public Accountant*, Vol. 13, No. 4 (April, 1914), pp. 65–67.

———. *The Public Accountant*, Vol. 28, No. 1 (July, 1928), pp. 1–6.

Fitzgerald, A. A. "Accounting Standards," *Proceedings of the Australian Congress on Accounting* (Sydney, 1949), pp. 7–49.

Fitzgerald, A. A. "Accounting—In Retrospect," *The Australian Accountant. Special Issue. 75 Years of Accounting 1887 to 1962*, Vol. 32, No. 6 (June, 1962), pp. 289–295.

Graham, A. W. *Without Fear or Favour* (Sydney: Butterworths Pty Ltd, 1978).

Howitt, Sir H. *The History of the Institute of Chartered Accountants in England and Wales 1880–1965 and of its Founder Accountancy Bodies 1870–1880* (London: Heinemann, 1966).

Latour, B. "Power, Action and Belief: A New Sociology of Knowledge," *Sociological Review Monograph 32*, J. Law, Ed. (London: Routledge and Kegan Paul, 1986).

Lubell, M. S. *The Significance of Organizational Conflict on the Legislative Evolution of the Accounting Profession in the United States.* Dissertation for the degree of Doctor of Business Administration, University of Maryland, 1978.

Marshall, N. J. *A Jubilee History 1928–1978*, (Melbourne: The Institute of Chartered Accountants in Australia, Victorian Branch, 1978).

National Companies and Securities Commission. *Third Annual Report and Financial Statements 1 July 1981 to 30 June 1982* (Canberra: Australian Government Publishing Service, 1982).

———. *Tenth Annual Report and Financial Statements 1 July 1988 to 30 June 1989* (Canberra: Australian Government Publishing Service, 1988–89).

Nixon, E. V. "The History of the Accounting Profession, and the Position of the Accountant in Commerce," *Proceedings of the Australasian Congress on Accounting 1936* (Melbourne:Australasian Congress on Accounting, 1936), pp. 255–271.

Poullaos, C. *Making the Australian Chartered Accountant 1896–1935.* A Dissertation in Fulfilment of Requirements for the Degree of Doctor of Philosophy (unpublished), (School of Accounting, The University of New South Wales, 1992).

Proposed Victorian Charter. [1905] "Copy of a Counter Petition," *The Public Accountant,* Vol. 5, No. 2 (December, 1905), pp. 38–39.

Royal Commission on the University of Melbourne. "Final Report on Government Administration, Teaching Work and Failures of the University of Melbourne," *Victoria, Votes and Proceedings,* 1904.

South Australia. *Report of the Committee to Inquire into the Registration and Conduct of Accountants* (Adelaide, 1979).

Selander, S. "Associative Strategies in the Process of Professionalization: Professional Strategies and Scientification of Occupations," in *Professions in Theory and History Rethinking the Study of the Professions,* M. Burrage and R. Torstendahl, Eds. (London: Sage Publications, 1990), pp. 139–150.

The Accountant. "English-Speaking Accountants in Paris," *The Accountant* (January 9, 1932), pp. 44–47.

The Public Accountant. "Copy of Charter Applied for by Victorian Accountants' Institutes," *The Public Accountant,* Vol. 5, No. 1 (September, 1905), pp. 20–26.

The Public Accountant. "Colonial Chartered Accountants," *The Public Accountant,* Vol. 6, No. 3 (November 26, 1906), pp. 39–40.

Victoria. Votes and Proceedings. "Companies Act. Further Amendment Bill," *Victorian Parliamentary Papers, [Assembly],* November 24, 1896.

Walker, F. "Regulation of the Accounting Profession," *The Australian Accountant* (May, 1981a), p. 235.

———. "Address to the Institute's NSW Branch Members' Luncheon," *The Chartered Accountant in Australia* (October, 1981b), pp. 23–26.

Zeff, S. A. "Forging Accounting Principles in Australia," *Society Bulletin* No. 14 (Melbourne pp. Australian Society of Accountants, 1973).

Part V:
Taxation

The Evolution of the US Income Tax:

The History of Progressivity, Influences from Other Countries and Comparison to the Canadian Experience[1]

William D. Samson
University of Alabama

1.0 ABSTRACT

US tax policy of progressivity has long been implemented through the rate structure of the federal income tax. Over the years, this relationship of the income tax with progressivity has become so closely linked that when one is mentioned, the other comes immediately to mind. However, this relationship has not always existed; the degree of progressivity of the federal income tax has continually been altered, reflecting changes in tax policy because of social, political and economic forces. Historically, Congress has run a long-term experiment, tinkering with the rate structure and other key income tax variables in the search for the right combination to allocate the tax burden while accomplishing other economic objectives. Given the current unsettled conditions in Washington, the US income tax is being reexamined, its progressivity will be reviewed and the distribution of taxes will likely change again.

Because dramatic modifications appear to be forthcoming, it seems appropriate to review the two-hundred-year-old US federal tax experiment. Noteworthy are the tax policy and economic forces that married the progressive rate structure with the income tax, as well as the international contributions and influences in this marriage.

After reviewing the early US tax experience and the initial attempts at utilizing the income tax and the progressive rate structure, the paper focuses on the progressivity of the federal income tax over the last eighty-two years, since its rebirth in 1913. Historical trends and relationships of the components of progressivity, such as the highest, the lowest, and the number of tax rates, and the amount of exempt income, are examined against the political, economic and national conditions at the time. Because similar circumstances and forces worked to shape the Canadian income tax, the Canadian experience with income tax progressivity offers a striking parallel to that of the United States. From this historical examination of income tax progressivity, insight about where these tax systems stand today can be more clearly seen. Tax debates and reform proposals should benefit from considering past experiences with the income tax experiment.

2.0 INTRODUCTION

During civilization's existence, there seems to have been a constant quest for an "ideal" tax. Civilizations have devised taxes on uncounted numbers of items, but the search for the perfect tax continues. Massive, frequent overhauls of our modern tax law reflect the trial-and-error search for equity and the continuing dissatisfaction with the current tax structure. Thus, in a sense, the history of the US federal income tax, with its frequent tax law changes that refine the measurement of ability to pay, represents the desire for a better scheme of taxing. After several initial experiments with the income tax in the US, the 1913 adoption of the Sixteenth Amendment, (which made the income tax constitutional) marked the rebirth of this "Great Experiment" (Prohibition being the "Noble Experiment"). The changes to the progressive tax structure are a major part of the Great Experiment.

Since the Republicans have now taken control over Congress, their "Contract with America" mandate is likely to cause dramatic alterations to the current income tax structure. Republican proposals are wide-ranging; some groups are arguing for a flat tax rate such as 17%, other groups are calling for much greater levels of exemption for families, while others wish to see the rate on capital gains reduced or the gain adjusted for inflation. Additional proposals contain exemptions for income from investment or deductions for savings. Any and all of these changes will redistribute the burden of tax and have a dramatic impact on the progressivity of the income tax.

Such tax reform proposals, particularly a flat-rate income tax, seem radical because progressivity and the income tax have long been synonymous, so that the major identifying characteristic that immediately comes to mind when the "income tax" is mentioned is the graduated rate structure. This marriage of progressive rates with the income base may have been a historical accident, although one that has been fitting and lasting. However, the income tax and the progressive rate structure have not always been so coupled; indeed, each initially had different partners.

Perhaps proposed tax modifications can best be analyzed and debated by taking a longer view of the income tax and examining how it evolved to what it is today. Such a review gives perspective and understanding of the current tax structure as well as providing insight concerning the impact of proposed changes. Now seems a particularly appropriate time to look back and contemplate why the progressive system of taxation came about, and how progressivity has been altered over the years. The parallel income tax experience in Canada offers clues as to what forces seem to drive progressivity as well as serves as a reminder that the issue of tax burden distribution is a worldwide problem. While this paper cannot answer the question of how progressive the income tax should be, the reader may gain insights and even an answer to this question from the examination of the historical perspective. Thus, this review of federal tax progressivity over the years offers suggestions for policy debate about tax progressivity and income tax reform.

2.1 Progressivity: A Definition

A tax is computed by applying a rate of tax to a tax base (the object of taxation). In equation form this computation can be stated as follows:

$$T = B \times R$$

Where T is the tax amount, B is the tax base and R is the rate of taxation. By rearranging the terms in the equation, the rate of tax can be computed as the tax amount divided by the tax base:

$$R = T/B$$

In classifying a tax as "proportional" (or "flat"), "progressive" or "regressive," the impact on the R term is examined when the B term (and the T term) changes. If R (the rate) remains constant for changes in B (the base), the tax is **proportional** because the total tax T increases proportionally with the size of the tax base B. If R increases because of increases in B, the tax is **progressive** because the tax T increased faster than the increase in the tax base B. A **regressive** tax is one in which the rate of tax R decreases when the base B is increased. Worth noting in these definitions of regressive and progressive taxes is that the focus is on what happens to the *rate, not to the tax amount*, when the base changes. Thus, a regressive tax includes taxes whereby the amount of tax increases, but at a slower rate than the increase of the tax base. Alternatively, a proportional tax rate collects twice as much tax from a taxpayer with a $50,000 tax base as from a taxpayer with a $25,000 tax base. Therefore, in describing a tax as proportional, progressive or regressive, the label provides information about the *rate* of taxation only, not the amount of tax owed by taxpayers with different amounts of base (income).

Also worth noting is the role that exemption and standard deduction amounts play in progressivity. An otherwise proportional tax rate structure may be effectively progressive if an exemption/standard deduction amount is used to exclude a portion of income from tax. This phenomenon can be illustrated in the following example:

Example 1:

Assumptions

- flat tax rate of 25%
- exemption/standard deduction amount of $10,000

Taxpayer A: gross income of $15,000
Pays taxes of:
($15,000 – $10,000) × 25% = $1,250
The effective tax rate for taxpayer A is:
$1,250/$15,000 = 8.33%

Taxpayer B: gross income of $30,000
Pays taxes of:
($30,000 – $10,000) × 25% = $5,000
The effective tax rate for taxpayer B is:
$5,000/$30,000 = 16.66%

As the base (gross income) doubled, the tax amount increased fourfold. Because the tax rate increases as the base increases, the exemption/standard deduction amount converts the flat proportional tax rate structure into a tax that is progressive. Policy experts label a uniform (proportional) tax rate with a large exempt level of income as a "degressive" rate structure.

3.0 HISTORICAL OVERVIEW OF PROGRESSIVITY: INTERNATIONAL INFLUENCE UPON AND ADOPTION OF THE INCOME TAX IN THE UNITED STATES

American institutions have long been influenced in many ways by European events. This is especially true in the case of the income tax. The adoption of the income tax in the US was greatly affected by its development in Great Britain; to a lesser extent circumstances in France and other European countries also had impacts.

While various societies had tried to use progressive taxes in the past, the most influential attempts were during the tumultuous late eighteenth century.[2] In the 1790s, the British were faced with continuous warfare with the French. Struggles with the financing of these emergencies led to innovations in taxation in both countries. Among the most noteworthy was the British adoption of a tax on the rental value of houses, a forerunner of a more comprehensive income tax. This British tax had a graduated rate structure. At about the same time, French revolutionaries also imposed a tax on houses; however, it was much more progressive than that of the British. This French tax was, in essence, class warfare that was intended to drive (and succeeded in driving) wealthy citizens from their homes. Large estates were broken up in France when nobles were forced into bankruptcy by the tax.

In Great Britain, William Pitt fathered the income tax as part of his "Triple Assessment" in 1798. This tax was expanded to a general income tax in 1799. Not by accident, Parliament chose income as the tax base in lieu of increasing the tax on property. The political makeup of the Houses of Lords and Commons, which were dominated by land interests, led Parliament to look for signs of ability to pay other than wealth. The rising class of merchants and professionals owned little real estate and earned income from sources other than rents. This class became the target of the British income tax which was essentially a flat rate tax. The tax ended with the Napoleonic Wars in 1816. Despite its class roots, the income tax was justified by the argument that the merchant class benefited greatly from the British war economy. Thus, to a degree, the tax was an attempt to tax "excess profits" created by the war. This, in turn, enabled the government to use the proceeds of the tax to pay for the war. The class tax and the war profits aspects of the income tax would be repeated later when the tax was adopted in the United States.

The British reinstituted the income tax in 1842. Again, the rate was essentially proportional. It remained a flat rate tax for the next 65 years, during which the debate over the concept of rate progressivity raged on in Great Britain. In 1880, under Gladstone's leadership, the British modified the income tax to include an exemption amount and "abatements" (reduced rate on wages) for lower income taxpayers. The debaters were divided, not surprisingly, along class lines, with the wealthy being the most opposed to any notion of progressivity. The British adopted a progressive rate structure for their income tax at the turn of the century, when the "super tax" rates on income beyond a relatively large threshold were introduced. Other European countries instituted the income tax in the latter half of the nineteenth century and also embraced progressive rate structures.

In America during the 1790s, the Federalists followed the British and French in proposing a progressive tax on houses with the tax rate determined by the value of the home. This proposal was initiated by Secretary of Treasury Wolcott and later modified by Alexander Hamilton to tax houses according to the number of rooms. Thus, in the US, progressivity was initially linked with real estate taxation.

The Napoleonic Wars between Great Britain and France spilled over to America. In 1812, the US formally declared war against Great Britain. As a means of raising revenue to fight the British, the Secretary of Treasury proposed that the United States utilize an income tax. While the British were already using an income tax to finance their war effort, this idea was premature for America and the income tax was not adopted at the federal level of government until several wars later.

Rather than the federal level of government, it was the states that first adopted the income tax in the United States. In the Southern states, the income tax evolved from a licence (occupation) tax during the 1840s. Because of economic booms primarily owing to westward expansion during the 1830s, several states had undertaken large road and canal building projects. Initially, these states had chartered private companies. In return for construction, the companies would operate the projects and charge tolls. However, private resources were quickly exhausted and the states stepped in to finish these undertakings. Like the private developers, the states continued to underestimate the completion costs and overestimate the revenues; thus states also faced bankruptcy from the project debts that were coming due. The solution was to raise taxes to pay off the heavy state debt burden.

The Southern states in particular were influenced by British developments which caused them to experiment with the income tax as a means by which to pay for the internal public works projects. Like the British Parliament, Southern state legislatures were dominated by large landowners who objected to taxing real estate or other property (slaves). Instead, in Virginia, North Carolina and Alabama, the legislatures enacted business taxes that were flat fees initially, the modern equivalent to a licence or occupation tax. This tax was changed to a proportional tax on revenue and finally evolved to a proportional tax on income. The targets of this tax were the merchants and professionals who were the backbone of growing towns. Soon the use of the income tax spread to most of the Southern states. By the time of the War Between the States, Virginia had begun to use a progressive rate structure.

The emergency of the Civil War caused the income tax to be adopted on a national basis. To fight the war, the North and the South had to find sources of revenue. Both the Union and the Confederacy imposed a tax on income, though with differing degrees of success. In the North, the tax was frequently evaded. In the South, the income tax experiment appears to have been more successful, perhaps because the citizens were more supportive since the plight was more desperate. Because a withholding system was used, tax administration and court systems were devised, and an excess profits tax was implemented. Despite having a better structure, the Confederate income tax ended with the surrender at Appomatox. The Union's income tax continued until 1872, when most debts from the Civil War had been paid. It is interesting to note that the income tax of the Civil War was the first time that a major national tax had been imposed on US citizens since 1818. Prior to the war, the federal government had relied on revenues from the sale of land and from *external* tariff revenue. The income tax was the nation's first major *internal* revenue and the income tax was selected over other tax bases.

Also noteworthy is the fact that the tax rate adopted for the first US federal income tax was initially a flat tax rate of 3% applied to all income in excess of $800. The revenue need of the Union to pay for the war forced this 1861 tax to be increased even before the original act had become effective. In 1862, the income tax was quickly modified to tax all income in excess of a $600 exemption. The tax rates were 3% on income in excess of $600 and 5% on income in excess of $10,000. Thus, with almost no debate, (1) the federal government adopted an income tax and (2) while initially a flat rate, the income tax was quickly changed to a progressive rate system. Obviously, the emergency of war along with Lee's threat to Washington, forced national attention to more important matters than tax policy arguments. As would often be repeated, economic considerations, particularly revenue needs of the government, dictated the rate structure of the tax, rather than tax policy and equity considerations. The linkage of the income tax with progressive tax rates was abandoned after the end of the Civil War, when the tax reverted to a flat rate of 5% on income in excess of $5,000. This coupling would not be rediscovered for almost fifty years.

The next attempt to establish an income tax was led by the Populist and Progressive parties which held political strength in the 1880s and 1890s among farm and working classes (especially in the South, the Midwest and the Far West). These groups felt that the tariffs were too high and protected Northeastern industry to the detriment of the rest of the country, which bore the cost of higher-priced goods. The income tax was seen as a replacement for reduced tariff revenues. However, it was clear that the incidence of the income tax would be quite different from that of the tariff. Indeed, the proponents of the income tax saw it as a weapon against wealthy monopolists and the Eastern industrialists who benefited most from the tariff. The income tax movement culminated in 1894 with the passage of a federal income tax. However, this success was short-lived because the Supreme Court, in *Pollack* v. *Farmers' Loan & Trust Co.* [1895], struck down the tax statute for being unconstitutional. The Court said that the income tax was a *direct* tax and as such was prohibited by Article I, Section 9, Clause 4, of the Constitution. The legal debate about whether the founding fathers really intended to prevent the federal government from taxing in such a manner has long been argued. It is sufficient to say that even today there is considerable confusion about what the Constitutional Congress meant by a *direct tax*. Particularly noteworthy is that the 1894 tax contained a flat rate structure: a relatively innocuous 2% rate applied to income in excess of a relatively large exemption of $4,000.

In 1909, Congress did succeed in passing the Corporate Excise Tax on the "privilege of doing business as a corporation." This tax was 1% of profits. Upon review, the Supreme Court upheld the tax as constitutional, ruling that since it was an excise tax, it was within the federal tax powers. Perhaps, the Court was more impressed with the form, rather than the substance of the tax, since it can certainly be seen as a tax on corporate income.

Also in 1909, proponents of the income tax began a drive for an amendment to override the constitutional limitations on direct taxes. By early 1913, thirty-six states had ratified the amendment, which reads simply, "The Congress shall have the power to lay and collect taxes on incomes, from whatever sources derived, without apportionment among the several states, and without regard to any census or enumeration."

After the adoption of the Sixteenth Amendment, Congress had to decide whether the 1913 income tax legislation should provide for progressive or proportional tax rates. Interestingly, in the intervening years after the Civil War income tax, there had been relatively little discussion of how the income tax should be structured; rather the focus was on whether an income tax should be reinstituted at all. As Paul reflected about this period in his 1954 book, "The average American who thought about income tax at all imagined a modest flat rate of tax with a high personal exemption; such a tax would be no great burden, it was something of a mere nuisance value, even if one were sufficiently fortunate to have the amount of income requiring the making of a return."[3] Perhaps the foremost authority during the era in which the 1913 income tax was being formulated was Edwin R. A. Seligman. An advocate of progressive taxation and author of the book *Progressive Taxation in Theory and Practice*, his thinking and writing certainly played a role in the actions that Congress took.

However, Congress was also influenced by the British income tax of the time, which was a model because of its success in collecting revenue with minimum administrative problems. The key to the British success was the "collection at the source" system, whereby the employer paying salary to employees, the corporation paying dividends or interest to security holders, the renter paying rent to the landlord, etc., all withheld a tax amount from the payment. The withholder then remitted the payment to the British government. This system was workable because one rate of tax was being imposed on income, thus the withholder did not need to know the taxpayer's total income to calculate the marginal tax rate bracket. Because the withholder did not bear the burden of the tax, there was no incentive for tax evasion. Further, the taxpayer did not have to file a tax return, thereby avoiding the need to educate the taxpayer and also avoiding the problem of public anger toward "officials" invading the taxpayers' private affairs to audit total income.

In 1910, the British instituted a *super tax* that subjected income in excess of £5,000 to additional (progressive) tax rates. However, most citizens regarded the super tax as a tax separate from the flat rate regular British income tax. This perception was probably attributable to the very high amount of income at which the super tax rates were applied. Thus, few British citizens were subject to the super tax; those few that were, also became audit targets of revenue officials.

The majority of the 1913 Congress held Populist sentiments, which included the concept of progressive tax rates. These congressmen were also practical and found the administrative simplicity of the British tax system very appealing. This administrative simplicity was based on the withholding at the source of income and the use of one tax rate. The outcome of Congress' philosophical leaning toward progressivity, balanced by practical concerns of administration, resulted in tax with a very low 1% flat tax rate for the *normal tax*, thus making feasible collection at the source. (Ironically, withholding of income tax was not actually instituted until World War II.) To achieve progressivity, the 1913 income tax also contained a *surtax* (the US equivalent of the British *super* tax) exempting all income under $20,000. The surtax rates went from 1% to 6%, with the 6% rate imposed on income in excess of $500,000. When combined with the normal tax, the 1913 income tax ranged to a maximum of 7%. In addition to the 1% tax rate on the first $20,000 of income, the law provided a relatively large exemption amount of $4,000 for married taxpayers and $3,000 for single taxpayers. Thus, only a small percentage of citizens were subject to any income tax, and a much smaller percentage were taxed at rates higher than 1%. This very large exemption was perhaps instituted for the purpose of administrative simplicity, since the Bureau of Internal Revenue was very limited and not prepared to deal with the complexity of the new income tax. This administrative simplicity theory for the large exemption is contrary to another possibility: that Congress was carrying out the will of the masses by installing a tax that would burden the rich. In any event, the belief persists that the 1913 income tax was a *class* tax aimed at extracting and confiscating wealth or, alternatively, rectifying the abuses of regressive tariffs by reducing the concentration of wealth, particularly of the Northern industrialists (who seem to have been direct beneficiaries of the high tax on imports that burdened the rest of the US citizens).

The new income tax, with its low rates and large exemption, represented a fresh source of revenue needed once America started preparing for World War I. In a rapid succession of tax acts, the *normal* tax was raised from 1% to 2% in 1916, to 4% in 1917, and to 6% in 1918. In addition, the exemption amount was reduced in 1917 to $1,000 for single taxpayers and $2,000 for married taxpayers. The *surtax* rates were increased rapidly by these World War I tax acts. Within a span of five years after the passage of the Sixteenth Amendment, the top income tax rate would climb to as high as 82%. In making changes, the attempt at administrative simplicity had to be abandoned. The Bureau of Internal Revenue became swamped as the number of tax returns grew at an exponential rate and as complexity grew. Also, conflicts between the taxpayer and the government multiplied because issues about items of income and deduction became so much more important at a high marginal tax rate. Additionally, the Bureau was pressured to collect all tax owed; so it adopted a policy of auditing every tax return. Worse, the Bureau reaudited returns previously audited when new Revenue Rulings came out, in order to produce consistency among all taxpayers. This further swamped the Bureau, increasing the uncertainty for taxpayers as closure became very hard to reach.

In summary, the adoption of the 1913 income tax proved to be a lucky coincidence given the revenue needs of World War I. While many citizens whose incomes were being taxed for the first time complained bitterly about the tax's unfairness for taxing only those with high incomes, for being "communistic" or "anarchistic," for being a violation of their property rights, or for being a confiscation of wealth, other citizens saw the tax as fair because it was a substitute for and a counter balance to the regressive protectionist tariff. Thus, perhaps one "class" tax replaced another. When the constitutionality of the progressive tax rate structure of the 1913 income tax was challenged in the Supreme Court in 1916, the Court upheld the use of progressive rates.[4]

Ironically, US rates of taxation soared in five short years to lofty heights never dreamed by even the most radical French revolutionist. As a further irony, the need for revenue during World War I had made far more people taxpayers than the era's social reformers considered to be targets. After the war, the income tax declined in importance until the Second World War. With the advent of this war, the income tax became truly a mass tax, since most American families became taxpayers during World War II and continued to pay an income tax through the next fifty years.

4.0 ANALYSIS OF HISTORICAL PROGRESSIVITY

Comparing the income tax across time is risky at best when changes in society, business, economics, inflation, etc., are considered. However, given the limitations, an attempt at assessing historical progressivity is made here. Progressivity is a relative concept and involves making comparisons between different taxpayers as to their effective tax rates. However, in this analysis, the historical statutory tax rates, exemption amounts, etc., will be used instead of effective tax rates.

The progressivity of the income tax structure is a function of several variables:

1. the tax rate on the highest income bracket (Figure 1)
2. the tax rate on the lowest income bracket (Figure 1)
3. the number of tax rates (the number of tax brackets) (Figure 2)
4. the amount of income exempt from tax (exemption and standard deduction amounts) (Figure 3)

5. the level of income at which the highest tax rate is imposed (Figure 4)
6. the width of the various tax brackets, i.e., how much income is taxed at each rate, how quickly the top rate is reached.

The analysis that follows focuses on the first five variables.

Figure 1

Highest and Lowest Individual Tax Rates: Historical Comparison of the Income Tax

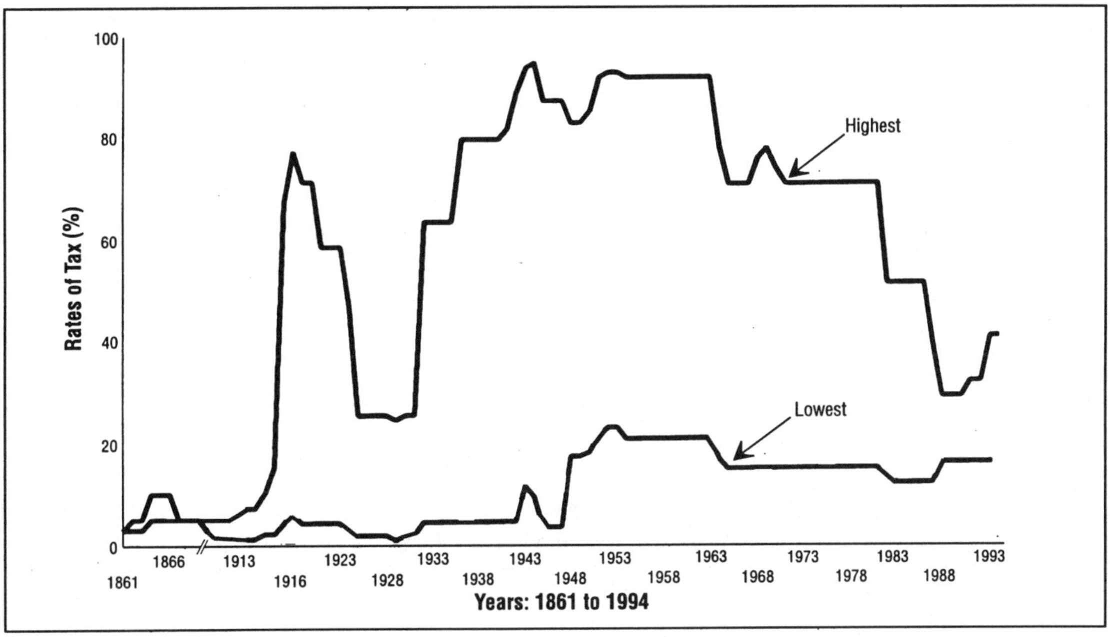

Figure 2

Number of Tax Rate Brackets: Individual Federal Income Tax from 1861

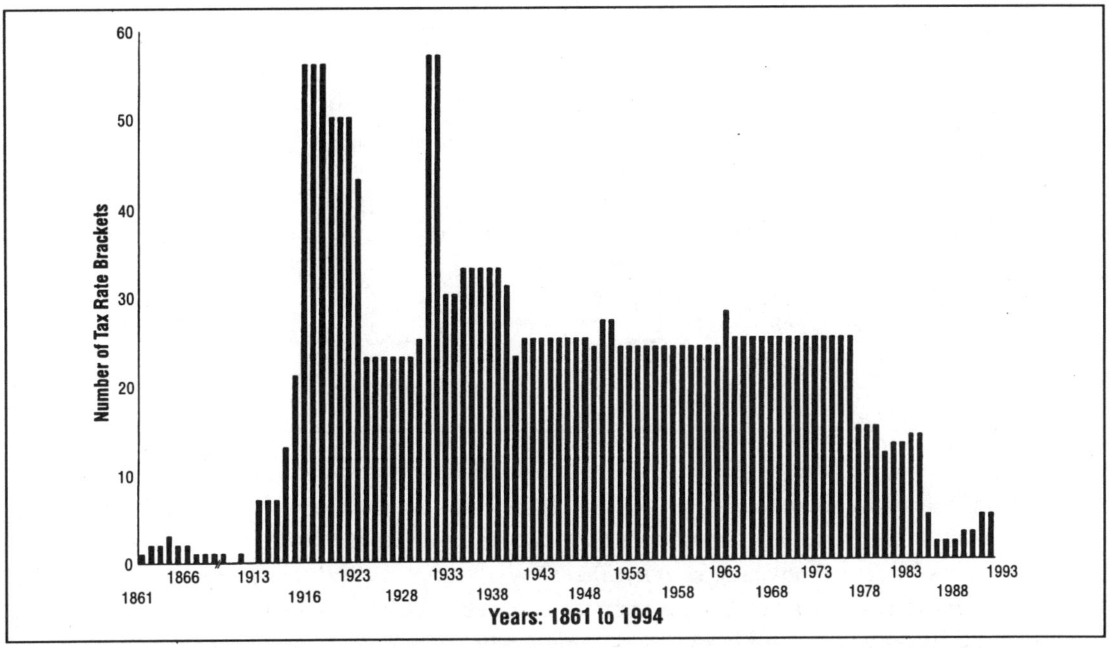

Figure 3
Amount of Exempt Income: Individual Federal income Tax from 1913

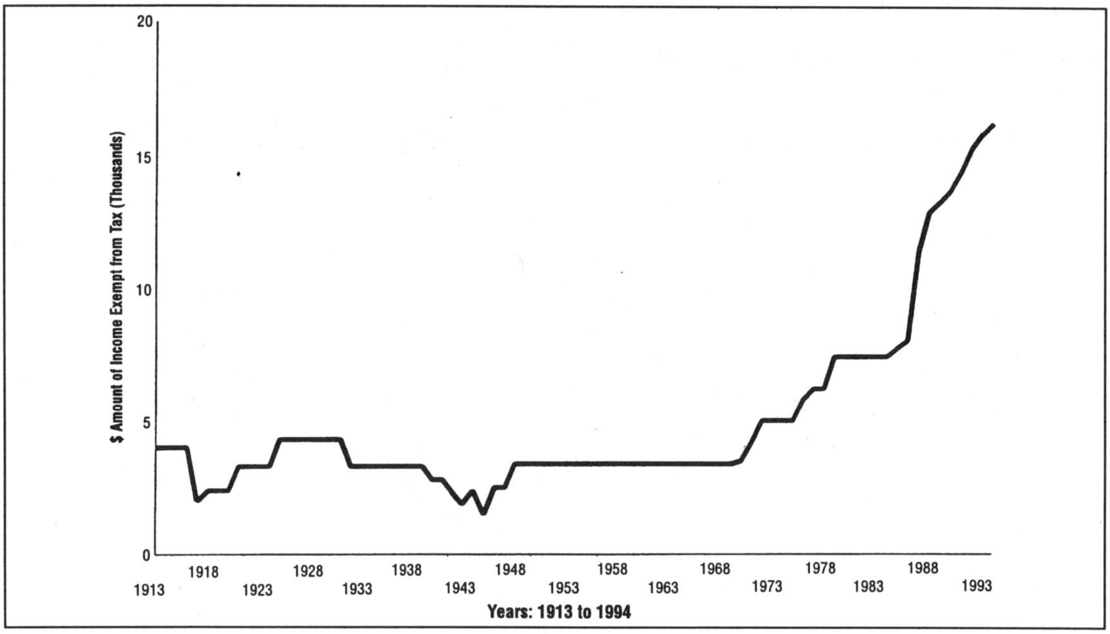

Figure 4
Income Level of Top Bracket: Individual Federal Income Tax from 1913

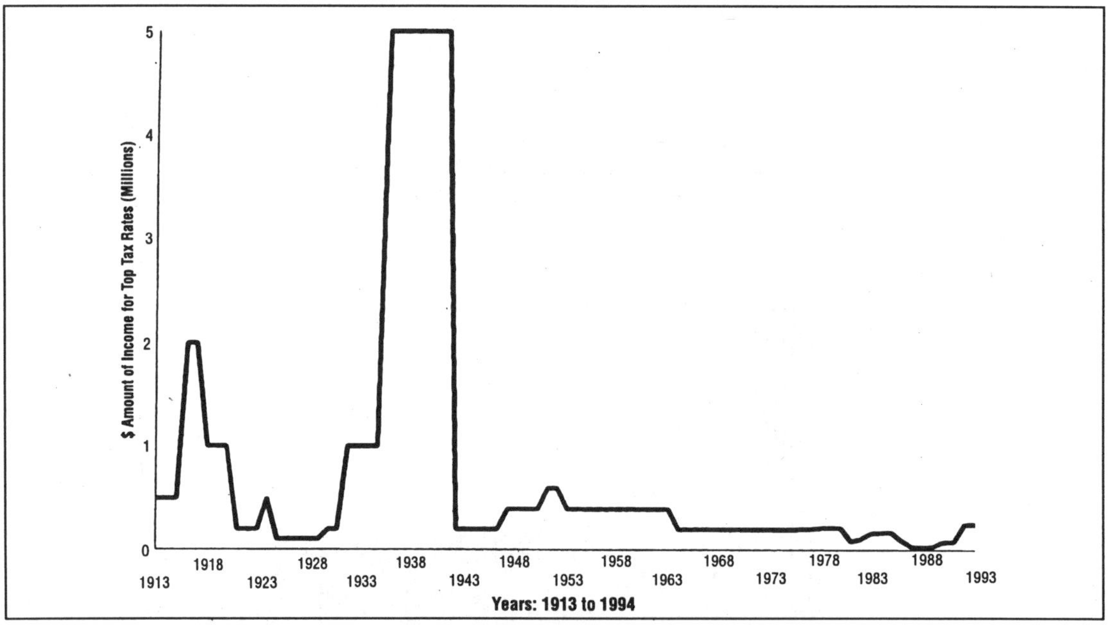

As indicated by Table 1 and Figures 1-4, these variables (hence progressivity) have fluctuated widely since 1913. The revenue needs of the government have had a major role in this variation; therefore, economic necessity seems to have been more important in determining the income tax rate structure than tax policy concerns about progressivity. Table 1 shows that the income tax has been used as a flexible economic device. This need-of-government explanation of the variables of progressivity seems more plausible than a trial-and-error approach to finding the "right" degree of progressivity.

Table 1
Individual Federal Income Tax: Progressivity from a Historical Prospective

Year	Number of Rate Brackets	Top Bracket Rate	Income Level for Top Rate	Exempt Income (Family of 4)	Lowest Bracket Rate	% High-Low Rate Difference	Ratio
1861	1	3.0%	$0	$600	3.0%	0.0%	1.00
1862	2	5.0%	$10,000	$600	3.0%	2.0%	1.67
1863	2	5.0%	$10,000	$600	3.0%	2.0%	1.67
1864	3	10.0%	$10,000	$600	5.0%	5.0%	2.00
1865	2	10.0%	$5,000	$600	5.0%	5.0%	2.00
1866	2	10.0%	$5,000	$600	5.0%	5.0%	2.00
1867	1	5.0%	$0	$1,000	5.0%	0.0%	1.00
1868	1	5.0%	$0	$1,000	5.0%	0.0%	1.00
1869	1	5.0%	$0	$1,000	5.0%	0.0%	1.00
1870	1	2.5%	$0	$2,000	2.5%	0.0%	1.00
1894	1	2.0%	$0	$4,000	2.0%	0.0%	1.00
1913	7	7.0%	$500,000	$4,000	1.0%	6.0%	7.00
1914	7	7.0%	$500,000	$4,000	1.0%	6.0%	7.00
1915	7	10.0%	$500,000	$4,000	2.0%	8.0%	5.00
1916	13	15.0%	$2,000,000	$4,000	2.0%	13.0%	7.50
1917	21	67.0%	$2,000,000	$2,000	4.0%	63.0%	16.75
1918	56	77.0%	$1,000,000	$2,400	6.0%	71.0%	12.83
1919	56	71.0%	$1,000,000	$2,400	4.0%	67.0%	17.75
1920	56	71.0%	$1,000,000	$2,400	4.0%	67.0%	17.75
1921	50	58.0%	$200,000	$3,300	4.0%	54.0%	14.50
1922	50	58.0%	$200,000	$3,300	4.0%	54.0%	14.50
1923	50	58.0%	$200,000	$3,300	4.0%	54.0%	14.50
1924	43	46.0%	$500,000	$3,300	2.0%	44.0%	23.00
1925	23	25.0%	$100,000	$4,300	1.5%	23.5%	16.67
1926	23	25.0%	$100,000	$4,300	1.5%	23.5%	16.67
1927	23	25.0%	$100,000	$4,300	1.5%	23.5%	16.67
1928	23	25.0%	$100,000	$4,300	1.5%	23.5%	16.67
1929	23	24.0%	$100,000	$4,300	0.5%	23.5%	48.00
1930	23	25.0%	$200,000	$4,300	1.5%	23.5%	16.67
1931	25	25.0%	$200,000	$4,300	1.5%	23.5%	16.67
1932	57	63.0%	$1,000,000	$3,300	4.0%	59.0%	15.75
1933	57	63.0%	$1,000,000	$3,300	4.0%	59.0%	15.75
1934	30	63.0%	$1,000,000	$3,300	4.0%	59.0%	15.75
1935	30	63.0%	$1,000,000	$3,300	4.0%	59.0%	15.75
1936	33	79.0%	$5,000,000	$3,300	4.0%	75.0%	19.75
1937	33	79.0%	$5,000,000	$3,300	4.0%	75.0%	19.75
1938	33	79.0%	$5,000,000	$3,300	4.0%	75.0%	19.75
1939	33	79.0%	$5,000,000	$3,300	4.0%	75.0%	19.75
1940	33	79.0%	$5,000,000	$2,800	4.0%	75.0%	19.75
1941	31	81.0%	$5,000,000	$2,800	4.0%	77.0%	20.25
1942	23	88.0%	$5,000,000	$2,300	4.0%	82.0%	22.00
1943	25	93.0%	$200,000	$1,900	11.0%	82.0%	8.45
1944	25	94.0%	$200,000	$2,400	9.0%	83.0%	10.44
1945	25	86.5%	$200,000	$1,500	3.0%	83.5%	28.83

Year	Number of Rate Brackets	Top Bracket Rate	Income Level for Top Rate	Exempt Income (Family of 4)	Lowest Bracket Rate	% High-Low Rate Difference	Ratio
1946	25	86.5%	$200,000	$2,500	2.9%	83.7%	30.35
1947	25	86.5%	$200,000	$2,500	2.9%	83.7%	30.35
1948	25	82.1%	$400,000	$3,400	16.6%	65.5%	4.95
1949	25	82.1%	$400,000	$3,400	16.6%	65.5%	4.95
1950	25	84.3%	$400,000	$3,400	17.4%	66.9%	4.85
1951	24	91.0%	$400,000	$3,400	20.4%	70.6%	4.46
1952	27	92.0%	$600,000	$3,400	22.2%	69.8%	4.14
1953	27	92.0%	$600,000	$3,400	22.2%	69.8%	4.14
1954	24	91.0%	$400,000	$3,400	20.0%	71.0%	4.55
1955	24	91.0%	$400,000	$3,400	20.0%	71.0%	4.55
1956	24	91.0%	$400,000	$3,400	20.0%	71.0%	4.55
1957	24	91.0%	$400,000	$3,400	20.0%	71.0%	4.55
1958	24	91.0%	$400,000	$3,400	20.0%	71.0%	4.55
1959	24	91.0%	$400,000	$3,400	20.0%	71.0%	4.55
1960	24	91.0%	$400,000	$3,400	20.0%	71.0%	4.55
1961	24	91.0%	$400,000	$3,400	20.0%	71.0%	4.55
1962	24	91.0%	$400,000	$3,400	20.0%	71.0%	4.55
1963	24	91.0%	$400,000	$3,400	20.0%	71.0%	4.55
1964	28	77.0%	$400,000	$3,400	16.0%	61.0%	4.81
1965	25	70.0%	$200,000	$3,400	14.0%	56.0%	5.00
1966	25	70.0%	$200,000	$3,400	14.0%	56.0%	5.00
1967	25	70.0%	$200,000	$3,400	14.0%	56.0%	5.00
1968	25	75.0%	$200,000	$3,400	14.0%	61.0%	5.36
1969	25	77.0%	$200,000	$3,400	14.0%	63.0%	5.50
1970	25	73.0%	$200,000	$3,500	14.0%	59.0%	5.21
1971	25	70.0%	$200,000	$4,200	14.0%	56.0%	5.00
1972	25	70.0%	$200,000	$5,000	14.0%	56.0%	5.00
1973	25	70.0%	$200,000	$5,000	14.0%	56.0%	5.00
1974	25	70.0%	$200,000	$5,000	14.0%	56.0%	5.00
1975	25	70.0%	$200,000	$5,000	14.0%	56.0%	5.00
1976	25	70.0%	$200,000	$5,800	14.0%	56.0%	5.00
1977	25	70.0%	$203,200	$6,200	14.0%	56.0%	5.00
1978	25	70.0%	$203,200	$6,200	14.0%	56.0%	5.00
1979	15	70.0%	$215,400	$7,400	14.0%	56.0%	5.00
1980	15	70.0%	$215,400	$7,400	14.0%	56.0%	5.00
1981	15	70.0%	$215,400	$7,400	14.0%	56.0%	5.00
1982	12	50.0%	$85,600	$7,400	12.0%	38.0%	4.17
1983	13	50.0%	$109,400	$7,400	11.0%	39.0%	4.55
1984	13	50.0%	$162,400	$7,400	11.0%	39.0%	4.55
1985	14	50.0%	$169,200	$7,700	11.0%	39.0%	4.55
1986	14	50.0%	$175,250	$7,990	11.0%	39.0%	4.55
1987	5	38.5%	$90,000	$11,360	11.0%	27.5%	3.50
1988	2	28.0%	$29,750	$12,800	15.0%	13.0%	1.87
1989	2	28.0%	$30,950	$13,200	15.0%	13.0%	1.87
1990	2	28.0%	$32,450	$13,650	15.0%	13.0%	1.87
1991	3	31.0%	$82,150	$14,300	15.0%	16.0%	1.94
1992	3	31.0%	$86,500	$15,200	15.0%	16.0%	1.94
1993	5	39.6%	$250,000	$15,750	15.0%	24.6%	2.64
1994	5	39.6%	$250,000	$16,150	15.0%	24.6%	2.64

As previously discussed, the income tax, enacted in 1913 to produce just the revenues needed to offset the reduction in the tariffs, was quickly converted to a revenue-generating source to finance World War I. As indicated by the top line in Figure 1, the marginal tax rate soared from 7% to over 80%. In addition, the level of income at which the top rate was applied decreased from $500,000 to $200,000. The revenue need also led to an increase in the lowest tax rate, from 1% in 1913 to 6% by 1918. A decrease in the income exemption level occurred simultaneously as well. Thus, not only was there a rise in tax revenues from soaring incomes during the wartime boom, but also tax revenues rose even more by the tax law changes that increased rates and cut the exempt level of income. As a result, both tax revenue and the taxpayer roll jumped as a greater number of taxpayers found themselves with taxable income. This phenomenon was to be repeated during World War II.

After World War I, the income tax rates were sharply reduced because the financial emergency had subsided. During the 1920s, the top marginal bracket was reduced to as low as 24% on the eve of the Great Depression. However, with the cuts in the top tax rate, there was also a reduction in the level of income to which these rates applied. By 1929, the top rate was reached at only $100,000 of income. During the 1920s, the lowest tax rate also was reduced. It reached its lowest point in 1929, when the bottom tax rate was only 0.5%. The amount of exempt income (standard deduction plus exemptions) for a family of four was $4,300 during this period.

Starting in 1930, the trend toward lower taxes reversed. In order to balance the federal budget during the Depression, the tax rates of all income brackets were increased. By 1932, the lowest tax rate was up to 4% (from 0.5% in 1929) and the highest tax rate rose sharply in 1932 to 63% (from 25% in the prior year). This top rate continued to climb during the 1930s. However, the increase in the top marginal tax rate was not as drastic as it might appear because the level of income that was subject to the top rate was increased from $200,000 to $1 million and later in the mid-1930s to $5 million when the top rate reached 79%.

On the eve of World War II, the income tax began to be used to generate more revenue to support the national "arsenal of democracy" and defence efforts. In 1942, the top rate climbed another 7% to 88%, while the lowest tax rate remained unchanged at 4%. However, a large increase in tax revenue came from a reduction in the amount of exempt income from $3,300 to $2,800 (family of four). With actual entry into the war, the top tax rate increased to more than 90%. This rate became effective at a relatively low income threshold of $200,000 (down from $5 million); thus many taxpayers became subject to very high marginal tax rates. During the war, the family income exempt from tax was reduced to being as low as $1,900, while the initial rate of tax climbed to more than 10%. The impact from lowering the level of exempt income coupled with the rise in salaries owing to the war was that, for the first time, the majority of American families were paying the federal income tax.

After World War II, the need for tax revenue was reduced such that tax rates were cut and exemption levels and bracket levels of income were increased. However, these changes were not nearly to the degree of those made after World War I. The Cold War era of world tension and military spending caused a continuing need for tax revenue. Most notable was the the lowest tax bracket rate which jumped from the 3% range to in excess of 20% with no corresponding increase in the exempt level of income. This combination produced very large amounts of income tax through the mid-1960s. Also, the 90% tax rate was reimposed during the Korean War. This top marginal tax rate, along with the $400,000 top bracket threshold amount of income, was maintained until 1965.

The year 1965 is noteworthy for the beginning of the trend to lower tax rates. In this year, the top tax rate dropped from 91% to 70%. However, the threshold income amount for the top rate was reduced as well, from $400,000 to $200,000; correspondingly, the benefit of this rate reduction was felt only in the case of very large income amounts. At the lowest taxable income level, the tax rate was cut from 20% in 1963 to 14% in 1965. The 70% range for the top rate and the 14% lowest rate were maintained for almost two decades until 1982. During this time, there were some temporary increases in the top tax rate to help finance the Vietnam War. Also, the exempt level of income rose regularly, from $3,400 in 1969 to $7,400 by 1981. This increase in the exempt level of income represents adjustments to the tax structure to offset the effects of inflation, rather than any tax policy or tax burden distribution (progressivity) reason.

The Economic Recovery Tax Act (ERTA) of 1981 cut the top tax rate from 70% to 50% and also reduced the lowest tax rate from 14% to 11%. This tax act decreased all of the other tax rates by a uniform percentage. In addition, the act lowered the income level at which the top rate was imposed to only $85,600 for 1982. This top income bracket level threshold was increased to $175,250 by 1986.

The rate cuts begun by ERTA were further continued by the Tax Reform Act of 1986. This act completed the Reagan tax revolution by instituting a much flatter tax rate structure on a broader tax base (fewer deductions). By 1988, the 1986 act had instituted a two-rate structure of 15% and 28%, with a much larger level of exempt income ($12,800 for a family of four). However, the 1988 tax structure had some new quirks not seen previously. First, there was a "phase out" of the benefit of the lowest tax bracket. This was accomplished by a "surtax" of 5% to "recapture" the 13% benefit (28% minus 15%) of the lowest bracket. In addition, the benefit of exemptions was also phased out for high income taxpayers. The novelty of these phase-outs was that for the first time, high income taxpayers did not enjoy the lower bracket tax rates or exemptions. This change caused a new form of class tax, a type of tax discrimination that for the prior seventy-five years had not existed. Overall, by the late 1980s, the income tax had become an almost proportional (degressive) tax rate structure.

The 1986 Tax Reform Act also removed the capital gains rate differential for the first time since 1921. The rate on capital gains, like other taxable income, was no more than 28%. Also, for the first time, the top individual income tax rate was less than that of corporations (34%).

The trend toward lower marginal tax rates and less overall progressivity was reversed by the passage of the 1991 Tax Act, which raised the top federal income tax from 28% to 31% on a fairly low level of taxable income ($82,150 for married, joint taxpayer). This rate increase was made by the Bush administration "to pay for" other tax changes under the balanced budget philosophy, rather than for any concerns about tax policy or desire for greater tax progressivity. Ironically, this small adjustment in tax rate cost Bush many votes and perhaps the 1992 presidential election.

With the Democratic victory and Clinton's election to the Presidency in the 1992 election, the trend toward greater tax progressivity was extended. The Democrat-dominated Congress passed (and Clinton signed) a new tax act in 1993 that raised the top marginal rate of tax to 36% and imposed an additional "surtax" of 10% (making another top marginal rate bracket of 39.6%). Thus, a three-rate bracket structure became five, with the 39.6% rate being imposed on taxable income in excess of $250,000 (irrespective of marital status).

5.0 1994 DOLLAR EQUIVALENTS OF INCOME TAX AND TOP RATE BRACKET THRESHOLDS

Figures 5 and 6 show the impact that changes in purchasing power have had on the exempt level of income and the top rate bracket thresholds, respectively. In each figure, the threshold amounts of each year have been adjusted to place the amounts in terms of the approximate 1994 dollar equivalent. These adoptions were based on the consumer price index. Thus, Figure 5 recasts the information in Figure 3, while Figure 6 reexamines the details of Figure 4.

With the adjustment for changes in purchasing power of the dollar, Figure 5 shows even more clearly than Figure 3 that Congress intended in 1913 to impose the tax only on citizens with income well above average. The 1913 exempt level of income (approximately $63,000 in 1994 purchasing power terms) excluded the great majority of citizens from tax. The 1913 income tax general rate of 1% was clearly designed to be the only tax rate for most taxpayers. The $20,000 bracket threshold that separated the 1% rate of tax from the surtax component of the 1913 income tax could only be attained when income reached the 1994 equivalent of approximately $380,000. Thus, all but a very few citizens experienced the progressive tax rates: for the majority, the tax rate was 0%, while those who were taxed were likely to have paid only the 1% tax rate.

At the other extreme, the 1913 highest tax rate bracket could be reached only if taxable income exceeded the modern equivalent of almost $8 million (Figure 7). By putting the 1913 7% rate-bracket threshold into this 1994 equivalent, two conclusions about the 1913 income tax become apparent. First, for the "poor" taxpayer who experienced this top tax rate, the income tax was hardly burdensome, if it was noticed at all, and thus the tax was not really "confiscatory," nor a "redistribution of the wealth," nor "communistic," nor "penalized success." Second, reaching the top tax rate bracket was viewed as a measure of success: an exclusive club of a handful of the very richest citizens, such as the Rockefellers, Carnegies, Vanderbilts, Dukes and Mellons.

Figure 5

Exempt Level of Income for Family of Four in 1994 Dollar Equivalents

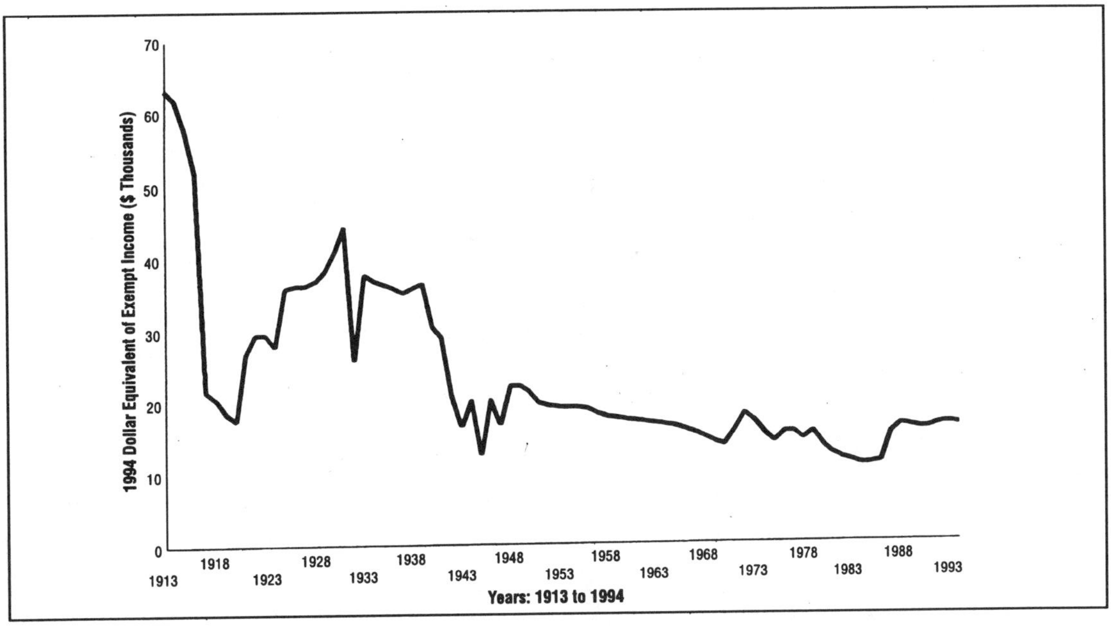

Figure 6
Top Bracket Level of Income in 1994 Dollar Equivalents

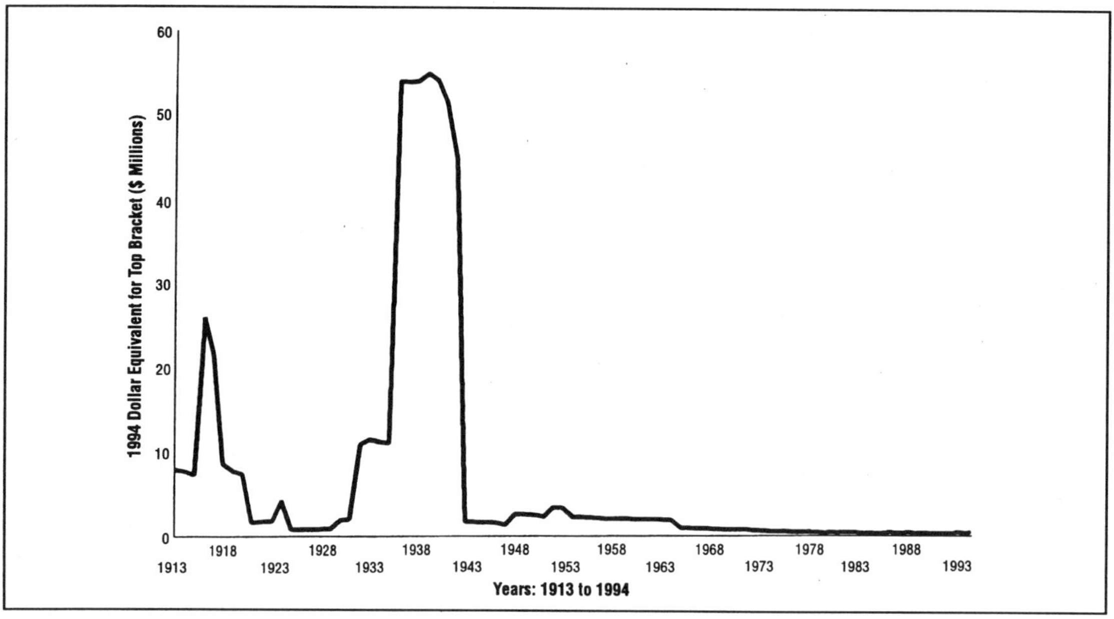

Figure 7
Ratio of High to Low Rates: Individual Federal Income Tax from 1913

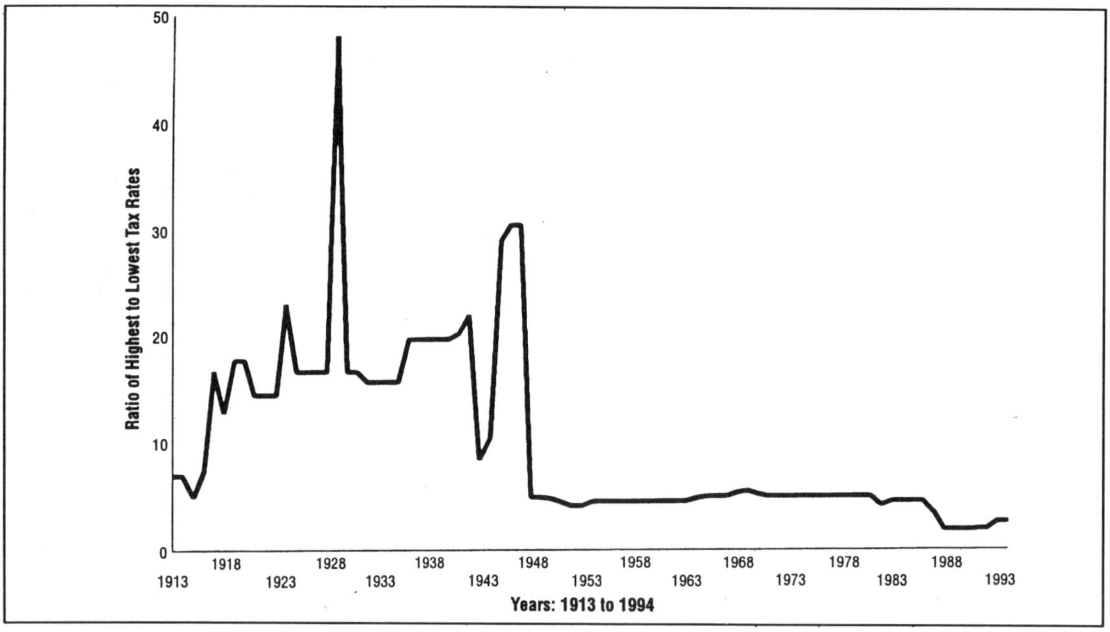

As Figure 5 indicates, the income tax was felt by many more citizens during World War I as the income tax threshold fell to the 1994 equivalent of less than $20,000. After World War I, this exempt level of income rose to the 1994 equivalent of the $40,000 range, before falling to the mid $30,000 range during the Great Depression Era. Thus, the income tax again was borne only by citizens enjoying above average incomes, with the majority of Americans not subject to any income tax.

Figure 6 further shows that only the very rich were subject to the top tax rates during the Great Depression. While the top rates during these years ranged from 63% to 79% and thus represented a heavy burden, almost to the point of confiscation, many millions of citizens were not as lucky as the taxpayer, since joblessness and hunger were all too common in those years. The charge that the income tax was a "class tax" used to confiscate wealth seems most relevant for the Great Depression Era. However, to be subject to the top tax rate during the 1930s, the 1994 equivalent income would be in excess of $50 million.

During World War II, the income tax became a mass tax; this fact is supported in Figure 5, where the 1943 threshold for the income tax begins at the 1994 equivalent of $16,379. By 1945, the exempt level income for a family of four had fallen to the 1994 equivalent of only $12,295. Thus, the income tax was first borne by the majority of US families during World War II. The 1994 dollar equivalents of the exempt level of income amounts since World War II indicate that even families with below median incomes have been subject to the income tax each year during the last half century. Figure 5 shows that the threshold for tax (exempt level of income) has remained relatively stable in 1994 dollar terms since World War II.

Finally, Figure 6 reflects that the top tax rates (90% during 1950 and early 1960s, 70% mid-1960s to 1981, 50% 1982–1986) have been imposed at successively lower 1994 equivalent dollar thresholds. For the 90% rate period, the 1994 equivalent bracket would start at between $2 million and $3 million. For the 70% top tax rate era from the mid-1960s to 1981, the 1994 equivalent of the threshold continuously declined from about $1 million in 1965 to $355,446 in 1981. The decline is almost uniform. Particularly startling in light of previous periods is how low the top rate bracket threshold became during the 1980s. The 28% top bracket brought about by the 1986 Tax Act was imposed on 1994 equivalent amounts of only $37,000, an equivalent income that would not have even been subject to tax during 1913–1916 and 1929–1931.

6.0 THE CANADIAN INCOME TAX EXPERIENCE: A COMPARISON

Many of the same economic, political, social and cultural forces that influenced the US federal income tax also helped shape the Dominion Income Tax of Canada. Therefore, it is not surprising that the Canadian experience with income tax progressivity has been similar to that of the United States. The following is a brief (albeit incomplete) examination of Canadian income tax history.

The Canadian income tax was instituted in 1917 to help finance the World War I effort. The "normal" tax rate was set at 4% on income above $1,500 (single taxpayers) or $3,000 (married taxpayers). A "super tax" with graduated tax rates was also imposed. The combined rates meant that income over $100,000 was taxed at 29%.

As with the US experience during World War I, the Canadian income tax increased annually. In 1918, the exempt level of income was cut to $1,000 for single and to $2,000 for married taxpayers. The super tax also was increased and reached 50% on income in excess of $1 million. In addition, a 35% surtax (a tax on the tax amount) was imposed, thus extending the tax rate to 72% on income over $1 million. These amounts were remarkably similar to those used in the US at the same time.

While the income tax was being lowered slightly in 1919 in the United States, the Canadian income tax rates increased in 1919 and 1920. However, in the early 1920s, both the Canadian and American tax rates were reduced, although the former's tax rates remained somewhat above the latter's rates.

As in the United States, the Canadian income tax was increased during the 1930s, with the first boost in 1932 from 2% to 3% for the lowest bracket and to 61% on income above $500,000. Again, the Canadian and American income tax rates, brackets and exempt levels of income seem very close in amounts during the Depression era. The degree of similarity, especially as to progressivity, between the Canadian and American income taxes was observed in a 1934 report to the US Congress by L. H. Parker, Chief Division of Investigation for the Joint Committee on Internal Taxation. In this report, Parker stated the following:

> The first fact that will impress the reader is that the Canadian income tax has much greater similarity to the Federal income tax than to the British income tax in respect to the burden on the individual taxpayer. This is plainly shown by the following table, computed for a married person with no dependents, whose income is all derived from salary:

Comparison of income-tax burden on individual
(Married man, no dependents, all earned income)

Net income before deduction of personal exemption	Total income tax			Net income before deduction of personal exemption	Total income tax		
	United States	Canada	United Kingdom		United States	Canada	United Kingdom
$1,000......	....	....	$7.99	$20,000.....	$1,589	$2,173.50	$4,893.96
$2,000......	....	....	100.29	$50,000.....	8,869	10,069.50	18,469.91
$3,000......	$8	$30.00	280.29	$70,000.....	16,104	16,390.50	29,019.91
$4,000......	44	70.00	460.29	$80,000.....	20,494	19,866.00	34,490.16
$5,000......	80	120.00	640.29	$100,000...	30,594	27,447.00	45,667.16
$10,000.....	415	546.00	1,677.64	$1,000,000	571,394	527,131.50	614,225.16

* Conversion unit £1=$4.86.

> It will be observed from the above table that the income-tax burden in Great Britain is much greater than in either the United States or Canada. This is especially true in cases of smaller income, where the tax burden in Great Britain is many times the burden upon individuals with equal incomes in the United States and Canada. It will be noted that there is no great disparity in the tax burden when we compare the United States and Canada. In Canada the taxes are slightly higher on net income up to $70,000 and somewhat lower in the case of net incomes larger in amount. The personal exemption allowed a single man in Canada is $1,000, as in the United States. In the case of a married man, the personal exemption is $2,000, compared with $2,500 in the United States. The credit for dependents in both countries is $400, but in Canada children are allowed the exemption up to the age of 21, while in the United States no credit [is] allowed for children over 18.[5]

During World War II, the Canadian withholding system was instituted, as in the US, to collect income tax from the pay cheques of workers. Similar to the US, the income tax was relied on to finance the war effort and tax rates became very high. After the war, the Canadian income tax rates remained high, as did the rates in the United States. The rates in 1963 of the two countries are compared in Table 2.

Table 2
Comparison of Canadian and American Tax Rates in 1963

	Canada	United States
Number of tax brackets	17	24
Top tax rate on income over	80% $175,000	91% $400,000
Initial bracket rate	11%	20%
Exempt income for family of four	$3,200	$3,400

Most interesting, the US income tax was reduced in 1964 to a top rate of 77% and the lowest bracket rate to 16%, certainly making the federal income tax even more Canadian-like.

The similarities of trends in Canadian and US income taxes have continued. In the early 1970s, the Canadian income tax top rate was 47% with a relatively low $60,000 income threshold, reached in a thirteen-step rate bracket from 17%. While this rate structure differed from the US at the time, it seems that Canada was ahead: it was not until the Reaganomics of a decade later that the US adopted a thirteen-step, 50% top tax rate structure. By this time, the Canadian income tax had been reduced to a top tax rate of 34%, with ten-rate bracket steps from a 6% initial rate. When the US utilized a two-rate bracket structure of 15% and 28% in the late 1980s, Canada was using a three-rate structure from 17% to 29%. Again, Canada may have been slightly ahead of US developments, because it was not until 1991 when the US began using a three-rate structure of 15%, 28% and 31%.

Because cultural, political, economic, and social forces are so similar between the two countries, the income tax histories are somewhat parallel. The variables that impact progressivity in both countries seem remarkably close at many points in time over the last seventy-five years.

7.0 SUMMARY

While the progressive rate structure and the income tax have been closely tied together, the income tax has utilized proportional rates at times during its history. The progressive rate structure had its beginnings with the property tax rather than with the income tax. Since 1913, the United States' income tax has utilized a progressive rate structure, but the degree of progressivity has changed numerous times. In addition, the rates chosen for the top tax rate and bottom tax rate have also fluctuated widely over the last eighty-two years. As shown by Table 1 and Figure 8, the statutory high-low rate differential has ranged from an initial 6% to a maximum of 91% during World War II to 13% in the late 1980s to 24.6% today. The ratio of high-to-low tax rates reached its all-time low in 1988 when this ratio stood at only 1.87. In other words, the top tax rate in 1988 was less than twice the lowest tax rate. Currently, this high-low rate ratio is still in a very low range of 2.64. In part, this low level for the ratio is attributable to a relatively high initial rate (15%) coupled with a relatively low top tax rate (39.6%). Noteworthy as well is the relatively low income threshold of $250,000 at which the top rate is reached. The ratio and the top bracket threshold support the criticism that the 1986 Tax Reform Act drastically reduced progressivity.[6] Thus, today the degree of progressivity of the rate of federal income tax remains low from a historical perspective.

Figure 8
High-Low Tax Rate Difference: Individual Federal Income Tax from 1913

It should be noted that the ratio of high-to-low tax rates did not reach its zenith during World War II (although the ratio—30—was very high), but during the time of the stock market crash in 1929 when the top bracket tax rate was 48 times the lowest tax bracket rate. This is attributable to the very small initial bracket rate, which perhaps is overly influential as the denominator in the comparison.

The search for the perfect tax has led to constant changes in taxation throughout the history of civilization. The frequency in modification to the income tax represents a continuation of this search. Historical variation in progressivity variables reflects a trial-and-error approach to refining tax equity. Income, as a tax base, does offer a way of taxing that is flexible to governmental needs and society's concept of fairness. The US federal income tax and the Canadian income tax experiences have been remarkably alike due to common economic, political, cultural, and social forces. As with the federal income tax, Canada frequently has altered tax rates and has shifted the distribution of its tax burden throughout recent history. Interestingly, the degrees of progressivity and even the variables themselves have often been amazingly similar during the last eighty years of US and Canadian usage of the income tax. While this fact seems to suggest a universality of seeking the perfect (optimal) distribution of tax burdens, the alterations to both the American and Canadian income taxes may reflect common economic necessities and political realities, rather than tax policy and tax equity concerns. Thus, given the fluctuations in rates, brackets, and levels of exempt income, it seems safe to conclude that the changes will continue in the future in both countries. With equitable distribution (redistribution of wealth) of tax considerations being balanced against other considerations, the income tax experiment continues.

8.0 CONCLUSIONS

The history of the income tax rate structure does not point to any ideal degree of progressivity underlying the income tax. Given the wide variation in the rate structure that has occurred over time, historical support for a strongly or moderately progressive income tax can be found equally, depending on what period of time debaters want to cite. More significantly, the history of the income tax can be used to validate both the argument for a flat rate (proportional) tax structure and that of a progressive structure.

Thus, the income tax, both in Great Britain and the United States, at the state and at the federal level in 1861 and 1894, started as a flat rate tax. Despite having only one rate, a relatively large exemption level was used with the flat rate to exclude the vast majority of citizens from tax. Only the rich were taxed under this "degressive structure." However, the revenue needs of the government in 1862 and again during World War I, the Great Depression, World War II and the Cold War eras caused the imposition of much more graduated rate structures. At the same time, the exempt levels of income were reduced to make the income tax more broadly applicable to a much greater number of citizens.

The income tax adopted in 1913 was clearly a class tax aimed at Northern industrialists who had grown wealthy from the highly protectionist tariffs of the turn of the century. While the large exemption level eliminated most citizens from the burden of tax, the 1% to 7% tax rates were probably too low to redistribute wealth as some people have suggested; others believed the rate structure was simply an application of the concept of taxation of the ability to pay. To many citizens at the turn of the century, the income tax of 1913 seemed fair because it offset the impact of the protectionist tariff, a tax borne directly and indirectly by the consumers, giving a distinct advantage to the US manufacturer.

Initially in 1913, administrative simplicity considerations moderated the Populist sentiments for a strong progressive rate structure. Thus, beyond the exempt level of income, those few citizens subject to the 1913 income tax paid, for the most part, only a 1% tax rate. Only the very few with income in excess of $20,000 experienced the "surtax" rate, which ranged to 6% (total 7%) on income in excess of $500,000. Rather than follow its tax policy mandate, Congress structured a tax system and tax rates that would be simple to administer. This early concern by legislators for the practical and this lack of philosophical tax policy debate characterizes the history of the income tax. Subsequent tax rate changes occurred because of increased revenue needs (or reduction of needs) of the federal government. Thus rates were driven by practical rather than tax equity concerns.

For forty years, from 1948 until 1987, the ratio of the top to lowest tax rates have remained at a remarkably constant four to five. This test of time implies that societal, economic, and political forces have reached a consensus about the appropriate degree of progressivity. This period of stability contrasts with the very volatile fluctuations in the index for the previous 35 years. During this period, 1913 to 1947, the ratio vacillated dramatically with a range of 7 (1913) to 48 (1929). The forty years of progressive structure tranquillity have been shattered by the 1986 Tax Act, which reduced the index to much lower (flatter rate structure) numbers. This new trend seems likely to be extended, as indicated by tax reform proposals now being discussed.

For virtually all years from 1913 to 1971 (an amazingly long period in tax history), the exempt level fluctuated between $3,000 to $4,000. As with the rate structure, there appears to have been universal acceptance of the level of exempt income as $3,000 to $4,000 for a family of four. Stability of the exempt income amount ended as inflationary pressures caused Congress to adjust the exempt level of income annually, now through an automatic adjustment of exemption and standard deduction amounts. In terms of constant (1994) purchasing power, the exempt level of income has remained very stable for fifty years at about $16,000.

The search of historical data for a fundamental agreement as to the degree of progressivity was not successful. What now seems apparent is that, rather than an underlying political, social and historical consensus as to the "correct" degree of tax progressivity, the tax rate structure of the income tax has been crafted according to government revenue needs and other economic considerations. Not the least of these other economic considerations has been the tax structure of the income tax in other countries. Thus, tax competition between countries such as the United States and Canada may be a factor of growing importance, since capital seems to have no borders in the global economy.

Throughout the many changes to the federal tax rate structure, there has been little discussion about the ideal burden distribution between taxpayers. No serious debate occurred about the amount of tax Citizen A with $25,000 of income ought to pay versus Citizen B with $50,000 versus Citizen C with $100,000, etc.

Currently, progressivity of the US income tax is near the historical low, with most progressivity achieved via the exempt level of income rather than via the rate structure. This trend seems likely to continue, given the flat rate structure being proposed. Indeed, the federal estate and gift tax represents a much more strongly progressive tax with its seventeen rate brackets that progress from 18% to a 55% rate as well as the credit which exempts the transfer of the first $600,000 of wealth from tax. Ironically, the current proposals for a one rate, no deduction of personal items and large exemption level seem remarkably close to the alternative minimum tax which has operated for two decades in the shadow of the "regular" income tax. Above all the changes, it is clear that the US income tax has been and remains remarkable for its flexibility and ability to meet the economic and revenue needs of the nation.

ENDNOTES

1 I appreciate the help and advice that Kathy Bindon, Mike Dugan, Mike Roberts and Jackie Stewart have given me in writing this paper.

2 See Edwin R. A. Seligman [1909].

3 Paul [1954], p. 714.

4 *Brushaber* v. *Union Pacific Railroad Company* [1916].

5 "Letter of Submittal" by L. H. Parker, published in *Income Tax in Canada* by Bernard, pp. xi–xii.

6 However, in fairness to the 1986 Tax Reform Act, it should be noted that the ratio compares just the top and bottom rates; the ratio ignores the progressivity effect of the amount of exempt income that was increased by the act.

REFERENCES

Arthur Andersen & Co. *Tax and Trade Guide—Canada* (Chicago, 1963).

Bernard, André. *Income Tax In Canada* (Washington: US Government Printing Office, 1934).

Blakey, Roy G. and Gladys S. Blakey. *The Federal Income Tax* (London and New York: Longman Green & Company, 1940).

Brushaber v. *Union Pacific Railroad Company*, 240 US 1, 25 (1916).

Paul, Randolph E. *Taxation in the United States* (Boston: Little, Brown, 1954).

Pollack v. *Farmers' Loan & Trust Co.*, 157 US 429 (1895).

Roberts, Michael L. "The Flat-Rate Tax: The Improbable Dream," unpublished paper, 1982.

Samson, William D. "The Income Tax Experience in Virginia: 1843–1913," *The Virginia Accountant* (December, 1983).

———. "The Nineteenth Century Income Tax in the South," *The Accounting Historian Journal*, Vol. 12, No. 1 (Spring, 1985).

———. "An Overview of Tax Revenue Sources and the Federal Tax Structure," Chapter 33 in *The Handbook of Governmental Accounting and Finance*, N. G. Apostolou and D. L. Crumbley, Eds. (New York: John Wiley and Sons, 1987).

Seligman, Edwin R. A. *Progressive Taxation in Theory and Practice*, Second Edition (Princeton: University Press, 1909).

Sommerfeld, Ray M., Hershel M. Anderson and Horace R. Brock, Eds. *An Introduction to Taxation* (New York: Harcourt Brace Jovanovich, 1983).

Taxation, Common Sense Implications and The Lower of Cost and Market Rule in the United Kingdom 1842–1925[1]

David M. Smith
Deakin University
Australia

1.0 ABSTRACT

It has been suggested that the desire of businesses not to pay taxes on unrealized gains would foster the use of a method of valuation of stock-in-trade (inventory) which prevents this from occurring. The use of the *lower of cost and market rule* will normally give a profit figure lower than that obtained by using either historical cost or market value alone. It is generally accepted that the use of the *lower of cost and market rule* was firmly established in the United Kingdom as the primary method of valuing stock-in-trade by 1925. This paper considers whether income tax considerations affected the development of the *lower of cost and market rule* for the period of 1842 to 1925. Research has found that there are few references to the use of the *lower of cost and market rule* in the United Kingdom prior to the introduction of a system of permanent income tax in 1842 and that its use increased progressively over the period to 1900. One suspects that the introduction of income tax would foster the use of a method of valuing stock-in-trade which prevents unrealized profit from being taxed and allows the deduction of unrealized losses. This paper investigates the available evidence to determine whether this intuitive reasoning can be validated.

2.0 INTRODUCTION

There are several possible catalysts which have been suggested as having fostered the development of the *lower of cost and market rule* (hereafter referred to as The Rule) for the valuation of stock-in-trade. This paper considers the possible impact of income tax upon The Rule's development in the United Kingdom. The importance of validating these possible catalysts is due to The Rule's underlying inconsistencies and lack of logic. Those commentators who looked at

The Rule have been critical of the effects of its application and of its structure.[2] The discussion has been divided into two time periods, 1850 to 1900 and 1901 to 1925. Most commentators agree that The Rule was firmly established in practice by the beginning of the twentieth century.[3]

A. C. Littleton [1941] has suggested the possible importance of taxation considerations in the development of The Rule, particularly in Europe prior to the twentieth century. The use of The Rule would be a convenient method of minimizing the impact of taxation, particularly income tax.[4] A trader or manufacturer by using The Rule would not be required to pay taxes upon profits which had not, as yet, actually been realized.[5] The possible link in the United States has been suggested by E. J. Filbey, based primarily on the fact that The Rule's use excluded *unrealized* gains from income.[6]

3.0 BACKGROUND

In the United Kingdom, the profits (income) derived from carrying on a business were first taxed with the introduction of income tax in 1795. The Income Tax Act of 1795 required a general return to be made. A major change was instituted with the introduction of The Income Tax Act of 1803, which required that returns be made for various classes of income received by a taxpayer. From that time on, income tax, being a tax charged on "any profession, trade or vocation" carried on by the taxpayer, has been levied under Case I of Schedule D of the Act. The top rate set by the 1799 Act was 10% for incomes £200 and upwards, with a graduated scale for incomes between £60 and £200. The 1803 Act was amended, but not so as to affect the question under discussion in 1805 and 1806, which was to become the Income Tax Act of 1806. After the end of the Napoleonic War, the income tax legislation was repealed. Income tax was not reintroduced in the United Kingdom until The Income Tax Act 1842. The 1842 Act was for all intents and purposes a reprint of the 1806 Act. The Act was later consolidated into The Income Tax Act of 1918.

4.0 PERIOD TO 1900

As pointed out in the preceding section, Case I of Schedule D specifically dealt with taxpayers carrying on any trade.[7] None of the Income Tax Acts to 1900 expressly referred to the necessity to take into account the value of stock-in-trade in-hand at the beginning and end of the year of income when ascertaining the *profits and gains* of a taxpayer.

While the income tax was an annual tax, the liability was not calculated with reference to the current year's income alone. A trader's liability under Case I of Schedule D of the Income Tax Act was calculated on the basis of the average of the preceding three years' income.[8] From the point of view of the Board of Inland Revenue, the valuation of stock was not a serious issue "because it was felt in the long run it would rectify itself." [Minutes of Evidence, 1920 (evidence of Mr. E. Stanford London, Board of Inland Revenue), para 12,488, p. 422.] This follows from the fact that one would expect in the normal course of events that the stock-in-trade would be realized in the following year. The effect of the use of The Rule would be one of the timing of income recognition and the consequent tax liability. It would not lead to a total avoidance or evasion of income tax. The effect of the three years' average was to minimize the effect of any undervaluation of stock-in-trade. This is because the undervaluations in years one and two would normally be brought in to account as higher profits in years two and three respectively.

The Board of Inland Revenue believed that the abandonment of the three years' average and the use of The Rule "would enable ... [the taxpayer] to work his profits advantageously." [Minutes of Evidence, 1920 (evidence of Mr. E. Stanford London, Board of Inland Revenue), para 12,425, p. 620.] A different interpretation on the effect of the use of the three years' average was expressed by W. L. Gough [1885, p. 8]:

> There can be no doubt that it would be much more simple to make the assessment on the profits of the preceding year, but the average of three years is clearly in the interest of the taxpayer. It may so happen that a heavy loss is sustained in a given year and moderate profits made in the following years.

If The Rule was firmly established by 1900, and its development had been influenced by income tax considerations, one would expect that there would be evidence of this in the taxation literature to 1900. It would be expected that a thorough search of the taxation columns and articles appearing on the subject of income in *The Accountant* would either support or refute the hypothesis. One would, of course refer to other professional journals, such as *The Incorporated Accountants' Journal* and to books on income tax.

None of the articles appearing in *The Accountant* or *The Incorporated Accountants' Journal* prior to 1901 specifically dealt with the issue of the valuation of stock-in-trade for income tax purposes. Nor did any of the requests for information or advice from members of the profession to the journals raise the question. The fact that stock-taking was necessary was mentioned on very few occasions, but without considering the issue of valuation of stock-in-trade. Consider the following comment as an example [Brierly, 1892, p. 465; see also Edwards, 1886, p. 13]:

> What could be simpler than this: On one side value of stock at the beginning of the year; next, the amount of purchases during the year; and then, in order, the expenses claimed, enumerating the same, so that the Commissioners may know whether or not they are all legitimate. On the other side would appear sales (cash and credit) during the year, and finally the value of the stock at the end of the year. The difference would be the total profit or loss on the year's workings. Surely traders ought to be in a position to give so simple an account.

Similarly, with respect to appeals, and information which needed to be supplied to support the taxpayer's argument when he/she claimed to have been over-assessed by the surveyor of taxes [Turquard, 1895, p. 76]:

> This involves the production of accounts showing the profits for each of the three preceding years, for which purpose particulars of the stock-in-trade are required for the three separate dates up to which these yearly accounts have to be prepared.

In a few cases, the amount of stock in hand was shown in examples. There was, however, no discussion of how the stock-in-trade figures had been ascertained [see McEwan, 1893, p. 204, Pitt, 1900, p. 96]. In an editorial note it was said:

> We cannot pretend that Mr. McEwan's paper forms interesting reading, ... The *pro forma* Trading Return is likely to prove most valuable in practice, for the explanations attached are extremely clear, and the list of possible contingencies is most complete. [*The Accountant* (May 27, 1892), p. 487]

An indirect reference was made with respect to the valuation of stock-in-trade in *The Accountant* in a paper by C. E. Mather [1893, p. 419]:

> The loss of stock, however, may be taken into account, because, to quote the lecturer's words, "it is an item which affects the balance of profit."

The only time anything like the issue of valuation of stock-in-trade arose was with respect to requests by the surveyors of taxes for the supply copies of balance sheets, etc., and the fact that the surveyors of taxes had no legal right to require a taxpayer to supply such information to them [Editorial note, *Income tax* (May 27, 1893), p. 488].

There was, however, a de facto requirement to produce books to the Commissioners when the taxpayer appealed. This was because it was up to the taxpayer to prove that the assessment was excessive. There were many comments about these two points in the literature.[9] In a reply to a query by "C&A" the Taxation Editor said

> On the whole we think you are right [that cannot force production], but the authorities may assess you at a high figure, and when you appeal your books will be demanded.—Lex. [Editorial note (Taxation Editor), *The Accountant*, 1897, p. 603]

Murray and Carter in their book also make reference to the fact that it was not necessary for a taxpayer to produce his books when submitting his income tax return [1895, p. 151; 1899, p. 216].

The textbooks and reference books published during the period provide little evidence that the valuation of stock-in-trade for income tax purposes was a burning issue. It does not appear to have been an issue at all! J. Rhodes makes this pertinent comment in his book that taking stock "is not generally looked upon as a *sine qua non*." In the examples of accounts there are figures for opening and closing stock — labelled as the "value" of closing stock. He points out that some taxpayers take stock only every three years because of the three years' average. Unfortunately, he does not further explain this comment about it being necessary only to take stock every three years. Clearly the annual profits which were used to calculate the three years average would require a valuation of stock-in-trade [1889–1890, pp. 12 and 13].

J. P. A. Long in the first edition of his text, refers to stock-in-trade only in an example, which is described as the "cost price of goods sold." In an edition published two years later, he points out that any increase in value of stock-in-trade increases taxable income and any diminution in value will reduce taxable income. The form reproduced on page 114 merely requires the amount of stock-in-trade on hand to be included [1876, p. 16; 1878, pp. 14–15, and 114]. Wm. Harnett Blanch [1890, p. 29] merely has a place for opening and closing stock figures.

Murray and Carter [1895, p. 74, explaining the figures in an example of a trading account, 1899, p. 97] also make scant reference to the valuation of stock-in-trade:

> stock has been analysed, and the amount of it appertaining to each item at the beginning and end of each year has been taken into account ...

This has the same effect as doing a stock take and using the figure ascertained as the opening and closing figures for stock-in-trade. They point out that one of the common errors made by taxpayers who keep accounts for cash transactions only is to forget that any increases and decreases in the value of stock-in-trade have to be taken into account to determine income for the period [at pp. 152 and 217, respectively]. The other authors who wrote during the period did not refer to the issue at all.[10]

5.0 PERIOD 1901 TO 1925

Between 1901 and 1925 there were several events which impacted upon income tax. During this period there were two inquiries into income taxation, there was the constitutional crisis of 1909–11, with the super tax being introduced in 1909; the First World War occurred, and with it the introduction of the excess profits duty. Several of these issues affected the rates of income tax paid (see Appendix I, p. 247). The requests for balance sheets by surveyors of taxes continued and during the First World War they started asking taxpayers to provide them with stock certificates to support their returns. The practice of using the average of the three preceding years' of income ceased with the passing of The Finance Act of 1926, which introduced yearly assessments, effective as of April 6, 1927.[11]

The 1904 Income Tax Inquiry had very limited terms of reference. It did not include the issues under consideration here. The Commission's limited terms of reference were regretable for the accounting profession [see Editorial, *The Accountant* (May 7, 1904), pp. 584–585]. The super tax added an extra six pence in tax in the pound on income over £5,000 "upon the amount by which such incomes exceed £3,000." This can be compared with the tax on land values of 20% on the increase in value. Despite all these stimuli there was very little discussion of the question of valuation of stock-in-trade for taxation purposes, except for problems caused by the termination of the excess profits duty.

The significance of the advent of World War I on the United Kingdom tax system cannot be underestimated. This can be seen from the following analysis by B. E. V. Sabine:[12]

> The financing of World War I can be split into two sharply contrasting periods. There was no attempt at first to put taxation on a truly war basis, although there was an all-round increase in rates in the November 1914 Budget: but this was effective for only a third of the year; and in the second Budget of May 1915 no new taxation at all was imposed. Before then, however, Lloyd Geroge [*sic*] had been translated [*sic*] to the Ministry of Munitions, and his successor, Reginald McKenna, an ex-banker, was forced to meet the challenge of daily expenditure on the £4.5 million mark. The Budget (1915) by which he did so ushered in the second period of war taxation. Income tax was raised to an unprecedented 3s.6d. in the £, supertax could reach an astronomical 6s.10d. and, a radical departure, wages were to be taxed by quarterly assessment made by the Surveyor (Inspector). The traditionalists were up in arms at this extension of bureaucratic power, but the original income tax scheme was never designed for weekly wage earners. In addition an Excess Profits Duty was imposed at 50 per cent on profits earned over a pre-war standard: retained until 1921, it accounted for no less than 25 per cent of the total tax revenue during the period.
>
> By the end of the war income tax had changed out of all recognition. No longer was it the simple Victorian mechanism with a uniform rate of pence in the pound. It was now a much more complex apparatus, admitting both differentiation in the form of an earned income relief, and graduation in the shape of a supertax, with the income tax rate at 6s. and the maximum supertax at 4s.6d. A limited range of personal releifs [*sic*] had also been introduced and, for industry, an embryonic system of capital allowances. The most remarkable change, however, was in yield from some £34 millions pre-war to nearly £585 millions in 1918. Equally radical were the parallel changes in administration, with an ever-growing wealth of judicial dicta. Day-to-day control now resided in the tax district not the General Commissioners' office: as Snowden put it: "Anybody who knows anything about the working of the income tax laws knows that 99 per cent of the disputes in regard to income tax are now settled by the Surveyor of Taxes...The real work is now being done by the Surveyors of Taxes."

5.1 The Royal Commission of 1919–1920

Evidence was given by several accountants representing the various professional accounting bodies. A Committee of the Institute [of Chartered Accountants in England and Wales] was set up to consider what evidence should be given to the Royal Commission. An editorial in *The Accountant* noted that [(May 24, 1919), p. 434]:

> It is gratifying to note that the Institute has decided to form a Committee to consider the evidence to be tendered to the Royal Commission on the Income Tax .... The profession is the only body that can offer comprehensive and complete evidence of the whole tax and the only body that will have the administration of the taxpayer's interests, so that the Commission must give extensive, and, in fact, exhaustive, attention to the Institute's recommendations.

It was stated that the Committee had "a comprehensive and interesting programme before it," and that [Editorial note, *The Accountant* (May 31, 1919), p. 458]:

> The best preventatives for the future are statutory requirements for all traders' income-tax returns to be certified by a *qualified* accountant, compulsory accounting on a specified basis, compulsory auditing by a qualified accountant, restriction of income-tax practice to a professional body such as that of accountants....

The editorial further considered that the three years' average rule was:

> another absurdity that the Committee should oppose. The basis of the preceding year is obviously the only sound method, as it results in a taxpayer being charged on his actual profits....

Given the above comments on the importance of the participation of the profession, the performance of accountants did not live up to these high expectations, particularly in the area of valuation of stock-in-trade. As is shown below there was no agreement on the method which should be used to value stock-in-trade; indeed, some accountants did not wish to discuss the issue at all.

In a leading article in *The Accountant* it was regretted [(April 10, 1920), p. 410]:

> that the Commission has not made a definite recommendation that the keeping of proper books should be made compulsory, and that the Revenue should only accept accounts prepared by a qualified accountant.

However, it was further reported that [Income tax notes, *The Accountant* (March 27, 1920), p. 359]:[13]

> The production of books is to be required when necessary, but subject to the taxpayer's right of appeal to the Special Commissioners.

According to evidence before the Royal Commission on Taxation (1919–1920), The Board of Inland Revenue did not find the valuation of stock-in-trade to be a problem until the rates of income tax began to rise [Minutes of Evidence, 1920, p. 628] (see Appendix I). It did not become a matter of concern until the onset of the First World War, although there is a reference to a significant number of cases of secret reserves having been created in respect to stock-in-trade in the cotton trade around 1910.[14] The most surprising fact is that the accountants who appeared to give evidence before the Royal Commission were reluctant to give any evidence at all with respect to the valuation of stock-in-trade. A cynic might suggest that accountants felt it the better part of discretion to say nothing as they could not present a logical argument for its use.[15]

G. O. Parsons (Incorporated Accountant, chartered secretary, and secretary of The Income Tax Reform League) only mentioned the matter in reply to a direct question, from Mr. Kerly, QC (Royal Commissioner), as to how stock-in-trade should be valued for income tax purposes. He replied by reference to accounting practice [Minutes of Evidence, 1920, paras 1817–1821, p. 89]:

> [*Mr. Parsons*] ... there are, of course, decided opinions as to how stock should be valued. It should be valued according to our idea of cost price, or at the customary market valuation if the market valuation is lower than the cost price, but you should not value it at the market price of the day, if more than cost, because you would be taking credit for profits not actually realised.
>
> ...[*Mr. Kerly*] ... is there any logic in not taking at that price? — [*Mr Parsons*] Simply that you would be taking credit for a profit you have not realised. The profit is not realized until you have sold the article.
>
> ...[*Mr. Kerly*] ... You do not desire to give any evidence about the valuation of stocks; you do not know that any difficulty has arisen about them? — [*Mr. Parsons*] I have not heard of any.

Parsons would not have given evidence on the matter except for the fact that he was specifically asked about it. Most of the discussion of the valuation of stock-in-trade occurred in relation to the wording of the stock certificate and desirability of making them mandatory.

E. Stanford London of the Board of Inland Revenue was questioned extensively on the proper way to value stock-in-trade for income tax purposes. He said that the practice was to accept accounts drawn up on the basis of The Rule, and that the Revenue usually requested signed statements from taxpayers stating the value of stock-in-trade and how it was valued.[16] The rule was only accepted by the Board of Inland Revenue because of its [assumed/claimed] long use in business, despite the inconsistencies in its application and its lack of logic. He described the use of The Rule as "an unsatisfactory practice."[17] He indicated that accounts which were based upon current "market values"[18] of closing stock-in-trade would be acceptable for income tax purposes, as would be accounts based upon historical cost values alone [Minutes of Evidence, 1920, at pp. 624 and 628]. Neither of these methods would lead to the types of manipulations and inconsistencies which were associated with the use of The Rule. He gave evidence that prior to the war and the introduction of the excess profits duty, the Revenue did not worry about stock certificates and the value of stock-in-trade, because "it was felt that in the long run it would rectify itself" [Minutes of Evidence, 1920, para 12,488, p. 622]. It was not common, so he said, to require stock certificates until the war years.

London believed it would be far more satisfactory if the method(s) of valuation of stock-in-trade was specifically dealt with in the income tax legislation.

The Accountant [Income tax note (July 12, 1919), p. 30] reported the evidence given on behalf of the London Chamber of Commerce. It had suggested that all businesses should be compelled to keep "proper books." It was stated that many of its members urged that businesses should be compelled to produce accounts audited by a qualified accountant for tax purposes. The editor commented that the problem of evasion of income tax would be very nearly solved if this suggestion were adopted. Certainly, in *The Accountant*'s opinion, the number of cases of evasion that are being "continually" discovered "must obviously be only a small proportion of the frauds existent."

The evidence given on behalf of the Association of British Chambers of Commerce was to a similar end [Income tax note, *The Accountant* (August 9, 1919), p. 127].

No specific legislation was forthcoming as a result of the Royal Commission on the Income Tax 1920, and it made no recommendations whatsoever with respect to the valuation of stock-in-trade, except that requests for stock certificates should be given the force of law.

5.2 The Literature 1900–1925

There was little attention paid to the issue of valuation of stock-in-trade for income tax purposes from 1901 to 1925. The use of The Rule was hardly mentioned until the introduction of the excess profits duty during the First World War. Most of the comments on the valuation of stock-in-trade were with respect to the excess profits duty.

Little was said on the question of stock-in-trade valuation for income tax purposes between 1900 and 1914, except with respect to the issue of the production of books and balance sheets to the surveyors of taxes or the commissioners.[19] There were many inquiries and comments on this issue in the letter to the editors of *The Accountant*.[20] The reasons given for asking for the production of balance sheets were to verify:

1. the amount of depreciation being claimed
2. the amount of interest paid on debentures to determine if the correct amount of tax had been deducted
3. if any amount had been claimed for doubtful debts and the amount of bad debts
4. if any reserve out of profits had been made or any secret reserves.[21]

It is to be noted that verification of the value and method of valuing of stock-in-trade was not included as one of the reasons. In one case the amount of stock was mentioned, but this was when discussing the production of the trading account [Rhodes, 1911, pp. 588–589].

The question of valuing stock for income tax purposes was raised by "Enquirer" [1909, p. 547]. The problem involved a retail ironmonger, whose stock-in-trade consisted of "thousands of articles." The taxpayer had only taken stock "every two or ... three years" due to the tremendous amount of work involved. The only other time when the issue of trading stock was raised was with respect to the taxation consequences of buying a business with stock value being greatly below actual value. Such profit was found to be of a capital nature.[22]

By 1914, the Board of Inland Revenue were asking taxpayers to supply copies of balance sheets, trading accounts and profit and loss accounts. These were to show:[23]

- the value of the stock at the beginning and end of each year
- the amount of purchases and sales of each year
- particulars of the several deductions claimed from gross profits each year
- particulars of the various assets and liabilities as at the beginning and end of each year.

The Board of Inland Revenue said the production of the balance sheet was to allow the surveyor to be satisfied with the taxpayers' return and to "obviate the possibility of an appeal ...."[24]

Between 1901 and 1910, the editorial comments in *The Accountant* were consistently in favour of the production of balance sheets as a means of preventing fraud and protection of the honest taxpayer.[25] In the long run, it would be of benefit to the taxpayers as it would force them to keep proper books and accounts.[26] This approach was not too popular with the profession [See Jenkinson, 1907, pp. 382–383; "A.C.A.," 1908, p. 525]. It was felt that a mere certificate by an accountant was not enough as there were "other classes of accountants ... whose certificate could not safely be accepted without due inquiry" [Editorial note, *The Accountant* (March 30, 1907), p. 413].

The requests for the production of balance sheets seem to have accelerated in 1908, and this appears to have coincided with the introduction of section 21 of the Companies Act, 1907, which dealt with the publication of accounts by public companies ["C," 1908, p. 74]. *The Accountant,* in an editorial invited discussion from readers on this "very important topic" [(July 4, 1908), p. 8].

This approach inexplicably changed in 1915, when *The Accountant* campaigned strongly against the production of balance sheets to surveyors of taxes.[27] This approach was reversed late in 1916 when *The Accountant* was advocating legislation requiring traders, etc., to submit "copies of such accounts as may be necessary to show the true profits" and that they be prepared from books "which are kept on proper accounting principles and shall be certified by a qualified accountant as showing the true and correct profit of the ... business." This would prevent evasion which "has been too rampant" [Leading article, *The Accountant* (October 7, 1916), p. 294].

None of the articles appearing in *The Accountant* during the period referred to the question of valuing stock-in-trade for income tax purposes.[28] In several cases there was an example which showed stock figures in the trading account and balance sheet, but without further comment.[29] Several authors emphasized the importance of keeping proper books of account, but did not deal with the issue of stock-in-trade valuation.[30]

The principles to be applied in determining the *balance of profits and gains* under the Income Tax Act and the valuation of stock-in-trade can be illustrated by the following situation discussed in *The Accountant.*

In an editorial note, the case of a timber merchant who had not taken stock for over ten years was discussed. Income (profits) had to be calculated by deducting purchases from gross sales. Due to the actions of the timber controller, it was impossible to purchase any timber during the current year. Therefore, all sales were out of the prior years' purchases. As a result, the current year's assessment was "unduly inflated." "F.C.B." asked if this could be avoided. The tax editor responded as follows [Editorial note, *The Accountant* (February 22, 1919), p. 138]:

> Rule I to Case I of Schedule D only charges the "balance of the profits or gains," and it was laid down in *inter alia Usher's case* that profits for income-tax must be computed on ordinary commercial principles, provided that where there is a specific provision in the Income Tax Acts disallowing a particular expense, that provision must be followed .... The income-tax is only an annual tax, ... an income-tax assessment for one year has no effect whatever on that of a subsequent year .... The position is, therefore, that ... profits for [each year] ... have to be ascertained on commercial principles quite separately and independently of what has been adopted [previously]. Now, as there are no stock figures, the profits must be estimated by estimating the difference in stocks ... the 1917 accounts do not give the "profits" without taking stock into account .... These accounts are incorrect by their incompleteness in not containing debits and credits for stock, so that without insertion of estimates for stock it would be a direct violation of Rule I to Case I to treat the profit at present shown as being the profit for income-tax.

In another case discussed in *The Accountant*, a taxpayer had valued his stock-in-trade at the end of the year at cost price. It was anticipated that there would be heavy losses due to the fall in prices. Could such anticipated losses be taken into account in the current period? The tax editor responded [Editorial note, *The Accountant* (June 16, 1917), p. 563] in a similar manner to the problem posed by "F.C.C.," that:

> Under *Usher's* case the profit for income-tax and, ... Excess Profits Duty also, must be ascertained on *commercial* principles so long as there is no specific prohibition in the Income Tax Acts ... from an ordinary commercial point of view, the stock would be reduced, that reduction must be allowed .... The fact of the loss coming in for income-tax when it actually occurs is irrelevant, as *Usher's* case substitutes the *commercial* profit, and, moreover, it would not necessarily come in for Excess Profits Duty.

The proper method of valuing stock-in-trade was also raised in the House of Commons. Sir A. Bird asked the Chancellor of the Exchequer about claims that Inspectors of Taxes were refusing to accept returns for excess profits duties in which current market prices were used to value stock-in-trade. The reply by Mr. Young [May 30, 1921], was a statement of general principle, that:

> The general rule for the valuation of trading stocks for taxation purposes is that they should be brought into account at cost or market value, whichever is the lower. [Editorial note, *The Accountant* (June 11, 1921), p. 778].

The tax editor of *The Accountant* claimed that use of cost prices alone was consistent with the application of The Rule. This comment arose in the context of a manufacturing company which had valued its stock-in-trade at cost for more than 20 years. They had changed to market value for part of the stock as the current prices were below their cost prices. Was this change permitted for income tax purposes? The tax editor replied that the difference in value for opening stock valued at cost and using The Rule (£12,000) should not be added back, as [Editorial note (June 4, 1921), p. 716.]:

> Valuation at market value where less than cost is the established practice for both taxes.

The tax editor [income tax note, *The Accountant* (December 13, 1919), p. 501] stated the approach to be taken with respect to the valuation of stock-in-trade for income tax purposes. This was in reply to a problem raised by "Audire," who cites an example where stock has been valued on a uniform basis for the past eight years. That method was now objected to by the Revenue and it was proposed to substitute another basis of valuation without altering the commencing valuation for the year and that:

> If the stock at 31st December 1918 is incorrect, that at 31st December 1917 must similarly be wrong, as the same basis was adopted at both stocktakings. If the Inspector's method is meant for an adjustment to cover past years, the more equitable course would be to adjust each year separately,....

A comment made in an editorial note replying to a query by "A.E.P." is of interest [Editorial note, *The Accountant* (January 27, 1917), p. 84]. Stock-in-trade had been "valued for many years at gross prices (estimated cost) less discounts, ... The gross price cannot be guaranteed to be the cost, as it is impossible to keep a record of the cost of all goods left in stock as prices vary at every purchase and no record is possible of the actual goods used." The Revenue wanted to use the gross prices for the value of stock-in-trade. It is commented that:

> the question is ... what is the correct *commercial* practice of valuing stock *in the particular trade* [emphasis added]. *Usher's* case laid down that the principles of ascertaining profits for income-tax must be the commercial principles .... The present year's assessment must be on the average profits of the three preceding years, ... as *Usher's* case, in its restriction of income-tax profits to the correct commercial profits of the years included in the average, avoids this.

In a comment [Editorial note, *The Accountant* (July 21, 1917), p. 46] on the "vexed" problem of valuing stock-in-trade it is stated, with respect to the White Paper, that it is in:

> agreement with The Rule that the lower figure of cost price or market value is the correct basis.

The Accountant considered that the participation of the accounting profession in the White Paper was an important step forward for the profession. The acceptance by the government and the Inland Revenue of the "general principle that Stocks should always be valued at cost price or market price (whichever be the lower of the two)" was to be welcomed. It was crucial to the profession that it had been consulted on this "important" matter [editorial, *The Accountant* (July 28, 1917), p. 63]:

> because it shows very clearly that the Government is taking full advantage of the fact that it is now in a position readily to obtain the best expert advice in all matters relating to questions of accounts.

A report in *The Accountant* [Editorial note (June 9, 1917), p. 544] shows that the use of The Rule was not the only way to reduce income tax liability, nor was it the most effective one. The report was as follows:

> A question has been asked in The House of Commons if relief can be given from demands of Surveyors of Taxes that, for Income-tax and Excess Profits Duty, stocks should be taken at cost or market value, whichever was the lower. It was urged that this acted unfairly, as many traders had been in the habit of taking their stocks below cost or market value, and that traders should be allowed to charge against present profits sums necessary to reinstate stocks to pre-war level ....

The opinion of *The Accountant* was that:

> It is impossible to lay down a general rule for treatment of stocks, but, on stock depreciating in a particular year, the above method [The Rule] gives a full allowance in that year by the credit for stock being reduced.

Books published during this period rarely mentioned the issue of stock-in-trade valuation. Those which did mention the issue were usually published towards the end of the 1920s. For instance Phillip Sulley [1927, p. 35] specifies the use of The Rule and that "the same system must be followed yearly." There was a further elaboration of the valuation of stock-in-trade. It was stated that [p. 117]:

> Items should be priced at cost. Where they have become damaged, or are out of date or fashion, to such an extent they are worth less than they cost, they must be entered at market value, what they may reasonably be expected to sell for.

Murray and Carter did not revise their scant treatment of stock-in-trade which they had used in the 1890s.[31] Usually stock-in-trade merely appeared in examples of the trading account or balance sheet, without further discussion. Indeed, many examples started from the gross profit figure.[32] Some authors made some additional comments on the valuation of stock-in-trade, but without referring to The Rule or any other method of valuation.[33] Harry

D. Myers points that "*Reserves and Reserve Funds* are not allowed" [1916, p. 23]. However, an example at page 14 is not explained. This is a general comment, and one presumes it includes any reserves made for diminution in the value of stock-in-trade. As with the period to 1900, many books on income tax did not refer to the stock-in-trade at all.[34] The issue of the production to surveyors of taxes of books and balance sheets by taxpayers continued. This is a point of some significance. The de facto need to produce the books and balance sheets upon an appeal by the taxpayer was also regularly discussed.[35] The matter of surveyors of taxes "demanding" the production by taxpayers of books for inspection was raised in the House of Commons by Captain Rankin (June 14, 1921). Young replied [Editorial note, *The Accountant* (June 25, 1921), p. 840] that the production of a taxpayer's books was never demanded and that:

> from time to time in which inspection of a taxpayer's books is desirable to resolve doubts or settle questions outstanding, but such an inspection is in no case made without the taxpayer's concurrence.

The issue of accountants being asked the question, "To what extent have you checked the stock and are able to certify as to the correctness of the valuation?" was raised by "Stocks" [1921]. He felt that it was time the profession "as a whole took a firm stand against this endeavour" by the Inland Revenue to:

> make accountants responsible for the stocktaking.
>
> I do not see that our responsibility to the Revenue Department is greater than that to the shareholders of the companies whose Balance Sheets we audit, and in that connection it has been held that accountants are "watchdogs and not bloodhounds." [Of course the Inland Revenue cannot make accountants responsible for anything they are unwilling to accept responsibility for: hence the query. — Ed. Acct.]

"Stocks" had obviously read something into the words that are not readily apparent to other readers.

5.3 Excess Profits Duty

The excess profits duty was introduced to limit the ability of businesses to make excessive profits out of the First World War and as part of the cost control structure for government contracts. This was achieved by introducing a penalty tax if profits varied by more than a given percentage of prewar profits. Part of the method for determining excess profits duty was the calculation of the capital base of the taxpayer. To do this the taxpayer had to submit balance sheets for the specified years. One of the items which was required by the Inland Revenue was the amount of stock-in-hand at balance dates. The tax editor of *The Accountant,* in reply to a question about the valuation of stock-in-trade for excess profits duty purposes, responded [Editorial note (September 10, 1921), p. 340] with a general statement of principle that:

> practice allows the adoption of cost or market value, whichever is the lower.

W. E. Snelling[36] points out the necessity of taking stock for excess profits duty purposes and that:

> Here, again, there should be no hidden reserve or writing down or up.

and that:

> the valuation is assumed to be on the same basis throughout the years concerned. The figures appearing in the balance sheet will therefore be taken.

Later when the impact on excess profits duty at the end of the war was being considered, following from the *Heads of Government Proposals upon the Valuation of Stocks for Purposes of Excess Profits Duty* and the resultant legislation, the commentary was updated for this occurrence with a quotation from an official memorandum issued by the Board of Inland Revenue,[37] emphasizing the introductory paragraph, which states:

> The Board of Inland Revenue are prepared to adopt the following modification of the *general principle* that stock should be valued at cost or market value, whichever is lower — (*Official Memorandum*).

Spicer and Pegler state that the normal method of valuing stock-in-trade for taxation purposes is by use of The Rule.[38] They point out in this context that "any depreciation below cost [is] covered by the phrase 'proper deduction for replacement.'" The taxpayer must declare any such reserve for loss in stock value in anticipation of the situation after the war when prices are presumed to fall significantly. Such reserves, they assumed, would not be allowable for excess profits duty purposes. However, this was still an open question [1916(a), pp. 76 and 86]. By 1918 the problem of stock valuation and the termination of excess profits duty was becoming clear. This was because of problems associated with wartime high prices as stock-in-trade is a "considerable asset" which "greatly increased in value" and its value will fall drastically after the end of the war. They refer specifically to paragraph 1 of an Inland Revenue document which followed from the White Paper and its recommendations, in a similar fashion to Snelling. They summarize their view on stock-in-trade valuation for excess profits duty purposes as follows [1918, p. 30]:

> The principle usually adopted has been to bring the stocks into account at cost or market value, whichever is lower, but the effect of this would be a considerable loss might be sustained if Excess Profits Duty terminated before stocks held at the last accounting period had been realized....

Harry D. Myers, when discussing the balance sheet for excess profits duty says that *assets* are to be "valued at cost, less proper deduction for wear and tear or replacement ..." [1916, p. 120]. This was one of The Rules issued by the Inland Revenue with respect to the excess profits duty. Roger N. Carter merely reproduces the *Heads of Government Proposal* without any substantive discussion of the question of stock-in-trade valuation [1921, pp. 109–110].

5.4 Stock Certificates

The introduction of stock certificates for income tax purposes may well have been a significant factor in the development of The Rule. This is because their use would have highlighted the other methods of manipulating stock values. Many of these methods would have been unacceptable to the Inland Revenue either because they did not show the true profits for the period or because their use led to the creation of secret reserves. It is to be noted that there was no obligation upon the taxpayer to provide a stock certificate when requested to do so by the surveyor of taxes. It is not precisely clear when stock certificates, for income tax purposes, were first used. The situation is complicated because use of stock certificates was not centrally developed. Rather, individual surveyors of taxes introduced them in their own districts.

At least two different types of stock certificates were used by the surveyors of taxes. Two examples are set out in Appendix II, p. 248. One certifies that stock-in-trade has been valued using The Rule, while the other merely requires the basis of valuation to be disclosed. It is to be noted that the one requiring the use of The Rule was rejected by the Royal Commission after being strongly criticized by one of the witnesses.[39] W. G. Rayner had strong objections to this form of stock certificate, as traders were not able to ascertain the exact cost or market value of their stock [Minutes of Evidence, 1920 , para 8867, p. 432]:

> Directly he breaks bulk in any large parcel of stuff, he does not know the value of his stuff.

and later under questioning by Mr. McLintock [Minutes of Evidence, 1920, para 9036, p. 436]:

> 9041. Is not that a common and every-day expression, well known to every trader as to what it means? — Yes, but it is not always clear when it is put into a certificate. You have to look at it in a different way. If you get down to the Law Courts and get that certificate overhauled by gentlemen at the Bar you will find it means something totally different to what it reads.
>
> 9042. Do you suggest that the average honest trader is in difficulty in granting that certificate? — I do; very great difficulty.
>
> 9043. That he does not know the cost price of his goods? — Manufactured or partly manufactured goods.
>
> 9044. A merchant knows the cost price of his goods? — A merchant knows it until he breaks bulk. If he breaks bulk he can never trace his exact cost.
>
> 9045. Give me an illustration of breaking bulk of a particular kind of goods that you refer to? — We will say soft goods.
>
> 9046. What kind of soft goods? — We will say silk.
>
> 9047. Right; go ahead with silk. He breaks bulk in what respect? He takes one of his rolls on to the board, and what happens? — He cuts it off and he starts selling it.
>
> 9048. Suppose he has taken out a roll, and he has sold half of it, do you suggest he does not know the cost price of the half that is left? — He does of that half. I am speaking now of it in bulk.
>
> 9049. Take your own illustration. I suggest that a roll of silk is rolled out on one of those lapping boards; when the goods come in each piece of silk has written on a ticket the cost price of it, taken from the invoice, and the number of yards that are in it? — Yes; but five years hence?
>
> 9050. Five years hence that ticket is still there? — How about the price?
>
> 9051. He is still entitled to value his stock at cost price, or market value if it is less? — Who is going to tell the market price?

He preferred a certificate which stated that stock-in-trade had been valued at "cost price or a fair value" [Minutes of Evidence, 1920 , para 9064, p. 437].

The use of stock certificates appears to have coincided with the introduction of the excess profits tax during the early stages of the First World War. No evidence of their use prior to the commencement of the War can be found.

The Accountant reported the evidence given on behalf of the Association of British Chambers of Commerce which suggested compulsory production of accounts audited by an accountant. They also suggested that taxpayers [Income tax note, *The Accountant* (August 9, 1919), p. 127]:

> should produce a certificate signed by himself, quite apart from the auditors' certificate, certifying ... [*inter alia*] that the valuation of the stock-in-trade is true and correct, both as to quantities involved and the basis of valuation.

It was pointed out by *The Accountant* that this suggestion was similar to the form of the "stock certificate used by *many* [emphasis added] Surveyors and willingly given by many accountants" and that there "is a clear necessity for such a certificate ...."

The Accountant believed that it was important that the correct figures should be used for stock-in-trade values for income tax purposes [income tax notes, *The Accountant* (March 27, 1920), p. 359]. To this end it was stated in an editorial that:

> The Stock Certificate now in use should be made statutory, and accountants should have to give a certificate showing the extent and nature of the audit.

This procedure would complement the new requirement to produce books when requested by the Revenue. It was noted, however, that some accountants objected to the form of the stock certificate which have been used freely "*recently*" by inspectors of taxes, however it was concluded that:

> much of this objection disappears on the certificate assuming a statutory form, as suggested by the Commission. From one point of view, the certificate has a value in removing from the accountant [the] responsibility ....

for stock-in-trade values used for income tax purposes [Leading article, *The Accountant* (April 3, 1920), p. 378].

Snelling [[1919], p. 303; [1920](a), p. 331] points out, when discussing an example, that "[a] stock certificate is usually required." This is the first reference to stock certificates which has been found in books published to 1920. It is in a book on excess profits duty and not a book on income tax law.

The preeminence of The Rule for income tax purposes can be questioned. Consider the following comment of the tax editor in reply to A. Bell who had raised the question of stock valuations. The tax editor [Editorial note, *The Accountant* (February 12, 1921), p. 177] responded with the comment that:

> Stock is one of the most difficult factors in accounts, and the only redeeming feature is that the matter adjusts itself over a period, but this point ceases to operate on the Excess Profits Duty being repealed. *The taking of stock at cost or market value is only a compromise*, and is adopted commercially, as there is [an] ultimate adjustment .... [emphasis added]

There would, however, be problems associated with having used The Rule for excess profits duty purposes. It would be necessary for "some allowance" to be permitted where values had fallen after the end of excess profits duty.

The notes, editorials and articles appearing in *The Accountant*, make it clear that many taxpayers tried to create secret reserves by undervaluing stock-in-trade and that the Revenue would not accept these for income tax purposes if they were discovered. This can be illustrated by an extract of a letter appearing in *The Accountant* ["Chip off the Old Block," (May 28, 1921), pp. 676–677]:

> Sir, — The questions now being asked about stock ... bring a memory reminder that common-sense reserves and anticipated losses have been disallowed and a thought that "it was not ever thus." Now the boot is on the other leg and deficiencies becoming the usual thing, ...
>
> [677] having tried to sell them and found no buyers the market value is "nil." What a problem! Market price or cost, whichever is lower; that is the accepted rule; ... as H.M. Inspectors have disallowed *anticipated losses* and *common-sense reserves* in the past for taxation purposes .... [emphasis added]

In this case the value of both the opening and closing stock-in-trade had been excluded when determining the profit for the period.

6.0 COURT CASES DEALING WITH THE VALUATION OF STOCK-IN-TRADE

The question of the valuation of stock-in-trade was first considered by the Courts in the United Kingdom in *Whimster & Co.* v. *Commissioners of Inland Revenue*, where Lord President Clyde made this statement [(1925) 12 T.C. 813, (1926) SC 25]:

> the profits of any particular year or accounting period must be taken to consist of the difference between the receipts from the trade or business during such year ... and the expenditure laid out to earn those receipts the account ... must be framed consistently with the ordinary principles of commercial accounting, so far as applicable, and in conformity with The Rules of the *Income Tax Act* .... For example, the ordinary principles of commercial accounting require that in the profit and loss account of a merchant's or manufacturer's business the values of the stock-in-trade at the beginning and at the end of the period covered by the account should be entered at cost or market price, whichever is the lower; although there is nothing about this in the taxing statute.

Lord Sands has observed in the same case that [(1925) 12 TC 813, at p. 827]:

> The consideration of how it would be prudent for a trader to act does not solve the question here presented to us as one of revenue law. Under this law the profits are the profits realised in the course of the year. What seems an exception is recognised where a trader purchased and still holds goods or stocks which have fallen in value. No loss has been realised. Loss may not occur. Nevertheless, at the close of the year he is permitted to treat these goods or stocks as of their market value.

The Courts thus endorsed the use of The Rule as being permissible for income tax purposes, but not until 1925.

7.0 CONCLUSIONS

From the investigations undertaken can the proposition be supported that income tax consideration fostered the development of The Rule in the United Kingdom? We are considering this question in the context of the three time periods of the study. Clearly during early development of The Rule to 1900 the answer is a definite "No." This assumes that it is, as it is widely claimed to be, common by the beginning of the twentieth century.

There is virtually no discussion in the taxation literature of the valuation of stock-in-trade before the First World War. Nor is there any discussion of the tax advantages or consequences of the use of The Rule in the accounting literature during this period. It is difficult to believe that there could be an interplay between the use of The Rule and income tax without a discussion occurring on the issue. After all, it would be a rational reason for the adoption of The Rule. It would be expected, therefore, to appear along with such comments (justification for the use of The Rule) as "its use is dictated by commercial prudence," "that profit should not be anticipated" or it is "a sound accounting practice."

Could the rates of income tax have fostered the development of The Rule? A careful examination of Appendix I indicates that no such inference can be made. If income tax was a factor, one would have expected that during the period around its reintroduction there would have been a rapid impact upon accounting practice. There is however, practically no discussion of The Rule during this period. Similarly, the doubling of the income tax rate in 1854 would, one would have thought, brought some reaction.

The table shows violent swings in the rates of income tax up until 1900. The period 1850 to 1900 is generally said to be the time in which the use of The Rule became common in the United Kingdom. Would a rational businessman defer recognizing income when there was an equal probability of an increase or decrease in the tax rate? The rule will only be an advantage where the rate of tax falls or remains constant.[40] The percentage increases during the period to 1900 varied from 7.14% to 80% and decreases 16.67% to 56.25%. Because of the variability in the rate of income tax, it is difficult to find any reason for businesses adopting The Rule for valuing their stock-in-trade for income tax purposes.

It is not as if the rates of income tax were very high during the period. The rate varied from a low of 0.83% from 1874–76 to a high of 6.67% in 1855–1857. Nor were the rates of income tax during the first decade of the twentieth century conducive to the development of The Rule. Income tax rates varied between 3.33% and 5.0% during the period 1860 to 1900.

The only time the taxation has fostered a debate on the use of The Rule was the impact of the excess profits tax and the consequences of its removal. The impact here, however, would be expected to be negative. The introduction of the excess profits duty during the First World War was effectively an increase in the rate of taxation. Coupled with the increase from the prewar rate of one shilling, two pence in the pound to three shillings in 1915–16; five shillings, from 1916–18, and from 1918, six shillings in the pound, one would expect that any method of stock-in-trade valuation which deferred income recognition would be a distinct disadvantage to taxpayers during this period.

The real problem was that if stock was realized after the termination of the War, for less than the value taken at the last stock-take, there would have been no offsetting credit for the extra excess profits duty paid in the last period.

The expectation that normal rates of income tax would fall after the end of the War would be anticipated to have a positive impact. There is another side to the problem. It was also expected that prices would fall significantly after the war. Both of these expectations were fulfilled to a significant extent. The decrease in the tax was later than expected. The rate remained at six shillings in the pound until 1922, fell to five shillings for the following year, four shillings, six pence for 1923–1925, and four shillings for 1925–1928. The price falls, however, came quickly and were followed by a period of severe economic depression.

The events discussed in the last paragraph occurred after The Rule is said to have become the popular or traditional method for valuing stock-in-trade. In any event, the literature gives no indication that the rate of income tax was a factor in stock-in-trade valuation. It was only the need for adjustments consequent upon the termination of the excess profits duty which raised the issue of stock-in-trade valuation in a substantive manner.

Why would one use The Rule when there were more effective ways of reducing income tax? If the Revenue could not force the production of books of account or balance sheets, and could not insist on taxpayers returning stock certificates, how would undervaluations ever be detected? It would have been extremely easy to create secret reserves from undervaluing stock-in-trade. Such reserves would have been far greater than those created by the use of The Rule. Such forms of tax evasion would appear to have been relatively common.[41]

The acceptance of the use of The Rule by the Courts in 1925 did not impact upon its use for accounting purposes. This would have been expected if there was any relationship between income tax considerations and the development of the use of The Rule.[42]

It is concluded that until 1925 there is no evidence to suggest that income tax factors influenced the development of The Rule.

Appendix I

Rates of Income Tax 1842–1928*

From Apr. 6 to Apr. 5.	Rate per £	% £	% increase	From Apr. 6 to Apr. 5.	Rate per £	% £	% increase
1842 to 1854	7d.	2.92		1880 to 1881	6d.	2.50	+20.00
1854 to 1855	1s.2d.	5.83	+100.00	1881 to 1882	5d.	2.08	-16.67
1855 to 1857	1s.4d.7	6.67	+14.29	1882 to 1883	61/2d.	2.71	+30.00
1857 to 1858	7d.	2.92	-56.25	1883 to 1884	5d.	2.08	-23.08
1858 to 1859	5d	2.08.	-28.57	1884 to 1885	6d.	2.50	+20.00
1859 to 1860	9d.	3.75	+80.00	1885 to 1887	8d.	3.33	+33.33
				1887 to 1888	7d.	2.92	-12.50
1860 to 1861	10d.	4.17	+11.11	1888 to 1893	6d.	2.50	-14.29
1861 to 1863	9d.	3.75	-10.00	1893 to 1894	7d	2.92	+16.67
1863 to 1864	7d.	2.92	-22.22	1894 to 1900	8d	3.33	+14.29
1864 to 1865	6d.	2.50	-14.29				
1865 to 1867	4d.	1.67	-33.33	1900 to 1902	1s.0d.	5.00	+50.00
1867 to 1868	5d.	2.08	+25.00	1902 to 1903	1s.2d.	5.83	+16.67
1868 to 1869	6d.	2.50	+20.00	1903 to 1904	1s.3d.	6.25	+7.14
1869 to 1870	5d.	2.08	-16.67	1904 to 1909	1s.0d.	5.00	-20.00
				1909 to 1914	1s.2d.	5.83	+16.67
1870 to 1871	4d.	1.67	-20.00	1914 to 1915	1s.8d.	8.33	+42.86
1871 to 1872	6d.	2.50	+50.00	1915 to 1916	3s.0d.	15.00	+80.00
1872 to 1873	4d.	1.67	-33.33	1916 to 1918	5s.0d.	25.00	+66.67
1873 to 1874	3d.	1.25	-25.00	1918 to 1922	6s.0d.	30.00	+20.00
1874 to 1876	2d.	0.83	-33.34				
1876 to 1878	3d.	1.25	+50.00	1922 to 1923	5s.0d.	25.00	-16.67
1878 to 1880	5d.	2.08	+66.67	1923 to 1925	4s.6d.	22.50	-10.00
				1925 to 1928	4s.0d.	20.00	-11.11

From 1842 to 1853 the tax was on £150 and upwards. From 1853 to 1863 incomes of £100 to £150 paid a tax of (about) 2d. less than the figures given in above table. From 1863 to 1876 incomes under £100 were exempt; and incomes between £100 and £200 were allowed an abatement of £60. Since 1876 incomes under £150 have been exempt, and those under £400 have been allowed an abatement of £120.

* This table is taken from McEwan [1893, p. 212], supplemented by Anonymous [1920] and Murray and Carter [1927].

Change in Tax Rate 1842–1928

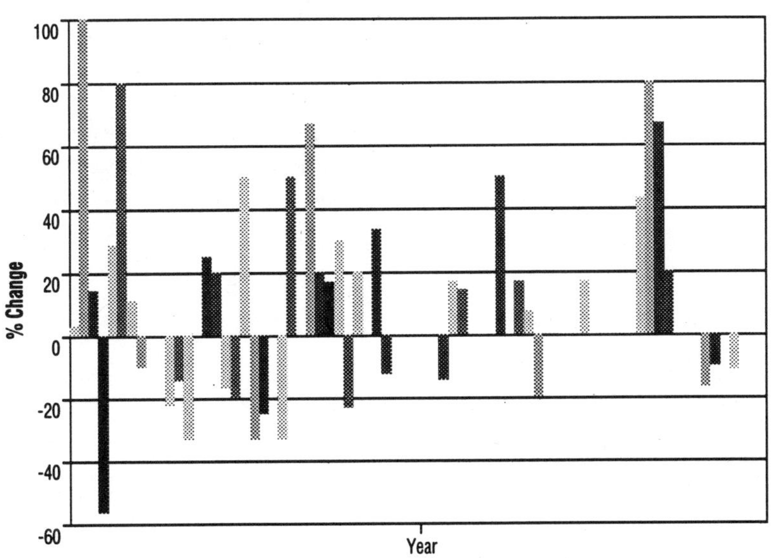

Appendix II

Examples of Stock Certificates

Stock Certificate Type A ["Auditors", 1921, p. 848]:

Stock.
State on what basis this stock was valued.
Has any reduction been made from the values so obtained before arriving at this amount?
Was the same basis adopted in previous years?
Have you certified that this figure includes the value of stock, the cost price of which has been charged against Revenue but which has not been actually delivered?
In arriving at the above figure, has any consideration been given to any change in prices or values since the above date?
Does this figure include any outlay incurred in connection with the stock, such as carriage?
Please state what steps you have taken to verify the quantities, values and calculations, leading up to the above figure."

Stock Certificate Type B [Minutes of Evidence, 1920, p. 531]:

Accounts. One year ended .... We hereby certify that the whole of our stock on hand on the .... is shown in our Stock Sheets produced to .... and amount to £ ......

We further certify that the Stock is valued at cost, or market price if under cost, on the same basis as hitherto, and that no deductions have been made from the value of the Stock in arriving at the above figures, which represent its total value to the best of our knowledge and belief.

We further certify that to the best of our knowledge and belief all transactions relating to the business of .... are correctly entered in the books of account during the period .... to .... which have been produced to Messrs .... and that we know of no other transactions which ought to be included and which would affect the Balance Sheet and Trading Account of the Company, or which should be brought into an account of the Company's dealings .

We further certify that no reserves whatever have been created (whether by writing down Stock, Book Debts, or otherwise) beyond those disclosed on the face of the Balance Sheet sent to the Surveyor of Taxes.

Dated this ....day of .... 19....

To be signed by an Acting Partner in a firm or a Managing Director of a Limited Company

ENDNOTES

1 The comments on an earlier version of this paper by the staff of The Department of Accounting and Finance, University of Glasgow, particularly Ken Shackleton and Simon Keane, are appreciated. The many insightful comments of Ray Chambers, Peter Wolnizer and Dick Edwards are acknowledged.

2 Scott (A. J.) [(undated), pp. 35–36]; Hatfield [1917, pp. 101–103; 1927(a), pp. 99–104; 1927(b), pp. 273–274]; Newman [1921, p. 10]; Paton [1922, reprinted in Baxter (1950), pp. 157–171, 167–169]; Scott [1926]; Edwards [1938]; MacNeal [1939(a) (see particularly "The Three Fables," pp. 1–19)]; MacNeal [1939(b)]; Littleton, [1941]; Vance [1943]; Chambers [1949, 1965]; Parker [1965]; Sterling [1967].

3 Edwards [1938]; Littleton [1941]; Vance [1943]; May [1954, p. 16]; Parker [1965].

4 It should be noted that for most of the last half of the nineteenth century the cost of goods was continually falling. However, as George O. May has noted, there was a "general tendency of price levels to rise, which existed between 1896 and 1913 ..." [1954, p. 8]. The use of The Rule would more likely to reduce tax when prices are falling, not when they are increasing.

5 Littleton [1941]; See also Littleton [1935, p. 271]. Littleton's approach has been strongly criticised by Vance [1943, pp. 221–227].

6 Commenting on *Conservatism in Inventory Valuations*, by D. R. Scott, *The Accounting Review*, March 1926, p. 24.

7 Case IV charged annual profit or gains not charged under any other Schedule.

8 Other classes of income were charged on different bases: collieries on a five years' average; manorial estates on a seven years' average; with railways and gas companies charged on the year preceding the assessment. The change from three years' average to assessment on a single year was recommended in *The Report of the Royal Commission on The Income Tax*, HMSO, 1920 (Section VII—Basis of Assessment under Schedule D) [Minutes of Evidence].

9 See editorial note, *The Accountant* (February 16, 1884), p. 8; Edwards [1886, p. 13]; Weekly note (on income tax), *The Accountant* (May 8, 1886), p. 269; Editorial, *The Accountant* (May 27, 1893), p. 487; McEwan [1893, p. 211]; Turquand [1895, p. 76]; Blunden [1897, p. 284].

10 See Muir [1861]; Senior [1863]; Dowell [1874, 1885, 1890, 1895]; Paton [1878].

11 This change was recommended by *The Report of The Royal Commission on The Income Tax*, HMSO, 1920 (Section VII—Basis of Assessment under Schedule D) [Minutes of Evidence].

12 Sabine [1980, p. 139]. More detailed comments to the same effect are made in *A History of Taxation* [1966, pp. 151–155], but without the spelling errors.

13 See also Leading article, *The Accountant* (April 3, 1920), p. 378.

14 See discussion of this occurrence, Minutes of Evidence, 1920 (E. Stanford London and Royal Commissioner, Dr. J. S. Stamp), para 12,631, p. 628.

15 See the interesting interchange between Mr. Birley, member of the Royal Commission and Mr. E. Stanford London of the Board of Inland Revenue, in the Minutes of Evidence

Before the Royal Commission [Minutes of Evidence, 1920, paras 12,535 to 12,544, pp. 624–625].

16 These statements were called stock certificates and are discussed later. It is to be noted that the type of certificate referred to did not require that any particular method of valuing stock-in-trade be used.

17 Minutes of Evidence [1920, p. 622]. At p. 628 he agrees with the statement that "the matter has only become acute by reason of the rise in rates during the war and the very rapid rise in prices...."

18 The words current "market values" could mean either replacement market or selling market.

19 See, for example, the articles by Isaacs [1901(a), p. 54, 1910(a), p. 283]; Carter (Eric M.) [1904, p. 8]; Johnston [1905, p. 649]; Richmond [1905, comment by Mr. Buckley, p. 22]; Anonymous [1907]; Jenkinson [1909, p. 787]; Stapleton [1911, p. 10, and discussants F. N. Hawnt, p. 13, and J. Boyd, p. 14]; Alban [1913, p. 174]; Walmsley [1913, p. 141]; Anonymous [1914, p. 291].

20 See for example Westcott, Maskall & Co. [1902, pp. 12–13]; "O.P." [1906]; "Seaside" [1906]; "Income Tax" [1906]; Jenkinson [1907]; "A Provincial Firm" [1908]; Davies Bros. [1908]; Payne [1908]; "C" [1908]; Grimson [1909, p. 644]; "Taxpayer" *The Accountant* (October 30, 1909), p. 645; "Anglo–Irish" [1909]; "X.Y.Z." [1909]; Cox [1910]; "Subscriber" [1910]; Rhodes [1911]; "Intax" [1911(a), p. 546]; "Intax" [1911(b), p. 589]; "Honi Soit Qui Mai [*sic*] Y Pense" [1914, p. 679]; "Interested" [1914, p. 614]; "X.Y.Z." [1914]; "Northern A.C.A.'s" [1914].

21 For point 1, see Westcott, Maskall & Co. [1902]; "O.P." [1906]; "Seaside" [1906]; Anonymous [1907, p. 524]; "A.C.A." [1908]; Davies Bros. [1908] "Anglo–Irish" [1909] "Subscriber" [1910].

For point 2, see: "Seaside" [1906]; Anonymous [1907, p. 524]. For point 3, see "O.P." [1906, p. 504]; Anonymous [1907, p. 524]. For point 4, see Anonymous [1907, p. 524].

22 See *J and M Craig (Kilmarnock) Ltd* v. *Cowperwaite* (1913) 13 TC 627, [1914] SC 388, referred to in an editorial note, *The Accountant*, Income Tax, February 21, 1914, p. 248 and the similar situation discussed in an Editorial, *The Accountant*, May 29, 1915, pp. 715–716. *J and M Craig (Kilmarnock) Ltd* v. *Cowperwaite* was in effect overruled by the Court of Appeal in *Steel Barrel Co. Ltd* v. *Osborne* (H.M. Inspector of Taxes), (1941–1942) 24 T.C. 293, (1942) 1 All ER 634.

23 According to an editorial note, *The Accountant*, November 14, 1914, pp. 563–564

24 See Geo Wingfield, Edwards & Goddard [1908, p. 899]. See also Rawlinson, [1909, p. 445] where an extract to answer a question raised by A. H. Scott, Lloyd George said that the Special Commissioners considered "that in many cases the information contained in Balance Sheets is essential in arriving at the correct liability." This was especially so with respect to claims for depreciation. This extract was also published as an editorial note in *The Incorporated Accountants' Journal*, June 1908, p. 206.

25 It was presumed that balance sheets would give a correct value for stock-in-trade as these were records used by the taxpayer for their own decision making. Surely if fraudulent values were being used for tax purposes the balance sheets produced for tax purposes could also use fraudulent values. This point was not addressed.

26 See for example Editorial note, *The Accountant*, November 3, 1906, p. 538, Editorial note, *The Accountant*, November 26, 1910, p. 722, Editorial, September 10, 1910, pp. 335–336, Cox, 1910, p. 266, Rhodes [1911], "Interested," 1914, Editorial, *The Accountant*, October 24, 1908, pp. 487–488 (qualified support), that complaints from the profession might be mitigated if certificates of accountants were accepted as to the accuracy of returns, Editorial, *The Accountant*, June 20, 1908, pp. 877–878.

27 See the leading article in *The Accountant*, November 14, 1914, pp. 553–554; Editorial note, July 11, 1914, p. 44; Editorial note, February 13, 1915, pp. 216–219, detailing correspondence between *The Accountant* and the Board of Inland Revenue on the topic. The latter brought an attack from *The Incorporated Accountants' Journal*, which was critical of *The Accountant*'s approach to the issue and giving a review of the area [*The Incorporated Accountants' Journal* (March 1915), pp. 121–123]. Not surprisingly *The Accountant* responded attacking *The Incorporated Accountants' Journal* view [(March 13, 1915), pp. 336–339].

28 See, for example, Carter [1903, 1910]; Ross [1904]; Wright [1907]; Isaacs [1909, 1912]; Edwards (H.) [1909]; Levie [1912]; Duxbury [1915].

29 See Carter [1902]; Smith [1902, p. 11]; Jenkinson [1909, p. 787]. Spicer [1911, pp. 109 and 110] gives examples which merely started from the gross profit figure.

30 See, for example, Isaacs [1901(a), p. 54; 1901(b), p. 407; 1910(b), p. 274; 1907, p. 651]; Alban [1913, p. 174]; Lunt [1915, p. 130].

31 Murray and Carter [1905, pp. 125 and 284, respectively; 1908, pp. 126-127 and 301, respectively; 1911, pp. 156 and 362, respectively; 1915, pp. 177–178 (the second point is not referred to in this edition); 1921, pp. 165 and 388, respectively; 1924, pp. 193–194 and 431, respectively; 1927, pp. 157 and 316, respectively].

32 Carter [1908, pp. 16–17 and 23; 1912, pp. 12–13, 21 and 37; 1916, pp. 13–14]; Spicer and Pegler [1910, 1912, pp. 80, 81, 82, 100 and 101; 1916(b), pp. 104, 105 and 143; 1928, pp. 122–124 and 165]; Fieldhouse [1908, 1913, p. 40 points out the need to keep proper books for taxation purposes; 1917, p. 20]; Anonymous [1910, pp. 80, 84, 90 and 91]; Snelling [1916 (d), p. 8; 1920 (b), p. 8].

33 Anonymous [1917], referring to the need to take care with stock. An "actual and careful estimate" of it should be used [p. 33]. In the index of the [1919] edition the following entry appears [p. 235]: "Stock in Trade, an account of, at the beginning and end of year of account, must be *properly shown* [emphasis added]. Any necessary expenses of stocktaking is a trade deduction." It is noted [p. 123] that the purchase of stock-in-trade is an allowable deduction.

34 Dowell and Piper [1902, 1908, 1913, 1919]; Spicer and Pegler [1909, pp. 25–30]; Snelling [1912, 1916(c), 1921]; Anonymous [1920].

35 Murray and Carter [1905, p. 284, 1908, p. 301; 1911, p. 361, 1921, p. 388; 1924, p. 431 1927; p. 316]; Fieldhouse [1908, p. 40; 1913, p. 65; 1917, p. 77]; Anonymous, [1919, p. 123].

36 Snelling [1916(a), pp. 117 and 122; 1916(b), pp. 139 and 144, respectively; 1917?, pp. 179 and 310, respectively].

37 See Snelling [1919, p. 208]. For the issue of stock-in-trade valuation gennerally see Chapter XI, pp. 206–230; [1918], Chapter XI, pp. 170–182; [1920]a p. 234 and Chapter XI, pp. 245–256.

38 If it was the general rule, why did they not refer to it in their books on income tax?

39 See the evidence of W. G. Rayner on behalf of the Society of Incorporated Accountants and Auditors [Minutes of Evidence, 1920, pp. 430–432].

40 Interest rates, and the time value of money, can be ignored, as they were extremely low during the whole period, far below the lowest percentage increase rate of 7.17%.

41 See the discussion of this issue at the Royal Commission and the extracted comments from *The Accountant* above.

42 The author's extensive research has shown that the use of The Rule did not become common until the middle decades of the twentieth century. This research is supported by the findings of *Methods of Valuation*, [1941 and 1940], Chambers [1949, 1965], Gibson [1971, pp. 181–189], Edwards (J. R.) [1981, pp. 31–33, 1989, pp. 136–137], and the author's earlier research [Smith (David. M.), 1987].

REFERENCES

"A Provincial Firm," *Re Income Tax Returns*, Letter to the Editor, *The Accountant* (May 30, 1908), pp. 486–487.

"A.C.A.," *Income Tax and Balance Sheets*, Letter to the Editor, *The Accountant* (October 31, 1908), p. 525.

Alban, F. J. "Income Tax," *The Incorporated Accountants' Journal* (April, 1913), pp. 168–177.

"Anglo–Irish," *Income Tax Surveyors and Balance Sheets*, Letter to the Editor, *The Accountant* (March 27, 1909), pp. 433–434.

Anonymous. *Income-Tax Accounts and How to Prepare them. With notes on Income Tax Law and Practice with specimen Statements Thoroughly revised to include the Finance (1909–1910) Act, 1910* (London: Sir Isaac Pitman & Sons Limited 1910).

———. *Your Income Tax. A Clear and Simple Guide. with hints on exemptions, abatements, etc., Invaluable for Business Men, Professional Men, Investors and all taxpayers* (London: Thomas Nelson & Sons Ltd., 1917).

———. *Your Income Tax. A Clear and Simple Guide. With hints on exemptions, abatements, etc., Invaluable for Business Men, Professional Men, Investors and all taxpayers* (London: Thomas Nelson & Sons Ltd., 1919).

———. "Accounts for Income Tax Purposes," *The Accountant* (October 26, 1907), pp. 523–524, at 524.

———. "Income Tax Appeals," *The Accountant* (February 28, 1914), pp. 290–292.

———. *Income Tax Year 1919–20*, Fredc. C. Mathieson & Son, London (London: Effingham Wilson, Trade Suppliers, 1920).

"Auditors," *Stock Valuation*, Letter to the Editor, *The Accountant* (December 19, 1921), pp. 848.

Baxter, W. T., Ed. *Studies in Accounting* (London: Sweet & Maxwell Limited, 1950).

Blanch, Wm. Harnett, *Shall I Appeal Against My Income Tax Assessment* (London: P.S. King & Sons, 1890).

Blunden, G. H. "The Income Tax," *The Accountant* (August 28, 1897), pp. 823–826.

Brierley, F. "Income Tax," *The Accountant* (June 4, 1892), pp. 464–465, at 465.

"C," *Re Income Tax Returns and the Production of Balance Sheets*, Letter to the Editor, *The Accountant* (July 18, 1908), pp. 73–74.

Carter, Eric M. "Income Tax Reform," *The Accountant* (December 31, 1904), pp. 799–808.

Carter, Roger N. "Income Tax," *The Accountant* (March 1, 1902), pp. 233–238.

———. "Income Tax—Some Practical Points," *The Accountant* (December 7, 1903), pp. 1375–1382.

———. *The Simplex Guide to Income Tax: Its Assessment and Repayment* (London: Gee & Co. (Publishers) Ltd., 1908)

———. "Some Practical Income Tax Difficulties," *The Accountant* (January 1, 1910), pp. 16–26.

———. *The Simplex Guide to Income Tax: Its Assessment and Repayment*, Second Edition (London: Gee & Co. (Publishers) Ltd., 1912).

———. *The Simplex Guide to Income Tax: Its Assessment and Repayment*, Third Edition (London: Gee & Co. (Publishers) Ltd., 1916).

———. *Excess Profits Duty and Corporation Profit Tax* (London: Gee & Co. (Publishers) Ltd., 1921).

Chambers, R. J. "The Spice of Accounting," *The Australian Accountant*, Vol. 19, No. 11 (November, 1949), pp. 398–401.

———. "Financial Information and the Securities Market," *Abacus*, Vol. 1, No. 1 (September, 1965), pp. 3–30.

"Chip off the Old Block," *E.P.D. and Deficiencies*, Letter to the Editor, *The Accountant* (May 28, 1921), pp. 676–677.

Cox, Cryl. *Surveyor of Taxes and Balance Sheets*, Letter to the Editor, *The Accountant* (August 27, 1910), p. 266.

Davies Bros. *Re Income Tax Returns*, Letter to the Editor, *The Accountant* (June 13, 1908), p. 873.

Dowell, Stephen (Assistant Solicitor Inland Revenue). *The Income Tax Laws at Present in Force in the United Kingdom. With practical notes, appendices, and a copious index* (London: Butterworths, 1874).

———. *The Income Tax Laws at Present in Force with reference to decisions on the subject*, Second Edition (London: Butterworths, 1885).

———. *The Income Tax Laws at Present in Force with reference to decisions on the subject*, Third Edition (London: Butterworths, 1890)

———. *The Income Tax Laws at Present in Force with reference to decisions on the subject*, Fourth Edition (London: Butterworths, 1895)

Dowell, Stephen (the late), and John E. Piper. *The Acts Relation to the Income Tax*, Fifth Edition (London: Butterworth & Co.,1902).

———. *The Acts Relation to the Income Tax*, Sixth Edition (London: Butterworth & Co., 1908).

———. *The Acts Relation to the Income Tax,* Seventh Edition (London: Butterworth & Co., 1913).

———. *The Acts Relation to the Income Tax,* Eighth Edition (London: Butterworth & Co., 1919).

Duxbury, Nathaniel. "Points Arising in Income Tax Practice," *The Incorporated Accountants' Journal* (April, 1915), pp. 152–154.

Editorial. "Balance Sheets and Income Tax," *The Accountant* (March 13, 1915), pp. 336–339.

———. "Income Tax and Balance Sheets," *The Accountant* (July 4, 1908), p. 8.

———. "Income Tax and Balance Sheets," *The Accountant* (October 24, 1908), pp. 487–488.

———. "Income Tax Returns and Balance Sheets," *The Accountant* (June 20, 1908), pp. 877–878.

———. "Income Tax Surveyors and Balance Sheets," *The Accountant* (September 10, 1910), pp. 335–336.

———. "The Income Tax Inquiry," *The Accountant* (May 7, 1904), pp. 584–586.

———. "The Valuation of Stock," *The Accountant* (July 28, 1917), pp. 62–64.

———. "Value of Stock," *The Accountant* (May 29, 1915), pp. 715–716.

Editorial note. *The Accountant* (May 24, 1919), p. 434.

———. *The Accountant* (June 11, 1921), p. 778.

——— (correspondence). *The Accountant* (August 27, 1910), p. 266.

———. "Income Tax," *The Accountant* (May 27, 1893), pp. 487–488.

———. "Income Tax," *The Accountant* (February 16, 1884), pp. 8–9.

———. "Income Tax," *The Accountant* (February 21, 1914), p. 248.

———. "Income Tax and Balance Sheets," *The Accountant* (November 26, 1910), p. 722.

———. "Income Tax and the Production of Balance Sheets," *The Incorporated Accountants' Journal* (June, 1908), p. 206.

———. "Income Tax Surveyors and Balance Sheets," *The Accountant* (November 3, 1906), p. 538.

———. "Income Tax Surveyors and Balance Sheets," *The Accountant* (March 30, 1907), p. 413.

———. "Inspection of Books," *The Accountant* (June 25, 1921), p. 840.

———. "Precept for Accounts," *The Accountant* (November 14, 1914), pp. 563–564.

———. "Royal Commission," *The Accountant* (May 31, 1919), p. 458.

———. "Stock," *The Accountant* (June 9, 1917), p. 544.

———. "Stock," *The Accountant* (February 22, 1919), p. 138.

———. "Stock," *The Accountant* (September 10, 1921), p. 340.

———. "Stocks," *The Accountant* (January 27, 1917), p. 84.

———. "Stocks," *The Accountant* (July 21, 1917), p. 46.

———. "Stocks," *The Accountant* (February 12, 1921), p. at 177.

———. "Stocks," *The Accountant* (June 4, 1921), p. 716.

——— (Taxation Editor), *The Accountant* (June 19, 1897), p. 603.

———. "Trading Stocks," *The Accountant* (June 16, 1917), p. 563.

———. The Incorporated Accountants' Journal (March, 1915), pp. 121–123.

Edwards, Allan. "Income Tax," *The Accountant* (February 2, 1886), pp. 7–15.

Edwards, H. (Surveyor of Taxes). "Income Tax," *The Incorporated Accountants' Journal* (March, 1909), pp. 144–145.

Edwards, J. R. *Company Legislation and Changing Patterns of Disclosure in British Company Accounts 1900–1940* (London: Institute of Chartered Accountants in England and Wales, 1981), pp. 31–33.

———. *A History of Financial Accounting* (London: Routledge, 1989), pp. 136–137.

Edwards, R. S. "The Nature and Measurement of Income," in *Studies in Accounting Theory,* W. T. Baxter, Ed. (London: Sweet & Maxwell Limited, 1962), at 227–320 (originally a series of articles in *The Accountant* (July–October 1938).

"Enquirer," "Stocktaking for Retail Accounts," *The Accountant* (October 30, 1909), p. 547.

Fieldhouse, Arthur. *Income Tax Simplified. Being a guide to the preparation of the return for Assessment ...* (London: Simpkin, Marshall, Hamilton, Kent & Co. Ltd., 1908).

———. *Income Tax Simplified. Being a guide to the preparation of the return for Assessment ...* (London: Simpkin, Marshall, Hamilton, Kent & Co. Ltd.,/Huddersfield: Fieldhouse, 1913).

———. *Income Tax Simplified. Being a guide to the preparation of the return for Assessment ...* (London: Simpkin, Marshall, & Co. Ltd.,/Huddersfield: Arthur Fieldhouse, 1917).

Geo Wingfield, Edwards & Goddard, *Re Income Tax and the Production of Balance Sheets,* Letter to the Editor, *The Accountant* (June 20, 1908), p. 899.

Gibson, R. W. *Disclosure by Australian Companies* (Melbourne University Press, 1971), p. 181–189.

Gough, W. L. "Income Tax," *The Accountant* (March 28, 1885), pp. 8–10.

Grimson, David M. *Income Tax Surveyors and Balance Sheets,* Letter to the Editor, *The Accountant* (October 30, 1909), p. 544.

Hatfield, Henry Rand, *Modern Accounting—Its Principles and Problems.* (New York: D. Appleton & Co, 1917 [reprinted by Arno Press Inc, 1976]).

———. "What is the Matter with Accounting?" *Journal of Accountancy,* Vol. 44 (1927), pp. 267–279, at 273–274. (a).

———. *Accounting—Its Principles and Problems* (New York: D. Appleton & Co., 1927 [reprinted by Scholars Books, 1971]). (b)

"Honi Soit Qui May [*sic*] Y Pense," *Income Tax,* Letter to the Editor, *The Accountant* (December 5, 1914), p. 679.

"Income Tax," *Income Tax Surveyors and Balance Sheets,* Letter to the Editor, *The Accountant* (October 13, 1906), pp. 409–410.

Income tax note. "Accounts," *The Accountant* (August 9, 1919), p. 127.

———. "Balance Sheets," *The Accountant* (July 11, 1914), p. 44.

———. "Balance Sheets," *The Accountant* (February 13, 1915), pp. 216–219.

———. "Royal Commission," *The Accountant* (May 24, 1919), p. 434.

———. "Royal Commission," *The Accountant* (July 12, 1919), pp. 30–31 at 30.

———. "Stocktaking," *The Accountant* (December 13, 1919), p. 501.

———. "Taxation (Trading Stocks)," *The Accountant* (June 11, 1921), p. 778.

Income tax notes. "Evasion," *The Accountant* (March 27, 1920), p. 359.

"Intax," *Income Tax Returns and Balance Sheets*, Letter to the Editor, *The Accountant* (April 8, 1911), p. 546. (a)

"Intax," *Income Tax Returns and Balance Sheets*, Letter to the Editor, *The Accountant* (April 15, 1911), pp. 588–589. (b)

"Interested," *Income Tax*, Letter to the Editor, *The Accountant* (October 25, 1914), p. 614.

Isaacs, C. E. (Surveyor of Taxes). "Popular Errors Concerning an Unpopular Tax," *The Accountant* (January 12, 1901), pp. 53–61. (a).

———. "Income Tax as Affecting Chartered Accountants," *The Accountant* (December 28, 1901), pp. 1404–1410. (b).

———. "Income Tax," *The Accountant* (May 11, 1907), pp. 649–655.

———. (Retired Inspectors of Taxes). "Income Tax Procedure," *The Accountant* (October 16, 1909), pp. 482–487.

———. "How Income Tax Difficulties Should be Met," *The Accountant* (February 19, 1910), pp. 278–284. (a).

———. "Income Tax, with Special Regard to Returns and Assessments," *The Accountant* (August 27, 1910), pp. 270–276. (b).

———. "Text Books in Relation to Income Tax," *The Accountant* (April 20, 1912), pp. 611–616.

J and M Craig (Kilmarnock) Ltd v. *Cowperwaite* (1914) 13 T.C. 627, [1914] SC 388.

Jenkinson, M. Webster. *Income Tax Surveyors and Balance Sheets*, Letter to the Editor, *The Accountant* (March 23, 1907), pp. 382–383.

———. "Income Tax," *The Accountant* (December 25, 1909), pp. 780–792.

Johnston, R. H. "Income Tax," *The Accountant* (December 2, 1905), pp. 646–654.

Leading article. "Balance Sheets and Income Tax," *The Accountant* (November 14, 1914), pp. 553–554.

———. "Income Tax and Accounts," *The Accountant* (October 7, 1916), pp. 293–294.

———. "The Income Tax Royal Commission—II," *The Accountant* (April 3, 1920), pp. 377–379.

———. "The Income Tax Royal Commission—III," *The Accountant* (April 10, 1920), pp. 409–410, at 410.

Levie, Geo. Elder. "Income Tax and Income Assessable Under Schedule D," *The Accountant* (June 29, 1912), pp. 972–984.

Littleton, A. C. "Value or Cost," *The Accounting Review*, Vol 10 (September, 1935), pp. 269–273, at 271.

———. "A Genealogy of Cost or Market," *The Accounting Review*, Vol. 16 (June, 1941), pp. 161–167.

Long, J. P. A. *A Popular Guide to Matters Relating to Income Tax ...* (London: Effingham Wilson, 1876).

———. *A Popular Guide to Matters Relating to Income Tax ...* Fourth Edition (London: Effingham Wilson, 1878).

Lunt, Walter. "Income Tax," *The Accountant* (January 23, 1915), pp. 130–139. (a).

———. "Income Tax (Cont)," *The Accountant* (January 30, 1915), pp. 169–174. (b).

MacNeal, Kenneth. *Truth in Accounting*, 1939 [Houston: Scholars Book Co., reprinted 1970] (a).

———. "What's Wrong With Accounting?" *The Nation* (New York: October 7–14, 1939). Reprinted in *Studies in Accounting Theory*, W. T. Baxter, Ed. (London: Sweet & Maxwell Limited, 1950), pp. 213–226. (b).

Mather, C. E. "Income Tax From a Student's Point of View," *The Accountant* (May 6, 1893), pp. 419–422.

May, George O. "Concepts of Business Income and their Implementation," *Quarterly Journal of Economics*, Vol. 68, No. 1 (February, 1954), pp. 1–18.

McEwan, M. C. "Income Tax," *The Accountant* (February 25, 1893) pp. 183–187; (March 4, 1893), pp. 204–211.

Methods of Valuation, Accounting Research Association, Report No. 5 (January, 1941). London: Gee & Co., 14 pages. Also published in *The Accountant* (August 24, 1940), pp. 161–167.

Minutes of Evidence. *The Report of The Royal Commission on The Income Tax*, HMSO, 1920.

Muir, Francis. *The Stamp and Tax Office Manual. [Muir's Manual]* (Edinburgh and London: William Blackwood and Sons, 1861).

Murray, Adam, and Roger N. Carter (Chartered Accountants, Manchester). *A Guide to Income-Tax Practice* (London: Gee & Co., 1895).

———. *A Guide to Income-Tax Practice*, Second Edition (London: Gee & Co., 1899).

———. *A Guide to Income-Tax Practice*, Fourth Edition (London: Gee & Co., 1905).

———. *A Guide to Income-Tax Practice* Fifth Edition (London: Gee & Co., 1908).

Murray, Adam (the late) and Roger N. Carter. *A Guide to Income-Tax Practice*, Sixth Edition (London: Gee & Co. (Publishers) Ltd.,1911).

———. *A Guide to Income-Tax Practice*, Seventh Edition (London: Gee & Co. (Publishers) Ltd., 1915).

———. *A Guide to Income-Tax Practice*, Ninth Edition (London: Gee & Co. (Publishers) Ltd., 1921).

———. *A Guide to Income-Tax Practice,* Tenth Edition (London: Gee & Co. (Publishers) Ltd., 1924).

———. *A Guide to Income-Tax Practice,* Eleventh Edition (London: Gee & Co. (Publishers) Ltd., 1927).

Myers, Harry D. *Income Tax For Businessmen—with special reference to various Deductions, Claims, and Concessions, and to recent legislation in connection with the War, including Excess Profits Duty* (London: Simpkin, Marshall, Hamilton, Kent & Co. Ltd., 1916).

Newman, E. W. *Theory And Practice Of Costing* (London: Sir Isaac Pitman & Sons, 1921).

"Northern A.C.A.'s," *Balance Sheets and Income Tax,* Letter to the Editor, *The Accountant* (December 12, 1914), p. 716.

Note. "Taxation (Trading Stocks)," *The Accountant* (June 11, 1921), p. 778.

"O.P.," *Income Tax Surveyors and Balance Sheets,* Letter to the Editor, *The Accountant* (October 27, 1906), p. 504.

Parker, R. H. "Lower of Cost and Market in Britain and the United States: An Historical Survey," *Abacus,* Vol. 1, No. 2 (December, 1965), pp. 156–172.

Paton, James M. *The Only Road to Entire Freedom of Trade* (London: William Ridgway, 1878).

Paton, W. A. "Valuation of Inventories," *The Journal of Accountancy* (December, 1922). Reprinted in *Paton On Accounting—Selected Writings of W.A. Paton,* Herbert F. Taggart, Ed. (Bureau of Business Research, Graduate School of Business Administration, University of Michigan), pp. 157–171.

Payne, Alex W. *Income Tax and Balance Sheets,* Letter to the Editor, *The Accountant* (November 7, 1908), pp. 554–55.

Pitt, G. S. "Income Tax, Schedule D," *The Incorporated Accountants' Journal* (February, 1900), pp. 92–97.

Rawlinson, Walter A. *Income Tax and Balance Sheets,* Letter to the Editor, *The Accountant* (October 9, 1909), p. 445.

Report of the Royal Commission on The Income Tax, The, HMSO, 1920.

Rhodes, George. *Income Tax Surveyors and Balance Sheets,* Letter to the Editor, *The Accountant* (April 15, 1911), pp. 588–589.

Rhodes, J. *Income Tax Assessments—A Practical Guide* (London: Simpkin, Marshall, Hamilton, Kent & Co./Birmingham & Leicester: Midland Press Co., 1889–1890).

Richmond, Edwin. "The System of Income-Tax and the Proposed Alterations," *The Incorporated Accountants' Journal* (October, 1905), pp. 14–24.

Ross, C. H. (Surveyor of Taxes). "Income Tax Practice," *The Incorporated Accountants' Journal* (December, 1904), pp. 68–71.

Sabine, B. E. V. *A History of Taxation* (London: George Allen & Unwin Ltd., 1966).

———. *A Short History of Taxation* (London: Butterworths, 1980).

Scott, A. J. *The Future of Company Accounts,* mimeographed book located in the Edinburgh Library of the Institute of Chartered Accounts in Scotland,.

Scott, D. R. "Conservatism in Inventory Valuation," *The Accounting Review* (March, 1926), pp. 18–30.

"Seaside, *Inspector of Taxes and Balance Sheets*, Letter to the Editor, *The Accountant* (October 27, 1906), p. 504.

Senior, Charles. *Handbook of Income Tax Law and Practice.* [*Senior's Handbook*] (London: Simpkin, Marshall & Co., 1863).

Smith, David. M. "The Lower of Cost and Market Revisited an Extensive Historical Survey (United Kingdom 1870–1925)—Some Preliminary Thoughts", a paper presented at 1987 Accounting Association of Australia and New Zealand Conference, Aukland, New Zealand.

Smith, W. Southwood. "Income Tax—Schedule D," *The Incorporated Accountants' Journal* (October, 1902), pp. 11–14.

Snelling, Walter Edward (of the Inland Revenue Department). *Income Tax and Inhabited House Duty Law and Cases—A practical exposition of the law, for the use of Income Tax Officials, Solicitors, Accountants, etc.* (London: Sir Isaac Pitman & Sons Limited 1912).

———. *Excess Profits (Including Excess Mineral Rights) Duty and Levies Under the Munitions of War Acts* (London: Sir Isaac Pitman & Sons Ltd., 1916). (a).

———. *Excess Profits (Including Excess Mineral Rights) Duty and Levies Under the Munitions of War Acts*, Second Edition, revised and enlarged (London: Sir Isaac Pitman & Sons Ltd., 1916). (b).

———. *Income Tax and Inhabited House Duty Law and Cases—A practical exposition of the law, for the use of Income Tax Officials, Solicitors, Accountants, etc.* Second Edition, revised and enlarged (London: Sir Isaac Pitman & Sons Limited, 1916). (c).

———. Practical Income Tax. *A guide for the preparation of Income Tax Returns.* (London: Sir Isaac Pitman & Sons Ltd., 1916). (d).

———. *Excess Profits (Including Excess Mineral Rights) Duty and Levies Under the Munitions of War Acts* Third Edition, revised and enlarged (London: Sir Isaac Pitman & Sons Ltd., 1917?).

———. *Excess Profits (Including Excess Mineral Rights) Duty and Levies Under the Munitions of War Acts*, Fourth Edition, revised and enlarged (London: Sir Isaac Pitman & Sons Ltd., 1918).

———. *Excess Profits (Including Excess Mineral Rights) Duty and Levies Under the Munitions of War Acts*, Fifth Edition, revised and enlarged (London: Sir Isaac Pitman & Sons Ltd., 1919).

———. *Excess Profits (Including Excess Mineral Rights) Duty and Levies Under the Munitions of War Acts*, Sixth Edition, revised and enlarged (London: Sir Isaac Pitman & Sons Ltd., 1920). (a).

———. *Practical Income Tax—A guide for the Businessman and the Commercial Student*, Fourth Edition (London: Sir Isaac Pitman & Sons Ltd., 1920). (b).

———. *Taxation Annual ... 1921* (London: Sir Isaac Pitman & Sons Ltd., 1921).

Spicer, Ernest Evan. "Some Remarks on Income and Super Tax and its Legal Evasion," *The Accountant* (January 21, 1911), pp. 105–117.

Spicer, Ernest Evan and Ernest C. Pegler. *An Examination Notebook for Accountant Students* (London: H. Foulks Lynch & Co., 1909).

———. *Income Tax in Relation to Accounts,* Second Edition (London: H. Foulks Lynch & Co., 1910).

———. *Income Tax in Relation to Accounts,* Third Edition (London: H. Foulks Lynch & Co., 1912).

———. *The Excess Profit Duty and Profit of Controlled Establishments* (London: H. Foulks Lynch & Co., 1916). (a).

———. *Income Tax in Relation to Accounts,* Fourth Edition (London: H. Foulks Lynch & Co., 1916). (b).

———. *The Excess Profit Duty and Profit of Controlled Establishments,* Fourth Edition (London: H. Foulks Lynch & Co., 1918).

———. *Income Tax in Relation to Accounts,* Tenth Edition, revised and enlarged (London: H. Foulks Lynch & Co., 1928).

Stapleton, M.J. "Income Tax—A Plea for Fair Play for Commercial Interests," *The Incorporated Accountants' Journal* (October, 1911), pp. 9–15.

Steel Barrel Co. Ltd v. *Osborne (H.M. Inspector of Taxes),* (1941–1942) 24 T.C. 293, [1942] 1 All ER 634.

Sterling, Robert R. "Conservatism: The Fundamental Principle of Valuation in Traditional Accounting," *Abacus,* Vol. 3, No. 2 (1967), pp. 109–132 .

"Stocks," *Stock Valuation,* Letter to the Editor, *The Accountant* (December 17, 1921), p. 848.

"Subscriber," *Re Surveyor of Taxes and Balance Sheets,* Letter to the Editor, *The Accountant* (August 20, 1910), p. 232.

Sulley, Phillip. *Nelson's New Income Tax Guide—The charged taxes of 1927* (London: Thomas Nelson and Son Ltd., 1927).

"Taxpayer," "Income Tax: Production of Accounts," *The Accountant* (October 30, 1909), p. 645.

Turquand, P. W. "Income Tax," *The Incorporated Accountants' Journal* (January, 1895), pp. 75–79.

Vance, Lawrence L. "The Authority of History in Inventory Valuation," *The Accounting Review,* Vol. 18 (July, 1943), pp. 221–227.

Walmsley, F. "Points in Income Tax Practice," *The Incorporated Accountants' Journal* (March, 1913), pp. 141–143.

Weekly note [on income tax]. *The Accountant* (May 8, 1886), pp. 268–269.

Westcott, Maskall & Co., *Income Tax and Balance Sheets,* Letter to the Editor, *The Accountant* (January 2, 1902), pp. 12–13.

Whimster & Co. v. *Commissioners of Inland Revenue,* (1925) 12 T.C. 813, [1926] SC 25

Wright, George E. "Income Tax," *The Incorporated Accountants' Journal* (May 1907), pp. 200–203

"X.Y.Z.," *Income Tax Assessments and Balance Sheets,* Letter to the Editor, *The Accountant (October 2, 1909), pp. 415–416*

"X.Y.Z.," *Balance Sheets and Income Tax,* Letter to the Editor, *The Accountant*

A USA/Canada Model of "Sin" and Other Excise Taxes

Brenda Yelvington
University of Mississippi

Tonya K. Flesher
University of Mississippi

William Shughart
University of Mississippi

Dale L. Flesher
University of Mississippi

1.0 ABSTRACT

The motivation for this study was to consider why proposals, such as US President Clinton's, to levy additional sin taxes, have failed in recent years. These proposals were thought to have a great chance to be enacted. In order to speculate on causes of recent failures, the authors sought to determine the reasons for past successes in promoting excise taxes. This paper summarizes the history of the excise tax in the United States, beginning shortly after the end of the American Revolution. The discussion covers both the specific types of excises levied on the American public and the reasons why particular items of consumption have been chosen for taxation. The reaction of taxpayers to the first excise tax, which erupted into the Whiskey Rebellion of 1794, serves as the paper's point of departure.

2.0 INTRODUCTION

Excise taxes became important revenue sources during each of the major wars in US history. The War of 1812, the Civil War, World War I, World War II, and the Korean War were all financed in part by raising existing federal excise taxes and imposing new ones. These levies were customarily scaled back or repealed at the conclusion of hostilities. An exception to this wartime-emergency-only rule occurred during Franklin Roosevelt's Administration. His New Deal excise taxes are considered following the discussion of the "war" taxes.

While excise taxes have contributed revenues throughout US history, they declined sharply in importance after 1913 when the federal income tax came into being. Following an evaluation of the passage of the income tax on the role of the excise tax, the purposes and effects of selective excise taxes in the postwar economic environment are reviewed. Particular attention is paid to the reasons underlying the 1980 windfall profits tax—possibly the most significant recent development in the history of sin taxation.

The paper continues with a brief summary of the Clinton Administration's sin-tax proposals, along with the alternative compromise plans proposed in the House and Senate. The resemblance between contemporary rhetoric and the reasons advanced to justify sin taxes earlier in American history is striking.

The US experience is then compared to the Canadian experience with excise taxes. The authors chose to explore the connection between the countries because of the recent problems Canada had when its cigarette excise taxes were higher than its neighbors. This incident raises the question of the impact of neighbouring countries on the development of an excise tax system. For this purpose, the authors drew extensively from a model of the fiscal history of Canada developed by W. Irwin Gillespie and presented in his 1991 book, *Tax, Borrow and Spend: Financing Federal Spending in Canada, 1867–1990.*

Finally, based on the US and Canadian experiences, a model is presented as an explanation of the development of the excise tax structure in the United States. A model should be helpful in explaining failures and predicting successes.

3.0 THE ORIGIN OF THE EXCISE (SIN) TAX

In order to understand the origins of the current system of federal excise taxes, one must begin with the American Revolution. The colonies incurred large war debts in the six years it took them to win independence from England [Forsythe, 1977, p. 17]. Because taxation without representation was at the heart of colonial grievances against the British government, it is understandable that the newly formed Congress was not given the power to tax under the Articles of Confederation ratified in 1781 [Charles Adams, 1993, p. 308; Forsythe, 1977, p. 14]. All taxing power was to remain at the state level where property taxes were the primary source of revenue.

When the federal government needed money, a requisition was made upon the states based on real property (land) values.[1] This system might have worked, but the states themselves were in desperate financial trouble [Charles Adams, 1993, p. 308].[2] Periodic requisitions consequently produced little revenue for the federal government, and its inability to raise funds directly through taxation made promises to pay off the war debts ring hollow. In fact, at one point, Congress was unable even to pay the interest on the debt. Charles Adams [1993, p. 308] states that "without money, the Congress became the laughingstock of the new nation," a reputation some might think it has yet to live down.

When delegates to the Constitutional Convention assembled in Philadelphia in 1787, "everyone now agreed the federal government must be able to tax" [Charles Adams, 1993, p. 309]. Hence, the first power granted to the new Congress in the Constitution adopted in 1789 was "to lay and collect Taxes" that were "uniform throughout the United States." The federal government was given this power "in order to pay the debts and provide for the common defense and general welfare of the United States." Congress initially raised revenue through import tariffs which were also protectionist in nature,[3] but tariff revenues were not enough. Prodded by Alexander Hamilton, Congress began to consider the first internal tax.

3.1 The First Sin Tax (1791)

Shortly after taking office in 1788, George Washington appointed Alexander Hamilton as his Secretary of the Treasury [Kirshon, 1989, p. 202]. Hamilton was a New York lawyer and banker who favored a strong central government [Kirshon, 1989, p. 191]. He devised a fiscal plan to establish sound credit for the new nation [Kirshon, 1989, p. 204]. At the heart of the plan was the repayment of the Revolutionary War debts. In order to raise the revenues necessary for achieving this goal, Hamilton supported the adoption of an internal excise tax, thus becoming the father of the "sin" tax in the United States.

In 1790, Hamilton, following Adam Smith's *Wealth of Nations*, proposed that an excise tax on whiskey be enacted [Forsythe, 1977, p. 39; Charles Adams, 1993, p. 315].[4] Excise taxes had historically been unpopular. When a temporary excise tax was levied in England in 1641, for instance, riots broke out [Forsythe, 1977, p. 39]. In 1734, another proposal for an excise tax was defeated in the House of Commons [Forsythe, 1977, p. 39]. Indeed, in his well-known eighteenth-century *Dictionary of the English Language*, Samuel Johnson defined the "excise" as "a hateful tax levied upon commodities, and adjudged not by common judges of property, but by wretches hired by those to whom the excise is paid."

Indeed, one might not go too far wrong speculating that the excise tax, which ultimately was imposed in England on a variety of items such as liquor, tea, coffee, soap, and salt [Charles Adams, 1993, p. 254], was one of the main forces that drove immigrants to America. Only a few years after the Revolution, however, Congress was contemplating inflicting this dreadful tax on the new nation.

Whiskey was a convenient commodity to be singled out for the new excise tax. Hamilton thought the consumption of whiskey to be a luxury and, moreover, to represent a threat to the nation's virtue. In Hamilton's words, "the consumption of ardent spirits particularly, no doubt very much on account of their cheapness, is carried on to an extreme, which is truly to be regretted, as well in regard to the health and the morals, as to the economy of the community" [Cooke, 1964, p. 34]. In answer to those who opposed the whiskey tax, Hamilton argued that import duties had been extended as far as the interests of trade would allow [Henry Adams, 1884, p. 45].

The first law imposing an excise tax in the United States was approved on March 3, 1791. A permanent tax on whiskey (distilled spirits) was passed in the House by a vote of 35 to 21 on May 8, 1792 [Henry Adams, 1884, p. 45]. Adams contends that many of those who voted for the tax were opposed to excise taxes in principle and, had the tax been extended to any article of consumption other than whiskey, it is doubtful the tax would have passed.

3.2 The Whiskey Rebellion of 1794

The whiskey excise tax levied a duty of seven cents per gallon on spirits distilled from materials produced in the United States (whiskey) and ten cents on spirits distilled from foreign materials (rum) [Henry Adams, 1884, p. 46]. New England's whiskey manufacturers were apparently able to shift the lion's share of the tax forward to consumers. However, farmers in western Pennsylvania, Maryland, Virginia, and North Carolina, for reasons given below, were forced to shoulder the tax directly [Ratner, 1942, p. 27; Paul, 1954, p. 6]. Adding to the general discontent with the new tax, many opponents of the whiskey tax (especially the farmers) believed that its adoption helped legislators avoid raising property taxes—taxes that would have hit the well-off New England area much harder than western and southern farmers with proportionately more undeveloped land.

The farmers in Pennsylvania rebelled. In their view, whiskey was not a luxury item. Rather, it was the basic medium of exchange in a largely barter economy [Weisberger, 1991, p. 22]. While the 7-cent per gallon tax might not have seemed excessive to Alexander Hamilton, it had to be paid in scarce hard currency. Farmers in western Pennsylvania would grow rye, distill it into whiskey, and then transport the whiskey across the mountains to Philadelphia [Charles Adams, 1993, p. 317], where it was then sold or used in barter transactions. The grain from which the whiskey was distilled was itself too bulky for transporting—wagon roads either did not exist or were impassable [Weisberger, 1991, p. 22].

The enforcement of the whiskey tax was delegated to private tax collectors enlisted under a tax-farming system.[5] The collectors, who had the authority to enter cellars and barns to search for bootleg whiskey, received four percent of their take [Weisberger, 1991, p. 22]. The more whiskey the collectors found, the more income they earned. Given the incentives for vigorous law enforcement created by the tax-farming system, it is not surprising that most collectors were hated and that some were tarred and feathered.

Encouraged by his Treasury Secretary, President Washington took a strong stand against the tax revolters. After giving the farmers two warnings, Washington called out 12,500 militiamen to enforce the new government's tax law [Kirshon, 1989, p. 212]. Washington actually led the troops in the field [Charles Adams, 1993, p. 319]. A military confrontation was averted at the last minute, though. The rebels surrendered and an anti-tax-committee signed a "solemn promise" to submit to all US laws in the future in exchange for pardons of any past offences [Weisberger, 1991, p. 23]. No farmers went to jail.

The events surrounding the first "sin" tax are important for several reasons. First, the new government demonstrated its ability to enforce the law. Second, taxpayers displayed their willingness to fight "unjust" taxes. Third, and possibly most important, Congress discovered a new source of revenue—the selective excise tax. It had been proved that taxes on articles of consumption could be successfully imposed if the articles themselves were portrayed as luxuries or if their use were pronounced harmful to individuals or the economy as a whole.

3.3 Excise Taxes Following the Whiskey Rebellion

The tax on whiskey opened the door for additional excise taxes on "luxury" items. A similar tax was imposed on carriages in 1794 [Henry Adams, 1884, p. 48]. The 1794 excise tax system was later expanded to include duties on the sale of certain liquors, the manufacture of snuff, the refining of sugar, the proceeds of auction sales, and the purchase of salt [Henry Adams, 1884, pp. 48–49]. Not all of these levies could of course be justified on the grounds that they represented taxes on luxuries or on products harmful to individuals. Congress had seemingly gone far beyond Hamilton's original plan by setting up an elaborate system of excise taxes whose chief purpose was to increase government revenues.

This objective was not met, however, largely due to the high cost of collection [Forsythe, 1977, p. 50]. In addition, the excise taxes were extremely unpopular with the voting public. Using the abolition of internal taxes as one of his key campaign promises, Thomas Jefferson became President of the United States in 1801. With the exception of the salt tax, Jefferson eliminated the excise taxes in 1802 [Pechman, 1987, p. 305]. The salt tax was repealed in 1807 [Paul, 1954, p. 6].

4.0 FROM "SIN" TAXES TO "WAR" TAXES

History reveals that with the exception of the period following the Great Depression, excise taxes were predominantly enacted as wartime emergency measures. The majority of the taxes were customarily repealed when hostilities ended.

4.1 The War of 1812

In 1812, the United States again found itself at war with England. Congress was at first hesitant to enact internal taxes to help finance the war. Customs duties were doubled, but the war's adverse impact on international commerce caused revenues from this source to actually decline by half in 1813 [Forsythe, 1977, p. 58]. Congress soon realized that it would be virtually impossible to rely on tariff revenues alone to pay for the war.

In August 1813, new excise taxes were approved by Congress. The tax structure was similar to that imposed under Alexander Hamilton's financing plan, and included excise duties on carriages, sugar refining, and distilled spirits. There was one major difference between the excise taxes of 1813 and their predecessors, though: the 1813 taxes were presented to the public as "war" taxes. In fact, the taxes were explicitly highlighted in italics in the body of the legislation as *war taxes* and were to be repealed automatically within one year following the end of the war [Henry Adams, 1884, p. 58].

The method of collection during this second period of excise taxation likewise departed from its earlier precedent. Tax farmers were replaced by tax collectors who were required to be "respectable freeholder[s] and reside in the district" [Henry Adams, 1884, p. 60]. In addition, the states were permitted to assume the amount assigned to them and to pay those amounts directly into the Treasury. A reduction of 15 percent in the total due was granted to each state for performing the collection service [Henry Adams, 1884, p. 68]. In 1814, seven states took advantage of this tax reduction opportunity.

The costs of collecting the excise taxes enacted in 1813 were, in fact, much lower than those associated with the earlier internal-tax levies. The average cost of collecting taxes had been 17.5 percent of revenues for the period of 1795–1800; the comparable figure was six percent during the War of 1812.

What caused such a dramatic decline in the cost of collecting taxes just 18 years after the infamous Whiskey Rebellion? According to Henry Adams, it was not due to a more efficient tax collection system. Adams instead attributes the large differences in collection costs to other factors. First, he argued that there was greater public enthusiasm for the War of 1812 and, hence, a greater willingness to pay taxes to help finance it than there had been to extinguish old debts during the relatively peaceful mid-1790s. Second, the temporary nature of the war taxes—they were in fact repealed in 1817—made them more palatable. Adams suggests that these observations should bring "again clearly to our view how important an element is public sentiment in the working of all revenue systems" [Henry Adams, 1884, p. 67].

After the War of 1812, the tariff regained its position as the federal government's primary source of revenue. Federal expenses were chiefly defrayed by customs duties, supplemented occasionally by the sale of public lands or the issue of Treasury notes [Smith, 1914, p. 1]. During the period of 1817 to 1857, the government usually ran a budget surplus. Any revenue shortfalls which occurred were covered by balances held over from previous years. There was no need for any form of internal taxes.

4.2 Civil War

Ratner [1942, p. 80] calls 1862 and 1863 "the darkest period in the financial history of the federal government." At the Civil War's outbreak, the government relied chiefly on borrowing as a method of finance. Collections of customs duties were at a standstill, largely due to the interdiction efforts of the Confederate Navy [Ratner, 1942, p. 82]. By 1861, the federal government collected only $1 in taxes for every $8.52 it borrowed [Kirshon, 1989, p. 367].

The Union's financial crisis called for drastic measures. President Lincoln signed the Internal Revenue Act of July 1, 1862 on the day Congress passed it [Paul, 1954, p. 9; Ratner, 1942, p. 73]. This legislation was the most comprehensive tax measure enacted in the 70 years since the nation's first revenue act in 1791. The 1862 law provided for the first tax on income ever put into operation in the United States.[6] In addition, the Act imposed an inheritance tax and included all of the excises, licence fees, and stamp duties levied by the federal government during the War of 1812 [Paul, 1954, p. 10].

However, the Internal Revenue Act of 1862 went further. The list of items subjected to federal excise taxes was expanded. Every manufactured article was taxed, and rates of 1.5 percent and 0.3 percent were applied to the gross receipts of railroads, ferryboats, steamships, toll bridges, and advertisers [Paul, 1954, p. 10]. The 1862 Act also covered a broader range of legal documents and financial transactions than the taxes of 1813.

As the federal government's revenue needs continued to grow, Congress demonstrated its willingness to raise excise taxes sharply. In the Internal Revenue Act of June 30, 1864, tax rates on distilled spirits were raised from 20 cents to $1.50 per gallon. Subsequent increases in the alcohol tax resulted in a top rate of $2.00 per gallon in 1865, which was ten times the original cost of the product [Paul, 1954, p. 13]. Other increases included the tax on loose tobacco, which more than doubled, and the tax on cigars whose maximum rate jumped from $3.50 per thousand to $40 per thousand.

As had been done following the War of 1812, the majority of the Civil War excise taxes were rescinded by Congress with legislation passed in 1867 and 1870 [Ratner, 1942, pp. 116, 124]. However, the liquor and tobacco taxes remained in place and became permanent fixtures of the federal revenue system [Pechman, 1987, p. 305]. A definite precedent had nevertheless been established for federal excise taxes. No longer were such taxes justified solely as ways of protecting the country's health and morals. Rather, excise taxes were rationalized as patriotic ways of raising additional revenues during wartime emergencies.

4.3 Spanish-American War

Following the sinking of the *Maine* in 1898, the United States intervened against the Spanish in Cuba. War revenues were again needed. The Chairman of the Committee on Ways and Means opposed the income tax and feared the political repercussions of raising tariffs, so the Committee again looked to excise taxes for funding a war effort. However, this time the burden of war financing was shifted from the business and professional classes to the working class. The war taxes were on theaters, circuses, bowling alleys, and billiard parlors and rates were doubled on tobacco, beer, and liquor. Stamp taxes were levied on bank checks, stocks, bonds, insurance policies, legal documents, chewing gum, and wine [Kennon and Rogers, 1989, pp. 243–244].

4.4 World War I

The country again found itself in financial straits during World War I. Although the Income Tax Act of 1913 was in place, it was new and the revenues it generated were not sufficient to compensate for declining tariff collections.

Congress once again turned to the excise tax. The War Revenue Tax Act of October 22, 1914, brought back the Civil War excise taxes and greatly expanded the list.[7] Federal excise taxes were levied on manufacturing, theatre admissions, telephone calls, and retail sales of jewelry, toilet preparations, luggage, and chewing gum [Pechman, 1987, p. 305; Ratner, 1942, p. 342]. With the exception of the tobacco, liquor, and stamp taxes, the World War I excises were repealed afterwards by the Revenue Act of 1924 and the Revenue Act of 1928 [Ratner, 1942, pp. 416, 432].

4.5 World War II

During World War II, the excise taxes still in effect from the early 1930s (discussed in a separate section below entitled "The New Deal Excise Taxes") were increased and new taxes were introduced. In particular, the tax on distilled spirits was increased from $2.00 per gallon to $9.00 per gallon, a hike of this magnitude being feasible as a result of the demand for liquor greatly exceeding the supply [Leff, 1984, p. 35].[8] By war's end, the list of new federal taxes included an admissions and dues tax, a manufacturers' excise tax, the retailers' excise tax, and excises on certain facilities and services [Anderson, 1951, p. 409]. Over the opposition of the Treasury, a tax was also imposed on freight [Due, 1956, p. 207]. Items subject to the federal excise tax ranged from automobiles and automobile tires to refrigerators, furs, and electrical energy.

As in all previous wars, the primary reason for imposing the World War II excise taxes was the raising of revenue. However, Anderson [1951, p. 409] contends that this was not the only reason. For the first time, excise taxes were justified for their supposed "anti-inflationary effects" and because they would "discourage the purchase" of "certain scarce items such as tires, tubes, and leather goods." Finally, Anderson states that the "intent was to place some additional burden on luxury goods such as furs, toilet preparations, jewelry, and luggage." Based on these considerations, "war" taxes were beginning to reincorporate elements of "sin" into the federal revenue system.

Keeping with the tradition of repealing wartime excise taxes after hostilities ended, Congress began work on a measure to reduce the taxes by up to 50 percent.[9] Just as a bill to accomplish this goal passed the House of Representatives, the Korean War began. Thus, the World War II excise taxes remained in effect for a few more years.

4.6 The Korean War

The Revenue Act of 1950 originally contained provisions substantially reducing the excise taxes levied to help finance World War II. The outbreak of war on the Korean peninsula caused the tax reduction provisions to be removed and tax increases to be substituted in their place. These changes converted a potential $910 million reduction in excise taxes into a $55 million increase [Paul, 1954, p. 557].

New items, such as television sets, deep freezers, and diesel fuel, were added to the excise tax roll [Anderson, 1951, p. 410, Pechman, 1987, p. 306]. However, the bulk of the revenue continued to come from a relatively small number of excises. The lion's share of total federal excise tax receipts was generated by liquor and tobacco taxes (47 percent). The gasoline tax (11 percent) and the taxes on automobiles and related products (16 percent) were also important revenue contributors; all other taxed items accounted for the remaining 26 percent [Due, 1956, p. 206].

By the Korean War, according to Due [1956, pp. 206–207], excise taxes had become "so well grounded in tradition that consideration of elimination of them is not worthwhile." The taxes, largely justified by the money they raised, were also widely accepted by society. The dominant point of view was apparently that the "consumption of ... particular commodities warranted the payment of a high tax penalty" [Due, 1956, p. 207].

As in previous periods, the logical basis for some of the excises as taxes on "luxuries" or "sin" was elusive. Critics objected particularly to the excise tax on freight imposed as a war revenue measure in 1942. Due [1956, p. 207], for instance, argued that it provided an artificial incentive for the transport of goods by private rather than public carrier, thereby hindering the development of an efficient transport system. Congress and the Treasury Department seemingly were determined to maintain high revenue levels regardless of the cost. In the words of Due, Congress would have supported the "retention of an excise on bread and milk if one had been levied during the war." As in the past, federal excise taxes were reduced after the Korean War ended. The majority of the tax rates were lowered to pre-war levels in April 1956 [Committee for Economic Development, 1955, p. 8]. Over the next ten years, many of the excise taxes, including (in 1958) the freight tax, were repealed [Pechman, 1987, p. 306].

In 1965, Congress pared the Korean War excise taxes down to just a few major ones including liquor, tobacco (cigarettes), and gasoline. Excise taxes accounted for nearly one-eighth of federal revenue in the postwar period, as much as ten billion dollars a year. Liquor and tobacco taxes produced forty percent of the total, with taxes on automobiles and fuels providing one-third. The purpose of the Excise Tax Reduction Act of 1965 was to overhaul the federal excise tax structure:

> The present excise taxes, for the most part, were initially levied as emergency revenue-raising measures at the time of the Korean war, or World War II, or the depression of the 1930's. As a result, they were not developed on any systematic basis and are often discriminatory in their application to the taxed industries or to purchasers of the taxed products. Your committee bill, either in the current fiscal year, or over the next 3 subsequent years, removes entirely this miscellany of selective excise taxes except those designed to serve certain specific purposes .... The excise taxes which are retained fall in one of three categories. Those remaining will, in effect, constitute user charges (where the tax paid is in effect a charge based on the use of a given governmental service), regulatory taxes (such as those on marihuana, opium, and wagering), or sumptuary taxes (namely, those on alcohol and tobacco products) .... The bill, by removing all other excise taxes, substantially improves the fairness of the Federal excise tax structure and simplifies the tax law, as well as contributes to the economic well-being of the Nation. [US Congress, House of Representatives, 1965, p. 211]

The Excise Tax Reduction Act cut excises by $4.7 billion between June 22, 1965 and January 1, 1969. The ten percent luxury tax on items such as jewelry and furs was eliminated, but the most controversial was the reduction of the excise tax on automobiles. Representative Martha Griffiths, a Democrat from Michigan and the first woman to serve on the Committee on Ways and Means, fought for the complete elimination of the auto tax. She argued that the tax savings would result in lower car prices and increased sales would stimulate the economy. Treasury estimated that the elimination of the auto tax would cost one billion dollars in lost revenues. As usual, Chairman Wilbur Mills succeeded in getting a four-year phase-out compromise that gave something to both Treasury and the auto industry [Kennon and Rogers, 1989, p. 347]. These arguments over economic impact are the same as those that accompanied the more recent luxury taxes.

5.0 THE NEW DEAL EXCISE TAXES

Prior to the Great Depression (1929–1933), and for most of the time afterwards, Congress enacted major excise tax increases only during wartime emergencies. Franklin D. Roosevelt's New Deal was an exception to this rule.

As in the earlier periods of heavy excise taxation, Roosevelt's primary justification for increasing taxes was to generate additional federal revenues to meet an emergency situation. The Depression had devastated the economy and tax receipts were consequently down. Just before the introduction of income taxes on the eve of America's entry into World War I, alcohol taxes had surpassed tariffs as the primary source of federal revenues. While the excise tax on distilled spirits technically remained on the law books, the passage of the 18th Amendment, ratified on January 29, 1919, mandated Prohibition [Kirshon, 1989, p. 613]. Realizing the revenue generating power of liquor taxes, Roosevelt pledged to repeal Prohibition in order "to provide therefrom a proper and needed revenue" [Johnson and Porter, 1973, p. 332]. The Democratic Party's platform had a very un-Keynesian theme: "If only given a chance, Americans might drink themselves into a balanced budget" [Leff, 1984, p. 31].

Roosevelt was elected President in 1932. The 21st Amendment repealed the 18th Amendment shortly thereafter, and in 1933 liquor was again legal [Kirshon, 1989, p. 661]. The House Ways and Means Committee proposed a liquor-tax schedule which was designed to generate the maximum possible revenue without at the same time perpetuating illegal liquor sales due to excessive rates [Leff, 1984, p. 33]. The pre-Prohibition federal alcohol tax of $1.10 per gallon was increased to $2.00.

Other New Deal taxes included a series of manufacturers' excises on automobiles, trucks, buses, appliances, and other consumer durables. Long-distance telephone calls were also added to the list. These federal excise taxes were extended at varying rates until 1965 [Pechman, 1987, p. 305].

It was also during Franklin Roosevelt's Administration that the federal gasoline tax was introduced. While all of the states had levied a gasoline tax by that time, 1932 was the first year in which the federal government began tapping this source of revenue.[10] The tax, levied on gasoline refiners, was set at one cent per gallon [Crawford, 1939, p. 9]. Unlike other taxes included as part of the New Deal, the federal excise tax on gasoline was explicitly submitted to Congress as a temporary revenue measure and subsequently adopted for only one year.

At the time, the federal tax on gasoline was characterized as a "nuisance" tax [Crawford, 1939, p. 13]. It was to be a special tax enacted only because Congress needed emergency sources of revenue. In addition, it was sold as a "benefit" tax that helped defray the expenses of a related spending program—building and maintaining roads [Leff, 1984, p. 18]. The states were strongly opposed to a federal gasoline tax on the grounds that it resulted in double taxation and placed too heavy a tax burden on a necessity. Ignoring these arguments, Congress continued to extend and to increase the "temporary" gasoline tax. At present, it is considered to be a permanent part of the federal tax system.

6.0 THE ROLE OF THE EXCISE TAX AFTER 1913

Before the Income Tax Act of 1913, the federal government relied almost exclusively on customs duties. During the initial period of excise taxation (1791–1801), these levies accounted for a relatively small share (10 percent at its highest point) of the federal government's total tax receipts. By contrast with the trend in customs revenue, excise taxes for the most part continued to decline in importance until the Civil War.[11]

The first individual income tax, enacted to raise revenues for the Civil War, was in effect from 1862 through 1871. Income tax receipts accounted for almost 25 percent of total federal revenue at its peak in 1866 [Pechman, 1987, p. 299]. After the tax lapsed in 1872, customs duties again became the government's revenue mainstay.

Following the passage of a tax on corporate income in 1909, the 1913 Income Tax Act imposed a tax rate of one percent on the taxable net incomes of individuals, with an additional surtax ranging from one percent to six percent on persons with annual incomes exceeding $20,000. An exemption of $3,000 was granted to single taxpayers; married taxpayers were granted a $4,000 exemption [Ratner, 1942, p. 333].

Because of the generous exemptions and low rates, for almost 30 years the personal income tax applied only to high-income individuals. In the prosperous late 1920s, however, the corporate and individual income tax contributed approximately two-thirds of all federal tax revenues [Leff, 1984, p. 13]. As a result, excise tax receipts were declining in importance. The Depression's onset caused a sharp decline in government income tax receipts and, as discussed above, selective excise taxes (specifically, the alcohol tax) were called on to make up the difference. Excise taxes provided more revenue for the federal government than did income taxes between 1933–1937. Not until 1938 did income taxes ($2.6 billion) exceed excise tax revenues ($2.3 billion) [Kennon and Rogers, 1989, p. 294].

In an effort to raise much-needed revenue during World War II, the individual income tax was given a major overhaul. Personal exemptions were reduced (to $750 for single individuals and to $1,500 for married individuals) and surtaxes on affluent taxpayers went as high as 77 percent [Paul, 1954, pp. 278–279]. Congress thereby converted the personal income tax into a "mass" tax.

Prior to the changes made in the income tax during World War II, the New Deal excise taxes contributed between 30 percent and 45 percent of total federal tax collections. Between 1941 and 1945, excise taxes accounted for 20 percent of the federal government's total annual receipts, on average. The excise tax has continued to decline in importance as a revenue source since then. In fiscal year 1994, excise taxes accounted for only 3.5 percent of total federal tax receipts.

7.0 EXCISE TAXES IN THE POST-WAR ENVIRONMENT

A major new development in federal excise taxation occurred in 1956. The revenue generated by a number of excise taxes was earmarked for the Highway Trust Fund, a special account established for the construction and maintenance of the federal highway system [Pechman, 1987, p. 306]. The dedicated revenue sources included the existing federal excise taxes on gasoline, diesel and other special motor fuels, trucks, and tires. New taxes were also imposed on tread rubber and on the operation of heavy trucks and buses on the highways.

A similar special-purpose program financed by earmarked excise tax receipts was created by Congress in 1970. The revenue generated by taxes on passenger tickets, air freight, general aviation fuels, and other aviation-related taxes was set aside for the Airport and Airway Trust Fund. Another such account, the Hazardous Substances Superfund, was established in 1980 to pay the costs of cleaning up chemically polluted sites in cases where the source of the pollution cannot be identified. Superfund is financed with excise taxes on crude oil, various chemicals whose production creates hazardous waste, and a tax on corporate income as defined by the alternative minimum tax.

Possibly the most significant postwar sin tax took effect in 1980. In the Crude Oil Windfall Profit Tax Act of 1979, Congress imposed a 70 percent windfall profits tax on domestic crude oil producers. The tax was assessed on the difference between the prevailing market price of oil and its price in May 1979. To fully understand the reasons for imposing the tax, it is necessary to briefly review federal oil price controls during the 1970s.

Crude oil prices had remained remarkably stable until 1970. However, with inflationary fears on the loose, oil prices were frozen by President Nixon when he imposed general wage and price controls in 1971. Following the 1975 Arab oil embargo and the sharp increase in world oil prices that ensued, oil price controls were extended until May 1979 [US Congress, House of Representatives, 1979, p. 89].

In April 1979, President Carter announced his intention to phase out oil price controls between June 1, 1979, and September 30, 1981. Congress apparently believed that both the demand for and the supply of oil was inelastic in the short run [US Congress, House of Representatives, 1979, p. 90]. In other words, neither consumers nor producers were thought to be very responsive to changes in oil prices in the short run and, because of this, the worry was that relatively small shifts in either supply or demand might produce large swings in prices. Congress anticipated that decontrol of domestic oil prices (along with expected further increases in world oil prices) would result in substantial—and largely unjustified—increases in the revenues of US oil producers and royalty owners.

The new windfall profits tax was justified in the House Ways and Means Committee's Report in the following terms:

> The revenues resulting from these higher prices would provide income to oil producers far in excess of what most of them originally anticipated when they drilled their wells and in excess of what they might now be expected to invest in energy production. Indeed, some producers are now using their excess revenues to acquire unrelated businesses.
>
> Thus, the committee believes that the additional revenues received by oil producers and royalty owners, ... are an appropriate object of taxation. [US Congress, House of Representatives, 1979, p. 91]

Demonstrating a complete misunderstanding of the concept of opportunity costs, federal tax policy was thereby applied to a new sin—the making of too much money. The windfall profits tax imposed on oil producers in 1979 had much in common with the excess profits taxes traditionally enacted by Congress during wartime emergencies.[12] In this case, revenue generated by governmental decontrol of oil prices was taxed away on the faulty theory that the profitability of investments in energy production was determined by historical costs rather than by current replacement costs.

The windfall profits tax was repealed in 1988. Federal excise taxes on cigarettes and distilled spirits were raised in revenue measures enacted during the 1980s. The cigarette tax was increased to its current rate of $12.00 per thousand (or 24 cents a pack), and the tax on distilled spirits was increased to $13.50 per gallon.

Another significant development in excise taxation occurred in the Omnibus Revenue Reconciliation Act of 1990. This Act imposed a ten-percent luxury tax on the sale of passenger vehicles selling for more than $30,000, boats selling for more than $100,000, aircraft selling for more than $250,000, and furs and jewelry with prices exceeding $10,000. The Omnibus Revenue Reconciliation Act of 1993 repealed the luxury excise taxes on jewelry, furs, boats, and aircraft. The tax on luxury automobiles remains in effect, but is now indexed to take account of inflation.

Under current law, federal excise taxes apply to seven general product categories. These categories are:

- retail taxes on automobiles, trucks, trailers, and certain fuels
- manufacturers' excise taxes on gasoline, mined coal, sporting goods, firearms and shells, alcohol, and tobacco
- facilities and services taxes, including local telephone service and air transportation
- documentary stamp taxes on foreign insurance policies, including casualty insurance policies or indemnity bonds, and life, sickness, or accident insurance policies
- wagering taxes which impose annual licensing fees on any person accepting wagers and taxes on wagers placed with bookmakers and lottery operators
- a highway vehicle use tax which applies to certain heavy motor vehicles such as trucks, truck tractors, and buses with taxable gross weights of 55,000 pounds or more
- environmental taxes on ozone-depleting chemicals, other chemicals and petroleum products which apply to all taxpayers, including all levels of government and nonprofit educational organizations.

8.0 THE CLINTON ADMINISTRATION'S "SIN" TAX PROPOSALS

In September 1993, President Bill Clinton announced health care reform proposals. Several funding measures, including increases in "sin" taxes, were suggested as ways of financing the administration's health care plan. The President indicated in his address to a joint session of Congress that tobacco would be one of the main sources of revenue. Specifically, the federal excise tax would be raised by between 75 cents and $1.00 a pack, thus placing the total federal cigarette tax in the range of 99 cents to $1.24 per pack.

The cigarette tax would have been increased by only 60 cents per pack in an alternative financing plan put forth by the House Ways and Means Committee [Rogers, 1994, p. A3]. Under yet another plan, authored by Senate Finance Committee Chairman Daniel Moynihan, the federal cigarette tax would have increased to $2.00 per pack and the levy on handgun ammunition sales would also be raised [Rogers and Stout, 1994, p. A3].

Hillary Rodham Clinton, testifying before the Senate Finance Committee about her husband's health care plan, asserted that "tobacco should be taxed as part of this package, largely for health reasons, and particularly to try to deter smoking among young people" [US Congress, Senate, 1993, p. 35]. In her testimony before the House Ways and Means Committee, Mrs. Clinton repeated these assertions, adding "that tobacco ... if used as directed can have damaging health consequences" and is "particularly damaging to young people" [US Congress, House of Representatives, 1993, p. 35].[13] Based on this reasoning, she said that the President believes "tobacco taxes are a fair way to support health care" [US Congress, Senate, 1993, p. 36]. The President's health care plan was to have been financed partially by "sin" taxes on tobacco.

The Bush Administration had also considered sin taxes, specifically excise taxes on alcohol and tobacco, as a way to finance health care. These proposals would have been modelled after the Canadian system, which is funded by high taxes on tobacco and alcohol. The Bush Administration was responding to surveys that showed that the public would accept an increase in taxes to pay for national health care and the most acceptable tax was a sin tax. This sin-tax strategy was an effort to counter health care proposals put forth by Democrats [Louden, 1992, p. 6].

Therefore, it is somewhat surprising that the Clinton proposal with its sin-tax financing did not pass. Public opinion polls favored this type of funding. A poll by the Cancer Society found that 66 percent of all smokers supported a $2-per-pack cigarette tax hike. Canadian anti-smoking groups hoped that an increase in American cigarette taxes would discourage smoking in Canada. Canadian consumption of cigarettes had been cut nearly in half since 1980 after increasing the cigarette tax [Press Watch, 1994, p. 207].

However, some warned that there was a danger that increased cigarette taxes would lead to increased smuggling in the United States. Indeed, Canada was forced to cut cigarette taxes to combat smuggling and bootlegging. As seen during Prohibition in the United States, the government has conflicting goals of wanting to stop consumption but at the same time needing the revenue generated by the aforementioned items [Bartlett, 1994, p. 1493].

9.0 THE CANADIAN EXCISE TAX EXPERIENCE

The Canadian excise tax experience is an outstanding source for comparison with the US history. It provides an opportunity to consider whether excise taxes were passed for the same reasons and under similar circumstances as in the United States. Also, it allows a search for any interdependence between the two systems.

The primary source of information on the Canadian tax experience was W. Irwin Gillespie's book [1991]. This book is vital to this study not only because Gillespie provides a thorough development of Canadian tax history, but because his book is organized around a model which he developed. Using a brief summary of the history of excise taxes and the parts of Gillespie's fiscal model that are relevant to excise taxes, the authors will present a model of US excise tax development.

Gillespie hypothesizes that citizens may have a preference between two revenue sources which will result in different political costs for a government.

> The political cost of introducing, maintaining or increasing a tax on a revenue source for which citizens have a tax preference will be lower than the political costs of introducing, maintaining or increasing a tax on a revenue source for which citizens do not have a tax preference. [1991, p. 26]

A variant of this hypothesis is that "voters have a preference for taxes on sinful products, such as alcohol and tobacco products, as compared with other products that are not viewed in such an unfavourable light" [Gillespie, 1991, p. 26]. Taxes from a revenue source are less politically costly if judged by taxpayers to have unhealthy, immoral or sinful connotation (expenditures on alcoholic beverages and tobacco products) than if viewed as healthy, moral or meritorious (expenditures on milk, footwear and clothing for children and expenditures on charitable donations) [Gillespie, 1991, p. 26].

Other parts of Gillespie's model that are relevant to excise tax development relate to horizontal and vertical tax competition; administration costs; political costs of legislating and collecting tax; and a tax preference for equitable taxes. Ancillary to the political costs hypothesis is the maxim that "an old tax is a good tax" because an old tax has a lower political cost at the margin than an untried new revenue source [Gillespie, 1991, p. 177]. Further, goods with an inelastic price demand provide more tax revenue potential than price-elastic goods and have lower political costs, particularly if the goods are widely judged to be sinful. Thus, alcohol and tobacco have always been taxed, and taxed heavily. Government officials claimed that these were voluntary taxes and the "real" or involuntary taxes were low [Gillespie, 1991, p. 63].

Gillespie provides support for his model with a detailed history of the development of Canadian fiscal policy. The first period of history begins with the formation of Confederation in 1867 when Confederation assumed the exclusive right to indirect taxation which had been the major source of revenues for the colonies in the form of customs and excise taxes [Gillespie, 1991, p. 49]. During this initial developmental phase, from Confederation in 1867 to the summer of 1917, a primary objective was to attract immigrants and persuade the remaining colonies to join the Union. These goals influenced the types and the rates of taxes in the fiscal mix. Excise taxes on alcohol and tobacco, the tariff, and deficit financing were the three most significant sources of governmental revenues during this period and income was not taxed [Gillespie, 1991, pp. 10–11]. The temperance movement of the 1880s and 1890s sparked increased reliance on sin taxes [Gillespie, 1991, p. 67]. Due to horizontal competition with the United States, the Minister of Finance closely monitored rates of excise taxes to keep them below the US rates, particularly on goods that were viewed as necessities by settlers. These goods, such as tea or sugar, were taxed at reduced rates or exempted from tax [Gillespie, 1991, p. 60]. Vertical competition with the provinces and municipalities also influenced the tax mix that relied on indirect taxes to the exclusion of income taxes.

Between 1917 and 1920, the Canadian government levied three major new taxes: the personal income tax, the corporation income tax and the sales tax. These three taxes became the primary sources of funding from 1918–1990 [Gillespie, 1991, p. 78]. However, during this period, the preference for sin taxes prevailed. In wartime, especially during World War II and the Korean conflict, the government relied on taxes on alcohol and cigarettes. Smuggling of cigarettes caused declines in revenues and eventual reductions of the tax [Gillespie, 1991, p. 103]. Luxury items were first taxed in 1915 and have been objects of taxation a number of times. Wartime excise and luxury taxes were reduced or eliminated after each emergency. Canada employed a windfall profits tax on the gold-mining industry after the President of the United States revalued gold in 1934. The Minister of Finance thought this tax would meet little opposition as a tax on extraordinary profits but instead it was viewed as a tax on production. The tax was changed three times due to pressure from industry and expired in 1935 [Gillespie, 1991, p. 176]. The relative significance of excise taxes as a revenue source declined during the Great Depression and never regained their original importance.

10.0 CONCLUSIONS

The motivating purpose for this study was to determine reasons why excise taxes have been levied and why they have recently failed in the United States. The investigation of the development of US excise taxes revealed a number of reasons for both success and failure. These will be highlighted and also compared to Gillespie's Canadian model.

The selective excise tax has played roles of varying importance throughout US tax history. The first excise tax enacted in 1791—the whiskey tax—gained the support of a majority in Congress on the basis of Alexander Hamilton's condemnation of whiskey as a luxury which corrupted the nation's morals and damaged its citizens' health. Made immortal by the rebellion it spawned, the whiskey tax was subsequently rescinded when Thomas Jefferson assumed the presidency, but the selective excise tax soon returned. Canadian Ministers of Finance were quite vocal in their preachings against alcohol and stressed that liquor taxes were voluntary liabilities that citizens could and should avoid. Gillespie's sin tax variant hypothesis holds true in both Canada and the United States.

During the War of 1812, astute politicians reinvented excise taxation as a wartime emergency measure and thereby began a tradition of increasing existing excise taxes and imposing new ones during every major war thereafter. The majority of these "war" taxes were temporary and were generally repealed at the conclusion of hostilities. The Canadian experience was similar. If the public perceives that an emergency situation exists and wants to be supportive of its financing, the political costs of increasing or adding new taxes is low. The repeated return to the use of excise taxes in an emergency is true to the maxim that "an old tax is a good tax."

Excise taxes were used to meet another type of emergency during the New Deal. Campaigning on a promise to repeal Prohibition, President Roosevelt saw liquor taxes as a way of helping the US economy recover from the Great Depression. While most politicians still thought that the consumption of liquor might be harmful to an individual's health, the purported benefits of the additional tax revenues to the health of the economy were apparently more important. Throughout the history of sin taxes, there is the quandary of raising taxes to discourage the sinful behaviour but knowing that if consumption drops significantly, then tax collections will decline substantially. Gillespie addressed the price-inelasticity issues. Further, Canada and the United States have both struggled to combat bootlegging and smuggling that rob the government coffers. These concerns were widely discussed during the recent debates over sin taxes.

The primary goals of early Canadian fiscal policy were to attract immigrants and to add provinces to the Dominion. Thus, vertical and horizontal competition were chief concerns. Horizontal competition focused on the United States and continues to the present, although to a lesser extent. Canada's recent problem with cigarette taxes is an example. Gillespie notes that horizontal tax competition "was not a significant determinant of tax structure in a large country like the United States, but it was a significant determinant of tax structure in a country like Canada, which was small in terms of population" [1991, p. 115]. According to Gillespie, there was considerable testimony that Canadian governments were extremely concerned about the effect of taxes on the migration of people and capital; whereas, there was little concern in the United States that taxes would discourage immigration and encourage emigration to Canada [1991, p. 115]. Of course, a greater percentage of the Canadian population lives near the US border than vice versa, which makes smuggling a greater concern in Canada. There have been only minor problems of vertical tax competition in US tax history.

The relative contribution of excise taxes to total tax revenues was reduced substantially following the passage of the Income Tax Act in 1913. Canada has experienced the same decline. Still, an elaborate system of excise taxes is in effect today and lawmakers continue to find ways to justify new ones.

In 1980, the windfall profits tax was enacted to slash the profits oil producers and royalty owners could earn following the decontrol of domestic oil prices. In 1990, a new luxury tax was created to tax the sale of expensive cars, boats, aircraft, yachts, jewelry, and furs. At present, only the luxury tax on automobiles remains in effect, but the message it sends is clear: if individuals can afford expensive consumer items, then they should be made to pay for their affluence.

Canada has also experimented with windfall profits and luxury excise taxes for the same reasons and with similarly limited success. Those with extraordinary profits and with the wherewithal to consume expensive items also have the ability to pay higher taxes. In both countries, politicians thought this would result in low political costs for them. However, the industries and the suffering workers protested loudly (something of a nonviolent Whiskey Rebellion). Apparently, the fairness campaign does not sell to the public when drowned out by the cries of the unemployed.

Gillespie's model relied on a number of hypotheses:

- tax preference and the sin-tax variant
- horizontal and vertical tax competition
- administration costs
- political cost of legislating and collecting tax (including the maxim that "an old tax is a good tax")
- and a preference for equitable taxes (fairness and ability to pay).

Taxes on "sinful" items had lower political costs because of inelastic price demand and the notion that they were voluntary taxes. The evidence from the US excise tax experience supports all of the hypotheses of the model with the exception of horizontal and vertical tax competition. Two variants of the political cost hypothesis may be added to the US model. One is the emergency variant that the public will pay if they support the emergency. Secondly, specific excise taxes that directly affect an industry face tough challenges led by business owners and workers. Protests from producers of "sinful" items that are subject to tax generally fail to gain public support. This US model can now be used to predict when excise tax proposals will be successful or to explain why one has failed.

The various reasons for imposing new excise taxes (or increasing existing excise taxes) has come full circle. Presidents Bush and Clinton planned to use the federal excise tax on cigarettes to help pay for health care reforms. The justification for increasing the tax was that smoking can have damaging health consequences. This is essentially the same argument Alexander Hamilton used to gain enactment of the first sin tax on whiskey over 200 hundred years ago. However, these recent attempts to increase excise taxes have not been successful in spite of the public's escalating disdain for smoking. Polls indicated that the public had a tax preference for cigarette taxes and judged them to be equitable because smokers are thought to have higher health care costs. The tax was promoted as a voluntary tax. There are probably many explanations for these failures. Ultimately, perhaps the American people did not perceive health care to be an emergency worthy of increased taxes and that made the political costs too high.

ENDNOTES

1 According to Charles Adams [1993], requisitions based on real estate values supplied a common denominator that avoided the definitional problems posed by the differential treatment accorded to slaves in the North (population) as opposed to the South (personal property).

2 Forsythe [1977, pp. 15–16] contends that the problems with the requisition system were complicated by the refusal of Congress to accept either supplies or the states' own currencies in payment. The fact that states were not credited for payments made directly to the troops created another complication. These problems were encouraged by individuals who supported giving Congress the power to tax and therefore wanted the state requisition system to prove inadequate.

3 The first tariff legislation was enacted on July 4, 1789. Between 1794 and 1816, 25 tariff acts were passed. Although the duties were protectionist in effect, they were enacted primarily as revenue measures [Ratner, 1942, pp. 26–27].

4 It is not surprising that Adam Smith influenced early law makers. Henry Carter Adams [1884, pp. 20–21] states that Smith's *Wealth of Nations* was a "work well known" during this time period and "quite generally endorsed." In fact, "the framers of the Constitution had in mind certain distinctions made by Adam Smith when they adopted into that instrument the words 'capitation, direct, and indirect tax'".

5 Tax collections were administered by the office of the Commissioner of the Revenue established in 1792 [Paul, 1954, p. 6]. The country was divided into 14 districts, each headed by a district director. Directors received one percent of the taxes collected in their districts. Agents, in turn, received four percent of the taxes they collected [Charles Adams, 1993, p. 317].

6 The Internal Revenue Act of 1862 was the second income tax law signed by President Lincoln. The first such act was signed by Lincoln on August 5, 1861; it was, however, not enforced. The 1862 Act materially extended the original law's income tax provisions and was actually put into operation [Ratner, 1942, pp. 67–68].

7 Note that the excise taxes were reimposed in 1898 (during the Spanish-American War) and subsequently were repealed in 1901 [Ratner, 1942, pp. 249–250].

8 The large discrepancy between the demand for and the supply of liquor was due to the wartime conversion of many distilling facilities to the production of grain alcohol [Leff, 1984, p. 35].

9 President Truman had indicated he would support a measure to reduce excise taxes. However, he wanted any resulting revenue reductions to be offset by closing loopholes in other taxes [Paul, 1954, p. 539].

10 The first state gasoline tax was enacted by Oregon in 1919. The tax was one cent per gallon. Within ten years, every state had adopted a tax on motor fuel. By the time the federal gasoline tax was passed in 1932, many states had increased their tax rates to between six and seven cents a gallon. State gasoline taxes were used primarily for highway construction and maintenance programs [Crawford, 1939, pp. 1–12].

11 One exception to the excise tax's dwindling importance as a revenue source occurred during the War of 1812. Due to the fall off in international trade, excise tax receipts

accounted for as much as 39 percent of total wartime federal revenues [US Bureau of the Census, Series P89–98].

12 Revenue collections during World War I, World War II, and the Korean War were supplemented by an excess profits tax. The tax applied to the excess of a corporation's profits over a designated prewar base period or over a "normal" rate of return (specified by statute) on invested capital. The tax rates reached as high as 95 percent during World War II [Pechman, 1987, p. 304].

13 Mrs. Clinton's claims respecting the salutary effects of tobacco tax increases on the incidence of smoking among "young people" are based on empirical estimates suggesting that the demand for cigarettes on the part of teenagers is much more elastic than it is among older smokers. The implication is that a given tax-induced price increase will reduce cigarette consumption among young people to a much greater extent than among other age groups and, moreover, that this will provide particularly important social benefits by providing incentives for young people to either quit before they become addicted or to prevent them from starting to smoke in the first place. Neither of these conclusions may be warranted. The cigarette demand elasticity estimates for young people may be substantially overstated because they fail to take account of the fact that many teenagers try cigarettes as a way of rebelling against social taboos. They smoke without any intention of taking up lifelong habits. Hence, reductions in cigarette consumption that appear on the surface to represent responses to increases in price may be nothing more than normal teenage experimentation.

REFERENCES

Adams, Charles. *For Good and Evil: The Impact of Taxes on the Course of Civilization* (London: Madison Books, 1993).

Adams, Herbert B., Ed. *Institutions and Economics.* Johns Hopkins University Studies in Historical and Political Science which includes "Taxation in the United States" by Henry Carter Adams (Baltimore: Johns Hopkins University, N. Murray Publication Agent, 1884).

Anderson, William H. *Taxation and the American Economy: An Economic, Legal, and Administrative Analysis* (New York: Prentice-Hall, Inc., 1951).

Bartlett, Bruce. "Cigarette Taxes, Smuggling, and Revenues," *Tax Notes,* Vol. 63 (June 13, 1994), p. 1493.

Becker, Robert A. *Revolution, Reform, and the Politics of American Taxation, 1763–1783* (Baton Rouge: Louisiana State University Press, 1980).

Bullion, John L. *A Great and Necessary Measure: George Grenville and the Genesis of the Stamp Act 1763–1765* (Columbia: University of Missouri Press, 1982).

Commerce Clearing House Tax Law Editors. *Federal Excise Tax Reporter* (Chicago: Commerce Clearing House, Inc., 1992).

Committee for Economic Development. *Federal Tax Issues In 1955* (New York: Committee for Economic Development, 1955).

Committee on Postwar Tax Policy. *A Tax Program for a Solvent America* (New York: The Ronald Press Company, 1945).

———. *A Tax Program for a Solvent America* (New York: The Committee on Postwar Tax Policy, 1947).

Committee on Taxation of the Twentieth Century Fund. *Facing the Tax Problem* (New York: The Twentieth Century Fund, 1937).

Comstock, Alzada. *Taxation in the Modern State*. Longmans' Economics Series (New York: Longmans, Green and Co., 1929).

Cooke, Jacob E., Ed. *The Reports of Alexander Hamilton* (New York: Harper and Row. 1964). Quoted in Dall W. Forsythe. *Taxation and Political Change in the Young Nation 1781–1833* (New York: Columbia University Press, 1977).

Crawford, Finla Goff. *Motor Fuel Taxation in the United States* (Syracuse, New York: By the author, 1939).

Due, John F. "The Role of Sales and Excise Taxation in the Over-all Tax Structure," *Journal of Finance*, Vol. 11 (1956), pp. 205–220.

Forsythe, Dall W. *Taxation and Political Change in the Young Nation 1781–1833* (New York: Columbia University Press, 1977).

Gillespie, W. Irwin. *Tax, Borrow and Spend: Financing Federal Spending in Canada, 1867–1990* (Ottawa, Canada: Carleton University Press, 1991).

Groves, Harold M. *Postwar Taxation and Economic Progress* (New York: McGraw-Hill Book Company, Inc., 1946).

Hansen, Susan B. *The Politics of Taxation* (New York: Praeger Publishers, 1983).

Hershey, Barry J. *The American Tax System: A Call for Reform* (New York: Philosophical Library, Inc., 1984).

Johnson, Donald B. and Kird H. Porter. *National Party Platforms 1840–1972* (Urbana: University of Illinois Press. 1973). Quoted in Mark H. Leff. *The Limits of Symbolic Reform* (Cambridge: Cambridge University Press, 1984).

Kennon Donald R. and Rebecca M. Rogers. *The Committee on Ways and Means: A Bicentennial History, 1789–1989* (Washington, D.C.: US Government Printing Office, 1989).

Kirshon, John W., Ed. *Chronicle of America* (New York: Chronicle Publications, Inc., 1989).

Leff, Mark H. *The Limits of Symbolic Reform* (Cambridge: Cambridge University Press, 1984).

Louden, Ian K. "Administration Eyeing 'Sin' Taxes to Fund Possible Health Care Plan," *Tax Notes*, Vol. 54 (January 6, 1992), p. 6.

"Luxury Excise Tax." *The National Public Accountant*, Vol. 36 (March 1991), p. 50.

Omnibus Trade and Competiveness Bill of 1988. 100th Cong., 2nd Sess. (1988), P.L., p. 418.

Omnibus Budget Reconciliation Act of 1990. 101st Cong., 2nd Sess. (29 November 1990), P.L., p. 508.

Omnibus Budget Reconciliation Act of 1993. 103rd Cong., 1st Sess. (10 August 1993), P.L. p. 66.

Paul, Randolph E. *Taxation in the United States* (Boston: Little, Brown and Company, 1954).

Pechman, Joseph A. *Federal Tax Policy,* Fifth Edition, Studies of Government Finance: Second Series (Washington, D.C.: The Brookings Institution. 1987).

Press Watch, *Tax Notes* ,Vol. 63 (April 11, 1994), p. 207.

Ratner, Sidney. *American Taxation: Its History as a Social Force in Democracy* (New York: W. W. Norton & Company, 1942).

Rogers, David. "Panel Offers Tax Concessions on Health Bill," *Wall Street Journal* (7 June 1994), p. A(3).

Rogers, David and Hilary Stout. "Moynihan Lays Out Health Proposals, Including Big Increase in Cigarette Tax." *Wall Street Journal* (10 June 1994), p. A(3).

Simonson, Kenneth D. "The Dubious Virtue of Higher 'Sin' Taxes," *Tax Notes,* Vol. 49 (1 October 1990), pp. 99–102.

Smith, Harry Edwin. *The United States Federal Internal Tax History from 1861 to 1871* (Boston: Houghton Mifflin Company, 1914).

Steuerle, Gene. "Postwar Changes in the Overall Tax System: Post-World War II," *Tax Notes,* Vol. 54 (2 March 1992), pp. 1163–1170.

"The Wages of Sin: Cigarette Taxes," *The Economist,* Vol. 326 (20 March 1993), pp. 28–29.

US Bureau of the Census. *Historical Statistics of the United States, 1789–1945* (Washington, DC: 1949).

US Congress. House of Representatives. Committee on Ways and Means. *Excise Tax Reduction Act of 1965,* 89th Cong., 1st Sess. (May 28, 1965).

———. Committee on Ways and Means. *Crude Oil Windfall Profit Tax Act of 1979: Report of the Committee on Ways and Means,* 96th Cong., 1st Sess. (22 June 1979), H.R. Rep. 304.

———. Committee on Ways and Means. *The President's Health Care Reform Proposals: Hearings before the Committee on Ways and Means,* 103rd Cong., 1st Sess. (28 September 1993).

US Congress. Senate. Committee on Finance. *President's Health Care Plan: Hearing Before the Committee on Finance.* 103rd Cong., 1st Sess. (30 September 1993).

Weisberger, Bernard A. "Seeking a Real Tax Revolt: Whiskey Rebellion of 1794," *American Heritage,* Vol. 42 (May–June 1991), pp. 22–24.

Whimster & Co. v. *Commissioners of Inland Revenue,* (1925) 12 T.C. 813, [1926] SC 25.

Wright, George E. "Income Tax," *The Incorporated Accountants' Journal* (May, 1907), pp. 200–203.

"X.Y.Z.," *Income Tax Assessments and Balance Sheets,* Letter to the Editor, *The Accountant* (October 2, 1909), pp. 415–416.

"X.Y.Z.," *Balance Sheets and Income Tax,* Letter to the Editor, *The Accountant*

Part VI:
Texts

The First Irish Accounting Publication: Ammonet, 1696

Peter J. Clarke
University College
Dublin

1.0 ABSTRACT

The first known accounting publication in Ireland is dated 1696. It was written, and printed, by S. Ammonet and was sold by him in Essex Street, Dublin. Three hundred years later, it is appropriate to analyze this publication. This paper examines the contents of the book and provides an overview of its economic and social background. The paper, adapting an approach by Vangermeersch [1988], is written in an A to Z format.

2.0 INTRODUCTION

To date, very little has been published on Irish accounting history. A possible reason for this is the lack of "good" source material. For example, Parker's [1994] comprehensive international bibliography of works on the history of accounting to 1987 cites just three Irish references available for consultation, as follows:

Early Irish Accounting

Freeman, A. M. (transcriber), "The Compossicion Booke of Conought"

Longfield, A. K. (Ed.), "The Shapland Carew Papers"

Longfield, A. K. (Ed.), "Fitzwilliam Accounts 1560–65, (Annesley Collection)"

A brief analysis of these sources is appropriate. *The Compossicion Booke of Conought* [Freeman, 1936] represents the results of a land survey undertaken in 1585. It was designed to identify, by verbal evidence under oath, the various owners of land in "counties Clare, Galway, Mayo, Sligo, Roscoman and the confynes thereof" in order to establish yearly rentals, payable to the Queen. Thus, it is a book of land tax assessments and is unlikely to be of great relevance to accounting historians.

The Shapland Carew papers [Longfield, 1946] relate to household accounts of the Carew family and their estate in County Wexford. The papers can be divided into three sections. The first section details rental income from various tenants and other expenses of various lands owned by the Carew family between 1740 and 1830. The second section provides details of household and other expense payments over the period 1746 to 1782 (e.g., the purchase of 70 galls of rum at 3/10 per gallon). The third section details some receipts, hire of and payments to servants (e.g., a dairy maid, Margaret Rossiter was hired at £3 per annum) and miscellaneous documents. These papers are likely to be of more relevance to economic and social historians than their accounting counterparts.

The Fitzwilliam accounts 1550–65 [Longfield, 1960] cover a period in which Sir William Fitzwilliam was treasurer at war in Ireland. Consequently, this record is dominated by expenses relating to army matters at that time and may be of assistance to those interested in various aspects of military history—such as details of pay for various ranks in the army (e.g., archers at six pence per diem), their overall numbers, together with details of expenses paid.

To Parker's bibliography one can add the many references to "accountancy" which can be found in Hayes [1965]. This includes, for example, a transcript of accounts of the treasurers of the City of Dublin, 1541–1613. Also, the National Archives Business Records Office in Dublin contains many business records, including wills, land deeds and leases, miscellaneous account books and reports. One can also add, for example, many of the account books of the various guilds which existed in Dublin during the 1500s and 1600s. A comprehensive directory of these guilds, together with a brief history of each which gives the location of surviving records and a list of repositories holding guild material is provided by Clark and Refausse [1993].

According to Yamey, Edey and Thompson [1963] and others, the first recorded publication in Ireland on accounting/bookkeeping is entitled *The Key of Knowledge etc.*, which was printed and sold by the author "S.A" in Dublin in 1696. At that time, Dublin (and Ireland) was relatively calm after the cessation of war between King James and King William. Indeed, the only item of note listed by Harris [1796] for that year was a proclamation for apprehending Henry Every the pirate and his crew. Remarkably, another publication was printed in virtually the same location and in the same year by J. Gibbon who provided us with the identity of "S.A", i.e., S. Ammonet and who was severely critical of Ammonet's method of bookkeeping.

This paper attempts to provide an holistic view of Ammonet's publication by looking not only at the content of the book and its criticisms by Gibbon but also at its commercial, economic and social context. The approach, in the form of an A-Z guide, is heavily influenced by Vangermeersch's [1988] discussion on Colinson's publication in Scotland, a few years earlier.

3.0 AMMONET

Ammonet describes himself as an "Accomptant" and also a "severe lover of bookkeeping." The surname "Ammonet" is not of Irish origin and does not appear in O'Hart's "Irish Pedigrees [1881] as being a family in Ireland in either the sixteenth or seventeenth century. However, in a subsequent edition [O'Hart, 1915] the name is listed as one of the Huguenot families naturalized in Great Britain and Ireland. The Huguenots were French Calvinists who fled to many countries in Europe to avoid religious persecution towards the end of the seventeenth century. Many thousands chose exile rather than compromise on religious principle [Caldicott, Gough and Pittion, 1987]. The name Ammonet appears in the London registers of the Huguenot on several occasions. However, the name does not appear in the major Irish publications of the Dublin Refuge [Lee 1936; Hylton, 1985; Caldicott *et al.*, 1987]. Neither was there any reference to such a person in various wills, cess tax returns or various records of the Genealogical Office in Dublin for the period.

4.0 BILLS OF EXCHANGE

The Ammonet publication consists of 32 pages, printed in octavo size and measuring 6 × $3^3/_4$ inches. It includes eight pages of dedication to "The Merchant Traders of the City of Dublin", with an additional three pages detailing the contents. The text consists of 41 articles or rules for recording various transactions, i.e., four articles for cash transactions, 17 articles concerning bills of exchange, 17 articles dealing with goods on commission or in company (partnership) and three articles dealing with closing accounts such as disposing with either the project or loss on a voyage.

The emphasis on bills of exchange is understandable since credit facilities in Dublin, at that time, were severely restricted and a bill of exchange was the usual method whereby money was transferred from one place to another [French, 1990].

5.0 COMMISSION AND COMPANY

In addition to indicating rules relating to bills of exchange, Ammonet also provides "instructuons upon goods by commission received, or sent, and others or in comnpany." Goods on commission are also referred to as "factorage" and company accounts are now more commonly referred to as partnership accounts.

Gibbon's main criticisms relate to Ammonet's method of keeping company accounts. Gibbon states that he "learned about twelve forms of company accounts, but none of them so mean and despicable as those two practiced by this Author .... In short, what he does, is evidently both without form, and imperfect." Gibbon further comments that "any person acquainted in any measure with business or book-keeping, upon perusal of his forms of company accounts (finding them to have so many statings and divisions) will be sensible that such forms are not practical."

6.0 DEDICATION

The most colourful part of Ammonet's publication is the dedication which runs for seven and a half pages—nearly a quarter of the book's 32 pages (which includes three blank pages). The dedication is addressed to the Merchant Traders of the City of Dublin who are all considered "Gentlemen."

The role of bookkeeping in commercial affairs is initially outlined. To Ammonet, man is "the most excellent of the sublunary creation ... with the imbellishing endowments of understanding, prudence and wisdom [for which] trade or traffick ... seems particularly adapted to humane capacity. This great mystery of trade, of vast extent and consequence ... [cannot] ... be carried on with effect without this excellent Art, which now hath with all obtained the name of book-keeping." He expressed the opinion that "without book-keeping trade would never stand long" and those who have neglected this particular art "have turned bankrupt to the disgrace of Merchants, the supporter of nations." He expressed his ambition "to prevent the same for the future not only in places which I personally converse, but also whereby small endeavours may hereafter happily arrive, in this following Treaty."

7.0 ESSEX STREET

Ammonet's book was printed and sold by the author in Essex Street, where he had his lodgings, but the precise location is not indicated. A handwritten addition to the cover suggests that it was sold "at the furriar [*sic*] shop." Essex Street was an important location at that time, due to its proximity to the Custom House and the Council-Chamber. Also, Essex Street was one of the principal streets of residence and property of the Dublin Huguenot community at that time [Hylton, 1986–87].

8.0 FRENCH TONGUE

The likelihood of Ammonet being a French citizen is enhanced by the fact that he offered to teach "the French Tongue" to his students. He also indicates that he is "a stranger to the English Tongue" and asks his readers to "pass over the many faults that may be found in my expressions." Furthermore, he indicates that his way of bookkeeping in "Double Partye" is taught after the "Italian, French and Dutch method."

9.0 GIBBON

It was mentioned previously that Ammonet did not print his name on the book, but twice used the initials "S.A." The identity of "S.A." is provided by J.A. Gibbon's "Reflections on a book published by Mr. Ammonet entitled the Key of Knowledge for all Merchants etc." Without Gibbon's reply we would not have discovered the identity of S. A(mmonet).

Gibbon's publication is, in effect, a severe rebuttal of Ammonet's rules. He claims that Ammonet "neither understands Merchants business or book-keeping, ... it being evident [that he] was never instructed in the very rudiments of bookkeeping, and has no true method." Gibbon, in writing, is trying to protect the Merchants of Dublin from Ammonet's "ignorance" so that Gentlemen should not lose their money or their children's education! He was also trying to protect the "deserved reputation of our merchants [lest] by their silence [they] approved of this pamphlet."

10.0 HUGUENOT

Ammonet was a French Huguenot. Research has revealed that a comparatively prosperous colony of French Huguenots settled in Dublin in the mid/late 1600s. Caldicott *et al.* [1987, p. 330] suggest that "a major ingredient of their success was access to and exploitation of the maritime network of coreligionists that flourished in France, Holland and England."

This group (refuge) is dominated by the more prestigious classes, noble and mercantile, which held at their disposal a considerable reserve of capital, and put it to work for the enrichment of their adopted city. The decade 1692–1701 marked the period of most intensive influx into Dublin. Some 1,800 individuals, comprising 452 families arrived, mostly via England [Hylton, 1985].

11.0 ITALIAN METHOD

The title of Ammonet's book includes reference to the Italian method. The first known printed treatise on double-entry bookkeeping was written by the Franciscan monk, Pacioli, and published in Venice in 1494. Pacioli's impact was enhanced by the moveable printing type and by the fact that he wrote in Italian rather than Latin, making the book available to a wide audience and bringing it into the modern era [Nobes, 1979]. Following Pacioli, writing on bookkeeping began to appear throughout the continent of Europe and elsewhere. Hatfield [1950, p. 4] says "It is nearly true to say that for a hundred years the texts appearing in England, France, Germany, Italy and the low countries were, at best revisions of Pacioli, at the worst, servile transcriptions without even the courtesy of referring to the original author."

12.0 JOURNAL

Ammonet mentions (but does not describe) the three books of record, i.e., the waste book, the journal and the ledger. However, his entire focus was "how to give the true title of Debtor and Creditor, out of the Waste Book into the Journal in Double partie after the Italian method ... but the Merchant that can title his Debtor and Creditor into the Journal, will with a little help, understand how to post any Article into his Ledger [*sic*]."

Towards this end, Ammonet presents "some short and easy rules wherein I plainly demonstrate by few examples." However, he mentions or provides no figures in his examples and there are no detailed illustrative examples showing how a series of transactions should be entered in the several account books; he provides no description of either the journal (or ledger) apart from the mention of a debit-credit convention; there are no ledger accounts or trial balance or balance sheet. There is only a passing reference to the profit and loss account.

13.0 KEY OF KNOWLEDGE

The full title of Ammonet's publication and cover sheet reads as follows:

> The key of Knowledge for all Merchants showing in short how to give the true title of Debtor and Creditor out of the Waste Book into the Journal in double partye, after the Italian, French and Dutch method.
>
> Dublin, printed; and are to be sold by the Author in Essex Street, 1696

It appears that Ammonet intended to publish additional material on accounting. He writes:

> the whole of it [i.e., the art of bookkeeping] is so great a mystery, that you'll need my further directions ... and that all true lovers of Merchants ... may attain to a great degree of perfection, I intend ... to have my whole set of books, by which I now teach, with the instructions thereof, by questions and answers, to be printed for the publick good, if out of your wanted generosity, for my further encouragement, will subscribe towards the charges thereof: for which advance, each Contributor shall have one of the said books were bound.

There is no evidence that Ammonet succeeded in his wish of having his set of books printed and published.

14.0 LODGING

Ammonet provided his teaching services at his "Lodging" in Essex Street. This suggests that he was not a property owner at that time and his name does not appear in any registry of deeds of Dublin property—although the available listings are incomplete. However, most Huguenots of the period tended to change locations on a regular basis. Hence, Ammonet adds that his clients will be attended "at my lodging in Essex Street, or else where you shall be directed." His name (or that of his descendants) does not appear on either of the maps dated 1751 and 1753 of the Essex Street area [Cosgrave, 1917].

15.0 MERCHANT

The title of Ammonet's book clearly shows the market at which it was directed—the Merchants of Dublin. At that time, Dublin was the political and social capital of Ireland. It was also an export and import gateway. For example, in 1726, half of the exports comprised cattle and sheep, whereas the main imports consisted of tobacco, silk, sugar, wines, coal, hops and fruit [Dobbs, 1729]. In effect, Dublin's merchants were catering to the landed gentry who were most able to afford imported luxuries [Mooney and White, 1987]. The jealous watchfulness of the British Parliament ensured that Ireland would never become a manufacturing base and therefore a possible threat to British industry [Beckett, 1966].

16.0 NEGOTIATOR

Ammonet indicates that his knowledge of the art of bookkeeping is based on "most accurate Observations of upward *forty* years standing, in all kinds of Trade, Traffick and Commerce, in which I was brought up as a negotiator." The compact edition of the Oxford English Dictionary [1971, p. 1910] gives three definitions of a negotiator, that is:

- a trader or business man
- one who carries out negotiations
- one who negotiates bills, loans etc.

Obviously, Ammonet had a business background of some sort, perhaps as a trader or trader's assistant rather than a bookkeeper.

17.0 OVID

The Roman poet, Ovid, is probably best known for the Metamorphoses, written in 15 books, about Greek mythology. In his dedication, Ammonet partially quotes Ovid as: *Os homini sublime dedit* which literally means "he gave to man a face looking upwards." However, the full English translation of the passage is more colourful and reads:

> Man was made to hold his head
> Erect in majesty and see the sky
> and raise his eyes to the bright stars above.

18.0 PLAGIARISM

It has been suggested by Dix [1905] and Murray [1930] that Ammonet may have "compiled" his book from an earlier publication. Dix's comment on Ammonet's book is revealing: "This work was probably compiled from an old treatise on the subject styled 'The pathway of knowledge, 1596, small 4to' ... it contains a treatise on book-keeping entitled

'The keeping of a merchants' books after the manner of debitor and creditor' (p. xxiv)." However, this claim of direct plagiarism by Ammonet is difficult to substantiate. The original "Pathway" contains 63 journal entries, with monetary values and specified transactions of fictitious persons, set out in logical order. Thus, there is a major dissimilarity between the layout and orientation of the two books. It is unlikely that Ammonet copied this edition of "Pathway" but he may have been influenced by it. Indeed, copyright law did not exist at that time, since the Copyright Act was not introduced until 1801.

19.0 QUICK

Ammonet's publication and Gibbon's response were both published in 1696. This is indeed a very quick response time by Gibbon, especially when one considers that the printing/publishing trade in Ireland did not develop until after 1709. This is because the Copyright Act of that year did not specifically mention Ireland and so Irish printers and booksellers began to reprint London editions since they were not legally bound to pay copyright [Cole, 1986]. Also, around 1696, a King's Printer's patent (monopoly) existed in Ireland which restricted printing in Dublin [Webb, 1929].

20.0 REFLECTION

This is the focus of Gibbon's publication. Its exact title is

> Reflections on a book published by Mr. Ammonet
> entitled The Key of Knowledge for all merchants, etc.
>
> by J.G.
>
> A well-wisher to all the lovers and practicers of the true
> Art and method of book-keeping.

"Reflections" was published by Mathew Gunn (a well-known Dublin printer) at Essex Street Gate in 1696—the same year and location of Ammonet's publication. Gibbon's method of rebuttal is "to quote the Instruction or Rule I am to reflect upon, then give you my observations and reflections upon the same." Gibbon, in fact, reflects on 17 of Ammonet's 41 rules. His reflections cover eleven pages whereas Ammonet outlined his 41 rules in eighteen pages.

21.0 SPENCER

Mention has previously been made of Gibbon's rebuttal of Ammonet's publication which he described as a "pamphlet" with a "haughty title page." Gibbon informs us that his knowledge was obtained from a "Mr. Spencer, one bred in Holland and practiser in this art 20 years." This reference reinforced the importance of the Dutch connection in the development of double-entry bookkeeping throughout Europe. As Edwards [1988] notes, "Holland became the training school for the Merchants of Britain and Ireland." Indeed, another early Irish accounting treatise was written by Elias Voster around 1725. This book on arithmetic contained a section on the operation of double-entry bookkeeping. According to Meagher [1994] his text enjoyed remarkable popularity and longevity and in 1785 a sixteenth edition was published.

Also, the reference to a Mr. Spencer allows us to revise the assertion by Robinson [1964, p. 10] who claimed that "Thomas Hogan, who carried on business as a merchant and accomptant at 46, South King Street, Stephen's Green, Dublin, was the first Irish public accountant of whom we have any knowledge." Robinson's claim was based on evidence of an entry in Wilson's Dublin Director for 1761. Gibbon's reference to Spencer, therefore, predates Hogan by about a hundred years.

22.0 TEACHER

Ammonet was a teacher. In addition to outlining some "short and easy rules" for recording transactions in double-entry, he also taught "a very easy method of book-keeping in single partie, fit for shop-keepers and others ... likewise if any county Gentlemen be desirous to have their children brought up in the ways of Commerce, I will undertake to teach them Writing, Cyphering, the French Tongue, and book-keeping." His clients would "find an exact performance of what may be reasonably expected by Gentlemen." Ammonet signed himself as being a "faithful and most obsequious servant."

23.0 UNCAPABLE [*sic*]

Gibbon clearly considered Ammonet to be incompetent. He refers to Ammonet's "ignorance" (on several occasions); how he "cumbers than assists the art of book-keeping" and has "no true method." Gibbon's final paragraph reads:

> I desire all judicious persons to consider how *uncapable* this author is of teaching, who himself makes false statings in proper accounts, and knows not the titles used and practised in book-keeping, as I have demonstrated in several particulars—If his ignorance has not been such, and so great as to appear in print, I should not have thus exposed him.

Gibbon states that he has "no prejudice against Mr. Ammonet." This could be an indication of religious tension. Alternatively, it could be professional rivalry since he requests readers to accept his reflections "as evidence of my zeal and forwardness to serve you."

24.0 VOSTER

While Ammonet may have written the first Irish publication on accounting, it is difficult to identify his contribution to the development of accounting practice in Ireland. Some years later, another Irish author [Deighan, 1807] provided a brief summary of previous accounting publications, starting with Oldcastle and Peel but there is no mention of Ammonet. Also, while other accounting books are to be found in sales catalogues of that time [Sadlier, 1721], there is no mention of Ammonet's publication. Meagher [1994] suggests that Elias Voster should be described as the father of Irish accountancy. The story of Elias Voster, therefore, needs to be retold [adapted from Meagher, 1994 and Voster, 1785].

> A Cork merchant named Browne, around 1696, sent his son Edward to Holland to learn more about various branches of the mercantile profession. Elias Voster, aged about 17, arrived with Edward Brown in Cork in 1699.
>
> Elias Voster eventually established a school in Brown Street—a street possibly named after his former employer. Many of the merchants of the city were educated by him in writing, arithmetic and the most regular method of book-keeping ....
>
> Amongst Elias Voster's most enduring achievements was his authorship of the earliest known textbook in this country which he wrote in order to meet the needs of his developing school ....

> The first edition was possibly published around 1725 ....
>
> The text enjoyed remarkable popularity and longevity ... in 1785 a sixteenth edition was published (revised by Daniel Voster).

In researching the background of Voster two amazing coincidences emerged. First, Elias's prosperity facilitated the building of Vosterburg which is now owned and occupied by John Meagher who is a member of the Department of Accounting at University College, Cork. The second is one of Voster's illustrations for the "sale of 9,465 lbs. of tobacco at 9d per lb—total value of £354-18-9d, sold to a *Peter Clarke*" (p. 263).

25.0 WORLD

The date of Ammonet's publication should be placed in a world context and especially in relation to accounting publications in the English language. Exhibit 1 shows how the dates compare with those of the first accounting book in various countries.

Exhibit 1

Dates of publication of first accounting book

English publications	
England (Oldcastle)	1543
Scotland (Colinson)	1683
Ireland (Ammonet)	1696
America (Bedford)	1737
Australia (Dimlow)	1871
and Non-English publications	
Italy (Pacioli)	1494
Holland (Ympyn)	1543
Spain (Solorzano)	1590
Denmark (Petraeus)	1673

26.0 EXTRAORDINARY

According to Ammonet all "house expense ordinary and extraordinary ... ought to be gathered weekly or monthly in one Article making profits and losses account Debtor to Cash." Is this one of the earliest accounting references to "extraordinary items which was the subject of two accounting standards (SSAP 6 and FRS 3)? It is not clear from Ammonet whether or not house expenses included private expenses which should have been treated as "drawings" rather than debited to the profit and loss account. However, the ultimate effect on the owner's capital account would be the same, regardless of which method was used.

27.0 YEARS (OF AGE)

Apart from his accounting publication in 1696, no other reference to Ammonet has been found in Dublin. However, there are two (English) references to a person of the same name. The first refers to the naturalization of a "Samuell Amonnett, born in Geneva, son of Samuel Amonnet" in 1665 [Proceedings, 1952–58]. Secondly, a Samuel Amonet was a sponsor at the baptism of Marie Phillibert Verbecq on 14 November 1669 [Registers, 1899].

The lack of uniformity in the spelling of the (Huguenot) surnames is noted by Shaw [1911] who argues that entries were made by clerks who were too busy to take the trouble of collating and verifying them and who must have been sorely puzzled by many of the names.

An English reference to Ammonet prior to his Dublin appearance is understandable since Ireland's geographical location on the western edge of Europe dictated that virtually all those who sought haven in Ireland would invariably have first travelled through England [Hylton, 1985].

We also know that Ammonet's accounting knowledge was based on "observations of upward forty years standing." Thus, it is plausible to argue that Ammonet was probably in his mid-fifties (if not older) when he penned his accounting "treatise."

28.0 Z

Z is the final letter of the alphabet. So, the final word is provided by Gibbon who partially quotes Seneca, the Roman philosopher as follows:

> *Nemo sibi tantummodo errat, sed alieni erroris et causa et auctor ets*

which translates as:

> No-one makes a mistake himself without also being the reason of someone else's mistake!

REFERENCES

Accounting Standards Board (UK). *FRS3; Reporting Financial Performance* (UK:ASB, 1992).

Accounting Standards Committee (UK). *SSAP 6; Extraordinary Items and Prior Year Adjustments* (UK: ASC, 1986).

Ammonet, S. *The Key of Knowledge*. Printed by the author, Dublin, 1696.

Beckett, J. C. *The Making of Modern Ireland 1603–1923* (London: Faber and Faber, 1966).

Caldicott, C., H. Gough and J. Pittion. *The Huguenots and Ireland: Anatomy of an Emigration* (Dublin: Glendale Press, 1987).

Clark, M. and R. Refausse. *Directory of Historic Dublin Guilds* (Dublin Public Libraries, 1993).

Cole, R. I*rish Booksellers and English Writers 1740–1800* (London: Mansell, 1986).

Cosgrave, E. MacDowel "On Two Maps Dated 1751 and 1753, of the Essex Street Bridge District of Dublin," *Journal of the Royal Society of Antiquaries of Ireland* (1917), pp. 140–149.

Deighan, P. *A Complete Treat on bookkeeping, Rational and Practical* (Dublin: Printed by Graisberry and Campbell, 1807).

Dix, E. *A Catalogue of Early Dublin-printed Books: 1601 to 1700* (Dublin: O'Donoghue & Co., 1905).

Dobbs, A. *An Essay on the Trade of Ireland* [Part 1] (Dublin: A. Rhames, 1729).

Edwards, J. D. "Early bookkeeping and Its Development into Accounting," *Business History Review* (1988), pp. 446–458.

Freeman, A. M. (transcriber). "The Compossicion Booke of Conought." Dublin Stationery Office for Irish Manuscripts Commission, 1936.

French, E. "The Origin of General Limited Liability in the United Kingdom," *Accounting and Business Research* (1990), pp. 15–34.

Gibbon, J. *Reflections on a book published by Mr. Ammonet, entituled The Key of Knowledge for all Merchants, &c* (Essex Street Gate: Mathew Gunn, 1696).

Harris, W. *The History and Antiquities of the City of Dublin, From the Earliest Accounts* (London: John Knox, 1796).

Hatfield, H. "A Historic Defence of Book Keeping," in *Studies in Accounting,* W. T. Baxter and S. Davidson, Eds. (Norwich: Fletcher & Son Ltd., 1962).

Hayes, R. *Manuscript Sources for the History of Irish Civilisation,* (11 volumes) (Boston: Hall, 1965).

Hylton, R. P. "The Huguenot Communities in Dublin, 1662–1745," (unpublished) PhD thesis, University College, Dublin, 1985.

Hylton, R. "Dublin's Huguenot Refuge: 1662–1817," *Dublin Historical Record* (1986–87), pp. 15–25.

Lee, Grace Lawless. *The Huguenot Settlements in Ireland* (London: Longmans, Green & Co., 1936).

Longfield, A. K., Ed. "The Shapland Carew Papers." Dublin Stationery Office, 1946.

———. "Fitzwilliam Accounts 1560–65, (Annesley Collection)." Dublin Stationery Office for the Irish Manuscripts Commission, 1960.

Meagher, J. "Elias Voster: The Father of Irish Accounting," *Journal of the Cork Historical and Archaeological Society,* Vol. 99 (1994), pp. 111–119.

Mooney, T. and F. White. "The Gentry's Winter Season," in *The Georgeous Mask: Dublin 1700–1850,* D. Dickson, Ed. (Dublin: Trinity Historical Workshop, 1987).

Murray, D. *Chapters in the History of Book-keeping, Accountancy and Commercial Arithmetic* (Glasgow: Jackson, Wiley & Co., 1930).

Nobes, C. "Pacioli—the First Academic Accountant?" *Accountancy* (September, 1979), pp. 66-67.

O'Hart, J. *Irish Pedigrees; Or The Origin and Stem of the Irish Nation* (Dublin: Gill & Son, 1881).

———. *Irish Pedigrees; Or The Origin and Stem of the Irish Nation* (Dublin: Gill & Son, 1915).

Oxford English Dictionary (Compact Edition) (London: Clarendon Press, 1971).

Parker, R. *Select Bibliography of Works on the History of Accounting to 1987.* Available over Internet using Mosaic, 1994.

Proceedings of the Huguenot Society of London (London: Publication of the Huguenot Society of London, No.3, 1952–1958).

Registers of the French Church (Threadneedle Street, London: Publication of the Huguenot Society of London, Vol. 11, 1899).

Robinson, H. *A History of Accountants in Ireland* (The Institute of Chartered Accountants in Ireland, 1964).

Sadlier, E., *A catalogue of books in all faculties to be disposed of at the lowest prices at Captain Edward's, next door to Doctor Smith's upon College Green* (Dublin: E. Sadlier, 1721).

Shaw, W. "Letters of Denization and Acts of Naturalization for Aliens in England and Ireland 1603–1700," Publication of the Huguenot Society of London (1911), reprinted by Kraus, Nendeln/Liechtenstein, 1969.

Vangermeersch, R. "Colinson's Idea Rationaria." Collected papers of the Fifth World Congress of Accounting Historians, published by the Accounting and Finance Foundation within the University of Sydney, A. T. Croswell, Ed. 1988, pp. 214–238.

Voster, E. *Arithmetic, in whole and broken numbers digested after a new method and chiefly adapted to the trade of Ireland to which are added instructions for book-keeping* (Dublin: Printed by Richard Cross, 1785).

Webb, J. *The Guilds of Dublin* (Dublin: Three Candles, 1929).

Yamey, B., H. Edey and H. Thompson. *Accounting in England and Scotland: 1543–1800* (London: Sweet and Maxwell, 1963).

The Making of the First English Book on Double-Entry Bookkeeping:

From Oldcastle to Mellis

J. J. Lanero
Universidad de León
Spain

1.0 ABSTRACT

The first English book on double-entry bookkeeping, by Hugh Oldcastle, published in London, in 1453, in many places corresponds very closely to Pacioli's text—so much that some scholars have described the former as a translation of the latter. However, there are significant differences between the two works. All we know about Oldcastle's book and its contents is obtained from John Mellis' "reproduction" published in 1588.

Mellis was a heavy borrower, that is evident in that part of his book for which he was directly responsible. Therefore, there is a hypothesis that any close correspondences between Mellis and James Peele's treatises, published in 1553 and 1569, are examples of borrowings by Mellis from Peele rather than of borrowings by Peele from Oldcastle. Nevertheless, it is possible to go well beyond this hypothesis. Examination of some of the correspondences clarifies our thesis: that Mellis must have been the borrower. It is obvious, too, that Mellis was inefficient as an editor or adaptor of Oldcastle's treatise.

However, correspondences between Pacioli and Oldcastle/Mellis provide support for a speculation of their dependence on a common source, but of course these numerous and pervading correspondences also support the much more credible assumption that it was the Pacioli printed text which Oldcastle used as his model.

In general, Mellis took liberally from Peele. The detectable resulting changes made to the Oldcastle text are significant. The Mellis edition of 1588 is therefore not to be considered as an even roughly faithful copy of the Oldcastle text.

The paper develops the following points: hypothetical use by Oldcastle of an Italian manuscript; Peele and Mellis as plagiarists; comparison and equivalence. Some correspondences between Peele and Mellis; the Inventory; the rule for debits and credits; the ruling of account-books; Peele's *The maner and fourme*; Peele's impact on Mellis; conclusion; and references.

2.0 INTRODUCTION

The first printed treatise of double-entry bookkeeping was Luca Pacioli's *Summa de arithmetica, geometria, proportioni & proportionalità* of 1494 [Pacioli, 1494], a compilation which includes a tractatus on the subject under the heading "Particularis de computis et scripturis." During this century the question has been debated whether Pacioli had taken this *tractatus* (or most of it) without acknowledgement from a Venetian manuscript. Fabio Besta [1929], with his masterpiece, *La Ragioneria*, was the foremost and prestigious spokesman of the charge of plagiarism. Balduin Penndorf [1930], with his *Geschichte der Buchhaltung in Deutschland*, and Federigo Melis [1950], with his *Storia della ragioneria*, were the main proponents of the opposing contention that Pacioli himself should be considered the author of the *Tractatus*.

It is not our purpose here to comment upon the controversy in all its features. Instead, the central idea of this paper is to illustrate that no confidence can be placed on one major piece of evidence given pre-eminence by Besta.

The first English book on double-entry bookkeeping was published in 1543: Hugh Oldcastle's *A Profitable Treatyce* ... [Oldcastle, 1543]. No copy of this treatise is known to have survived. All we know of its contents is obtained from another sixteenth-century book, John Mellis's *A briefe instruction* ..., published in 1588 [Mellis, 1588]. In his foreword "To the Reader," signed "Iohn Mellis Schole-maister," the writer admits that:

> And knowe ye for certaine, that I presume ne vsurpe not to set forth this worke of mine owne labour and industrie, for truely I am but the renuer and reuiuer of an auncient old copie printed here in London the 14. of August, 1543.

and he says that the original was "collected, published, made and set forth by one Hugh Oldcastle Scholemaster." Mellis did, notwithstanding, add an exemplary set of account-books after the text: "for the better vnderstanding and practise of these rules, I haue hereunto added a little Inuentorie, Iournal, and Leager." He also added *A Short and Plaine Treatise of Arithmeticke in whole numbers* ... [Mellis, 1588]. Mellis had been the author of "a thirde part of Rules of Practize, abridged into *a briefer method then hitherto hath been published*, with divers necessary Rules incident to the Trade of Merchandise: with Tables of the valuation of all Coynes, as they are currant at this present time. By John Mellis," an appendix to Robert Recorde's Treatise, *Records Arithmetick: or The grounde of artes*, in the edition of 1582 [Recorde, 1582].

The Mellis text in many places corresponds very closely to Pacioli's text—so much that some scholars have described the former as a translation of the latter. J. Row Fogo states:

> The treatise which introduced Italian bookkeeping into England is the earliest work on the subject in our language of which we have a record. It is a translation of Pacioli, and was produced in 1543 by Hugh Oldcastle, a teacher of arithmetic and book-keeping in London. Unfortunately no copy of this oldest English treatise on bookkeeping is known to exist. We can form an opinion of it only by a reprint which was issued in 1588 by John Mellis, also a schoolmaster in London. [Fogo, 1905, p. 126]

Arthur H. Woolf says that the year 1543 was an eventful one in the history of bookkeeping, for it saw the introduction of Pacioli's work into three countries; according to him, translations of the *De Computis* appearing almost at the same time in Dutch, French and English:

> The English translation of Pacioli ... appeared in England in 1543. It was written by Hugh Oldcastle, a teacher of arithmetic, and is the first treatise on bookkeeping in our language of which we possess any record. No original copy of Oldcastle's work is, unfortunately, known to exist, and our knowledge of it is derived from a reprint issued in 1588 by John Mellis, who describes himself as a 'Scholemaister'. [Woolf, 1913, p. 131]

John B. Geijsbeek defines Mellis's book as "nothing more than a translation of Pacioli's book" [Geijsbeek, 1914].

However, there are significant differences between the two works. For instance, several chapters in Pacioli are not to be found in Mellis, and several passages, sentences and words in Mellis have no counterpart in Pacioli. In some places, Oldcastle seems to have mistranslated individual words used in his Italian source. For example, the word *monte* used in Pacioli is rendered literally in Mellis, chapter five, as "mountaine," whereas it was used here in the sense of an aggregation of totality. In chapter fifteen, the word *casa* is translated as *chest* (i.e., cash), instead of as "house" or "firm." The word *cassa* was confused with *casa*.

Besta identified and discussed several examples of differences between the two works. His interpretation of some of these differences was advanced as a main pillar of support for his speculations that Pacioli's *Tractatus* was in large extent not an original piece of work, and that both Pacioli and Oldcastle had drawn heavily on a Venetian manuscript, of which Oldcastle's rendering was the more accurate reflection. Besta went so far as to suggest the identity of the author of this document: one Troylo de Cancellariis, of whom there is documentary evidence for the period 1421–1454, and who, being expert in accounts, may well have compiled a manuscript manual on double entry for use in mercantile academies in Venice. The Italian scholar claimed that Oldcastle's text was a translation of the supposed Venetian manuscript, and he believed that in turn the Mellis reissue was an exact reproduction of the Oldcastle text [Besta, 1929, Vol. III, pp. 369–376]. Besta also wrote that probably the decisive blow to Pacioli's reputation as an author on bookkeeping was given by the evidence of Oldcastle's book, which clearly was a translation not of Pacioli's work but of that earlier manuscript [Besta (a), Ceccherelli, 1913, p. 8].

The Dutch historian, P. Kats, was the first to point out that several of the additional passages in the Mellis text were substantially identical to passages in the works of James Peele: *The maner and fourme how to kepe a perfecte reconyng ...* of 1553 [Peele, 1553] and *The Pathe waye to perfectnes, in th'accomptes of Debitour and Creditour ...* [Peele, 1569]. Kats was inclined to subscribe to Besta's general speculation about Pacioli's lack of originality; nevertheless he was doubtful whether the Mellis text could give it any support. In a paper written in Dutch, Kats noted that Besta could not have known that Mellis had taken from Peele a number of passages where Mellis differs from Pacioli, and consequently that these passages could be ascribed neither to Oldcastle nor to the Venetian manuscript and, by implication, that other changes to the Oldcastle original may have been made by Mellis [Kats, 1925–1926, pp. 168–176]. He noted that Besta seemingly was not familiar with the contents of Peele's books, although he did quote them [Besta, 1929, Vol. III, p. 394].

However, Kats' considerations of the correspondences between Mellis and Peele seem to have had no repercussions on the Pacioli debate. They were not noted by either Penndorf or

Melis or Yamey.[1] Maybe they have been neglected because Kats made the main point most explicitly in a footnote to an article in Dutch. Even in that article he did not substantiate that the borrowings must have been by Mellis from Peele, rather than by Peele from Oldcastle. Perhaps, also, the point made by Kats has been overlooked because Kats was much more guarded in a more readily accessible paper. In this article he said that where Oldcastle/Mellis and Peele "agree but differ from Pacioli, it is uncertain which of the English authors had borrowed from the other" [Kats, 1926, p. 483]. Nevertheless, in an article published in the following year, 1927, Kats wrote:

> In 1588 John Mellis published a little treatise entitled "A Briefe Instruction and Maner hovv to keepe Bookes of Accomptes after the order of Debitor and Creditor," & c. This title is reminiscent of Peele's first book and of Ympyn's "Notable Woorke." Though it is said to be a reprint of Oldcastle's treatise of 1543, it is certain that Mellis altered it here and there by taking passages from Peele and enlarging it with a set of examples in which he followed not only that author but indirectly also Ympyn, e.g. in the valuation of the items in the inventory itself and the summation of the sections. [Kats, 1927, p. 263]

There is no statement here that Mellis was the plagiarist.

In this paper we study more closely some instances of correspondence between Mellis and Peele, after we have summarized the general background. In the penultimate section we also refer to another feature of the Mellis book which helps to establish the dependence of Mellis on Peele.

3.0 PEELE AND MELLIS AS PLAGIARISTS

Mellis tells his readers that he added the exemplary set of account-books to the text taken from Oldcastle. It is certain that in this part of the work Mellis took heavily from earlier authors, including Peele. In fact, Kats came to the conclusion that Mellis's illustrative material was manifestly under the direct influence of Peele [Kats, 1925–1926, p. 172]. Mellis also borrowed from John Weddington, whose *A Breffe Instruction, and Manner, Howe to Kepe, Marchants Bokes, of Accomptes After the order of Debitor and Creditor* ... was published in Antwerp in 1567 [Weddington, 1567]. Thus the entry in the inventory for "lands and rents" is very similar in the two books. In Weddington the asset is a farm purchased from "one Maister Iohan Hayes gentilman to me and my eyres for ever, after the rate of 16 yeres pourchase, wher unto ther is belonginge 50 ackers of lande." The sequence is the same in Mellis, except that the previous owner is "one M. Iohn H. Gentleman." Let us see a case of correspondence between Peele and Weddington, and a far closer one between Weddington and Mellis:

Peele (1553)	*Weddington* (1567)	*Mellis* (1588)
Item my farmehouse with thappurtenaunces therunto belonging, standing in Colchestre in the countie of Estsex, called the blacke hounde in the parish of Saint Bernardes, the fee simple thereof purchased to	More in landis and rentis within this countri of Brabant to saie- One ferme place, with all the apertenancis ther unto belonginge beinge or lyinge in the lordeship of the lorde	Item, in Lands and Rents within the Countie of Norf. That is to say, one Farme with all thapurtenances thereunto belonging: set, lying, and being in the parish of Wraxam, in the Lordship of Sir William

me, and mine heires of Master Fraunces Lambart Stapler, as by the writing thereof in my cheste more at large dooeth appere, and cost me ... £157.	of Barrow namyd the grove, within the perrishe of Santflet the whiche I have porchasid of *one Maiestter Iohan Hays gentilman to me and my eyres for ever, after the rate of 16 yeres pourchase, wher unto ther is belonginge 50 ackers of lande,* as by the indentors therof more plainly aperethe ... whereof the yearly rent is £12 fls. and cost me in redy mony £179 fls. which I do now exs teme al £200 fls.	Woodhouse knight, which I purchased of one *M. Iohn H. Gentelman, to me and my heires for ever, after the rate of xvi. yeares purchase: whereunto there is belonging fiftie Acres of lande,* as by the Indentures thereof more plainely appeareth ... whereof the yerely rent now is xv. li. And cost me in redy money Clxx xxii. li which I doe nowe esteeme at CCC li.

The correspondences between Peele's and Weddington's entries may perhaps be explained in terms of the use of common legal formulations. Those between Weddington's and Mellis's entries are too numerous and close to suggest any explanation other than direct copying. There are several examples of similar treatment or wording in certain ledger accounts of Weddington and Mellis. Thus in both cases the closing debit entry (for profit) in the lands and rents accounts appears, oddly, as "net rest and balance of this account" (in modern spelling). In the account of household goods both authors have an entry for what we would call depreciation. In Weddington the entry is "for so myche as I do finde, at this daye to be wholly consumyd or worne"; in Mellis it is "for so much as I doe finde at this day to be consumed and worn" (with Mellis omitting "wholly").

Peele also borrowed from some of his predecessors; like his contemporaries he did not acknowledge the sources of his borrowings, but unlike Mellis, Peele never borrowed slavishly. He altered, adapted or embellished the ideas or expressions he appears to have taken from others. All the cases of patent borrowing by Peele—the Peele-Mellis correspondences are considered more fully in the following section—are such as to suggest, paraphrasing Kats, that Peele was someone who scorned the use of words other than his own [Kats, 1925–1926, p. 176]. It may be noted that Mellis took as the title of his book the first twenty-five words of Weddington's title, excluding the word "marchantes" and adding, redundantly, "&" after "creditor." The title of Peele's first book has in it one element of the title of the English version of Ympyn's book (1547): *A notable and very excellente woorke, expressyng and declaryng the maner and forme how to Kepe a boke of accōptes or reconynges ...*, [Ympyn, 1547] and a hint of part of Oldcastle's title.

Let us see a few examples, which should make things clearer.

First, in *The Maner and fourme* Peele seems to have followed an instructional method introduced by Manzoni in his *Quaderno doppio* of 1540 [Manzoni, 1540]. Manzoni numbered consecutively the entries in his illustrative journal, a technique also to be found in contemporary practice, the sixteenth century journal of Zuan Antonio Barbarigo [Besta, 1929, p. 350]. In the text there is a table (*tavola*) listing the various types of transaction, in each case with a reference to the numbered journal entry which exemplifies the type of transaction and another to the folios of the ledger accounts involved. Each entry in the journal also has a description of the type of transaction in the margin. Peele seems to have adopted Manzoni's technique; however, he improved upon it in that he replaced the table with a long section in which the treatment of each type of transaction is set out, say, the accounts to be debited and credited, with appropriate references to the numbered entries in the journal.

Second, in the *Nieuwe instructie* ..., Ympyn [1543] introduced several unusual features in the procedures for closing a ledger. One of these was to bring together all the remaining balances on the various goods accounts in a single collective account. Its balance was transferred to the final balance account. The collective account was reopened in the new ledger, and from it the individual goods accounts. Peele referred to this practice in his first book, but he did not follow it in his model set of accounts. In *The Pathe waye*, however, Peele described as well as illustrated this treatment. Again he improved on his model. In Peele's second book there are two posting reference columns on each side of the balance account in the first ("A") ledger, headed "A" and "B" respectively. It is explained that in the A column one inserts the folio number of the account in the A ledger whence the particular entry came; and in the B column one inserts the folio number of the account opened in the new (B) ledger. In this way the same closing balance account served also as the source for the opening entries in the new ledger, thereby avoiding the need for an opening balance account or opening journal entries in the new ledger. Peele writes that in this fashion "I have used as muche brevite as maye posible be put in practice, and have rejected the tediousnes that divers use therin." He went further than Ympyn in this direction; in that he also furnished his "goodes remayninge" account with two posting columns and therefore had no need to raise an (opening) collective account in the new ledger.

Third, Pacioli did not include money values in his inventory book or record, partly because others besides the owner of the business could write in it or have access to it. Pacioli says in his tenth chapter that the entries in the inventory book or records should be entered in the journal and that, because the journal is "your secret book" (*per essere tuo libro secreto*), the merchant could record all his possessions, including his non-trading assets, in full detail. It should be understood that in Pacioli the entries in the inventory book do not include values, except where value is the only unit of measure as for cash or debts, and that others besides the merchant could make entries in the inventory book of records (*Referendote sepre al ditto foglio che per te o per altri fosse scritto*). In this manner the merchant who kept his own journal could withhold from his staff information about his private assets and wealth. In the ninth chapter of Mellis, the Journal is said to be "a secrete booke," and, as in Pacioli, it is said therefore to be safe "therein" to "shew write and expresse al your goods moveable and immoveable ...." Here Mellis forgot that in the third chapter he advised the insertion of values of some of the (non-monetary) assets in the inventory, and that values are shown for all items in the inventory in the worked example. He evidently was inconsistent in his modification and augmentation of Oldcastle's original text.

Ympyn handles the matter somewhat differently. In the fourth chapter he advises that the entries in the inventory book or records, which include the values of all the assets, should not be recorded in the memorial or waste-book: "There are some that write in the beginnyng of this boke of Memoriall the Inventory, whiche I cannot praise, forasmuche as this boke commeth daily into the handes of every persone ...." The treatment in the journal is not quite clear. The inventory entries are to be transferred to the journal, "reservyng the boke of your Journall Inventory to be locked in a cheste, that it be not made comon and knowen to all suche as shall handle or write in your boke ..." (chapter ten). Thus for Ympyn the journal was not a secret book; secrecy was secured by apparently segregating and detaching the inventory entries. It is not obvious why it was necessary for the inventory details to be entered in the journal at all, since the ledger entries could have been made directly from the inventory itself. In any event, in his model journal Ympyn treats the opening inventory entries the same as subsequent entries; there is no hint of their segregation. Peele addressed himself in the eleventh chapter of *The maner and fourme* to the problem of "What is to be done of suche as will have their substaunce kepte in secrete, and of circumspect hede to be taken, that eche parcel of the Jornall be truly cast before it be borne into the quaterne." The solution is similar to that suggested by Ympyn: "They maye binde their inventorye and the parcels therof whiche are borne into the Jornall, in the formost ende of their quaterne [ledger] before the kalender [index], and beare the same parcels orderly bothe debitors & creditors into the same quaterne." Peele's first book has money values. In addition, however, the assets are totalled and also the liabilities; finally, the net balance, the "substaunce of the owner" is shown.

Sporadically in Peele's works one detects echoes of Pacioli's *Tractatus*. Generally these refer to minor matters on which there was little space for originality of exposition or expression. But on more interesting matters closer examination shows once again traces of Peele's originality, even when he might have been influenced by Pacioli either directly or else through Oldcastle. Here are two examples.

First, in his opening chapter Pacioli explains that a merchant needs three things and, as expressed in Mellis, the "first and principall" thing is "money or other substance" (*la pecunia numerata e ogni altra faculta sustantiale*). He adds, however, that some wealthy merchants in Italy began their careers without any other assets than their credit. Peele also refers in *The maner and fourme* to the merchant who starts a business without assets, but he does so in his discussion of the inventory in chapter two: "but he that hath no gooddes (but suche as at his beginnyng, he taketh on credite) nedeth no Inventorie." The same point is made in Weddington, and the words used by him suggest he had Peele as a model.

Second, in Pacioli's fifteenth chapter the point is made that if a merchant were to lose his ledger "by infortune of thieves, fire or water & c. (*p alcun caso de robaria o incēdio di foco, o naufragii & c.*), he could from the journal (to quote from Mellis) "againe renew & make another Leager, with all the contentes and parcels from day to day, and put them in the same number and leafe in which they were found in before" (*refare vnaltro q̈derno cō le medesime ptite a di pdi. E ponerle al numero di le medesine che i q̈l pso si retrouauano*). Peele in *The maner and fourme* addresses himself to another implication of the correspondence between journal and ledger. At the end of the eighth chapter he advises that in the case of disagreement between the merchant and his account-keeper factor, the merchant should take custody of the ledger, "and the Journall havyng all thynges agreable therunto, to remain in the others custody whereby there can be no maner of subtletie wrought, of neither part, by any alteracion: for these two bookes ought alwaies to agree, as indentures."

The second treatise of Peele's has in it virtually no echoes of the Paciolian exposition. Nothing included in the body of its text is both surprising as well as being possibly explicable in terms of its inclusion in the treatise of Pacioli or of one of his close successors. The nearest example of a Paciolian echo is to be found near the end of the dialogue between the merchant and the schoolmaster. The schoolmaster remarks: "and accordinge to the proverbe, whear order is not kepte, ther must nedes be confucion." The same feeling is expressed in Paicoli's first chapter, in Latin: *Iuxta comune dictum ubi non est ordo ibi est confusio.* Oldcastle has it in his corresponding chapter as follows: "according to a common saying: Ubi non est ordo, ibi est confusio. Whiche is to meane: there must needes follow much confusion, where is no order."

In general, Peele's books, and much more remarkably *The Pathe waye* of 1569, impress one with the quality of exposition and the clarity and comprehensiveness of the examples. Peele strikes one as an author who by 1569 had mastered his subject, had absorbed the innovations introduced by several of his predecessors, and had reflected profitably on the problems of exposition. *The maner and fourme* is a good work, but has its faults. *The Pathe waye* is much better. One can agree on Kats's opinion that the second book is an important advance, not only on Peele's earlier work, but also on every other book which by then had appeared in print [Kats, 1925–1926, p. 170]. Kats expressed this view before a copy of Weddington's book of 1567 had became accessible for study. Until 1957 the fact of its publication was known only from its inclusion in bibliographical lists. In 1957, however, a copy of the work, the fourth book on accounting to appear in the English language, came to light in the Library of Blairs College, Aberdeen, Scotland [Yamey, 1958, pp. 124–133; Yamey, 1978]. Peele clearly borrowed from Weddington. Weddington advises that, where there are many cash transactions, the cash account in the ledger should not be debited or credited separately for every item, but that the entries should be accumulated in a separate "boke of the pourse." Presumably, totals would be transferred periodically from this book to the cash account in the ledger. If this procedure were not followed you "wolde consume your great boke of marchandize [business ledger] to[o] fast."

In an interesting digression Peele explains how, if the master requires a servant to handle his cash, transactions, the latter can keep a "chest booke." There are two ways of handling the matter in the master's own ledger. In the first method, the master enters all the individual items in the chest book appropriately in the ledger accounts affected, including the cash account. In the second method, the master peruses the chest book daily, and enters the individual items directly in the various ledger accounts, other than the cash account. The master balances the servant's book weekly, but no entry is made in the cash account in the master's ledger until the "closynge up of the Masters booke." Then the balance on the chest book is "to be borne into the ballaunce of the Masters booke on the debitour syde." The pupil had correctly observed of the first method, "Hearein is the Master eased of the payinge and receavinge of the monie but no whit of the writinge." The second method, like Weddington's analogous treatment, also reduces the writing.

That Mellis was a heavy borrower is evident in that part of his book for which he was directly responsible. Therefore, there is a hypothesis that any close correspondences between Mellis and Peele are examples of borrowings by Mellis from Peele rather than of borrowings by Peele from Oldcastle. Nevertheless, it is possible to go well beyond this hypothesis. Examination of some of the correspondences illustrates our thesis: that Mellis must have been the borrower. It is obvious, too, that Mellis was inefficient as an editor or adaptor of Oldcastle's treatise.

4.0 COMPARISON AND EQUIVALENCE: SOME CORRESPONDENCES BETWEEN PEELE AND MELLIS

4.1 The Inventory

Our first example of a correspondence between Peele and Mellis relates to the inventory, and it is particularly instructive.

Pacioli taught that the merchant's inventory should include all his worldly belongings (*cio che se ritrova haver al mondo de mobile e di stabile*), and should begin with those items most costly and most liable to be mislaid or lost. His example of an inventory in the third chapter consequently includes both business and personal assets, and begins with money. No money values are attached to items other than cash and debts.

In his first treatise, *The maner and fourme*, Peele also includes all the merchant's possessions and liabilities in the inventory. For each item a money value is assigned. The liabilities are shown last, as it was in Pacioli, and their total is deducted from the previous subtotal of assets, to yield a final sum: "and the remain is the substaunce of the owner, whiche remain muste in one totall somme, with expresse woordes be set out at large, as in the ende of the Inuentorie, dooeth well appere." In his second book, *The Pathe waye*, Peele organized his bookkeeping in a rather different way. Business assets and transactions are segregated from the owner's private concerns. There are, accordingly, two inventories, two journals and two interconnected ledgers; in this, Peele was almost certainly following a proposal for the preservation of secrecy made by Weddington two years earlier. Peele's first inventory is limited to assets and liabilities in the business, and accordingly is titled:

The Inuentorie of
Employmentes for trafique in mar
chaundies, contayninge readye monie,
detts, & goodes, with the creditors of
that accompte, for so muche by my Master Fraun
cis Ewyford Cittizen and Mercer of Lōdon (as
percell of his stocke generall) cōmitted to
thorder of me Anthony Ryce his ser
vante here in this citie of Lon-
don as followeth

In the text Peele writes:

> and then subtracte the somme totall of the creditours, from the totall somme of money, debtes & goodes, and the remayne is the net substaunce, stocke, or capitall, by the owner putt in trafique of marchaundise.

A separate inventory, referred to in the text as the "inventorie generall," comprehends not only this "saide net rest, or stocke for trafique before spoken of," but also "divers other thinges" including the owner's "landes, rentes, anuities, plate, Jewelles, & readie monie, reserved in his owne proper keping."

We now come to Mellis. In the second chapter Mellis explains that the inventory includes "all his substance moueables and unmoueables, alwayes beginning first at thinges of great valure, as golde, siluer, and iewelles." In the next chapter a specimen inventory is presented, the order of items being the same as in Pacioli's corresponding chapter. Business and personal assets are both included. Money values are attached to cash and debts and, haphazardly, to a few other items, but not, for instance, to the items of merchandise, "grocerie wares." The chapter ends as follows:

> Thē gather together the whole summe of your ready money, debtes and goods, And therefrom Substract the totall summe of your Creditours, and the remaine is the net rest, substance or capitall of the owner to be put in a trafique, & c.

In chapter thirteen, Mellis again used a similar structure of words. He explains that, seemingly after all entries for the opening inventory have been ported to the ledger, the credit balance on the stock or capital account is "the traffique, & c." To arrive at this balance to

> make the summes equall, gather the total hereof [debit entries] in a peece of paper aparte, and subtray it from the totall summe of your Creditor opposite, and the rest is the net substaunce or Capitall of the owner to bee put in traffique & c.

The purpose of the calculation is not clear, but apparently it was intended as a check on the postings to the ledger—since the balance on the stock account should equal that net balance established in the inventory itself. There is no counterpart to this passage in Pacioli. Peele in *The Pathe waye* also has a check on the opening entries in the ledger. A trial balance is drawn up:

> The percelles of the Inuentorie being all thus entered, then for *triall*, whether the debitours, and the creditours be like and of equall ballaunce, or not, you shall *in a paper aparte* adde together all the debitour percelles (that is to saye) the monie debts & goodes, all into one totall somme, and the creditours into an other totall some (the stocke being accompted with the creditours) and if those two sommes be bothe one in totall, then is the *state of thacompte perfectlie ballaunced*, and as before, after a certayne maner, euery debitour hathe his creditour, and euerye creditour his debitour. [emphasis added]

An indirect influence of Peele on Mellis appears to be manifest here. Mellis's exposition is rather clumsy. In addition, it is discussed before the explanation, in the next chapter of the ledger entries for the items of merchandise in the inventory.

It is obvious that Mellis, in his third chapter, having followed a Paciolian model in the main part of it, plausibly reproducing Oldcastle, changed direction towards the quite different treatments of the inventory in Peele, and tacked on to the original some slightly altered and distorted sentences taken from Peele's *The Pathe waye*. Kats noted merely that Mellis grafted this feature of Peele's "rather thoughtlessly, upon the original of 1543" [Kats, 1926, p. 484]. What is correct and proper in Peele would have been incoherent or misleading to readers of Mellis.

It should be noted that Mellis did not use the word "goods" restrictively in the sense of merchandise only. For instance, the opening remarks to the model inventory, in the third chapter, refer to "this my present Inuentorie of all my goods, moueables and immoueables, debts and creditors which I find in this world this foresayde day." Also the heading of chapter fourteen, which deals with the entry into the ledger of the opening items of goods to be traded, reads: "Hovv the parcels of marchandises ought to be entered and written, which by inuentorie or otherwise a man findeth himselfe to haue in the Leager, in the Debitor, and in the Creditor part." The readers, then, would have received little help if they turned to the inventory in the illustrative set of account-books, for the example includes assets employed in "trafique" as well as personal assets such as plate, lands and rents, dwelling house and household stuff. In addition, the order of items does not accord with the order in the text chapter; instead, it follows the order in the example in Peele's *The maner and fourme*. Mellis here calls his inventory the "inventory general," a correct use, obviously taken from Peele's *The Pathe waye*:

Peele
In the name of God. Amen.
1566
December the xxxj. daye.
The Inuentorie ge-
nerall of me Frauncis Twyforde Cit-
tezin and Mercer of London dwellinge
in the parishe of saint Swithens con-
tayninge my whole estate in Landes, Rentes,
Goodes, ready monie, Debtes and Creditours as
well
in myne own custody as also in Trafique of Mar-
chaundies in thorder of my seruante An-
thonie Rice, as by the sayde Inuen-
torie appearethe.

Mellis
In the name of God Amen.
1587
August the viii. day.
The Inuentorie generall of
me N. A. Citizen and N.
of London, dvvelling in the parish
of S Swithins, Contayning my whole
estate generall in lands, rents, goods,
readie money, debtes and Creditors
which I haue in this world
at this present
day.
As by the saide Inuentory particu-
larly appeareth.

4.2 The Rule for Debits and Credits

The second example of a correspondence between Peele and Mellis to be considered here concerns the rule for debits and credits, referred to both by Besta and Kats.

In *The maner and fourme*, Peele writes:

> Then as touchyng the enterying of your Inuentorie, into the Journall, as the order of this accompt requireth, you shall in eche parcell of the said Journall, expresse two denominacions: whereof the first shalbee the name of the Debitour, receivour or borrower, and the other of the Creditour, deliverer, or lender.

One of the canons presented in a piece of verse preceding the model journal elaborates the point:

Rules to be ob-
serued.
Yf that in this accompt, these preceptes ye obserue,
than I you well assure, no part thereof shall swerne.
To make the thinges Receiuyd, or the receiuer,
Debter to the thinges deliuered, or to the deluever.
And to receive before you write, and write before you paye,
So shall no parte of your accompt, in any wyse decaye.
Obserue welthese few rules, your Iournall boke throughout,
So shall you make sure worke, of that you go about.
I.P.

This is the first appearance in the accounting literature of a general rule for determining the accounts to be debited or credited in the recording of a transaction, assuming that it was not already in the lost Oldcastle. The rule appears again in *The Pathe waye*, early in the instructional dialogue between the schoolmaster and his eager "scholler." The schoolmaster says:

> Yt is a certayne rule to be learned by rote, and also by reason, and is to be practised in all causes of entring percelles into the Journal for the moste parte, which being well understanded, is a greate, furtherance to that which is yet to learne, and thus it is. All thinges receaued, or the receauer, must owe to all thinges deliuered, or to the deliuer.

At the pupil's request, the schoolmaster explains the "reason" for the rule. He does this in a longish paragraph, by analyzing a few simple transactions.

The sentences and passages in question are to be found also in Mellis's ninth chapter, which in its title, but not in all its contents, corresponds to Pacioli's tenth chapter. The first part deals with the marking of the journal, the numbering of its leaves, the privacy of the book, and the requirement that journal entries should be "written, ordered and indited in shorter sentence, without superflous words, than be the parcels in y Inuentory or Memorial as hereafter you shal by diuers examples have information." Then follows this passage in Mellis, which is not to be found in Pacioli:

> but first it is to be noted, that yee know the two termes used in the saide Journall after the maner as is used in the same, which as the order of this account requireth, is expressed by *two denominations: to wit, by Debitor, and Creditor*, whereof the first is the name of the Debitor, receiver or borrower; and the other of the Creditor, deliverer, or lender. To the furtherance whereof there is a Rule, which beeing well understood, will aide you greatly: which Rule is to bee learned as well by rote, as by reason, which is thus.
>
> *All thinges receiuved, or the receiuer mus owe to all thinges deliuered, or to the deliuerer.* [emphasis added]

As in Peele's *The Pathe waye*, the rule is printed in roman type, as distinct from the black-letter type which is otherwise used. After the rule comes a paragraph which is almost identical to Peele's explanation of the rule, the main distinction being that different proper names are used:

Peele	*Mellis*
As for example, Imagine that you haue bought clothes of william Jones, then to obserue the rule, you must enter the percell in your Journall sayinge, Clothes oweth to william Jones. & c. Yf you receaue monie of anye man, accordinge to the same rule you must saye, Monie oweth to Frauncis Taillor. & c. and hereby it apperes in that parte, howe the same rule is obserued, contrariewise if you sell goodes, or paye monie to anye, then to the obseruinge of the same rule, you shall saye, william Thomsone & c. oweth to clothes, or Jhon Ball & c. oweth to monye.	As for example: imagine you haue bought clothes of Thomas Long, then to obserue the Rule, you must enter the parcel into the Journall, saying: Clothes oweth to Thomas Long, & C. If you receiue money of any man: according to the same Rule you must say, money oweth to William Hall, & c. And hereby appeareth that part, how the same Rule is obserued. Contrariwise, if you sell goods, or pay money to any: Then to the obseruing of the same rule, you shal say, Henry Par, & c. oweth to clothes. Or James Welch oweth to money & c.

It is obvious that Mellis, when working from Oldcastle's Paciolian text, decided at this point to "bewtify" the original, and he did so by appropriating and cobbling together a piece from each of Peele's two works.

Pacioli's tenth chapter ends with a reference to *doi termini* (two terms) used in the Venetian journal: *doi termini che in ditto giornale si costuma vsare nela cita maxime excelsa de Vinegia. Di qualli immediate diremo.* The eleventh chapter explains that these two terms are "Per" and "A" to denote respectively the debtor and the creditor involved in each transaction recorded in the journal: *Per lo. Per. sempre se dinota el debitore. o vno o piu che se siẽno. E per lo. A. se dinota lo creditore o vno o piu che se siẽno* [Yamey, 1976, pp. 156–61; Yamey, 1978].

Mellis did not use this terminology in his journal entries. Occasionally Mellis seems to have forgotten to remove all traces of the Venetian form of entry; this is the case in chapter fifteen: "How ye shal order in your bookes the parcelles of voiages in your owne handes, or else in the guyding of another, as factor. by commision"; chapter sixteen: "The manner of the keeping of the famous accompt of companie, how it ought to bee ordered in al the 3 bookes"; and chapter twenty-three: "The manner to know and hold the accompt of a retayling shoppe in your owne hand, or else in the charge of another person." However, there is no chapter in his book corresponding to Pacioli's eleventh chapter: *Deli doi termini nel ditto giornale vsitati maxime ī venetia: luno ditto Per: laltro ditto. A e quello che per loro se habia a denotare.*

If we go back to the quotation in Mellis which is not to be found in Pacioli, we have to note that the first twenty-seven words in the paragraph are derived from Pacioli or from a Paciolian model. Then the "two terms" corresponding to Pacioli's *doi termini* become the quite different "two denominations" of the earlier Peele, and the passage from Peele is rendered less comprehensible by the gratuitous insertion of the words "to wit, by debitor and creditor". It is gratuitous and misleading, since the two terms "debitor" and "creditor" do not both appear in journal entries in Venetian practice, in Pacioli or indeed in Mellis. Surprisingly, the words "to wit, Debitor and Creditor" appear also in the heading of Mellis's chapter ten: "Of the manner of knovvledge, the enditing of parcelles into the Iournal, as well the Debitor, as the Creditor, and of the two other termes vsed in the Leager: whereof one is named capsa, and that other Capitali, and what by them is to be vnderstoode, to wit, Debitor and Creditor." This chapter is close to Pacioli's chapter twelve: *Del modo a saper ponere e dittare le ptitte ī lo giornale del dare e del auere cō molti exempli: e de li doi altri termini nel quaderno usitati luno detto Cassa e laltro Cauedale: e quello che per essi se habia intendere.* The Mellis *capsa* appears to be a misreading of *cassa* (cash) in the original, whether a manuscript or Pacioli. The last five words in Mellis appear to be an innovation by Mellis, or perhaps by Oldcastle. It is unskilled. The text of the chapter both in Pacioli and Mellis makes it clear that "cash" is not to be understood as "debitor," but as "the chyst" or ready money. Rather, it is said that the cash account in the ledger should always have a debit balance (or zero balance), and could not be in credit. The explanation of "capital" is as follows in Mellis:

> and by Capitall is understoode the substance of a mans goods, or his stocke, which stocke shal alwayes bee Creditor, aswell in your Journall, as in your Leager …

We wonder what the reader would have made of this prescription. The corresponding passage in Pacioli is also cryptic. At this point, after having inexpertly grafted a bit of the earlier Peele on to the Venetian or Paciolian body, Mellis switched over to the later Peele, and took from it material for a long passage, including a substantial passage with essentially no alteration.

4.3 The Ruling of Account-Books

The third example of close correspondence between Peele and Mellis to be examined here is about illustrative account-book rulings.

In Peele's *The Pathe waye* the sample rulings appear early in the dialogue between the schoolmaster and his pupil, who, as apprentice ("couenaunte seruaunt") to a merchant ("for smale wages, but in hope of good preferment and creadite, having as yet very little of myne owne, and therefore haue thoughte it so best"), had some familiarity with counting-house matters. The teacher briefly describes the various account-books to be kept, and explains that the inventory and the memorial "shall not nede to be ruled." He then, for practical purposes, shows the pupil sample rulings. In the book these take up the next three pages, which are introduced by this rubric:

> This page cominge next, declareth howe eureye leafe,
> and side in the Journal must be ruled, an the other two sides
> folowinge, declare howe every face of accompte in the leager or greate
> booke (lyinge open) shall be ruled, the one for the dibitour
> side, and the other for the creditour.

The scholar, having said that "This I haue perused, & understand you verie well," is asked to "utter unto me howe you understand of the same." Then he explains the purpose of the various spaces into which the ruled pages are divided. Thus the introduction to the subject, the demonstration and the explanation are developed consistently and clearly.

In Mellis, the sample ruled pages come abruptly at the end of the twelfth chapter. There is no introduction to these pages, which in essentials as well as in most of the detail are the same as in Peele. They come after the rulings of both journal and ledger have been described in words in chapters nine and eleven; after sample entries in the journal have been presented in chapter ten; and after having given an account "Of the vvay and manner of bringing the parcels out of the Iournal into the Leager, and why one parcell in the Iournall maketh two in the Leager, and the maner of striking out the parcels of the Iournall, and of the two numbers of the leaues of the Leager that bee set in the margent of the Iournal, and wherfore" (chapter twelve). The only novelty in Mellis's sample pages is the inclusion of a specimen index to the ledger, with four specimen entries in it. This specimen index extends to four pages. It has no heading or introduction. In addition, there are no cross-references in these pages to any of the samples in the chapters dealing with the rulings of the various account-books or with the index (eleventh and thirteenth chapter).

It is clear from their placing and the lack of integration with the rest of the text that the sample ruled pages were added by Mellis to an existing expository text. It is also clear that Mellis had taken the new material from Peele.

Besta was interested in the terminology used by Mellis/Oldcastle. In particular, he noted the absence of the terms "Per" and "A," or their English equivalents, in the journal entries. Also, he observed that while in Pacioli the two sides of a ledger account were expressed by the words *deve (devone) dare* (must give) and *deve (devono) avere* (must have), in Oldcastle they were distinguished by the titles "debitor side" and "creditor side," respectively. As to the latter, Besta was mistaken. For the headings "debitor side" and "creditor side" are not, as he thought, integral parts of an actual ledger opening, but are, instead, no more than descriptive headings to the sample rulings borrowed by Mellis from Peele.

However, Besta's discussion is relevant to the main theme of this paper. He pointed out that these differences between Pacioli and Oldcastle were alterations made by Oldcastle and constituted the original part of Oldcastle's work, and that Oldcastle in the frontispiece of his work had referred specifically to the fact that he was introducing some modifications [Besta,

1929, pp. 371–372]. Again, Besta was mistaken. The only prologue in the Mellis book is signed by Mellis himself, and the modifications referred to are clearly those made by Mellis to Oldcastle:

> for such persons as are disposed to learne the same, here ensueth sufficient Cannons and rules whereby a diligent Learner may attayne his desire which rules in diuers places, I haue bewtified and enlarged according to my simple knowledge.

It is more interesting however, that Besta should have made the point that Oldcastle had made amendments to the presumed Venetian manuscript which he was supposed to be translating. For once it is admitted that parts of Oldcastle's text may be Oldcastle's own original contributions, the text cannot be relied on in any part as being a translation or faithful rendering of the hypothesized manuscript. Therefore, no observed differences between Pacioli and Oldcastle/Mellis can support Besta's presumption that both Pacioli and Oldcastle worked from the same presumed manuscript, but that the latter did so more closely than the former. Oddly enough, correspondences between Pacioli and Oldcastle provide stronger support for a speculation of their dependence on a common source, but of course these numerous and pervading correspondences also support the much more credible assumption that it was the Pacioli printed text which Oldcastle used as his model.

4.4 Peele's *The maner and fourme*

The fourth example of a correspondence between Peele and Mellis to be considered here involves Peele's *The maner and fourme* and it has to do with partnership accounts.

Pacioli's twenty first chapter deals with *De laltra partitta famosa ditta Compagnie: commo se debino ordinare: e dittare in tutti li modi ocurrenti in ciascuno libro*; that is, the accounts to be kept for a partnership. Mellis's sixteenth chapter treats the same subject, under a similar heading: "The manner of the keeping of the famous accompt of companie, how it ought to bee ordered in al the 3 bookes." Pacioli explains that the partner in question can keep the partnership accounts in his own books, or that a separate set of books can be opened. Mellis also deals with the two works. Kats overstated the similarities when he wrote that Mellis here "compares closely with the Italian tract" of Pacioli [Kats, 1926, p. 585]. In one paragraph Oldcastle or more likely Mellis, misunderstood the original, and the assets introduced by the other partners to the joint venture are debited to the "stocke of the companie." Pacioli's exposition in his chapter is by no means clear, and neither is Mellis's.

Peele examined partnership or joint-venture accounts in the tenth (misnumbered eleventh) chapter of his *The maner and fourme*. He seems to have done this as an afterthought, in a chapter which refers to the opening of a new journal to replace the one completed. He explains "the maner howe to charge or discharge your bookes in any accōpt, partable for vyages or otherwyse by compacte." A "partable" account is opened and debited/credited for assets disposed of/received on partnership business. He explains that each partner should have such an account in his own ledger. In addition, he continues with his explanation in a long passage, which also appears, as the concluding paragraph, in Mellis's chapter, introduced only by the word "item." There are some small changes in wording; the wholly unhelpful and confusing omission of twenty words; and the characteristic addition of the symbol "&c" after the concluding word "gaine":

Peele	*Mellis*
... it is needefull that euery partener doo keepe thereof a Jornall and quaterne, declaryng therby howe thynges have passed or chaunced in tyme of that theyr *partable accompt,* wherein they must fyrst make an Iuentory, declaryng what eche man dooth put in. Then entre into theyre *Jornall,* makying eche thyng debitor to theyr partable stocke and bear the parcelles into their great booke of that compact, as you haue in this ordre before bene instructed. And then as the reste of your occupyeng in the sayd accompt chaunceth, so ordre your bookes. And at your viages returne or ende of your compactes, ballance up the bookes. And your parte therein as well as that you put in as your gaynes, beare into *the Jornall of your principall accompt,* be it money wares or debtes, and *make it debitor to the partable accompte, as is in the second parcell* bearyng it to your greate booke, whereon the creditour syde of partable accompt you shall fynde your principall answered with a gayne.[2] [emphasis added]	Item it is necessary that euery partner doe keepe thereof a Journall and Leager, declaring thereby how thinges have passed or chaunced in time of that partible accompte, making each thing Debitor to their partible stocke, and beare the parcels into the greate booke of that accompt, as I have before instructed you. And as the rest of your occupying in the said accompt chaunceth, so order your bookes: and at your viages returne, or end of your compacts, ballance up the books, and your part there as well that you put in as you gaines: beare into the Journal of your principall accompt, be it money, wares, or deptes, & c. and make it Debitor to the partible accompt, as in the second parcel, bearing it to your great booke: where on the Creditor syde of partible accompt you shall finde your principall answeared with a gaine, & c.

As Kats had noted, Mellis refers in his paragraph to the "second parcel": he slavishly followed Peele, in a manner which must have puzzled his readers, since in the illustrative journal in Mellis the entries are not numbered as they are in Peele, and there is no entry in Mellis's journal involving a partable account. Mellis's borrowing from Peele is evident here in other ways too. Thus it is only in the final paragraph of his partnership chapter that he uses the word "partable" rather than "company," or refers to voyage in connection with partnership.

5.0 PEELE'S IMPACT ON MELLIS

In two examples, chapter headings in Mellis closely remind one of the corresponding headings in Pacioli, and in each case includes a reference to a matter not discussed in the chapter itself.

The first is Mellis's twelfth chapter: "Of the way and manner of bringing the parcels out of the Iournal into the Leager, and why one parcell in the Iournal maketh two in the Leager, and the maner of striking out the parcels of the Iournall, and of the two numbers of the leaues of the Leager that bee set in the margent of the Iournal, and wherfore." This chapter deals primarily with the posting of entries from the journal to the ledger. Pacioli, in his fourteenth chapter: *Del modo a portare le ptite del giornale in q̃derno: e p che de vna ĩ giornale se ne facia doi in q̃derno: e del modo a depennare le partite in giornale e de li doi numeri de le carti del quaderno che in le sue margine si pone: e p che*, instructs how the journal entry is to be cancelled when it is posted: two transverse lines are to be drawn across the narration section of the journal, one for the posting to the debit of a ledger account, and the other for that to the credit of an account. This Venetian practice is not included in Mellis. The heading of the chapter, however, contains the words "and the maner of striking out the parcels of the Iournall," in Pacioli: *e del modo a depennare le partite in giornale.*

The second instance is Mellis's twenty-first chapter: "Hovv to make the balance of the booke, and the manner of the examinatiō of the old Leager for the concordãce of the new. And the manner of examination by pricks, and perusing with the Memoriall, Iournall, and Leager," which deals primarily with the calling-over and "pricking" of the ledger entries against the journal entries preparatory to the balancing of the books. In his thirty-second chapter: *Commo se debia fare el bilancio del libro e del modo a reportare vn libro in laltro: cioe el q̃derno vechio nel q̃derno nuouo e del modo a pontarlo con lo suo giornale e memoriale e altri scontridẽtro e difuor del ditto quaderno,* Pacioli concludes with the observation that the ledger entries should also be checked against the memorial and any other books kept. Mellis does not have this observation. However, as in Pacioli, the chapter heading includes the following: "And the manner of examination by pricks, and perusing with the Memoriall, Iournall, and the Leager."

This is an indication of negligent editing. More to the point, it suggests the influence of Peele, for Peele's works discuss neither the cancellation of posted journal entries nor the checking of the ledger against records other than the journal. It is possible that Mellis followed Peele's example in omitting references to these two practices, but failed to modify the Paciolian chapter headings consequentially. Although these omissions are about minor matters, they serve us by providing some further endorsement for the main points of this paper, that is that Mellis was influenced by Peele when revising the Oldcastle text, and that he was a poor editor or improver. At times, however, the corresponding chapter headings in Pacioli and Mellis both announce something which is not done in the chapter. For example, the headings of Pacioli's chapter thirteen: *Del terço e vltimo libro principate mercantesco detto el q̃derno commo debbe esser fatto e del suo alfabeto cõmo se debbia ordinare vgniolo e dopio,*" and Mellis's chapter eleven: "Of the last and thirde principall booke, called the Leager, and how it ought to be made & ordered, and of his Calender single and double," both promise to tell us how the index to the ledger can be made single or double. The double index is not described in either book.

6.0 CONCLUSION

In general, Mellis took liberally from Peele. The detectable resulting changes made to the Oldcastle text are significant. We must assume that Mellis made other changes as well. The Mellis edition of 1588 is therefore not to be considered as an even roughly faithful copy of the Oldcastle text. It is paradoxical, in the light of Besta's theory, to suggest that it might well be that the Mellis text is closest to the lost original Oldcastle only in those passages where it is closest to the Pacioli text. This is so, because differences between Pacioli and Mellis may have a far easier justification than that announced by Besta. They may be changes made by Mellis himself. After all, Robert Colinson [1683] was right when he wrote his *Idea Rationaria*, almost a century after Mellis's book and said: "The Art of Book-Keeping is the very Scale of Commerce .... It is a science absolutely necessarie for all Accomptants."

ENDNOTES

1 Penndorf [1933, pp. 63–68]; Melis [1950, pp. 620–23]; Antinori [1959, pp. 7–10]; Antoni [1970, pp. 87–88]; Yamey, *et al.* [1963, pp. 155–159]; Yamey [1967, pp. 64–68]; Yamey [1978].

2 "partable accompt" means here partnership business; "Jornall": the partnership journal; "the Jornall of your principall accompt": your own journal; "make it debitor to the partable acompte, as in the second parcell" [in the illustrative journal].

REFERENCES

Antinori, C. *Luca Pacioli: Summa di Arithmetica ....* Milan, 1959.

Antoni, T. *Fabio Besta.* Pisa, 1970.

Besta, F. (a), *Rivista dei Ragionieri,* Vol. 9, No. 4.

Besta, F. *La Ragioneria,* Second Edition (Milan, 1929).

Ceccherelli, A. *I Libri di Mercatura della Banca Medici e l'Applicazione della Partita Doppia a Firenze nel Secolo Decimoquarto* (Florence, 1913).

Colinson, Robert. *Idea rationaria, or The Perfect accomptant, necessary for all merchants and traffiquers; containing the true forme of book-keeping, according to the Italian methode ...* (Edinburgh: D. Lindsay, 1683).

Fogo, J. Row. "History of Bookkeeping," in Richard Brown, *A History of Accounting and Accountants* (Edinburgh: T.C. & E.C. Jack, 1905).

Geijsbeek, John B. *Ancient Double-Entry Bookkeeping.* Lucas Pacioli's Treatise (A.D. 1494—the earliest known writer on bookkeeping) (Houston, TX: Scholars Book Co., 1914).

Kats, P. "De Invloed der Nederlanders der 16de en 17de Eeuw op de Engelsche Literatur van het Boekhounden," *Maandblad voor het Boekhounden,* Vol. 32, No. 5 (1925–1926), pp. 168–176.

———. "Hugh Oldcastle and John Mellis," *The Accountant* (March 27, 1926), pp. 483–487; (May 1, 1926), pp. 641–648.

———. (1927), "The 'Nouuelle Instruction' of Jehan Ympyn Christophle," *The Accountant* (August 20, 1927), pp. 261–269; (August 27, 1927), pp. 287–296.

Manzoni, Dominico. *Quaderno doppio col suo giornale, novamente composto, & diligentissimamente ordinato, secondo* il costume di Venetia. Opera a Ogni Persona vtilissima, & molto necessaria. Di Dominico Manzoni Opitergiense. Cvm Gratia et Privilegio del Illustrissimo Senato di Venetia, per Anni diece. MDXXXX. Qui Se Hvmiliat Exaltabitur, 1540.

Melis, F. *Storia della ragioneria; contributo alla conoscenza e interpretatione delle fonti pi_ significative della storia economica* (Bologna, 1950).

Mellis, J. *A briefe instruction and maner to keepe bookes of accompts after the order of Debitor and Creditor, and as well for proper accompts partible, & c.* By the three bookes named the

Memoriall Iournall & Leaguer, and of other necessaries appertaining to a good and diligent marchant. The which of all other reckoninges is most lawdable for this treatise well and sufficiently knowen, all other wayes and maners may be the easier & sooner discerned, learned and knowen. Newly augmented and set forth by John Mellis Scholemaister. 1588. Imprinted at London by Iohn Windet, dwelling at the signe of the white Beare, nigh Baynards Castle.

———. *A Short and Plaine Treatise of Arithmeticke in whole numbers, comprised into a briefer method than hetherto hath bin published*. Adioyned to this small Treatise for the ayde of Leaners. By Iohn Mellis Schoolemaster. Anno Domini, 1588.

Oldcastle, Hugh. *A Profitable Treatyce called the Instrument or Boke to learne to knowe the good order of the kepyng of the famouse reconynge called in Latin, Dare and Habere, and in Englyshe, Debitor and Creditor* (London: John Gough, 1543).

Pacioli, Luca. *Summa de arithmetica, geometria, proportioni et proportionalità*, "Particularis de computis et scripturis," Frater Lucas de Burgo Sancti Sepulchri, Ordinis Minorum et sacre theologie magister, in arte arithmetice et geometrie. Vinegia: Paganino de Paganinis, 1494. (Part I, Section 9, Treatise 11).

Peele, James. *The maner and fourme how to kepe a pefecte reconyng, after the order of the moste worthie and notable accompte, of Debitour and Creditour*, set foorthe in certain tables, with a declaration therunto belongyng, verie easie to be learned, and also profitable, not onely unto suche, that trade in the facte of Marchaundise, but also unto any other estate, that will learne the same. Imprinted at London, by Richard Grafton, printer to the kinges Maiestie. Cum priuilegio ad imprimendum solum, 1553.

———. Fame do the for aye: Eche vertue displaye. *The Pathe waye to perfectness, in th'accomptes of Debitour, and Creditour*: in manner of a Dialogue, very pleasaunte and proffitable for Marchauntes and all oth' that minde to frequente the same: once agayne set forthe, and verie muche enlarged. By Iames Peele Citizen and Salter of London, Clercke of Christes Hospitall, practizer and teacher of the same. Imprinted at London in Paules Churchyarde. By Thomas Purfoote, dwellinge at the signe of the Lucrece. 16. August. Wisdome and Science Preuent Indigence. Practice procuereth perfection: Ia. Peele, 1569.

Penndorf, B. *Geschichte der Buchhaltung in Deutschland* (Leipzig, 1930).

———. *Luca Pacioli: Abhandlung über die Buchhaltung 1494* (Stuttgart, 1933).

Recorde, Robert. *Records Arithmetick*: or The grounde of artes: teaching the perfecte worke and practise of arithmetike, both in whole nubers and fractions, after a more easie and exact forme the in former time hath been set forth: Afterward, augmented by M. Iohn Dee. And now lately … corrected … with some newe rules and necessarie additions: And further endowed with a thirde part of Rules of practize, abridged into a briefer methode than hitherto hath bene published … By Iohn Mellis …. [London] Imprinted by I. Harrison, and H. Bynneman, 1582.

Weddington, John. A *Breffe Instruction, and Manner, Howe to Kepe, Marchantes Bokes, of Accomptes After the order of Debitor and Creditor*, as well for proper accomptes, partable, factory, and other & c. Verry nedefull to be knowen, and usid of all men, in the feattis of marchandize. Nowe of late newly, set forthe, and practisyd, by Johan Weddington Cytizen of London. MDLXVII. The trewthe sekethe no corners. Prenttyd in Andwarpe, by Petter van Keerberghen, dwellinge by owre Lady Charche, at the signe of the golden Sonne, 1567.

Woolf, Arthur H. *A Short History of Accountants and Accountancy* (London: Gee & Co. (Publishers) Ltd., 1913).

Yamey, B. S. "John Weddington's 'A Breffe Instruction,' 1567," *Accounting Research,* Vol. 9 (1958), pp. 124–133.

Yamey, B. S., H. C. Edey and H. W. Thomson. *Accounting in England and Scotland: 1543–1800. Double Entry in Exposition and Practice* (London: Sweet & Maxwell, 1963).

Yamey, B. S. "Fifteenth and Sixteenth Century Manuscripts on the Art of Bookkeeping," *Journal of Accounting Research,* Vol 5 (1967), pp. 64–68.

———. "Two Typographical Ambigüities in Pacioli's 'Summa' and the Difficulties of Its Translators," *Gutenberg-Jahrbuch* (1976), pp. 156–61.

———. *Essays on the History of Accounting* (New York: Arno Press, 1978).

Ympyn Christoffels, Ian. *Nieuwe instructie Ende bewijs der looffelijcker Consten des Rekenboecks, ende Rekenninghe te houdene nae die Italiaensche maniere,* allen Cooplie den, Rentmeesteren ..., Jan ympyn Christoffels ... Antwerpen, Gillis Copyns van Diest voor Anna Swinters, 1543.

———. *A notable and very excellente woorke expressing and declaryng the maner and forme how to kepe a boke of accōptes or reconynges,* verie expedient and necessary to all Marchantes, Receiuers, Auditors, Notaries and all other. Translated with greate diligence out of the Italian toung into Dutche and out of Dutche, into French, and now out of Frenche into Englishe, 1547.

This appendix contains abstracts of all papers presented to the 7th World Congress of Accounting Historians, Queens University, Kingston, ON, August 11–13, 1996.

Abstracts

AN HISTORICAL PERSPECTIVE ON FRAUDULENT FINANCIAL REPORTING IN THE UNITED STATES

M. J. Abdolmohammadi, Bentley College, Massachusetts
Paul J. McMann, Boston University
Mai E. Iskandar, Northern Illinois University

Detection of fraudulent financial reporting (FFR) was part of the responsibility of auditors in early years of audit practice in the United States. However, as the complexity of the business entities increased through mergers and acquisitions and as auditing formally became a profession, detection of FFR was pushed aside from the auditors' responsibility. This phenomenon has cost the profession dearly in terms of reduced credibility and heavy monetary losses in a number of scandalous audit failure cases involving FFR in the last three decades. This papers provides an historical perspective on FFR by critically reviewing the literature. In addition, several strategies are suggested for consideration in dealing with FFR.

THE DEMISE OF THE COST ACCOUNTING PROFESSION IN AUSTRALASIA

Ray H. Anderson, Victoria University of Technology, Australia

This paper traces the history of the Australasian Institute of Cost Accountants. This body was formed in 1921, following establishment of similar bodies overseas. Its formation reflected a desire by practising cost accountants in Australia and New Zealand to have a professional body catering exclusively for their interests.

Its early years were difficult, with lack of recognition within the profession and industry. Following reorganization, an active promotion program was undertaken, although the professional accountancy bodies refused to grant it equal status. By the mid-1930s, the Institute faced threats of a competing body being created by the Commonwealth Institute of Accountants, a reflection of disharmony within the profession.

The outbreak of World War II and associated growth in manufacturing, heralded an era of growth in membership for the Institute and the formation of a New Zealand body reflecting the emerging national identity within that country and greater professional standing. In Australia, professional disharmony still existed, and ultimately under the guise of unification of the profession, the Cost Institute was affiliated and then integrated into the Society of Accountants. A similar process occurred in New Zealand on the grounds of enhancing services provided to members. The actions taken in each country are believed to have been detrimental to the cost (management) accounting branch of the profession and each respective country.

DOUBLE-ENTRY BOOKKEEPING APPLIED TO ACCOUNTING IN THE *HACIENDADE BIENES DE DIFUNTOS EN INDIAS* DURING THE SIXTEENTH AND SEVENTEENTH CENTURIES

Rafael Donoso Anes, University of Seville, Spain

In 1510, when the second regulation for the *Casa de la Contratacion de Indias de Sevilla* was passed, accounting regulations were established for the administration and control of the belongings of the citizens who died in the *Indias* or in the journey to or from them. A "*Libro de cargo y data*" was a ledger kept in the same style as the book used to account for the transactions in the *Real Hacienda,* in which the origin and destination of the goods should be registered.

Consequently, accounting for the goods belonging to the dead experienced a similar development to that of the accounting for the *Real Hacienda.* As early as in 1550 the double-entry accounting system was used (method of the *Libro de Caxa y Manual*). There was a strong reason for its implementation: the administration of the goods required a strict control of the debit balances of the accounts assigned to the owners of the goods accounted for.

This paper presents a summarized analysis of the development of the accounting system as well as of the accounting practices resulting from the implementation of the double-entry bookkeeping system.

HOW TO STIMULATE ACCOUNTING STUDENTS WITH EXAMPLES FROM AMERICAN HISTORY

Robert Bloom, John Carroll University, Ohio
Jayne Fuglister, Cleveland State University, Ohio

This paper provides several ideas on incorporating history into accounting courses. These ideas include the use of:

- oral history projects and videotapes
- examples of accounting records in early American history
- examples of early annual reports.

PREINREICH'S CONTRIBUTIONS TO ACCOUNTING THEORY

Richard P. Brief, New York University

While names like Canning, Hatfield, Littleton, Paton and other early writers are well-known, Preinrich, who should be recognized as an important accounting theorist, has not achieved similar status. His work on goodwill and valuation models is the foundation for an important area of current-day research. He also made significant contributions to depreciation theory. The bibliography at the end of this paper contains an impressive list of publications on these and other subjects.

Why hasn't Preinrich been given greater recognition? His contemporaries might have viewed him an outsider; he was a sole practitioner and not a member of the academic community. Also, his research was based on mathematical models applied to accounting, economic and financial problems, and this kind of work did not appear in accounting literature until the 1960s and 1970s. Too, Preinreich often was extremely critical of others and this behaviour probably did not increase his popularity. But what about the present? Why isn't Preinreich better known today?

ENVIRONMENTAL PERFORMANCE, LEGISLATION AND ANNUAL REPORT DISCLOSURE: THE CASE OF ACID RAIN AND FALCONBRIDGE

Nola Buhr, Binghamton University, New York

This paper examines the relationship between environmental performance, legislation and annual report disclosure in an exploratory manner using the case of Falconbridge and sulphur dioxide emissions over a period from 1964 to 1991. Legitimacy theory and the political economy of accounting theory are used as a theoretical basis to examine corporate performance and the disclosure presenting that performance. Two key questions are addressed:

- How did the corporation respond to changing government regulations for sulphur dioxide abatement?
- How did the corporation choose to present these abatement activities in its annual reports?

These questions are examined through the methodologies of historiography, interviews and content analysis. Falconbridge has always been in compliance with sulphur dioxide regulations (albeit with a government extension in the late 1970s) and has consistently provided disclosure discussing the technological aspects of sulphur dioxide abatement. However, economic discussions presented in the 1970s were largely replaced with political discussions in the 1980s. Throughout the entire time period very little disclosure focused on the social issues of sulphur dioxide abatement.

BARRIERS TO ENTRY — AN ECONOMIST'S APPROACH TO THE EXPERIENCE OF WOMEN IN US PUBLIC ACCOUNTING

Anne Bunton, Cottey College, Missouri

This study offers an economic model to explain the historical experience of women in public accounting in the United States. Barriers to entry by female workers into a male-dominated profession can be optimal for the dominant male group; changes in the economic environment bring about a response in those behaviors through changes in optimization. It is proposed that the experience of women in the accounting profession may be explained by examining the self-interested choices of men in the profession. This case study of the accounting profession and the activities of the professional groups and organizational structure associated with that profession examines the motives of groups of male accountants and specifies the mechanisms by which these groups imposed barriers to entry of women into the profession.

Qualitative archival data from the period 1880–1965 supports the hypothesis that the principal architects of barriers to entry were the Big Eight public accounting firms. They accomplished the exclusion of women from accounting positions by coordinating a policy of refusal to hire women into positions for which they were qualified as long as there were qualified males to fill the positions. Large firms also coordinated a policy of hiring women into low skilled jobs where they were complementary with high skilled male accountants because it was beneficial to male partners in the firms. Occupational segregation occurred within firms by skill and among firms by size and was the result of a deliberate and coordinated policy of exclusion of women from high skilled jobs with large firms.

Increasing demand for accounting services during World War II combined with decreasing supply of male accountants to provide a change in the economic environment such that large public accounting firms reversed their stance and began to hire women because the opportunity cost of not doing so became too high. Women hired by large public accounting firms were paid lower wages for the same work as men, or they were required to be more highly qualified than men for the same job. The mechanism used by employers was occupational segregation of women into lower skilled job titles even if they were performing high-skilled work. When the supply of male accountants began to increase after the end of the Second World War, women found their position in the profession more difficult to protect, as it became less beneficial to the controlling male group to hire them into high skilled positions.

The model used in this study predicts the treatment of women accountants found in the historical accounts. The study proposed to find out whether there truly is evidence in the public accounting profession of male collusion to benefit professionally at the expense of females. The study represents an advance in accounting history in that it seeks an economic analysis of women's documented historical experience in the profession.

ACCOUNTING CHANGE AND MANAGEMENT CONTROL: EVIDENCE FROM EIGHTEENTH CENTURY SPAIN

Salvador Carmona, Universidad Carlos III de Madrid, Spain
Mahmoud Ezzamel, University of Manchester Institute of Science and Technology
Fernando Gutierrez, Universidad de Sevilla, Spain

This paper draws upon original archival evidence (Archive de Tabacalera, SA) during the period 1758–1780 in Spain to examine the complex relationship between changes in factory premises and changes in accounting system design. The archival evidence relates to the operation of the Royal Tobacco Factory (RTF) in Seville, and the period of study covers the last year of operation in the Old Factory (San Pedro) and the early years of operation in the New Factories (Nuevas Fabricas). The paper is initially informed by the institutional theory perspective developed by Fligstein (1990) who views conceptions of control as totalizing world views that cause actors to interpret the situations they face from a given perspective, with the aim of controlling, or at least mediating, their internal and external environments. Using this basic framework Fligstein develops a typology comprising four conceptions of control:

- the direct conception (which seeks to reduce competition)
- the manufacturing conception (which aims to stablize production processes and create oligopolistic pricing conditions)
- the sales and marketing conception (which focuses on finding/creating and keeping markets)
- the finance conception (which emphasizes control through financial measures based on profit rates).

We utilize the archival material to shed further light on Fligstein's control typology. The size (space) of the New Factories of the TRF was 2 1/2 times that of the Old Factory. The RTF received cash from the *Direction General de la Renta* and this was recorded via a single-entry bookkeeping system called *cargo* and *data* (charge and discharge). In addition, the accounting system reported on raw materials, work in-progress and finished goods , as well as payrolls and other "direct" and "indirect" overheads. The accounting system in the RTF operated on the basis of a number of series, each containing specific details of how to account for a particular transaction/activity. Before 1760, 31 accounting series were used in the RTF (while being located in the Old Factory). Two decades later, 87 new series were launched while four of the old series were eliminated. A new accounting series was typically initiated by the *Direction General de la Renta*. The development of these new accounting series can be linked to attempts by the *Direction General de la Renta* and the management of the RTF to improve work discipline and control. The paper seeks to explore the extent to which the move to the large premises of the New Factories made possible the development of new accounting series, or whether the pressure for larger factory premises was exerted by knowledge of accounting techniques whose implementation required new premises.

The paper goes on to suggest that, given the archival evidence, the management of the RTF developed a manufacturing conception of control which engendered stability in its organizational field. This conception of control was deployed by the management of the RTF to demonstrate to the *Direction General de la Renta* that management had expert knowledge in the tobacco business that made possible the securing of high levels of income for the Royal Treasury. Moreover, the manufacturing conception of control made it possible for the RTF, as the sole authorized producer of tobacco in Spain, to create significant entry barriers which sustained the monopoly for a long period.

THE EVOLUTION OF MANAGEMENT CONTROL AND NATIONAL CULTURE

Giuseppe Catturi, Vice-President of the Italian Society of Accounting History
Angelo Riccaboni, Member of the Steering Committee of the Italian Society of Accounting History

This paper analyzes the relationship existing in Italy between anthropological culture, corporate culture, goals being pursued and the control systems used.

It is divided into three parts. In the first one, the problem is faced from a general point of view. In order to explain such a relationship, a helicoidal pattern is proposed. The evolution of the main accounting concepts in Italy is described, considering seven phases. Attention is particularly given to the evolution of double-entry bookkeeping and to the present need for wider accounting information, taking into consideration also environmental and ethical issues.

In the second part, the analysis focuses on the evolution of management control in Italian literature, with reference to the last four phases. A strong relationship with the evolution of national culture emerges.

The use of management accounting instruments in the Italian firms is the topic of the third part of this paper. The results of some field studies on the "best practice" are considered, together with those of a survey on small and middle-sized firms and some considerations on a sector typically characterized by poor management control systems.

Finally, some conclusions are drawn on the existence of the relationship being studied, and on the need for further research on management control in the small and medium-sized firms.

LUCA PACIOLI'S *TRACTATUS MATHEMATICUS AD DISCIPULOS PERUSINOS*

Gianfranco Cavazzoni, University of Perugia, Italy

The aim of the paper is to investigate the origins and the content of Luca Pacioli's *Tractatus Mathematicus ad discipulos Perusinos* and its effects on the later *Summa*.

The work is divided into 17 parts. It contains elements of pure maths and its application to the different problems which may occur to the merchant. The treatise can be divided into two main parts: in the first one, Pacioli deals with business mathematics in order to teach how to count; in the second part, the author investigates mathematics and geometry referring, whenever it is possible, to merchants' activities.

As far as the contents of the *Summa* are concerned, it's possible to notice that most of them are taken from the treatise Pacioli had written in Perugia before. The discovery in the *Tractatus mathematicus ad discipulos perusinos* (issued 16 years before the publication of the *Summa*) of many subjects developed in the *Summa* itself, allows to date Pacioli's intuitions back to a previous period and to discharge him of some accusations of plagiarism.

COLONIALISM, CLOSURE, AND DISTANCE: AN EPISODE FROM AUSTRALIAN ACCOUNTING HISTORY

Wai Fong Chua and Chris Poullaos, University of New South Wales

This paper argues that the neo-Weberian perspective can be better exploited to develop a more nuanced and dynamic understanding of the cross-border professionalization projects of accountants and accounting. The activities of the Incorporated Institute of Accountants, Victoria (VIC) from 1886 to 1903 illustrate the benefit of extending Weber's class-status-party model. The VIC's professionalization project was significantly shaped by multiple and changing lines of social cleavage within the association, between that association and competing colonial and imperial associations, the actions of "autonomous" state agencies and wider political and communal tensions. In particular, imperial discourses and institutions, which mutated when transplanted from the metropolitan centre to the penal periphery, were significant. Finally, the concept of monopolistic closure is shown to be too blunt a descriptor either of associational intent or outcome.

THE FIRST IRISH ACCOUNTING PUBLICATION: AMMONET, 1696

Peter J. Clarke, University College, Dublin

The first known accounting publication in Ireland is dated 1696. It was written, and printed, by S. Ammonet and was sold by him in Essex Street, Dublin. Three hundred years later, it is appropriate to analyze this publication. This paper examines the contents of the book and provides an overview of its economic and social background. The paper, adapting an approach by Vangermeersch [1988], is written in an A to Z format.

INVITED SESSION

The Critical Potential of Accounting History

Session Chair: David Cooper, University of Alberta

FROM CHARLATAN TO DOYEN: THE LEGITIMIZATION OF AUSTRALIAN ACCOUNTANCY

Kathie Cooper, University of Wollongong, Australia

It is one thing for an occupational group to designate itself a profession but quite another to attain public recognition of this status. Accomplishing publicly recognized professional status was a prime task of Australian accountancy during the course of this century.

This task was, perhaps, more difficult for Australian accountancy than, for example, their United Kingdom counterparts. One factor contributing to the difficulty of the task was that many of the unexpected corporate failures in the wake of the Victorian land boom of the late eighteenth century cast many members of the early Australian accountancy associations in the role of charlatan or rogue. This occurred because subsequent investigation revealed that the accounts of many of these companies were grossly misleading even though they had been prepared and audited by so-called "qualified" accountants. Despite this ignominious start, two Australian accountancy associations, the Institute of Chartered Accountants in Australia and the Australian Society of Certified Practising Accountants (formerly the Australian Society of Accountants), have achieved a dominant position in the regulation of external financial reporting through control of the setting of legally backed accounting standards.

In this paper, a translation model of power will be used to explain some of the professionalization activities of Australian accountancy associations. In particular, it will demonstrate that the accountancy associations used traditional professionalization activities such as education, examination and training requirements to exclude the "unqualified" from membership. However, nontraditional strategies were also employed when necessary.

Nontraditional professionalization strategies included the formation of alliances and agency relationships with others interested in the activities of accounting associations, for example, the financial press, business interests, federal and state governments and the United Kingdom government and chartered accountants. Dissidence within Australian accountancy also had to be overcome by alliance strategies.

The translation model of power shows that achieving a dominant position, or for Australian accountancy, the transition from charlatan to doyen, was not so much a matter of proving claims to specialized knowledge and skill used in the public interest but an ability to form alliances and create agency relationships: in other words, an ability to win friends and influence people.

THE RISE AND FALL OF HIDDEN RESERVES

Jorgen Dahlgren, Linkoping University, Sweden

An established purpose for accounting is that of producing financial information to parties outside the company. The definition of target group differs but investors and creditors are certain to be included (sometimes together with employees, the public, etc.). The information should be relevant in the sense it should match the target groups' need for data relevant to decisions about whether to deal with the company or not. Any distortion in the financial information as a result of deliberate actions by the accountant is therefore regarded as a violation of the principle of legitimate access to relevant facts.

For decades, Swedish companies intentionally undervalued their assets and overvalued their liabilities. The scale of particularly the undervaluation was such that it went way beyond what is commonly understood as conservatism. Since the extent of undervaluation could not be ascertained by outside parties, the concomitant reserves were hidden. A more precise definition of a hidden reserve would be, to outside parties unascertainable, the difference between value according to the balance sheet and value as a result of applying conventional accounting principles.

Today the practice of using hidden reserves would be looked upon as a violation of the disclosure principle, but at the time it was not only accepted but also strongly recommended practice among Swedish companies. The use of hidden reserves even tied in with tax laws which in a reverse linkage process actually supported it. Finally this use also, in accordance with sound financial logic, also made sense for and was accepted by investors.

The reason for writing a paper on the use of hidden reserves is the importance this well-established and accepted practice once had in the financial reporting of Swedish companies. Since the reserves involved large amounts, they had a substantial effect on reported earnings. The subject has to our knowledge never been analyzed before and we want to discuss the economic logic behind the use of hidden reserves from a company, investor and government perspective. We further include a section on the corresponding phenomenon in Germany, where it once was much debated both in practice and in theory. Since much of the development of Swedish accounting was influenced by the German tradition, this debate presumably had its effect in the Swedish arena. Finally we also present some data from France. We conclude by discussing the national differences in a contrastive perspective.

THE INTERACTION BETWEEN ACCOUNTANTS AND NON-ACCOUNTANTS IN THE CREATION OF MANAGERIAL REPORTS: CASES FROM THE BELGIAN COLLIERY INDUSTRY

Ignace De Beelde, University of Ghent, Belgium

Cost and management accounting grew significantly in the nineteenth and twentieth centuries. Part of this development can be attributed to accountants, but engineers also seem to have played an important role. This paper focuses on the interaction between accountants and non-accountants in the creation of managerial reports in a number of Belgian colliery companies. The period studied is the first half of the twentieth century. The paper describes the results of an archival investigation of the managerial reports in these firms, lists the contents of these reports and looks for indications with respect to their origin. Overall, practice in these firms seems to have been variable, but in many firms the involvement of production departments appears to have been significant.

PROFESSIONALIZATION IN COLONIAL AUSTRALIA: A STUDY OF SOCIAL BACKGROUNDS AND BUSINESS OPPORTUNISM

John Richard Edwards, Cardiff Business School
Garry D. Carnegie, Deakin University, Australia

Britain exported accounting technology to colonial Australia. The transfer of accounting technology occurred through a variety of means, including the export of British accountants. Even though Australia adopted the British model of the accounting profession, there has been little empirical research to substantiate the claim that accountants qualified in Britain were responsible for founding Australian professional accounting bodies [Johnson & Caygill, 1971]. This prosopographical study of 45 founding members of the Incorporated Institute of Accountants, Victoria (c.1886) examines the common background characteristics of these founders to elucidate this issue and to augment our understanding of the interests which converged to shape the structure of professional accounting in Australia at that time. We also explore the unique circumstances which led to the formation of the accounting body which is the earliest antecedent body of the Australian Society of Certified Practising Accountants.

A THEORETICAL PRIMER FOR EVALUATING AND CONDUCTING HISTORICAL RESEARCH IN ACCOUNTING

Richard K. Fleischman, John Carroll University, Cleveland
Patti Mills, Indiana State University
Thomas Tyson, St. John Fisher College, New York

Historical research in accounting is flourishing as prestigious journals worldwide encourage authors to incorporate history into their submissions. Although a number of accounting academics are aware of these opportunities, others may be reluctant to participate because they lack an understanding of the rudiments of historical scholarship. This paper is geared to those scholars who seek to write about accounting's past but are unacquainted with historical methods, unsure how to begin, and generally unfamiliar with the debates that are now taking place in the field.

In this paper we discuss the formal theoretical structures of history as a discipline. These structures incorporate an organized body of mutually-connected elements and the relations and dissonance amongst them. We differentiate history as event, story, and way of knowing. We consider the problem of historical facticity and the subjectivity of the historian, and we examine the role historical evidence plays in the reconstruction of the past. We identify the forms of historical construction, alternate historical methods, historians' fallacies, and rhetorical devices. We discuss the distinctions between history and social science and summarize the current debate between conventional and critical accounting historians. We identify publication possibilities and address other professional issues.

TURN-OF-THE-CENTURY CPAs AND THE ACCOUNTING EDUCATION MOVEMENT

Dale L. Flesher, Tonya K. Flesher, University of Mississippi
Gary John Previts, Case Western Reserve University, Ohio

The year 1896 marks the 100th anniversary of the Certified Public Accountant (CPA) examination in the United States. The first law establishing the CPA designation was passed in New York on April 17, 1896. The motivation for this study was to determine the role played by early CPAs in the accounting education movement. This paper outlines and analyzes the careers of the educators among the first group of CPAs—those who were certified in 1896 and 1897. Although the first CPAs were all practitioners, many academic types emerged from the first group of CPAs. Indeed, some of the first CPAs were the pioneers of academic accounting as it is known today. In fact, all of the academics at major schools were involved in the CPA exam movement.

INVITED SESSION

DECIMALIZED CHARTS OF ACCOUNTS

Session Chairs:

David Forrester, Royal Philosophical Society of Glasgow
Alicja Jaruga, Head of Department of Accountancy, University of Łódź, Poland

Plans Comptables or *Kontenrahmen* are structured codes of accounts adopted by industries or countries to assist in cost comparisons, uniformity in financial reports and aimed often also at additive data for macro-accounting.

Their history during the first half of the twentieth century has been reviewed, not least in the European Accounting Review, 1995. J. Richard wrote there on accounting chart models in Europe, 1900–1945; B. Chauveau on the Spanish Plan General; W. Bechtel on German charts; and J. Richard on Russian and Romanian charts.

At the Kingston Congress, this and other work will be introduced—with special reference to differences between the standardizations of accounts, "top-down" by the Anglo-Saxon approach or "bottom-up" from Day-book codings. Polish charts will be studied by A. Jaruga; ordering problems of knowledge in general and accounting data in particular since Paul Otlet by D. Forrester; and comparisons between French PCG practice and structured databases will be reported from E. Anglia.

AN EVOLVING MODEL OF RESEARCH METHODOLOGIES IN ACCOUNTING

R. Michael Garner, Salisbury State University, Maryland
Tommie W. Singleton, University of North Alabama

Beginning with Aristotle and the Greeks and progressing through the medieval period, the Renaissance, the Industrial Revolution, the nineteenth century, and the modern era, scientific thinking has exploded in an ever-evolving, dynamic process. Cycles fixated on either inductive or deductive emphasis repeated themselves in ever greater complexity. Interestingly, each major way point on the journey has been populated by a large number of people who were convinced their particular paradigm was the sacrosanct "ultimate" answer. In each case, including the "modern era" they were patently wrong.

There are two key sets of players in every step of the evolutionary process: scientists (who explain facts) and scientific philosophers (who analyze the procedures and logic of scientific explanation). Actually the two elements are mirror images of one another. Each must exchange places regularly with the other if they are to be successful. This paper takes a brief look at the early parts of the evolution to establish a philosophical foundation, then explores the exponential rise of the reductionist approach to the pinnacle of research methodology.

ACCOUNTING FOR SUSTAINABLE DEVELOPMENT: LESSONS FROM ABORIGINAL SOCIETIES

Kathy Gibson, University of Tasmania

Corporate policies of "sustainable development" have been a major response of commerce and industry to societal demands for greater environmental responsibility on the part of commercial enterprises. This follows "almost universal acceptance of the goal of sustainability and sustainable development" at government level in developed countries, and reflects in commercial terms the environmental concept of intergenerational equity.
The large majority of production and investment decisions are made on the basis of accounting information, and the accounting language therefore has a paramount role in commercial decision-making. To the extent of any deficiencies in this language, issues of sustainable development may be excluded from the decision-making process. Whilst some of these exclusions arise through deficiencies in the lexicon, many are the result of the artificial definitions within which accounting practice is constrained.

In this paper, the author explores alternative definitions of accounting terms such as assets, liabilities and wealth, by examining an ancient economic system in which intergenerational equity was a fundamental principle. In traditional Aboriginal societies, "assets" had an entirely different meaning from the present concept, as to own an item was to have the obligation to share, or the right to be asked for it. Exclusive possession was not a feature of the assets of such societies, particularly in the case of land. The cultural basis of "claims" or "rights" lay in the ontological priority of The Dreaming, and custodianship was a transhistorical concept which placed no boundaries between past, present, and future generations.

In such societies, human capital in the form of training, knowledge and wisdom was more important than physical capital, and land ownership consisted of "control over the stories, objects and ritual associated with the mythological ancestors of The Dreaming at particular places". Thus, ownership carried both rights and obligations to future generations, and land, which to current commercial enterprises signals mining rights, pastoral leases and building sites, was to them "the source and locus of life and everlastingness of spirit".

It is proposed that by revisiting our accounting definitions in the light of ancient wisdom we can learn from the past and at least do no harm to the future.

ADMINISTRATION AND ACCOUNTING IN THE WARSHIPS OF THE SPANISH ROYAL NAVY ORDINANCE OF 1735

Esteban Hernandez-Esteve, Banco de Españo, Spain

During the sixteenth century, the Spanish State had an impressive administrative organization that was implemented by the first two kings of the House of Habsburg, especially by Philip II, to manage and control their extensive territories. In this sense, a great variety of ordinances, rules, regulations and instructions were issued to govern the smallest and most dissimilar aspects of public activity. In the seventeenth century the power of the Spanish monarchy declined progressively, in particular in the last third of the century. However, the administrative apparatus was not reduced or simplified. The accession of the Bourbons to the throne of Spain at the beginning of the eighteenth century carried many changes in the structure and organization of the State but it did not diminish the Spanish inclination to issue regulations. The consolidation of Philip V as the first monarch of the House of Bourbon in Spain generated an important revival of the Spanish military power and economic and cultural life. The administrative reforms and the restored fiscal income allowed to reconstitute an effective army and a powerful navy. In this last respect, the Minister of the Admiralty, Jose Patino, played a decisive role: he centralized trade with the Indes in Cadiz and reorganized the navy.

The Ordenanza e Instruccion de Escrivanos y Maestres de los Vageles de el Rey, formada para la cuenta y razon que se edeve llevar a sus Bordos en viage y en Puerto (Ordinance and Instruction for Registrars and Masters of the King's ships to rule the keeping of accounts on board during the voyage and in the harbour), approved on July 19, 1735, was precisely issued by Jose Patino. Among other things, this Ordinance established that a registrar should travel on each ship of the navy to manage and control the goods and purveyances delivered on board. This registrar, half accountant and half public notary, was responsible for supervising the reception and delivery of mentioned goods, keeping the account of stocks and consumption. For this purpose, he had to keep three books: a Book of Military Equipment, Artillery, Weapons and Ammunition; a Book of the Crew; and, finally, a Book of Provisions and Medicines. Moreover, every registrar had to keep a Book of Last Wills in which any testament made by members of the crew was to be registered. In the first book, to be kept according to the Castilian Charge and Discharge—i.e., single entry—method, he was required to register, in the first place, an initial inventory of all the supplies available on board and, later, all ingoing and outgoing items. At the end of each month, the registrar would draw a statement of recorded movements and, at the end of the voyage, a final inventory. In the second book, a section was open for each member of the crew in which all of his personal details were recorded: particulars, date of recruitment, origin, date of discharge, new destination, review, shore leaves, diseases, etc. In the third book, kept in a similar way to the first one, the registrar would keep the account of all the provisions and medicines stored on board for the crew.

This paper studies in detail the way in which the registrar was required to keep the books and supervise the goods and purveyances of the ship in accordance to the Ordinance of 1735.

THE LAWRENCE MANUFACTURING CO: A NOTE ON EARLY COST ACCOUNTING IN US TEXTILE MILLS

Keith Hoskin, University of Manchester Institute of Science and Technology
Richard Macve, University of Wales

This paper scrutinizes the Lawrence Manufacturing Co. accounts in the 1840s and challenges the inferences that have been drawn in previous literature both about the degree of sophistication of cost accounting practice that they exhibit and about their use for management purposes. It suggests that the accounting computations, which have been taken as evidence that a modern managerial approach was already being adopted in manufacturing contexts, for the purpose of developing a regime of cost control and performativity within the factory, have a different explanation: as calculations made for classic mercantile purposes, in order to track flows of money spent and received in manufacturing. It thereby contributes to a debate in which Yamey has been a leading figure, concerning the dangers of anachronism when considering the accounting practices of earlier times, and the importance of allowing modern intent in such accounting only after the most stringent scrutiny of the evidence.

GOVERNMENTAL ACCOUNTING IN THE PHASE OF STATE REGIME RESHAPING FROM CAPITALISM TO SOCIALISM: THE POLISH CASE

Alicja Jaruga and Wojciech A. Nowak, University of Łódź, Poland and
Barbara Bakalarska, Minister of Finance, Poland

The history of Polish twentieth century governmental accounting dates back to 1918, the year of restitution of the Polish state. The landmarks in the course of the governmental accounting developments were successively:

- Nazi occupation 1939–45
- imposition of the Soviet type political and economic system in 1945–53
- radically accelerated in 1989 transformation of this socioeconomic system, consisting of transition from the domination of state ownership of production and centrally planned economy, accompanied by a monoparty political system, to a free market economy and liberal democracy with private ownership of production as a basis and Soviet ideology rejection.

During the initial period of the raising of Polish governmental accounting, the integration of three accounting traditions from the beginning of twentieth century, i.e. the German, the Austrian and the Russian ones, was precondition. The 1939–45 war brought the imposition of the German system of accounting. However, in spite of differences, the first two stages in the development of Polish governmental accounting took place in a capitalistic socioeconomic context. The turning point came with the imposition of the Soviet-style accounting. This type of accounting was the point of departure for all recent changes, which determines largely their character and scope. Another factor determining the direction of current governmental accountancy development in Poland is governmental accounting of Western states which followed different ways of development. For the reasons set out above, the paper provides an analysis of reshaping of Polish governmental accounting from capitalist-type system to a socialist one. The characteristics of measurement and reporting standards of this period are also presented and changes in standard-setting procedures are described. Moreover, the paper attempts to judge whether and to what extent changes that happened during the analyzed transition period are favourable to current Polish transformations. The explorations are based on a generalized model of public sector accounting innovations, developed by A. Jaruga and W. Nowak on the basis of Luder's "contingency model" of governmental accounting innovations.

ORIGIN AND EVOLUTION OF PLANS OF ACCOUNTS IN POLAND

Alicja Jaruga and Anna Szychta, University of Łódź, Poland

Legal regulations in the field of accountancy in Poland over the past half-century have undergone changes related to political and economic system transformations. An important factor in the evolution of the accounting system in Poland have been the mandatory charts of accounts.

This paper aims to give a synthetic presentation of causes and effects of successive reforms of Polish plans of accounts as well as current practice concerning individual companies' accounting plans.

The first normative regulation to be introduced on the Polish territory was the Uniform Chart of Accounts for industrial enterprises operating in General Guberniya (German-occupied Poland) enforced by Nazi authorities during World War II. This chart served as a model for the development of the first Polish Uniform Plan of Accounts obligatory for state - owned industrial and trading enterprises in the years 1946–1949.

The shortcomings of this plan along with new requirements of the "socialist" economy led to the introduction in 1950 of several uniform charts of accounts for particular sectors of the economy. Difficulties which arose in the course of organizing accountancy according to the new plans, on account of their excessive complexity, called for speedy changes. The new solution consisted of the development and introduction of nine framework charts of accounts for state enterprises and banks and two charts for co-operatives. They were in operation from 1951 to 1959 and were based on Soviet models.

As a result of a subsequent reform of 1960, one obligatory plan of accounts came into use. It provided a basis for the development of standard charts of accounts (for enterprises in specified sectors of national economy) and branch charts of accounts (for enterprises belonging to specified lines of industry or trade).

Growing information needs at all levels of national economy management as well as changes in the financial system of enterprises resulted in the introduction of a General Uniform Plan of Accounts in 1976, modelled upon the French Plan of Accounts. It involved not only state-owned enterprises, but also budgetary units, and provided a framework for standard and branch charts of accounts.

As a result of the early 1980s economic reforms, enterprises could adopt individual accounting plans. Subsequent modifications in the structure of standard charts of accounts were made in 1985 and 1989.

The return to a market economy in Poland entailed a fundamental reform of accounting, which began in 1991. Since that time all business entities (except budgetary units) have been able to draw up freely their chart of accounts approved by the manager in the company's overall accounting plan, and define the principles of their functioning. However, under the January 1, 1995 Act on Accounting, authorized bodies may prescribe standard plans of accounts for specified types of business entities.

ACCOUNTING POLICY FOR AGRICULTURAL ASSETS

Roger Juchau, University of Western Sydney, Australia

The issuing of professional accounting policy statements and guidelines for the financial reporting of agricultural assets (self generating and regenerating) has a recent history. These assets have a natural capacity to grow and or to procreate and have unique economic attributes. The purposes for which these assets are controlled and developed can change dramatically. Natural production or market factors alter the economic value of these assets in a matter of hours.

This paper examines the history of the policy statements and discussion documents of three professional bodies (Australian, American and Canadian) on the financial reporting of agricultural assets. It analyzes the validity of policy guidelines and statements given the nature of both the agricultural industry and agricultural assets.

The period under review is 1985–1995.

The paper has special significance given that the International Accounting Standards Committee is currently preparing a statement on accounting for agriculture assets.

ACCOUNTING FOR PUBLIC MONIES

Patricia Kennedy, National Archives of Canada

This paper anatomizes the public accounts presented for audit in the colonies of British North America, circa 1760–1840. The public accounts of Quebec, Lower Canada and Upper Canada will be used to illustrate the public accounting systems developed in the colonies under imperial direction; the types of records created and preserved in the colonies and imperial archives; and the wealth of detail offered for research—in accounting no less than in material culture, legal history or archival science and other disciplines. A comparison with the financial records of the government printers, Brown & Gilmore [later, John Neilson] will serve to illustrate the relationships between public and private systems of accounting for expenditures on public business.

THE FORGOTTEN WARS - SOME REFLECTIONS ON CONTROVERSIES IN AUSTRALIAN AND UK PENSION ACCOUNTING RULE-MAKING

Paul J. M. Klumpes, Lancaster University, UK

In recent years, pension plans have affected financial planning decisions of an increasing proportion of the population both in Australia and the UK. This paper reviews controversies surrounding the development of pension plan accounting rules in these countries. Such disputes typically involved interests representing the:

- pension industry and
- pension plan members, and often arose from apparent financial abuses (e.g.: Maxwell's

looting of pension plans, misleading advice on personal pensions) causing members to sustain economic losses.

These disputes centred on:

- the nature and recognition of pension plan assets and liabilities
- the extent of disclosure of financial information contained in reports distributed to pension plan members.

While the outcomes of these rule-making disputes significantly affected the kind of financial information provided to members, they did not attract the interest of professional accounting rule-making bodies. Alternative plausible explanations for this phenomena are explored.

MANUAL DE CUENTA Y RAZON DE RAMON VALDES 1817

Fernando Martin Lamouroux, Universidad de Salamanca, España

The history of accounting in Spain during the nineteenth century, is still a pending matter as regards to the purely historiographic aspects as well as in the most important topics of accounting theory and practice.

In this last aspect, Valdes' contribution is fundamental through his book entitled *metodo de Llevar y Uniformar la Cuenta y Razon en las Contadurias Principales del Reino y Tratado Teorico y Paractico Para las Casas de Comercio* published in 1817 in Madrid by Repullés' printer. This book constitutes the first *theoretical accounting* work written in Spain, establishing already value judgments about accounting logic. It is important for several reasons:

- It summarizes Spanish accounting knowledge until the year 1817, when this book was published. Valdes' work was mainly based on Bartolome Salvador de Solorzano's book, but also on other Spanish authors like the bachelor Luis de Luque y Leiva with his book *Arte de partida doble* printed in Cadiz in 1774; Sebastian de Jocano y Madaria, Ministro del Tribunal de Contaduría Mayor: *Disertación crítica y apologética del arte de llevar cuenta y razón*, published in Madrid in 1793; that of J. Rodrigues, printed in Bordeaux in 1810 entitled *Tratado Teorico Practico de Comercio.*

  Valdes also cites other foreign authors as Laporte, Larue and Migueret. We believe that he knows them by references of Jocano and that, in reality, they correspond to De La Porte, La Rue and P. J. Migneret respectively. Valdes does not make reference to Pacioli as either makes it Solorzano.
- Its pedagogic character, with attempts to divulge accounting knowledge in the most correct way, abounding not only in reflections and very appreciable explanations, but also with numerous illustrative examples (more than 700).
- Valdes' status of Oficial del Giro de la Tesorería General, which connects him with the Hacienda de la Corona. We consider this to be an original contribution, since published works focused on administration or trading and banking activities, but not both at the same time.

THE MAKING OF THE FIRST ENGLISH BOOK ON DOUBLE-ENTRY BOOKKEEPING: FROM OLDCASTLE TO MELLIS

J. J. Lanero, Universidad de León, Spain

The first English book on double-entry bookkeeping, by Hugh Oldcastle, published in London, in 1453, in many places corresponds very closely to Pacioli's text—so much so that some scholars have described the former as a translation of the latter. However, there are significant differences between the two works. All we know about Oldcastle's book and its contents is obtained from John Mellis' "reproduction" published in 1588.

Mellis was a heavy borrower, that is evident in that part of his book for which he was directly responsible. Therefore, there is a hypothesis that any close correspondences between Mellis and James Peele's treatises, published in 1553 and 1569, are examples of borrowings by Mellis from Peele rather than of borrowings by Peele from Oldcastle. Nevertheless, it is possible to go well beyond this hypothesis. Examination of some of the correspondences clarifies our thesis: that Mellis must have been the borrower. It is obvious, too, that Mellis was inefficient as an editor or adaptor of Oldcastle's treatise.

However, correspondences between Pacioli and Oldcastle/Mellis provide support for a speculation of their dependence on a common source; but of course these numerous and pervading correspondences also support the much more credible assumption that it was the Pacioli printed text which Oldcastle used as his model.

In general, Mellis took liberally from Peele. The detectable resulting changes made to the Oldcastle text are significant. The Mellis edition of 1588 is therefore not to be considered as an even roughly faithful copy of the Oldcastle text.

The paper develops the following points: hypothetical use by Oldcastle of an Italian manuscript; Peele and Mellis as plagiarists; comparison and equivalence: some correspondences between Peele and Mellis; the Inventory; the rule for debits and credits; the ruling of account-books; Peele's *The maner and fourme*; Peele's impact on Mellis; conclusion and references.

IDENTIFYING THE FOUNDING FATHERS OF PUBLIC ACCOUNTANCY: THE SOCIETY OF ACCOUNTANTS IN EDINBURGH

Tom Lee, University of Alabama

Despite histories of the early Scottish professional accountancy bodies (e.g., Brown, 1905; Stewart, 1979; Walker, 1988; and Kedslie, 1990b), there has been little research to identify the small group of men who felt compelled to form the first body in 1853 (The Society of Accountants in Edinburgh [SAE]). This paper attempts to address this historical omission. It describes the sequence of formation events and meetings in 1853 and 1854, identifying those individuals most closely involved with the planning of the SAE. The main achievements of the study are to record the men and events of the SAE formation in a detail not previously attempted, and to demonstrate the élitish nature of the formation. The overall conclusion is that the emergence of the SAE in the mid-nineteenth century was as much the creation of a social élite as it was an economic monopoly.

INTRODUCING DOUBLE-ENTRY IN PUBLIC FINANCE, A FRENCH EXPERIMENT AT THE BEGINNING OF THE EIGHTEENTH CENTURY

Yannick Lemarchard, Université de Bretagne-Occidentale Brest, France

In 1716, the French government introduced a reform in the administration of public finance, based on an interesting technical innovation: double entry was used to control tax collectors' activities.

Tax-collecting was a private business and tax collectors were the bankers of the monarchy. Using fiscal receipts, they lent money to the crown, instead of giving it as soon as possible, so the state paid interest on public funds! The control exerted by the *Chambre des comptes* was useless, because tax collectors reported several years after the end of the fiscal year.

The goals of the reform were to accelerate the receipts of the Royal Treasury and to diminish the interests paid by the King. For this purpose, new accounting procedures were introduced. Each tax collector was obliged to hold a journal of his expenses and receipts, and to send a monthly copy of this journal to the central administration. Accounting for flows of funds between *financiers* (a *financier* was someone who received, held or spent government funds), these books permitted a control which was meant to deter the tax collectors from fraud. The data gathered by this procedure were consolidated at the central level in a double-entry accounting system. In the ledgers of the central administration, accounts were opened to each financier and to each sort of expense and receipt. So it was possible to know the balance of each tax collector with the state, and to consolidate their expenses and receipts on an analytical basis.

This rationalization was progressively extended to the various tax sectors, but it was interrupted in 1726, following political changes at the head of the government, and most of the controls instored were suppressed. It seems that it was impossible to establish a serious control on the management of royal funds, insofar as it was mostly a private profitable activity, placed at the heart of a short-term credit system which made the state prisoner of the *financiers*.

The technical innovation—the use of double-entry to give a representation of the whole system of public finance—is noteworthy. It gave the state a powerful instrument of control, by offering a wide overview on tax collectors' fund management. Rejected by those whose interests might be threatened, that experiment foreshadowed the procedures that would be implemented, a hundred years later, when a genuine public finance administration would be constituted in France.

CONSTRUCTING REGULATORY SPACE: THE PUBLIC ACCOUNTANTS COUNCIL FOR ONTARIO: 1950–1964

Laura MacDonald, Queen's University, Canada

The question of whether professionals should be regulated by licence has plagued most professions throughout the world. Theories suggest regulation of professions is in the public interest and solves market failure, while others suggest regulation is only in the profession's best interest [Posner, 1974; Stigler, 1971]. Many researchers have explored the question of regulation of practice rights from both a theoretical and empirical basis [Walker and Robinson, 1993]. In contrast to this literature which asks why regulation could exist, this paper aims to answer the question of how a regulatory body constructs itself given its mandate of regulating the practice rights of public accountants. It considers how a regulatory body constructs itself by handling the ambiguity of the law, dealing with interest groups, fulfilling its mandate and staking out its regulatory turf.

To achieve this end, the paper borrows two concepts from the well-developed literature on accounting standard-setting bodies. This literature examines how standard-setting bodies function, how standards are set and the consequences of setting standards [Cooper and Sherer, 1985, Tinker, 1984, O'Leary and Boland, 1987, Zeff, 1978]. From this literature, the concept "regulatory space" and "logic of appropriateness" are borrowed to investigate how a specific regulatory body socially constructs itself. By embracing the notion that regulation of practice rights and the operation of the regulatory body occur within a regulatory space, this paper examines how the Public Accountants Council constructed its regulatory space and moreover, how its actions were driven by a "logic of appropriateness".

This paper examines how the Public Accountants Council for Ontario, established in 1950, interpreted its mandate, created a regulatory space and controlled practice rights for public accountants in Ontario. The period examined is from 1950 to 1964, a period which encompasses the birth of the Council, several years of administering the regulation and the amendments in 1962. This paper is primarily based on an archival study of fifteen years of the minutes of the meetings of the Public Accountants Council for Ontario, augmented by other archival sources such as court cases, newspaper clippings, correspondence and reports.

ASPECTS OF EARLY ACCOUNTING SYSTEMS (AFTER 3000 B.C.) AND THEIR RELATION TO OUR TIME

Richard Mattessich, University of British Columbia

While some previous papers of mine investigated prehistoric token accounting (i.e., from ca. 8000 B.C. to 3000 B.C.), analyzing and interpreting Schmandt-Besserat's archeological research from an accountant's point of view, the current presentation extends this research by dealing mainly with the "early *historical* period" of accounting (i.e., from ca. 3000 B.C. to 300 B.C.). I have selected four items particularly worthy of further exploration:

1. A discussion and interpretation of some passages from other archeologists: *Archaic Book-keeping—Early Writing and Techniques of Economic Administration in the Ancient Near East* by Nissen, Damerow and Englund (1993). So far, this work does not seem to have been discussed in the academic accounting literature (except for a reference in Japanese). After a concise comparison with Schmandt-Besserat's (1992) *magnum opus*, my emphasis here is not on token accounting, but on newly disclosed proto-cuneiform and cuneiform accounting aspects.

2. A short reference to Chinese accounting, mainly during the Shang (1600 B.C.–1100 B.C.) and Chou (1121 B.C.–255 B.C.) periods, as well as to accounting in ancient Rome and Greece. These references only serve to connect the temporal gap (and its major accounting events) between the periods of items 1 and 3. This item 2 does not raise any claim to interpretative or other originality.

3. A discussion of accounting as it emerged in India during Maurya period (ca 322 B.C. to 183 B.C.), based on exciting evidence submitted by Bhattacharyya (1988) in his *Modern Accounting Concepts in Kautilya's Arthasastra*. This book, little known in the Western accounting literature, deals with the bookkeeping and related aspects of the ancient treatise *Arthasastra* (ca. 300 B.C.). The latter contains a series of accounting concepts that appear to be surprisingly modern. I will here concentrate on three of those aspects:

- Kautilya's various types of income (including aspects of inflation accounting and a possible distinction between real and fictitious holding gains, etc.) as well as their possible relation to modern concepts
- his classification of expenditures or costs (including possibly fixed vs. variable costs)
- his notions of capital.

These aspects indicate a surprisingly long-standing need for, and use of, relatively sophisticated accounting concepts. Thus Battcharyya must be praised for drawing the attention of Western scholars to those particular aspects of an important ancient treatise; hence Bhattacharyya's work deserves to be critically investigated and further interpreted from the point of view of modern accounting.

4. The fourth item refers to a later period (the seventh century A.D. or before), but also concerns a major breakthrough achieved by Indian scholars. Therefore, I have included it under the section "Early Accounting Notions of India" (see item 3 above). It pays tribute not only to the fact that Indian mathematicians were the first to give recognition to negative numbers but, above all, that the impetus to do so might have come from accounting. There is evidence that the insight that debts are negative assets helped to convince Indian mathematicians of the legitimacy of negative numbers. This is hinted at in Kline's *Mathematics—The Loss of Certainty* and seems to be confirmed by reference to the writings of such well-known early medieval scholars as Brahmagupta and Bhascara. Undoubtedly, here is another surprising possibility worthy of further exploration.

THE FALL OF MANAGEMENT ACCOUNTING: THE NIRA AND THE HOMOGENIZATION OF COST PRACTICES IN THE UNITED STATES

C. J. McNair, Babson College, Massachusetts
Richard Vangermeersch, University of Rhode Island

This paper explores the impact of societal trends on cost practices, and the management techniques used to support business structures, within the United States. Specifically, the influence of the National Industrial Recovery Act [NIRA] on the development of the competitive market, and the costing and pricing policies within it, is explored from the perspective of social rule system theory. It is argued that the NIRA, as enforced through the symbol of the "Blue Eagle" displaced the free market economy in the United States, leaving in its wake a pseudo-competitive market structure where full cost recovery and the earning of a fair and reasonable profit became the basis for market pricing and business management. The displacement of the competitive market by the NIRA is argued to account for the apparent loss of relevant costing theory and practice during this period, as well as the economic shocks currently hitting the United States in the wake of the developing global marketplace. The paper concludes by suggesting that relevant management accounting theory has to be reconstructed from a true competitive market framework.

TASKS OF A SOCIAL HISTORY OF ACCOUNTING

D. Neu, University of Calgary, Canada
A. J. Richardson, Queen's University, Canada

The need for an historical understanding of accounting practices and institutions is increasingly being recognized by practitioners and educators. As the Accounting Education Change Commission in the United States asserts, "a successful practitioner requires ... an understanding of the flow of events in history" (1990, p. 7). Such an understanding is integral to "a strong fundamental understanding of accounting and auditing" (p. 8).

This plea for academics and practitioners to understand accounting history presumes that historical research is designed to provide a critical interpretation of the evolution of accounting practices and institutions, thereby providing a starting point for evaluating current practices [Edward 1989]. In fact, prior historical accounting research has been largely narrative (i.e., descriptive) rather than analytic and has tended to focus on the details of accounting practice without commensurate attention to the context in which those practices evolved [Miller, Hopper & Laughlin 1991; Previts, Parker & Coffman 1990]. Recognition of the current relevance of history thus presumes the existence of a form of historical research in accounting which is only now emerging.

The purpose of this paper is to summarize and synthesize prior historical research on the evolution of Canadian accounting practices and institutions. This preliminary work is necessary in order to provide a basis for the critical interpretation of the evolution of Canadian accounting practices and institutions, and the assessment of current accounting practice. Specifically, our analysis examines the following issues:

- professional governance (i.e., divisions of labour, regulation of the lay membership, commercial practices)
- demographic issues (i.e., the role of occupational elites, gender and equity issues, career paths)
- professionalization (i.e., emergence of a "profession", intra-professional competition, market structures)
- accounting practice (i.e., standard setting, legal issues, variations in practice).

HARRINGTON EMERSON'S STANDARD COSTING RECONSIDERED: HIS CRITICAL VIEWPOINTS ON COST ACCOUNTING

Hiroshi Okano, Osaka City University, Japan

As is well known, Emerson, a pioneer in standard costing, has been studied in a number of historical papers on management accounting. His theories were later revised by his followers, including G. C. Harrison, into standard cost systems. Critics agree that it was only after this stage that standard costing was established as a "control device."

While being acclaimed as the first to present standard costing theory by those who favour this evolutionary process, Emerson encountered criticism by D. Solomons (for the inconsistency of his concept of standard costing and for the inaccuracy of his analysis on the variance between standard costs and actual costs) whose view is generally followed by most critics both in and outside Japan.

This paper considers standard costing as a part of the efficiency improvement system proposed by Emerson. His main idea was that "efficiency may be converted to cost but cost cannot be converted to efficiency." This means that even if the efficiency of finished operations may be quantified by costing, it is impossible to improve efficiency by varying costs: efficiency can only be improved through "preliminary surveys" (task management). Accordingly, Emerson's standard costing theory should be regarded as a means of measuring *a priori* the degree of improved efficiency attained through task management. Emerson's standard costing may appear similar to "standard costing as a control device," systematized by his followers, but the former is in fact different from the latter. Thus, criticism of Emerson in D. Solomons [1952], Matsumoto [1961], Okamoto [1969] and Tsuji [1971, 1988] requires reevaluation.

Such misunderstanding is caused by paying too much attention to the computational aspects of standard costing without putting it into perspective within Emerson's efficiency theory.

ACCOUNTING SYSTEMS AND ORGANIZATION OF SPANISH TRADING COMPANIES IN THE EIGHTEENTH AND NINETEENTH CENTURIES

M. Garate Ojanguren, University of the Basque Country, Spain

Spanish trade with its colonies during the eighteenth and nineteenth centuries gave birth to various trading companies. Their organization and size had a widespread range. Some of them were made up of a low number of shareholders. On the other hand, other companies had many shareholders. In both of them, but mainly in the latter, the accounting system established from the beginning of deals was basic.

It's of great interest to analyze these systems which were related not only to the way in which accounts had to be dealt with, but also the control upon them.

Moreover, it also regulated the organization system of the company, its functions, the roles of the shareholders, different ways to sell the shares of the company, etc. In the paper, several matters are analyzed:

- the accounting system used by Spanish trading companies in the eighteenth and nineteenth centuries.
- the changes and evolution in accounting system and methods
- the control tools of the shareholders upon the accounts of the company (on those societies by shares).
- the different managing flowcharts at the time.
- roles played by the shareholders, chairmen, chief executives, etc.
- the deployment of the different company representatives in different places, due to the trade.

The latest point is of great importance as these companies had activities at both sides of the Atlantic, forcing them to have representatives both in America and in Spain, and even in Europe. This network will show the trading and financial exchanges that took part between the different sites.

A CRITIQUE OF THE NON-EXISTENCE OF ACCOUNTING IN ANGLO-SAXON ENGLAND

D. Oldroyd, University of Newcastle, UK

The Anglo-Saxon period has been characterized as playing no part in accounting history. Government accounting commenced in England in the eleventh century, and manorial accounting in the thirteenth. In Europe, accounting was preserved in the Roman Church following the eclipse of the Roman Empire, and at the court of Charlemagne in the ninth century. Apparently, neither source influenced the development of accounting amongst the Anglo-Saxons. They remained an illiterate society, dependent on the spoken word [Chatfield, 1977, p. 20].

This paper appraises whether the established view, that accounting was virtually nonexistent in Anglo-Saxon England, still seems tenable in the light of current knowledge. The answer is a cautious negative; although the prime aim of the paper is to highlight those areas that warrant further investigation, rather than to provide definitive solutions. This type of study, which touches both the ancient and modern worlds, helps answer Lister's [1983, p. 68] criticism that accounting history is a series of disconnected episodes.

THE CPA EXAMINATION IN THE UNITED STATES: ITS BEGINNINGS

Mary Ellen Oliverio, Bernard H. Newman, Pace University, New York

The first examination for accountants was scheduled to be administered in New York State in Buffalo and New York City in December 1896. That first examination reflected the efforts of a small group of practitioners in accounting to gain professional status in one state. Efforts followed in other states in the United States; within a decade seven states had passed legislation and had granted certificates based on examinations or waivers.

This historical review has as its objectives the following:

- to identify conditions for the first CPA examination administered in the United States
- to describe briefly the business society at the time of emerging professionalism in accounting
- to discuss and assess the nature of the first examination administered in New York State
- to discuss criticism of the first examination
- to identify some implications for further historical investigations.

There are limitations to this effort. The review is based primarily on publications of the American Institute of Certified Public Accountants and its predecessor organizations. This review, therefore, is basically based on the documentation as developed by the professional associations. The period for consideration is generally from the early 1890s to approximately 1905.

PROFESSIONAL SEGMENTATION: THE CASE OF CO-MEMBERSHIP OF AUSTRALIAN AND BRITISH ACCOUNTANCY BODIES TO 1914

R. H. Parker, University of Exeter, UK

During the period c.1880 to 1914, Britain "exported" to Australia both British accountants and British accountancy qualifications. While numerous British and Australian accountancy bodies were established during this period, some accountants resident in Australia held both British and Australian qualifications. Based on surviving membership records to 1914, this paper establishes a list of such persons. It aims to explain why some accountants of the time should seek co-membership of Australian and British accountancy bodies and thus to elucidate the contingent nature of the structure of professional accountancy in Australia during and since that time.

ACCOUNTING AT ECCLESIASTICAL DEPOSIT BANKS IN CATALONIA (THIRTEENTH TO NINETEENTH CENTURIES)

Jose M. Passola, CCI S.A., Barcelona, Spain

The most important long-term lending source in Europe during Middle and Modern ages came from the ecclesiastic state. In general, churches received large donations from individuals, from bishops, from the nobility and also from the members of the communities themselves. This capital was administrated by the ecclesiastical deposits banks regarding its maintenance, its control and its investment in long-term loans.

In the most secure places of the cathedrals and churches, within the sacristies, rooms were built as real safe rooms where treasures (chalices, gold and silver crosses, etc.) and money were kept. This money was put in wooden boxes that were usually strengthened with iron bandages, known as *thecas*. They were closed with three locks and the keys were kept by two *clavigerius* and the treasurer. The function of the latter consisted of administrating this capital and investing it buying perpetual annuities.

Kings and popes granted various privileges in order to protect these ecclesiastic treasures that made the deposits in the *thecas* non-embargable and inviolable (not even the king could touch them) and any damages done to them was punished with excommunication. Municipal authorities also left their money in these *thecas*, as well as the nobility and outstanding members of towns. The pope's money that came from bulls and the king's money that came from some taxes were kept in them until public banks were created. As a result, although the property of these banks was private, they turned into semi-public deposit banks keeping money and jewelry.

The offer of ecclesiastical long-time loans was not speculative and it only sought after the attainment of some rents from which the different ecclesiastic communities could afford their living, allowing them to dedicate themselves to the cults (groups of canons, groups of beneficiaries, monasteries, convents, etc.). They usually invested in public debt or in long-term loans to the nobility and richest citizens, to handicraftsmen and especially to farmers. They used accounting books, many of which still exist nowadays, particularly those belonging to the fifteenth up to the nineteenth centuries.

The purpose of this paper is to study the books of accounts of ecclesiastical deposit banks in Catalonia and the accounting techniques employed.

ORIGIN AND DEVELOPMENT OF SURVIVORS' PENSIONS IN THE SPANISH ARMY:THE FIRST MILITARY PENSION FUND

M. Pilar Pérez, University of Valladolid, Spain

The Ordinances of April 20, 1761 created the First Military Pension Fund with official character founded in Spain and immediately extended to its American colonies. It is also the first system of compulsory social foresight which recognizes the right to a pension for military widows and orphans, and which also served as a model for other similar associations created during eighteenth century.

With our present work, we develop an introductory analysis of the Military Pension Fund: its organization, the most relevant tasks it had and the funds which it administered. We have chosen the first 30 years of its history because it coincides with the period during which *Diego Jose de Cosa* was facing the Treasury; he was in charge of presenting the annual countable information about the movement of the funds which would serve to demonstrate the progress of the institution. We also have some of the documents elaborated by *Antonio de la Portilla*, Accountant of the Military Pension Fund, whose mission was now reduced to supervising the accounts presented by the treasurer, However, he had a definite part in the analysis and control of the development of the Military Pension Fund by justifying reasonably and via documents the need for and movements of resources which took place since the opening of the institution.

THE ROYAL EXCHEQUER'S BOOK OF CURRENT ACCOUNTS WITH THE CAPITAL PROCEEDING FROM PEPPER THAT SUNDA PAID IN THE YEAR 1743

Manuel Rodrigues Benavente, Director
Associaçao Portuguesa de Tecnicos de Contas, Lisbon, Portugal

This small book written by hand, not even bound, is catalogued with the number 47-*Casa dos Contos* (House of Accounts), in the Historical Archives of the Audit Department of the Exchequer in Lisbon.

It is a book of accounts that covers a period between 1743 and 1760 and it tells us, in a remarkable way, not only how commercial exchanges were made, but also gives us an idea about the unusual way in which accounts were made at the time.

The Portuguese State in India had ancient matters of contention with its neighbours—the Indian leaders—who were either allies or enemies. They were fighting over several issues; however, almost all these issues were a consequence of a clash of cultures and mentalities between the European colonists and the east natives.

In this context and after a long war with the King of Sunda—a territory near Goa—which would continue for many years, the Portuguese defeated the Sunda—as he was known—and he was obliged to make the necessary investment required to reconstruct the two provinces, Ponda and Zambaulim. The Portuguese mediated that payment which consisted of 40,000 *xelins* (shillings), Goa's local currency.

This book describes precisely the accountancy of these 40,000 *xelins*.

THE EVOLUTION OF THE US INCOME TAX: THE HISTORY OF PROGRESSIVITY, INFLUENCES FROM OTHER COUNTRIES AND COMPARISON TO THE CANADIAN EXPERIENCE

William D. Samson, University of Alabama

US tax policy of progressivity has long been implemented through the rate structure of the federal income tax. Over the years, this relationship of the income tax with progressivity has become so closely linked that when one is mentioned, the other comes immediately to mind. However, this relationship has not always existed; the degree of progressivity of the federal income tax has continually been altered, reflecting changes in tax policy because of social, political and economic forces. Historically, Congress has run a long-term experiment, tinkering with the rate structure and other key income tax variables in the search for the right combination to allocate the tax burden while accomplishing other economic objectives. Given the current unsettled conditions in Washington, the US income tax is being reexamined, its progressivity will be reviewed and the distribution of taxes will likely change again.

Because dramatic modifications appear to be forthcoming, it seems appropriate to review the two-hundred-year-old US federal tax experiment. Noteworthy are the tax policy and economic forces that married the progressive rate structure with the income tax, as well as the international contributions and influences in this marriage.

After reviewing the early US tax experience and the initial attempts at utilizing the income tax and the progressive rate structure, the paper focuses on the progressivity of the federal income tax over the last eighty-two years, since its rebirth in 1913. Historical trends and relationships of the components of progressivity, such as the highest, the lowest, and the number of tax rates, and the amount of exempt income, are examined against the political, economic and national conditions at the time. Because similar circumstances and forces worked to shape the Canadian income tax, the Canadian experience with income tax progressivity offers a striking parallel to that of the United States. From this historical examination of income tax progressivity, insight about where these tax systems stand today can be more clearly seen. Tax debates and reform proposals should benefit from considering past experiences with the income tax experiment.

EVOLUTION OF THE APPLICATION OF PRESENT VALUE TO VALUATION OF NON-MONETARY RESOURCES

Michael E. Scorgie, La Trobe University, Australia

In this paper we address a historical research question: What were the significant steps in the evolution of the application of present value to valuation of non-monetary resources? An important outcome of the research is that we modify the contention that the pioneering application of net present value to economic problems involving non-monetary resources did not occur until the nineteenth century.

We present a synthesis of previously cited and uncited evidence and set forth significant steps in the evolution of the application of the concept of present value to monetary and non-monetary resources prior to the mid-eighteenth century. We suggest that a take-off in the application of present value to non-monetary resources occurred in the 1540s when auditors were required to set sale prices for ecclesiastic estates that had been confiscated by the crown. We show that the rulers who followed Henry VIII stimulated the evolution by selling freehold and leasehold property, and that in the aftermaths of the execution of Charles I and the Great Fire of London, property transactions were accompanied by a heightened understanding and use of the concept of present value.

In respect of fungible non-monetary resources we cite an entry made by Robert Loder in his farm journal. This early seventeenth century Berkshire farmer attempted to apply the concept of present value and thereby improve his management performance. He sought to measure in present money the value of increased production resulting from spreading dung. We draw attention to a continuing discussion about the need to establish plantations of native and exotic trees and the impact of this nationwide discourse on the application of present value. We cite evidence that shows how a surveyor from Exeter in the 1730s addressed the problems of valuation of standing timber under both sustained and intermittent management. That is, the same economic problems that the well-known German forester, Martin Faustmann considered more than a hundred years later.

PROGENITORS OF MODERN MANAGEMENT ACCOUNTING CONCEPTS AND MENSURATIONS IN PRE-INDUSTRIAL ENGLAND

Michael E. Scorgie, La Trobe University, Australia

Edwards and Newell [1994, p. 407] noted that "the application of accounting techniques in business management continues to be a largely unexplored area of business history." Outcomes of this lack of research and knowledge are simplistic conclusions such as "accounting systems for managerial decisions and control can be traced back to the origins of hierarchical enterprises in the early nineteenth century" [Johnson and Kaplan, 1987]. In contrast, the case and conclusion presented in this paper holds that innovative measurements for decisions and control attributed to industrial revolution managers were adaptations of concepts used for centuries by lords of the manor and their auditors, stewards and bailiffs who controlled agricultural activities on landed estates. In addition, evidence is presented which shows that concepts of production standards and standard costs were used in pre-industrial England to control the manufacture and sale of bread.

Much of the evidence used to build the case was drawn from translations of medieval management, accounting and legal treatises and is presented under six headings. Under each heading evidence of the use of a progenitor of a modern management accounting concept and associated mensuration (action of measurement) is presented and discussed. The headings are: i) Production Capacity; ii) Production Standards; iii) Standard Costs; iv) Cost Allocation; v) Performance Analysis; and vi) Relevant Costs.

THE CLERGY IN ITALIAN LITERATURE OF ACCOUNTANCY

Luigi Serra, Consiglio Nazionale Ragionieri, Italy

The Church has always had a considerable place in the history of accountancy, for the administration of plentiful properties. Consequently, several clerics taught and published various works about that subject, in the course of ages. This paper includes only those clerics who dealt with accountancy in a strict way, omitting the others who wrote about business mathematics, these last being much more numerous.

Luca Paciolo, author of the first treatise about double-entry, was a Franciscan friar. He taught mathematics in several Italian universities and was also interested in accountancy, when the latter was confused with the former. In many places, but above all in Venice during his youth, he came into contact with merchants' world.

Secondly, the Benedictine Angelo Pietra who, with a large leap on the previous works, wrote a volume on the administration of monasteries: it is another milestone in the history of accountancy. He also left to us a manuscript about the administration of a public undertaking. Other authors, with time, followed his work, so it was completely reproposed after 238 years since its publication for its up-to-dateness.

The first one who drew his inspiration from Pietra was the Jesuit Lodovico Flori who took a further step forward in the administration of property of ecclesiastical body. He completed several points of his predecessor even as he repeated some of his errors.

The three mentioned clerics are certainly the most important authors in the history of

Italian accountancy of the first centuries about double-entry.

Giamcomo Venturoli, on the contrary, is one among minor, followed by Pellegrino Balugani and Carl'Antonio Monti.

Near the end of the nineteenth century, another fierce priest—Francesco Alberigo Bonalumi—wrote over 20 works to divulge and defend logismography from the contrary attacks: it was a new form of recording in double-entry excogitated by Giuseppe Cerboni, whose doctrine was fervently followed by Bonalumi. This priest attended the fights among the schools of his time and treated diffusely in all his books also a little history of accountancy.

FEDERALISM IN BRITISH ACCOUNTING: A STUDY OF POLITICAL REFORM, 1968–1972

Ken Shackleton and Stephen P. Walker, University of Glasgow

This study, established in the social, economic and professional context of its time examines the attempt through the 1960s to create a UK accountancy profession based on a federal structure. The research extends the examination of the reformation and amalgamation of the accountancy bodies in the British Isles during 1942–1957 [Walker & Shackleton, 1995]. The principal bodies involved were the three chartered societies (ICAEW, ICAI, ICAS) and the second tier organizations (Certified [ACCA], Cost [ICWA], Public sector [IMTA]). The study examines:

- the process of policy formulation and political negotiation at institutional levels
- the debate amongst institutions and with their memberships on a major constitutional proposal
- the consequences of failure at institutional and membership levels.

The arguments for integration were stated as attempting to:

- dispel confusion and misunderstanding causes in the public mind by a multiplicity of professional designations
- allow the profession to speak with a united voice on matters of professional national and international importance
- allow the profession to respond to great changes which are taking place in the scope and emphasis of the work of professional accountants.

The subsequent debate identified significant divisions of opinion amongst the members of the bodies involved in the scheme, and ultimately the ICAEW membership rejected the integration proposals [Willmott, 1986].

THE ORIGIN OF ACCOUNTING

R. M. Singhvi, Indian Accounting Association

I have tried to trace the account of the double-entry system through ancient Indian literature in this article. In this way I had to use the script of other Indian languages named Parkrit and Sanskrit. Without using these scripts my article will have no authenticity, I have also translated the scripts in English.

India has a long history and traditions. It is believed in India that accounting is prevailed in its present form of double entry for more than 2,500 years. All the sole traders still use the Indian System of Accounting in their regional languages in India.

Shukracharya and Kautilya have described in their writings about the system of debit and credit. They have also described a sound system of taxation. If we believe that a sound system of taxation and revenue was prevailed then we are bound to accept that in olden days we had a sound accounting system also. India had its long business relations with Greece and with Roman and Ottoman Empire. If Indians in ancient period had their business relations with West they might have a developed system of accounting. In this article, I have given references to believe that there was a system of accounting in ancient period in the form of double entry. Indians are treated as the originator of zero and mathematics. In the second part of my article I have given some features of Indian mathematics which is known as Mahajani Ganit.

SOME HISTORICAL PERSPECTIVES AND MORE RECENT DEVELOPMENTS IN WORKING CAPITAL MANAGEMENT

M. Beaumont Smith, University of South Africa

This paper looks at some developments in working capital management over the years. The study commences with a historical background to the concept of working capital. Thereafter, working capital theory advancements are discussed, examining the ideas propounded by authors such as Walker, van Horne and Beranek. Finally, attention is given to more recent working capital concepts developed, specifically to measure corporate liquidity. The paper concludes with remarks on the paucity of research in working capital in South Africa, and the need for empirical confirmation of the normative theorems in this dynamic area of financial management.

TAXATION, COMMON SENSE IMPLICATIONS AND THE LOWER OF COST AND MARKET RULE IN THE UNITED KINGDOM 1842–1925

David M. Smith, Deakin University, Australia

It has been suggested that the desire of businesses not to pay taxes on unrealized gains would foster the use of a method of valuation of stock-in-trade (inventory) which prevents this from occurring. The use of *the lower of cost and market rule* will normally give a profit figure lower than that obtained by using either historical cost or market value alone. It is generally accepted that the use of *the lower of cost and market rule* was firmly established in the United Kingdom as the primary method of valuing stock-in-trade by 1925. This paper considers whether income tax considerations affected the development of *the lower of cost and market rule* for the period 1842 to 1925. Research has found that there are few references to the use of *the lower of cost and market rule* in the United Kingdom prior to the introduction of a system of permanent income tax in 1842 and that its use increased progressively over the period to 1900. One suspects that the introduction of income tax would foster the use of a method of valuing stock-in-trade which prevents unrealized profit from being taxed and allows the deduction of unrealized losses. This paper investigates the available evidence to determine whether this intuitive reasoning can be validated.

HELOISE BROWN CANTER: HER CAREER, HER CONTRIBUTIONS TO PUBLIC ACCOUNTING, HER INFLUENCE ON WOMEN IN ACCOUNTING

Wanda G. Spruill, State University of New York at Geneseo
Charles W. Wootton, Eastern Illinois University

Heloise Brown Canter is one of the women who laid the framework for gains that women have achieved in public accounting. She was the first woman CPA in Houston, the fifth in the State of Texas, and the first to be licensed in Arkansas. The purpose of this paper is to examine the life of Heloise Brown Canter, her career, her contributions to public accounting and her influence on women in public accounting.

Helen Cantor Brown became a CPA at a time when few women practised as CPAs. She has enjoyed a long and successful career in the business world at a time when many women in business were restricted to secretarial duties. Throughout her career she has been active in professional organizations and has written and published articles in the journals of those organizations. Her influence on the accounting profession was eloquently stated by President George Bush: "Your efforts have inspired those around you and have set an example for others to follow." She was and is a role model for women and men who seek to succeed in accounting.

IS STATE OF AFFAIRS, FINANCIAL POSITION?

Julie Tabart-Gay, Deakin University, Australia

"State of affairs" is an expression which has been used in accounting at least since the sixteenth century and by the legal system up to the present time. Historically, the term was used to explain the financial capacity of a merchant, businessman or individual to describe what they owned, what they owed, and what was owing to them. At some stage in the twentieth century or earlier the term "state of affairs" has been replaced by "financial position" in accounting literature. And the term "financial position" has since been used in a more nebulous way than its predecessor "state of affairs" was ever used. It is of importance to determine the era over which this transition occurred, but it is more important to identify elements which contributed to the change in order to understand the use and meaning of "financial position" in contemporary accounting. An entity requires up-to-date knowledge of its financial situation to determine capacity to pay debts, purchase commodities, make economic choices to maintain liquidity in the short-term and solvency in the long-term. Conventional accounting practice periodically provides interested parties with dated financial statements of an entity's operating results, a statutory requirement for publicly listed firms. Conventional wisdom implies that these statements contain information about the financial position of the entity at a specified date. This paper examines the meaning of "financial position" as currently used in accounting literature and concludes it is not synonymous with the implied meaning of "state of affairs" as used in a historical or contemporary context.

THE CURRENT LEDGER OF F. W. READ & CO: 1904–1908

Joel E. Thompson, Northern Michigan University

This study examines the current (i.e., general) ledger of F. W. Read & Co., a lumber business, from January 1, 1904, through November 30, 1908. The purpose is to better understand the evolution of bookkeeping techniques as well as methods of income determination. This is partly accomplished by comparing the current ledger of F. W. Read &

Co. with the ledger described 500 years ago by Luca Paciolo. Many of the changes in bookkeeping techniques over the intervening 410 years can be considered refinements to improve efficiency. However, there is a substantive change in income determination to a periodic basis, reflecting the change in the accounting entity.

THE EVOLUTION OF CANADIAN TAX POLICY FOR PREFERRED DIVIDENDS, 1975–89: AN APPLICATION OF THE COASE THEOREM

Dan Thornton, Queen's University, Canada

The Coase theorem suggests that, if there are no transaction costs, people can "plan around" tax laws, nullifying their intended effects. This paper uses the theorem, in tandem with the Pareto principle, as a framework for analyzing the evolution of the complicated tax rules relating to preferred dividends in Canada from 1970 until 1989. It is concluded that the analysis provides a useful framework for explaining the historical development of tax rules in this important area and in financial markets generally. Political and social factors appear to play no systematic role in influencing such tax policies.

The analysis underscores the fact that the government relies on transaction costs to give its rules teeth. As financial technology improves and the transaction costs of financing fall, it becomes increasingly difficult for governments to maintain their tax revenues from the corporate sector. The framework proposed in the paper should be helpful in analyzing the evolution of tax rules relating to derivative securities, a current pressure point in the tax system.

ACCOUNTING TECHNIQUE AND THE DUAL CHARACTER OF MAN

Eamonn Walsh, New York University and University of Limerick
Ingrid Jeacle, Dublin City University

To date, examinations of accounting and the social have generally perceived the social as synonymous with the world of work and accounting as a phenomenon rather than a series of techniques. This essay represents an imperfect attempt to invert this broad tendency. We attempt to unravel the nature and consequences of a specific accounting technique which gives rise to a framework that incorporates the two faces of generic man—man as producer and consumer.

INSCRIBING THE WORKERS' EXPERIMENT IN FACTORY DISCIPLINE OF THE INCULCATION OF MANNERS

Robert Williams, University of Wollongong, Australia

The establishment of the factory system during the beginning of the Industrial Revolution created a demand for labour—labour that was unused to the confines and rigours of factory life. In an attempt to encourage punctuality and conscientiousness, the industrialists of the late eighteenth century resorted to a number of practices designed to encourage their employees to give up their old habits and take on a new rhythm of life tied to the demands of the factory. At the same time, the guiding principle of improvement of product and factors of production led many industrialists to devote considerable energy to improving their human capital.

Samuel Oldknow was one of these industrialists and this paper is concerned with his attempts to exert discipline through the surveillance and recording of the behaviour and output of his employees.

ASSETS AS PROPERTY AVAILABLE FOR THE PAYMENT OF DEBTS

Sarah Williams, Deakin University, Australia

The word "asset" was originally taken into the English language, from the Latin *ad satis* and French *asez*, as a term used at law meaning sufficient estate or effects to discharge debts. It later came to be used in the sense of property available for the payment of debts. Assets were understood to be property (objects owned and rights of ownership) that could be exchanged for cash. The importance of factual knowledge of the money equivalents of property and debts, in managing mercantile affairs, was emphasized in accounting manuals during the eighteenth and nineteenth centuries. The rights of investors and creditors to factual up-to-date information about the financial state of affairs of companies, given the advent of limited liability, underscored the early company legislation that required the preparation and auditing of statements of property and debts. Existing company law requires the preparation and auditing of statements of assets and liabilities. Asset has a very specific meaning at law—property available for the payment of debts. To use the word in any other sense in accounting is to misrepresent the situation. Property, or ownership, is an interest protected at law. Property rights are transferable or exchangeable. Only where assets represent the money amounts of exchangeable property will dated statements of assets and liabilities represent a realistic picture of an entity's financial position at that date, its ability to enter into exchanges, to pay its debts, to continue in the future. Such information is vital to the protection of creditors' and investors' interests. Where statements of assets and liabilities are not representative of the money equivalents of property and debts, investors, creditors and other users are denied a reliable and informative basis for action.

A USA/CANADA MODEL OF "SIN" AND OTHER EXCISE TAXES

Brenda Yelvington, Tonya K. Flesher, William Shughart, Dale Flesher
University of Mississippi

The motivation for this study was to consider why proposals, such as Clinton's, to levy additional sin taxes, have failed in recent years. These proposals were thought to have a great chance to be enacted. In order to speculate on causes of recent failures, the authors sought to determine the reasons for past successes in promoting excise taxes. This paper summarizes the history of the excise tax in the United States, beginning shortly after the end of the American Revolution. The discussion covers both the specific types of excises levied on the American public and the reasons why particular items of consumption have been chose for taxation. The reaction of taxpayers to the first excise tax, which erupted into the Whiskey Rebellion of 1794, serves as the paper's point of departure.

Biographies

Mohammad J. Abdolmohammadi is primarily interested in behavioural auditing research. He has published regularly in *Accounting and Business Research, The Accounting Review, Advances in Accounting, Asia Pacific Journal of Accounting, Auditing: a Journal of Practice and Theory, Behavioral Research in Accounting, Contemporary Accounting Research, Expert Systems With Applications, Internal Auditing, International Journal of Accounting, Iranian Accounting Review, Issues in Accounting Education, Organizational Behavior and Human Decision Processes, Research in Accounting Regulation and Advances in Quantitative Finance and Accounting*, among others. He has served on several editorial boards including that of *The Accounting Review.* Having taught at Indiana University, Boston University, and the University of Illinois at Chicago before joining Bentley College in 1988, Dr. Abdolmohammadi's areas of teaching include financial and managerial accounting, cost accounting, accounting systems applications, auditing, financial statements analysis, and methods and practices of professional research.

Ray H. Anderson is professor of accounting and finance at Victoria University of Technology, Melbourne, Australia. He has published widely in both domestic and international professional and academic journals. He is a member of the editorial board of *Accounting Forum* and has just completed a joint research project with Marc J. Epstein on the usefulness of corporate annual reports to investors in Australia, New Zealand and the United States. It is to be published by Jai Press.

Ignace De Beelde is assistant professor of auditing in the Faculty of Applied Economics and Vlerick School of Management at the University of Ghent. He has a masters degree in history, a qualified teacher's degree, a degree of advanced studies in accounting and auditing, and a PhD in arts and letters. He is also director of two postgraduate programs in accounting and auditing at the University of Ghent. Major areas of interest are accounting history and auditing.

Peter Clarke, FCA, PhD is a statutory lecturer at the Department of Accountancy, University College, Dublin, Ireland. He has published many articles on various accounting topics in academic and professional journals and has presented papers to the annual conferences of the European, Irish and American Accounting Associations. He has also written three accounting textbooks. He is a former winner of the "Accountancy Ireland" award from the Institute of Chartered Accountants in Ireland.

Kathie Cooper, PhD, has been a lecturer with the Department of Accounting and Finance at the University of Wollongong, Australia, since 1988. Her teaching responsibilities at the undergraduate level include intermediate and advanced financial accounting and accounting theory. Postgraduate responsibilities include lecturing in accounting history and regulation and the supervision of research students. Her research interests include financial accounting, accounting history, regulation, corporate failures, critical theory and interdisciplinary approaches to the study of accounting, history and regulation including autopoiesis, sociology of professions and power frameworks.

Dale L. Flesher is the Arthur Andersen Alumni Professor and associate dean in the School of Accountancy at the University of Mississippi. He holds CPA, CIA, CMA, and CGFM certificates. Dr. Flesher received his PhD from the University of Cincinnati. Dr. Flesher has authored 30 books and over 180 journal articles. He is an active member of numerous professional organizations and was the 1988 president of the Academy of Accounting Historians. He is a former editor of both *The Accounting Historians Notebook* and *The Accounting Historians Journal.* He received the University of Mississippi's 1987 Burlington Northern Award as the outstanding faculty member on campus. In 1990, he received the Leon Radde Award from the Institute of Internal Auditors as the Outstanding Audit Educator worldwide. During the past year, he has been working with an AICPA task force developing a video on the history of the CPA profession in the United States.

Tonya K. Flesher is professor of accountancy and former dean of the School of Accountancy at the University of Mississippi. To date, she is still the only woman to ever hold a deanship in the 148-year history of the university. She holds a PhD from the University of Mississippi. She is the author of eight books and more than 70 articles. She was the recipient of the Mississippi Society of CPAs 1995 Outstanding Educator of the Year Award. Dr. Flesher is past president (1993) of the Academy of Accounting Historians and has served on numerous committees of the AICPA and other professional organizations. Dr. Flesher received the University of Mississippi's 1986 Burlington Northern Award as the outstanding faculty member on campus. She has been a departmental editor for two accounting journals: *The Tax Adviser* and *The Woman CPA.*

Mai Iskandar received her doctorate from the University of Missouri at Columbia in 1986. She has been a prolific researcher, with publications spanning a broad range of finance topics such as corporate bankruptcy, mergers and acquisitions, divestitures, initial public offerings (IPOs) of securities, corporate pension funding decisions, insider trading, capital structure decisions, issues related to convertible bond financing, internal corporate governance and restructuring. She has numerous articles published in top quality refereed finance journals such as the *Journal of Financial and Quantitative Analysis, Journal of Banking and Finance, Journal of Business Finance and Accounting, Journal of Financial Research, The Financial Review*, etc. One of her articles won the outstanding paper award at the 1995 Southern Finance Association's annual conference. *The Wall Street Journal* recently carried a full length article drawing attention to her investigation of the impact of insider trading on bondholders. Dr. Iskandar is an associate professor of finance at the University of Massachusetts at Dartmouth.

Paul J. McMann is a CPA and CMA. He is finishing his doctorate at Boston University and is a visiting lecturer at Babson College, Massachusetts. He has taught management accounting courses at both the graduate and undergraduate levels. He has written articles on performance measurement and Japanese management accounting methods and has been published in *Management Accounting, Emerging Practices in Cost Management, Management Accounting Research* and *EDP Auditor Journal*. Paul McMann also is a course leader for the Institute for International Research and for the American Management Association on the subject of performance measurement. He is currently working on several field research projects on performance measurement.

C. J. McNair, CMA, is the Chandor Term Chairholder and professor of accounting at Babson College, Massachusetts. She received a PhD from Columbia University in 1986 under the tutelage of Gordon Shillinglaw. McNair has authored *The Profit Potential: Taking High Performance to the Bottom Line* and *World Class Accounting and Finance*. She has coauthored *Benchmarking: A Tool for Continuous Improvement* and *Crossroads: a JIT Success Story*. She lectures extensively on state-of-the-art management accounting systems, performance measurement, capacity accounting and management, and continuous improvement for organizations such as the Institute of Management Accountants, the American Production and Control Society, the American Institute of CPAs, and the Financial Executive Institute. McNair also consults for organizations such as Digital, Polaroid, and Caterpillar. She has been on the accounting faculty of the University of Rhode Island and the Pennsylvania State University.

Bernard H. Newman, CPA, PhD is a professor of accounting in the Lubin School of Business, Pace University, New York City. He is coauthor of the continuing professional education self-study textbook for Certified Public Accountants titled *The Role of the Internal Auditor*, published by the American Institute of Certified Public Accountants, and numerous professional articles. He has presented papers at many American Accounting Association regional meetings. Newman earned his PhD at New York University. He is a member of the AICPA, the Institute of Internal Auditors and the New York State Society of CPAs.

Hiroshi Okano is an associate professor, Graduate School of Business, Osaka City University, Japan. He has a strong interest in cost management, especially target costing and its history, and his recent publication is *Japanese Management Accounting: A Historical and Institutional Perspective Toward Target Cost Management* (Tokyo: The Chuo Keisaisha, 1995). (Japan Institute of Certified Public Accountants Award, 1996.)

Mary Ellen Oliverio, CPA, PhD is a professor of accounting in the Lubin School of Business, Pace University, New York City. She has written textbooks and professional articles and has lectured at seminars throughout the United States and in Puerto Rico, Canada, Peru, and Italy. Oliverio earned her PhD at Columbia University. She is a member of the AICPA, the Institute of Management Accountants, the American Accounting Association, and the New York State Society of CPAs. She serves currently as chairperson of the Audit Sampling and Analytical Techniques Committee of the New York State Society.

Pilar Pérez is a professor of accounting and financial economics at the College of Business Studies in the University of Valladolid, Spain. Pérez, whose expertise is in accounting history, has written several articles and two books in the area: *The Royal House of Coinage of Valladolid and Its Accounting Records* and *The Bankruptcy of the Bank of Valladolid*.

Gary John Previts is professor of accounting and former chairman in the Weatherhead School of Management at Case Western Reserve University, Ohio. He is a CPA and is currently serving on the board of directors of the AICPA. He is a past president of the Ohio Society of CPAs. He received the Federation of Schools of Accountancy 1991 Joseph Silvoso Award as the outstanding accounting educator nationwide. He was recently selected as the recipient of the 1996 AICPA Outstanding Educator Award. Dr. Previts was the founding president of the Academy of Accounting Historians and is the coauthor of the acclaimed *History of Accounting in America*. He has written numerous books and articles and has served as editor of *The Ohio CPA Journal, The Accounting Historians Journal*, and *Research in Accounting Regulation*.

Alan J. Richardson received his PhD from Queen's University in 1985 and has been a member of the School of Business, Queen's University, Ontario since 1987. He currently serves as associate dean and executive director of the CGA-Ontario International Business Research Centre at Queen's University. He is active in the profession, serving on the CGA-Canada Education Advisory Council. His research maintains an institutional focus and has included studies of professionalization, regulation, standard-setting and financial disclosure. He has published in *Accounting Organizations and Society, The Accounting Review, Journal of Accounting Research, The Accounting Historians Journal* and other academic and practitioner journals. He is also editor of the CGA-Canada Research Foundation Monograph entitled *Research Methods In Accounting: Issues and Debates*.

Manuel Rodrigues Benavente is director of *Apotec-Associaçao Portuguesa de Tecnicos de Contas*, the Portuguese Association of Accountants. A professional accountant, he has collaborated on several magazine and newspaper articles about accountancy, auditing and accounting history.

William D. Samson is the Roddy-Garner Professor of Accounting at the University of Alabama. He is currently serving as secretary of the Academy of Accounting Historians and has served as a co-editor of *The Accounting Historians Journal* from 1990 – 1994. His main research interests include tax history and financial accounting, especially cash flow studies and development of cases. Samson teaches undergraduate and graduate tax courses as well as MBA financial accounting courses. He received his PhD in 1981 from the University of North Carolina. He has taught previously at Louisiana State University and at Old Dominion University. He is a CPA and has passed the CMA exam.

William Shughart is professor of economics and holder on the Self Chair of Free Enterprise at the University of Mississippi. He holds bachelors, masters, and PhD degrees from Texas A & M University.

N. M. Singhvi has been an associate professor for 22 years and has a teaching degree as well as a postgraduate degree. Three persons have been awarded a PhD under his guidance. Four people are currently working towards their PhD under his guidance. Dr. Singhvi has published three books: *Toward Excellence, Bhartiya Lekhankan* (in Hindi) and *Accounting Education.* He has delivered lectures and had discussions in more than two dozen countries. Dr. Singhvi has published 21 articles in English and Hindi journals and newspapers.

David M. Smith has degrees in accounting law and taxation from the University of New South Wales. He qualified for admissions as barrister, Supreme Court of New South Wales (1977). He has been a full-time academic since 1978, teaching mainly in the areas of revenue law, constitutional law, and legal process. Smith has published widely in the areas of taxation law and legal process, tax accounting and valuation of trading stock (inventory). His work has appeared in *Taxation in Australia, Australian Tax Review, Accounting History, Deakin University Law Review,* and *Prometheus.* Smith is the principal author of commentary on taxation of trading stock in *Australian Tax Practice* and author of *Tax Accounting* and *Tax Accounting for Trading Stock* in Volume 31 of Laws of Australia (in press) [both encyclopaedic works]. He is a Fellow of Australian Society of CPAs, Fellow Taxation Institute of Australia, member of Australian Tax Research Foundation, Institute of Public Administration Australia, Accounting Association of Australia and New Zealand, Australasian Law Teachers Association, Australasian Tax Teachers Association and Academy of Accounting Historians.

Richard Vangermeersch, CPA, CMA is a professor of accounting at the University of Rhode Island. He received a PhD from the University of Florida in 1970. He has edited, authored, and coauthored many books on the history of accounting, including *Alexander Hamilton Church: A Man of Ideas for All Seasons* and *The History of Accounting: An International Encyclopaedia* (with Michael Chatfield). He and C. J. McNair have just published *Measuring the Cost of Capacity, Management Accounting Guideline* 42 of the Society of Management Accountants of Canada. Vangermeersch received the Hourglass Award of the Academy of Accounting Historians in 1988 for the work he coauthored with Peter McMickle on *The Origins of a Great Profession.* Vangermeersch has served a five-year term as treasurer of the Academy of Accounting Historians (1979–84), was president in 1987, and chaired its trustees from 1990–92, of which he is still a member.

Daniel A. Wren, PhD, University of Illinois, is David Ross Boyd Professor of Management and curator of the Harry W. Bass Business History Collection at the University of Oklahoma. He has served as president of the Southern Management Association and as chairman of the Management History Division of the Academy of Management and is a fellow of the Southern Management Association of the Academy of Management. He has been honoured with the Merrick Foundation Award for teaching excellence and recently received the Distinguished Educator Award from the National Academy of Management for his contributions "as foremost management historian of his generation."

Brenda Yelvington is a doctoral student at the University of Mississippi. She is currently ABD and lives in Little Rock, Arkansas. She is a CPA and was formerly with the firm of Ernst & Young in the Little Rock office. She was the 1995 representative to the American Accounting Association Doctoral Consortium at Lake Tahoe. She holds a bachelors degree from Hendrix College and an MBA from the University of Central Arkansas.